AF802114

European Union and its Neighbours in a Globalized World

Volume 7

Series Editors

Marc Bungenberg, Saarbrücken, Germany

Mareike Fröhlich, Saarbrücken, Germany

Thomas Giegerich, Saarbrücken, Germany

Neda Zdraveva, Skopje, North Macedonia

Advisory Editors

Başak Baysal, Istanbul, Turkey

Manjiao Chi, Beijing, China

Annette Guckelberger, Saarbrücken, Germany

Ivana Jelić, Strasbourg, France

Irine Kurdadze, Tbilisi, Georgia

Gordana Lažetić, Skopje, North Macedonia

Yossi Mekelberg, London, UK

Zlatan Meškić, Riyadh, Saudi Arabia

Tamara Perišin, Luxembourg, Luxembourg

Roman Petrov, Kyiv, Ukraine

Dušan V. Popović, Belgrad, Serbia

Andreas R. Ziegler, Lausanne, Switzerland

The series "The European Union and its Neighbours in a Globalized World" will publish monographs and edited volumes in the field of European and International Law and Policy. A special focus will be put on the European Neighbourhood Policy, current problems in European and International Law and Policy as well as the role of the European Union as a global actor. The series will support the cross-border publishing and distribution of research results of cross-border research consortia. Besides renowned scientists the series will also be open for publication projects of young academics. The series will emphasize the interplay of the European Union and its neighbouring countries as well as the important role of the European Union as a key player in the international context of law, economics and politics.

Unique Selling Points:

• Deals with a wide range of topics in regard of European and International Law but is also open to topics which are connected to economic or political science

• Brings together authors from the European Union as well as from accession candidate or neighbouring countries who examine current problems from different perspectives

• Draws on a broad network of excellent scholars in Europe promoted by the SEE | EU Cluster of Excellence, the Europa-Institut of Saarland University as well as in the South East European Law School Network

Roman Maydanyk • André den Exter •
Iryna Izarova
Editors

Ukrainian Healthcare Law in the Context of European and International Law

Springer

Editors
Roman Maydanyk
School of Law
Taras Shevchenko National University of Kyiv
Kyiv, Ukraine

André den Exter
Erasmus School of Law
Erasmus University Rotterdam
Rotterdam, The Netherlands

Iryna Izarova
School of Law
Taras Shevchenko National University of Kyiv
Kyiv, Ukraine

ISSN 2524-8928 ISSN 2524-8936 (electronic)
European Union and its Neighbours in a Globalized World
ISBN 978-3-031-05689-5 ISBN 978-3-031-05690-1 (eBook)
https://doi.org/10.1007/978-3-031-05690-1

© The Editor(s) (if applicable) and The Author(s), under exclusive license to Springer Nature Switzerland AG 2022
This work is subject to copyright. All rights are solely and exclusively licensed by the Publisher, whether the whole or part of the material is concerned, specifically the rights of translation, reprinting, reuse of illustrations, recitation, broadcasting, reproduction on microfilms or in any other physical way, and transmission or information storage and retrieval, electronic adaptation, computer software, or by similar or dissimilar methodology now known or hereafter developed.
The use of general descriptive names, registered names, trademarks, service marks, etc. in this publication does not imply, even in the absence of a specific statement, that such names are exempt from the relevant protective laws and regulations and therefore free for general use.
The publisher, the authors, and the editors are safe to assume that the advice and information in this book are believed to be true and accurate at the date of publication. Neither the publisher nor the authors or the editors give a warranty, expressed or implied, with respect to the material contained herein or for any errors or omissions that may have been made. The publisher remains neutral with regard to jurisdictional claims in published maps and institutional affiliations.

This Springer imprint is published by the registered company Springer Nature Switzerland AG
The registered company address is: Gewerbestrasse 11, 6330 Cham, Switzerland

Preface

This book is the product of a project initiated by Ukrainian legal scholars interested in health issues. Ukraine, as other Eastern and Central Europe have been confronted with various challenges in their health care systems. For instance, the introduction of 'market-oriented' elements in the health care systems of the European countries in transition reflects some of the characteristics towards a more Bismarckian health care model upgraded with managed competition tools.

In line with the health system reforms, subsequent governments have revised the health sector's legal framework frequently and it is expected to continue in the coming years. For instance, medical (reproductive) technologies raise various ethical and legal concerns on the legal status of the human embryo, regulating the freezing and storage of human gametes and embryos, and most recently CRISPR-Cas gene-editing technologies in health care. Since these medical-ethical issues raise human rights concerns, legislative intervention is required.

But apart from regulating health care technologies, health system reforms address the organization, planning, and financing of health care services, as well as the need for revising quality of care issues (qualification of health professionals, monitoring complaint and professional review mechanisms, patients' rights, etc.).

Simultaneously, the ratification of international and European treaties by Ukraine also affects its national health system, and thus its regulatory framework. For instance, the Oviedo Convention (1997) including Additional Protocols imposes member states to harmonize their national patients' rights legislation with the Council of Europe's minimum standards. In addition, the so-called Europe Agreement[1] concluded with the European Union will also require the implementation of the health EU acquis (public health, health data protection, market access rules, and health products and services, pharmaceuticals, etc.).

The urgency of revising and alignment of the national legal framework in health care is not unique to Ukraine, as other Central and Eastern countries have been

[1] Ukraine-European Union Association Agreement, OJ EU L161/3, 29 April 2014.

confronted with similar developments, particularly those entering the European Union since the 1990s. What we know from previous system reforms is that there is no universal 'blue print' that should be followed when revising the health care system. But the complexity of the reform process requires an overall and coherent strategy, introducing a step-by-step revision of the legislative framework. Such an incremental approach is based on underlying principles and concept of health law, national priorities of law-making, and legal instruments steering and monitoring the reform process.

Being confronted with the Covid-19 pandemic, a new dimension was added to this research project. The global pandemic has confronted national governments with introducing restrictive measures on human rights that were unthinkable before. Public health protection and prevention justifies restrictive measures such as Covid-track and tracing measures, seizure of nursery homes, postponing non-emergency medical interventions, as well as the debate on voluntary or mandatory vaccination, and emergency scenarios for critical care admissions in hospitals. As the health crisis increases, it becomes painfully clear that national measures are not sufficient and the call for regional and global collaboration becomes more eminent. The exchange of health data, the need for joint procurement of both preventive and curative health equipment, vaccines and pharmaceuticals create unprecedented legal challenges in terms of health data security, the mutual recognition of national standards, as well as potential constitutional challenges derived from newly developed joint actions.

The key objective of 'Europe towards a Globalization of Healthcare Law' is to provide an overview of current developments in Ukrainian health law and health legislation, with an emphasis on the Eastern and Central Europe in terms of Globalization, ranging from the unified model of healthcare, patient's rights, concept of patient autonomy to post-mortem organ and cell donation, biobanks, medical liability and alternative disputes resolution in health care, vulnerable groups (children), new (reproductive) technologies, intellectual property in medicine and pharmacy, intellectual property protection of the DNA sequence, pan-European treatment contract, managed entry agreements, and prevention of occupational morbidity as a component of public health.

Each contribution examines the applicable norms, identifies legal obstacles and (future) challenges, and suggests recommendations for improvement. Occasionally, it includes valuable lessons learned from other legal systems, adopting international and European values in health care. Although far from complete, the editors hope this book will contribute to increase the understanding of health law in Ukraine, both at national and international level.

Kyiv, Ukraine — Roman Maydanyk
Rotterdam, The Netherlands — André den Exter
Kyiv, Ukraine — Iryna Izarova

Acknowledgements

This book arose from the work on the Conference 'Private Healthcare Law: Challenges and Prospects', held on 17th September 2020, hosting the Taras Shevchenko National University of Kyiv with the participation of the National Bar Association of Ukraine. Among the panels were 'Medical Code and European experience of Systematization of Law in the field of Healthcare', 'Treatment contract: legal nature and standards of medical services, challenges and prospects', and 'Globalization of Right of Person with mental disorders: adaptation of Ukrainian Law to European standards'. Mostly the results of studies, prepared by reporters of this conference, substantive improved and amended, are represented within the structure of this book. Therefore, the following parts were consistently placed in this collection: 'General Provisions of a Healthcare' (Part I), 'Human Autonomy. Circulation of the Deceased's Organs' (Part II), 'Protection of Rights and Medical Dispute Resolution' (Part III), 'Reproductive Rights' (Part IV), 'Intellectual Property in Medicine and Pharmacy' (Part V), and 'Healthcare Contracts' (Part VI). All the chapters, presented in this collection, are logically divided among the abovementioned parts. It helps to create the full general presentation of the chosen topic—how Europe moves towards a globalization of healthcare law with the particular attention to the Eastern and Central European countries legal doctrine.

We are indebted to Iryna Izarova for her help with this work preparing and finalizing, to Julia Baklagenko and David Phelan for their comments which enabled us to correct language errors and clarify the presentation.

We would like to thank the staff at Springer, in particular Anja Trautmann, Manuela Schwietzer, and Abdus Salam Mazumder, for their help and support.

Kyiv, Ukraine — Roman Maydanyk
Rotterdam, The Netherlands — André den Exter

Contents

Editors and Contributors

About the Editors

André den Exter Dr., Associate Professor of Health Law, Erasmus School of Law, Erasmus University Rotterdam, Burg. Oudlaan 50, Rotterdam, the Netherlands. e-mail: denexter@law.eur.nl

Iryna Izarova Dr. Sc. (Law), Full Professor, Professor at the Law School, Taras Shevchenko National University of Kyiv, Volodymyrska str. 60, 01030 Kyiv, Ukraine. e-mail: irina.izarova@knu.ua

Roman Maydanyk Dr. Sc. (Law), Full Professor, Professor of the Department of Civil Law at the Law School, Taras Shevchenko National University of Kyiv, Volodymyrska str. 60, 01030 Kyiv, Ukraine. e-mail: roman.maydanyk@knu.ua

Contributors

Svitlana Batychenko Law School, Taras Shevchenko National University of Kyiv, Kyiv, Ukraine

André den Exter Erasmus School of Law, Erasmus University Rotterdam, Rotterdam, The Netherlands

Anna Golovashchuk Kyiv, Ukraine

Iryna Izarova School of Law, Taras Shevchenko National University of Kyiv, Kyiv, Ukraine

Oksana Kashyntseva Centre for Harmonisation of Human Rights and Intellectual Property Rights of the Scientific and Research Institute of Intellectual Property of National Academy of Law Sciences of Ukraine, Kyiv, Ukraine

Nataliia Kvit Department of Civil Law and Procedure, Ivan Franko National University of Lviv, Lviv, Ukraine

Liubov Maidanyk Intellectual Property and Informational Law Department, Law School of Taras Shevchenko National University of Kyiv, Kyiv, Ukraine

Nataliia Maydanyk Department of Civil and Labour Law at the School of Law, Vadym Hetman National Economic University of Kyiv, Kyiv, Ukraine

Roman Maydanyk Department of Civil Law at the Law School, Taras Shevchenko National University of Kyiv, Kyiv, Ukraine

Kateryna Moskalenko Civil Law Department at the Law School of Taras Shevchenko National University of Kyiv, Kyiv, Ukraine

Galyna Myronova Academician F. H. Burchak Scientific Research Institute of Private Law and Entrepreneurship of the National Academy of Legal Science of Ukraine, Kyiv, Ukraine

Vitalii Pashkov Department of Civil, Commercial and Environmental Law, Poltava Law Institute, Poltava, Ukraine

Oleksandra Pohorielova Department of Labour Law and Social Security Law at the Law School, Taras Shevchenko National University of Kyiv, Kyiv, Ukraine

Nataliia Popova Department of General Legal Disciplines, Civil Law and Tourism Legislative Regulation at the Economics and Law School, Kyiv University of Tourism, Economics and Law, Kyiv, Ukraine

Olha Rozghon Leading Researcher of the Scientific and Research Institute of Providing Legal Framework for the Innovative Development of National Academy of Law Sciences of Ukraine of Kharkiv, Kharkiv, Ukraine

Iryna Sakharuk Department of Labour Law and Social Security Law at the Law School, Taras Shevchenko National University of Kyiv, Kyiv, Ukraine

Iryna Senyuta Department of Medical Law at the Faculty of Post-graduate Education of Danylo Halytskyi Lviv National Medical University, Lviv, Ukraine

Oleksandr Shyshka Department of Civil Disciplines, Kharkiv National University of Internal Affairs, Kharkiv, Ukraine

Sviatoslav Slipchenko Department of Civil Disciplines, Kharkiv National University of Internal Affairs, Kharkiv, Ukraine

Vigita Vėbraitė Faculty of Law, Vilnius University, Department of Private Law, Vilnius, Lithuania

Abbreviations

ADR	Alternative Dispute Resolution
AHR	Assisted human reproduction methods
ART	Assisted reproductive technologies
BGB	German Civil Code (*Bürgerliches Gesetzbuch*)
CC of Ukraine	Civil Code of Ukraine
Community acquis, EU acquis	Acquis communautaire
Convention on Human Rights and Biomedicine, Oviedo Convention	Convention for the Protection of Human Rights and Dignity of the Human Being with regard to the Application of Biology and Medicine
COVID-19	Coronavirus infection SARS-CoV-2
CRC	Convention on the Rights of the Child
CTR	EU clinical trial rules
DCFR	Principles, Definitions and Model Rules of European Private Law: Draft Common Frame of Reference
DRC	Declaration of the Rights of the Child
ECHR	Convention on Human Rights and Fundamental Freedoms
ECOSOC	United Nations Economic and Social Council
ECtHR	European Court of Human Rights
EMA	European Medicines Agency
EPO	European Patent Office
EWCA Crim	England and Wales Court of Appeal (Criminal Division)
FC of Ukraine	Family Code of Ukraine
FDA	U.S. Food and Drug Administration
Fundamentals	Fundamentals of the legislation of Ukraine on health care

GAVI	Global Alliance for Vaccines and Immunization
ICESCR	International Covenant on Economic, Social and Economic Rights and Cultural Rights
ILO	International Labour Organization
MEAs	Managed Entry Agreements
MHRA	Healthcare products Regulatory Agency
The EU-Ukraine Association Agreement	Association Agreement between the European Union and the Ukraine
TRIPS, Agreement TRIPS	Agreement on Trade-Related Aspects of Intellectual Property Rights
UDHR	Universal Declaration of Human Rights
WHO	World Health Organization
WIPO	World Intellectual Property Organization

Part I
General Provisions of a Healthcare

Europe Towards a Unified Model of Healthcare

Roman Maydanyk and Nataliia Maydanyk

Contents

Abstract The pan-European unified legal model of the healthcare is a system of legal norms, which are provided by the legal instruments of European unification and contain principles and decisive characteristics (determinants) of healthcare in European countries at national and international levels. These determinants combine recognized values and operative principles in the EU with principles of acceptable economic efficiency and growth of healthcare of any European country, taking into account common and distinctive features of the European countries, developed economies and countries in transition. This healthcare model should be the basic

---

This chapter is prepared on the basis of the report for the Conference 'Private Healthcare Law: Challenges and Prospects'.

R. Maydanyk (✉)
Department of Civil Law at the Law School, Taras Shevchenko National University of Kyiv, Kyiv, Ukraine
e-mail: roman.maydanyk@knu.ua

N. Maydanyk
Department of Civil and Labour Law at the School of Law, Vadym Hetman National Economic University of Kyiv, Kyiv, Ukraine

© The Author(s), under exclusive license to Springer Nature Switzerland AG 2022
R. Maydanyk et al. (eds.), *Ukrainian Healthcare Law in the Context of European and International Law*, European Union and its Neighbours in a Globalized World 7,
https://doi.org/10.1007/978-3-031-05690-1_1

healthcare standard, setting a minimum level of healthcare for European counties, combining universal health coverage with public and private hospital and ambulatory care to secure a high level of healthcare provision. This model provides for equal participation of consumers in the payment for medical services, necessary to avoid excessive use of medical services as well as other tools of managed competition under tight control and regulation of the state, taking into account European values and principles, financial and institutional ability, mentality and other national traditions of European healthcare systems. The instruments of unification of European law should provide a common frame of reference for the pan-European unified healthcare model, which will define the basic principles, characteristics (determinants) of said unified model, principles of international policy. It should also secure the exclusive competence of national law, the interrelation of international and national healthcare policies based on the exclusivity of the competence of national law and the subsidiarity of the norms of the international healthcare law.

1 Introduction: Background and Objectives of the Study

The need for sustainable development of European health care in terms of globalization necessitates the approximation of national law through the use of legal instruments of harmonization and unification at different levels to better succeed in combining European values and principles with economic efficiency and growth. EU Member State and countries within the Association Agreements and European Neighborhood should have effective and predictable systems (models) of healthcare.

Despite the diversity of healthcare models, the system of legal characteristics (determinants) of the European unified model determines the primary and derivative characteristics, which are inherent to different European countries and reflect the common development of health care systems.

The ideological basis of any health care model is a system of basic characteristics (determinants) of the model comprising a general understanding of medical services as a social good. The legal uncertainty of such a system hinders the efficiency and predictability of the health care model.

At present, EU acquis and national law of the European countries on the model of healthcare law and their decisive components are not unified.

The acute relevance of these issues is due to the differences between the national Law of EU-member states and other European countries in terms of variety of healthcare systems and set of their decisive characteristics. This makes it difficult to define unified approach to achieve acceptable efficiency and growth of all European healthcare systems.

To approximate and harmonize the national law of European countries and EU-healthcare law, it is essential to form a common frame of reference of the pan-European model of healthcare, in particular, principles, decisive determinants (characteristics) of this model, which combine European values and principles with acceptable economic efficiency and growth of the healthcare of any European country.

Thus, in this chapter, we will try to outline the concept and basic provision of the European unified model of healthcare law in terms of globalization to better succeed in combining European values and principles with economic efficiency and growth. The comparative component of this study should help identify the peculiarities of healthcare models in European countries, developed economies and countries in transition to formulate the relevant balanced characteristics (determinants) to be taken into account in the unified model of healthcare.

2 Legal Analysis of the Pan-European Model of Healthcare

2.1 Concept, Principles, and Levels of Healthcare Models

The healthcare model should be considered as a system of legal norms that determine the main characteristics (determinants) of healthcare based on the principles of affordability of price, affordability of providing, and reliability of healthcare services.

The mentioned three principles are the key principles of health care, which correspond (correlate) with the values and principles of healthcare recognized in the EU.

The healthcare systems in the European Union contribute to social cohesion and social justice and are treated as an important element of 'a social state' and the key part of Europe's high level of social protection and.

Council Conclusions on Common values and principles in European Union Health Systems (2006/C 146/01)[1] recognize the overarching values of universality, access to good quality care, equity, and solidarity as values of healthcare which have been widely accepted in the work of the different EU institutions. Together they constitute a set of values that are shared across Europe.

Universality means that no-one is barred access to health care; solidarity is closely linked to the financial arrangement of national health systems and the need to ensure accessibility to all of them; equity relates to equal access correspondent to the needs and regardless of ethnicity, gender, age, social status or ability to pay. EU health systems also aim to reduce the gap in health inequalities, which is a concern of EU Member States; closely linked to this is the work in the Member States' systems on the prevention of illness and disease by inter alia the promotion of healthy lifestyles. All health systems in the EU aim to make the provision which is patient-centered and responsive to individual needs.

---

[1]Council Conclusions on Common values and principles in European Union Health Systems (2006) C 146/01. https://eur-lex.europa.eu/LexUriServ/LexUriServ.do?uri=OJ:C:2006:146:0001:0003:EN:PDF.

The operating principles of health care consist of principles of (a) Quality: All EU health systems strive to provide good quality care, (b) Safety: Patients can expect each EU health system to secure a systematic approach to ensuring patient safety; (c) Care that is based on evidence and ethics; (d) Patient Involvement: All EU health systems aim to be patient-centered; (e) Redress: Patients should have a right to redress if things go wrong; (f) Privacy and confidentiality: The right of all EU citizens to the confidentiality of personal information is recognized in EU and national legislation.

It is important to understand that the healthcare model is dynamic by nature and should take into account important social changes in the healthcare sector, including the impact of global challenges. One of the manifestations of globalization is the pandemic coronavirus COVID-19 which at present is not a fully controlled global challenge. This global challenge significantly affects the general understanding and unification of the model of healthcare law, necessitates a reconsidering of the concept, characteristics (determinants), and legal instruments of approximation and unification.

Reconsidering the concept, approximation and unification of the healthcare law model implies the need to understand them at different levels: national and international (regional and global), public and private. At the national level, the model of healthcare law shall be a system of basic and derivative characteristics (determinants) provided by national law, which are decisive for the formation of the national healthcare system.

At the international level (regional and global), the healthcare model of law shall be defined by international legal acts, other sources of international law, and legal provisions that define international healthcare policy and the principles of interaction with national healthcare systems. The model of healthcare law should be considered at the public and private levels, which provides for the existence and consideration of public and non-state (private) healthcare. As a result, the healthcare system aquires a two-level character.

At the level of public law, healthcare shall be understood as a healthcare system provided by public (state and municipal) healthcare facilities and physicians who are government employees providing state-funded healthcare services.

At the level of private law, healthcare shall be a system of private healthcare provided by private healthcare individuals and entities and private healthcare insurance. Medical and other healthcare in private healthcare are paid at the expense of consumers, first of all, for better and additional services. Private healthcare fills the gap in the supply of healthcare insurance and in healthcare in general.

Thus, the pan-European unified model of the healthcare law is a system of legal norms of 'strict' and 'soft' law, which are provided by the instruments of unification of European law and contain decisive characteristics (determinants) of public and private health care in European countries at national and international levels. These norms correspond to the recognized EU values (universality, access to good quality care and solidarity) and the operative principles of health care (quality, safety, evidence and ethics, redress, privacy, and confidentiality), take into account common and distinctive features of European countries, developed economies and countries in transition.

2.2 *Types of Healthcare Models*

Generally, the typology of healthcare (i.e., the division of healthcare into types, or models) determines the main characteristics (determinants) of the health care that ensure affordability of price, affordability on the provision of medical services, and reliability of health services.

Usually, in legal doctrine, there are four major models for health care: the Beveridge Model, the Bismarck model, the National Health Insurance model, and the out-of-pocket model.[2]

The Beveridge model is known as 'socialized medicine' because all citizens of a country will have healthcare that is financed by their government using tax payments. Since the government owns hospitals and other medical centers, most physicians are considered government employees. Healthcare costs are also low because the government is the sole payer, which eliminates market competition. The idea behind this system is that healthcare is a human right and citizens are guaranteed universal coverage. Because patients contribute through taxes, they do not have to pay anything out of pocket for medical services. Additionally, a disadvantage of a system that provides equal access to everyone is long waiting lists and over-use that can lead to higher costs. In times of a crisis, a decrease in public revenue can lead to a decrease in funding for services while patient numbers increase, causing a burden on the system. This model was developed in the United Kingdom and has spread to Northern Europe and other countries such as Spain, New Zealand, and Cuba.[3]

Bismarck model 'All Payers' uses a workplace insurance system, quite often through semi-private 'health insurance funds'; the insurers are called 'sickness funds,' usually financed jointly by employers and employees through payroll deduction. These insurance funds may operate within one or more sectors of the economy.

At the same time, the number of contributions and payments are set by the state. Quite often such contributions are just a kind of payroll tax and are paid directly to the appropriate fund. Unlike the U.S. insurance industry, Bismarckian health insurance plans have to cover everybody, and they don't make a profit. Doctors and hospitals tend to be private. The amount of remuneration they receive for services is set as a result of negotiations with the funds, sometimes on an individual basis and sometimes on a national scale. Beveridge Model envisages tight regulation that provides the government with a significant impact on the cost control. German

---

[2] Chung (2017).

[3] Shikha (2020).

healthcare had long been regarded as a model of this system. This model usually includes France, Belgium, the Netherlands, Japan, and Switzerland.[4]

The National Health Insurance model 'Single Payer' has elements of both the Beveridge and Bismarck models. It uses private-sector providers, but payment comes from a government-run insurance program that all citizens fund through a premium or tax. These universal insurance programs tend to be less expensive and have lower administrative costs than American-style for-profit insurance plans. The National Health Insurance system also controls costs by limiting the medical services they pay for and/or requiring patients to wait to be treated.

The state tends to develop a total budget for healthcare when deciding how much of the budget should be allocated for this purpose, and sets the price or volume of compensation to those who provide medical services. In some cases, physicians are government employees who receive salaries. In others, they remain independent and receive compensation on the volume of services provided and treatment measures taken. Within the strictest version of the single-payer system, private healthcare insurance and other ways to 'move beyond voluntary' public medicine are prohibited. The classic National Health Insurance system can be found in Canada; such healthcare model has spread also in some other countries (Taiwan, South Korea).[5]

Out-of-pocket model—'Pay-to-Play' is used in rural areas of India, Africa, China, South America). Only the developed, industrialized countries—perhaps 40 of the world's 200 countries—have established health care systems. Globally, most nations are too poor and too disorganized to provide any kind of mass medical care. The basic rule in such countries is that the rich get medical care; the poor stay sick or die.

As a separate healthcare model sometimes the Patchwork model—'A Little of this, a little of that' is considered, such as model, applies in the US. The patchwork model is an informal term because this model has elements of all four previously mentioned systems in this fragmented national health care apparatus. When it comes to treating veterans, this model is British, for Americans over the age of 65 on Medicare it is Canadian model, for working Americans who get insurance on the job it is German. For the uninsured or underinsured, the US model is rural Indian, with access to a doctor available if you can pay the bill out of pocket at the time of treatment or if you're sick enough to be admitted to the emergency ward at the public hospital.[6]

It is worth noting the classification of the model of a single-payer, the model of health insurance at work, and the model of managed competition. The first two models correspond to the Beveridge and Bismarck models. The latter one—the model of managed competition—involves the provision of medical services by

[4]Tanner (2008).

[5]Wallace (2013).

[6]Summary of international health systems (2011). http://caphysiciansalliance.org/wp-content/uploads/2011/11/International-Comparison.pdf.

private providers, but this market is 'artificial' because it is under tight control and regulation by the state.[7]

In most cases, the state requires citizens to purchase a healthcare insurance policy, which is often combined with the obligation of employers to insure their employees. Patients can choose an insurance company as well as a healthcare provider within a regulated market. Although the standard insurance 'package' is set by the state, insurance companies are allowed to compete with each other on prices, the level of equity participation in the payment of services, and additional coverage. In its purest form, a comprehensive insurance system based on managed competition operates in Switzerland, and recently the healthcare system of the Netherlands has also transferred to a similar basis.[8]

There are some significant differences within these general categories. In some countries, such as France and Japan, the share of consumers in the financing of healthcare is quite significant—so they try to avoid unnecessary requests for medical care and excessive costs for these needs. In other countries, the amount the consumer is obliged to pay out of his/her pocket is limited. Sometimes citizens are allowed to choose medical facilities and the purchase of alternative or additional policies from private insurers is widespread, while in other countries private insurance is prohibited or underdeveloped. Resource allocation and prioritization also vary widely. In Japan, for example, substantial sums are being invested in new technologies, but compensation for surgery is limited, and France has an unusually high level of prescription drugs.[9]

While in theory these categories have distinct policy separations, in reality, most countries have a blend of these approaches, though they generally have a single health care system.[10] The latter may include the following models: 'the southern model',[11] 'the Nordic model',[12] 'budget-insurance model of countries with economies in transition.'[13]

2.3 *Primary and Derivative Characteristics of Healthcare Model*

Despite the diversity of healthcare models, the system of legal characteristics (determinants) of the European unified model is determined by the primary and

[7] Enthoven (1993).

[8] Tanner (2006).

[9] Tanner (2008).

[10] Reid (2009); Summary of international health systems (2011) http://caphysiciansalliance.org/wp-content/uploads/2011/11/International-Comparison.pdf.

[11] Ferrera (1996).

[12] Andersen et al. (2007).

[13] Voronenko and Skorohod (2014).

derivative characteristics, which are inherent in different European countries and reflect the common development of health care.

The principle underlying the model, i.e. the recognition of the nature of medical services as a social good, should be considered as a decisive primary characteristic of the healthcare model.

Derived characteristics (determinants) of the healthcare model are: (1) the scope, quality, availability, and range of available medical services; (2) sources and methods of financing healthcare (according to the rules of social insurance, etc.); (3) unification of general provisions for providing medical services; (4) dualism and/or monism of contracts for providing medical services; (5) control of funds spending efficiency; (6) the legal status of providers of healthcare services as subjects of private or public law; (7) the share of healthcare expenditure in the gross domestic product; (8) use of new technologies; (9) price regulation, other permissible restrictions of the state on medical services.

Each of these healthcare models is based on a different understanding of what healthcare goods are. The principle underlying the model of healthcare concerns both the role of the state and the understanding of the 'goods' in the field of healthcare and the social essence of medical services for society. World practice has formed three main approaches to understanding medical services: as a public, quasi-public, and private goods, which determines the existence and scope of the state's obligation to control the healthcare system.

The state-funded and social insurance models of healthcare recognize a medical service as a public or quasi-public good, which is bought and sold under state control in accordance with restrictions established by law (state-regulated prices, etc.) and taking into account the social purpose of this service. In the market model of healthcare, medical service is considered as private goods that are bought and sold like any other product, regardless of their social purpose and with minimal restrictions by the state.

The attitude to medical services as a private, public or quasi-public good determines the role of the state in the healthcare system, the formation of prices for medical services, and the remuneration of employees in this field.

One of the decisive characteristics of the healthcare model is related to the legal models of medical services applicable in the national healthcare system, which differ in the legal grounds for their providing and the turnover of medical services under the rules of private law or public law.

In European countries two main models for the rendering of medical services can be roughly distinguished: monistic and dualistic. The monistic model for medical services stipulates that the relevant medical services are provided according to the rules of civil (private) law services, and medical services, provided on behalf of a public authority (state or regional community)—according to the rules for providing of public services, to which the provisions of public law apply unless otherwise stipulated by law. The dualistic model for rendering medical services lies in the ability to provide medical services according to the rules on rendering of civil (private) services, or according to the rules on rendering of public (administrative) services.

An example of a monistic model for rendering medical services is the law of Ukraine, where medical services are mainly provided based on contracts (contract for rendering of medical services, contract of medical care under state medical guarantees) under the rules on civil law services. Even if the medical service is provided by the state or municipal healthcare entity based on a public healthcare contract, these medical services are subject to the general provisions of the CC of Ukraine on services and performance of obligations, not the provisions on public (administrative) services and administrative contracts.

The dualistic model for rendering medical services is provided by the law of some European countries (in particular, Germany), which implies dualism and/or monism in models of healthcare delivery. Thus, German law provides rules for classifying the legal relationships for the provision of emergency medical care in the field of public law or private law according to the dualistic system and model of accession. The Accession model ('Eingliederungsmodel') provides for the provision of public emergency medical care on behalf of, at the expense of, and at the disposal of the respective federal state with which private entrepreneurs can cooperate. The Dualistic System (Dualistisches System) provides for the existence, along with the public, emergency medical care with the participation of private entrepreneurs acting on their behalf and at their own expense.[14]

The affiliation of the relevant national model of healthcare to centralized or decentralized healthcare systems, or their combination, in some respects, determines the social demand for the formation of the defining characteristics (determinants) of the European unified model of healthcare, which acknowledges the affiliation of healthcare to private good or quasi-public good.

Medical service is a private good in the case of its provision based on a contract for rendering of paid medical services, the party to which are private persons (for example, a private hospital-provider and a patient or other customer), or on other legal grounds based on legal equality and free will of the parties, if between the participants of the obligation there are no relationships of public power and subordination.

Medical service is a quasi-public good in case it is provided on the ground of an administrative act/order, on behalf of the subject of administrative power (state, municipal community) based on administrative power subordination between the participants of these legal relationships. The provision of medical services on the ground of an administrative act does not turn such services into a public good.

Obligations regarding medical services provided on the ground of an administrative act are of a civil nature, at least in part of the performance of such obligations, as comply to the general rules of performance of obligations under the Civil Code, given the administrative legal grounds for their provision.

[14]Martis and Winkhart-Martis (2014), p. 122.

2.4 *Effectiveness of the Healthcare Model: Towards a Unified Hybrid Healthcare Model in Europe*

The healthcare in each country is a product of its unique characteristics, history, the political process, and the national character of the people; many of these systems are currently undergoing major reforms.

An analysis of the best European healthcare models gives grounds for the general conclusion, that the strength of any national health and welfare system is the domestic people's adherence to the fundamental principle of contribution based on the ability to pay, and the receipt of care on the basis of need. This type of system ensures solidarity and freedom; for patients, freedom in choice of physician and for health care professionals, the freedom to set up practice and prescribe.[15]

At the same time, today, in many European countries, there is a general trend towards the formation of hybrid nature of the healthcare, which makes it possible to avoid some of the most serious problems inherent in other models,[16] including public and market healthcare systems.

The use of state-funded centralized healthcare in all European countries causes the need for mechanisms of managed competition to avoid excessive regulating of medical services and the threat of increased costs.

Managed competition in health care is defined as a purchasing strategy to obtain maximum value for consumers and employers, using rules for competition derived from microeconomic principles, according to which a sponsor (either an employer, a governmental entity, or a purchasing cooperative), acting on behalf of a large group of subscribers, structures and adjusts the market to overcome attempts by insurers to avoid price competition.[17]

Finding a compromise solution to competition in state-guaranteed health care is a complex process involving sometimes the inconsistent, even paradoxical, behavior of their actors.

The irony is that those who most loudly called for competition as the ultimate means of achieving a sustainable, affordable health care system are the very same players who are now opposing any change. Competition is fine as long as it affects everybody except oneself.

Compromise on this issue extends to the limites of achieving certain incentives to improve the quality and efficiency of health care in order to strike a balance in the form of an agreement that meets the needs of all parties—patients, health care facilities and the state, which guarantees the health care.[18]

To avoid the excessive regulating of medical services and the threat of increased costs, the most of the European countries try within of their healthcare reforms to

[15] Cases (2006).

[16] Tanner (2008).

[17] Enthoven (1993).

[18] Lisac and Schlette (2006), Cases (2006).

modernise hospitals, and improve health systems organization and management. They aim to change the behaviour of key actors and place a special emphasis on the monitoring of health care expenditure by health care professionals. The reforms, in particular, focus both on the renewal of the organisation and management of the health system on one hand, and financial measures and incentives on the other.[19] Moreover, the reforms will have strong implications for modernising hospitals and other health facilities. The Modernising hospitals usually has several tiers: firstly, the use of an approach based on a key concept—complementairity; secondly, an important reform of hospital funding with activity based payment; and finally, structural reforms placing more emphasis on clinical services in hospitals.

In this context, the most successful experience of building an effective healthcare model among European countries (in particular, France)[20] shows that the effectiveness of the pan-European unified model should be associated with such a feature as a significant share of patients in the payment for medical services aiming at avoiding excessive use of medical services.

The ability of the state-funded healthcare model to contain rising medical costs is largely due to the possibility of an innovative solution by the national healthcare system of one of the most difficult policy issues in this area: the phenomenon of economic nature called ‘moral risk.’ Moral risk is the tendency of people to overconsume goods and services if it provides them with higher benefits without a corresponding increase in costs. In other words, it means that people eat more at all inclusive buffet because they can get additional portion for free, likewise, they tend to seek medical services more often because they have paid for them in advance in the form of insurance premiums, rather than upon receipt.

The obvious solution is to transfer a larger share of the cost from premiums in the share participation or insurance deduction, thereby increasing consumer’s awareness of the real costs of each ‘unit’ of healthcare service they receive.[21]

An important role in the formation of an effective healthcare system plays the availability of a largely unregulated market of private healthcare insurance that fills the gaps of supply on medical insurance market. Besides, consumers should be allowed to pay extra for better and additional services, as a result of which the healthcare system aquires a two-level character. These features do not correspond to the most common notions of what public healthcare should be.

The healthcare model should provide mechanisms for resolving the general contradiction related to healthcare services provided by the state: most people do not want to pay more for them (either by raising taxes or directly from their own pockets), and at the same time, citizens are concerned that cost containment measures may lead to a deterioration in the quality of services in the future.

In this regard, the healthcare model should take into account the peculiarities of the national character of the relevant country. Thus, two-thirds of the consumers of

[19] Cases (2006).
[20] Tanner (2008).
[21] Klein (2007).

healthcare services in France expressed the view that the quality of healthcare services is not as important as comprehensive and equal access to these services. This means that the French experience would probably be difficult to implement in another country, whose citizens are characterized by a much less egalitarian ethic.[22]

Thus, the European unified healthcare model should combine universal coverage with a public-private mix of hospital and ambulatory care and a broad service provision taking into account financing and institutional ability of the national healthcare system.

Unlike countries with a liberal healthcare model, all European countries predominantly use a public healthcare system, which determines their differences and main characteristics (determinants).

In contrary to the liberal model and other healthcare systems, the undoubted advantages of state health care models used by European countries (Beveridge, Bismarck, budget and insurance, etc.) are: less expenditure on health care administration in comparison with other systems, better than in other systems healthcare output, the issue of the fundamental moral decision to provide health care coverage to all citizens. European countries that have embraced universal health coverage for their citizens have outperformed the other health care systems on indices of cost, quality, and choice—three key principles of an effective health care model.[23]

However, compared to the US-healthcare system, the disadvantages of European state-funded healthcare models include: insufficient use of advanced medical technology, prescription drugs and research in the field of healthcare; less effective healthcare measures for patients with cancer, pneumonia, heart disease, and AIDS.[24]

The disadvantages of healthcare normativity, provided by state funding, may be eliminated by managed competition rules by combining economic efficiency and growth of healthcare with a peaceful labour market, a fair distribution of income and social cohesion, taking into account present challenges to the healthcare model, including globalization and demographic change. This model will remain viable and successful only if the challenges and the need for reform are understood—and if action is taken. In particular, productivity in healthcare services could be enhanced by having them subjected to competition from other public or private providers. Raising efficiency in the provision of public healthcare services is indeed essential for resolving the fiscal dilemma. Increase in privatization and/or outsourcing of public healthcare services may in some cases help raise efficiency if difficult and important issues of governance can be successfully dealt with. Growth increases the tax base and tax revenues—but also the public sector wage bill and transfers as well as the demand for welfare services.[25]

Any healthcare model that exists in European countries has its advantages and disadvantages, which makes it impossible to determine which of them is the most

---

[22] Rodwin (2003).

[23] Reid (2009).

[24] Tanner (2008).

[25] Andersen et al. (2007).

effective: market, governmental, or social insurance. Determining the effectiveness of the healthcare model and taking into account its provisions as a general guideline or a unified—pan-European—healthcare model should be based on the idea of a balance of basic characteristics (determinants), which reflect often conflicting goals of maximizing quality, efficiency and equality of access, as well as the effectiveness of healthcare system in conditions of limited governmental resources and demographic and technological changes.[26]

Thus the main but not the only criterion for evaluating the effectiveness of the healthcare model should be the right to universal access to healthcare without discrimination and, consequently, improvement of the overall health performance of health and well-being of the entire population.

In this regard, the reform of the healthcare model of any country should be based on a system of key determinants (characteristics) that provide the social relationships to maintain, restore and improve private and public health, taking into account the state, features, and resources of national healthcare to be reformed.

An effective national healthcare model aims to balance public and private interests by taking into account the peculiarities of a centralized and pluralized healthcare sectors and a dualistic understanding of healthcare services as a public good.

In particular, given the existence of a centralized model, it is primarily a matter of revising the presumption of governmental supremacy and introducing elements of decentralization (increasing the institutional capacity of healthcare facilities at the local and regional levels, legitimizing public-private partnerships).

Instead, the market healthcare models are improved by the state acting as a kind of referent-monitor in the relationships between authorized governmental and private subjects.[27]

Thus, the pan-European unified model of healthcare should combine universal coverage with public-private hospital and ambulatory healthcare to provide a high level of medical services, envisage a relevant share of consumers in the payment of medical services necessary to avoid excessive use of medical services, other mechanisms of managed competition under tight governmental control and regulation, taking into account the financial and institutional capacity, mental traditions of national healthcare systems of the relevant European countries.

---

[26] Reform of Healthcare systems in Europe—harmonization of requirements for equity, quality and efficiency: recommendation of the Parliamentary Assembly of the Council of Europe 1626 (2002). http://www.coe.int/T/r/Parliamentary_Assembly/%5bRussian_documents%5d/%5b2003%5d/%5bSept_2003%5d/Rec%201626%20Rus.asp#TopOfPage.

[27] Pronevych (2017).

2.5 *Peculiarities of Healthcare Models of European Countries in Transition*

A majority of Central-Eastern European countries, which are countries in transition, are faced with carrying out health-care reforms and examining the relevance of a theoretical model of health care law-making. Confronted with the legacy of the previous regime, the mentioned countries have shifted away from a ‘socialist’ model towards a more ‘market-oriented’ health care system. From a legal perspective, this change of system imposed the need for drastic reforms on the government, starting with the introduction of a compulsory health insurance scheme based on the notion of solidarity. Future accession to the EU, requiring the incorporation of the EU acquis, has increased the complexity of legal reforms. Strengthening the reform process increases the importance of a developed method of law-making based on the legal theoretical understanding. Case study research in the selected European countries justifies the conclusion that the analytical model rationalizes the law-making activity, including the ‘EU law approximation process.’ What is more, it became apparent that the importance of this theoretical model is not restricted only to the selected countries but may also be a valuable instrument for other European countries.[28]

At the same time, the analytical model of healthcare should take into account the differences in understanding the essence of healthcare that exist in European countries with developed market economies and countries in transition in Southeast, Central, and Eastern Europe.

The macroeconomic environment in European countries in transition has a huge impact on healthcare services. The socio-economic crisis has worsened the healthcare situation in these European countries. Healthcare in many transition countries has faced significant challenges, indicating a close link between social and health status. The globalization of markets widens the gap between the rich and the poor. Poverty, regardless of its causes and manifestations, is one of the main factors in poor health. Both unemployment and uncertainty about the future contribute to deteriorating of health, increasing the risk of psychological and physical disorders, and suicide.

Social inequality in European countries in transition is increasing along with the cost of healthcare and medicine. The public health-based care system, which guarantees full and free access to all healthcare services regardless of income, is currently being reformed under pressure from both the market and international financial institutions.[29]

The policy of reforms in many European countries in transition is aimed at increasing market elements in the healthcare system, decentralization, strengthening the role of healthcare. Decentralization is a key principle of healthcare reform in

---

[28] Den Exter (2002).

[29] Tadevosyan (2000), item 19.

many of these countries. It is seen as an effective way to improve the quality of services, greater involvement of resources according to needs. Privatization is the ultimate form of decentralization. Governments with financial difficulties view privatization as a means of raising private capital in healthcare, thus reducing the need for meager public funds.[30]

The experiences in the early 1990s however, revealed certain devastating effects of transposing the general concept of market competition to the field of health care. One valuable lesson of those developments was that liberalising relations in health care necessitates a certain degree of government intervention. Furthermore, the nature and the scope of Central and Eastern European healthcare reforms differed from country to country with no readily available uniform 'blueprint' for reform derived from emulating Western European experiences. Nevertheless, previous experiences in reforming health care may provide us with some valuable lessons. Their significance needs, nonetheless, to be reviewed taking into account specific national features.[31]

In this context, for European countries in transition, which are now moving from a 'socialist' model to a 'market-oriented' healthcare system, it is necessary to take into account the European experience, in particular, of Germany, France, and Great Britain, as well as the peculiarities of healthcare reform of similar in general social, economic and legal traditions transition countries of Central and Eastern Europe.

The decisive principle that should underlie the national healthcare model of any European country concerns the understanding of the 'good/goods' in the field of healthcare and the social nature of medical services for society, which determines the existence and scope of the state's obligation to control the healthcare system.

The orientation of European transition countries to the formation of a market and social society has created the inadmissibility of concepts of medical services as an exclusively public or private good and the need to understand medical services as a private good (based on contracts of rendering medical services) and quasi-public good (based on state-funded contracts or acts of state authority), acquisition and alienation of which is carried out according to the rules of civil turnover under the control of the state and with the restrictions established by law.

A unified understanding of healthcare services as a private and quasi-public good and financing of the latter mainly through budget funds under healthcare public run insurance rules determines the social insurance type of the national healthcare model based on comprehensive healthcare insurance and unacceptability for countries of Central and Eastern Europe of exclusively public or market (private) healthcare system.

The expediency of legislative implementation in the Central and Eastern Europe law of legal provisions for a unified understanding of medical services as private and quasi-public goods and general provision for providing medical services is noteworthy along with the dualistic and/or monistic model of contracts for rendering medical

[30] Tavedosyan (2000), items 15–20.

[31] Den Exter (2002).

services and the resulting features of state-funding of medical services and legal status of medical services providers as subjects of private law and public law.

2.6 Common Frame of Reference and Legal Instruments of Unification of the Pan-European Healthcare Model

Despite the diversity and differences in healthcare models, Europe is developing common frame of reference for a unified, pan-European healthcare model that is in line with the EU's common legal values, such as fundamental rights, democracy, and the rule of law.[32]

In the condition of information society with market and social orientation, the priority of human rights protection and globalization, the modern approach to the typology of healthcare systems determines the main characteristics (determinants) of universal legal relationships in maintaining, restoring and improving private and public healthcare, which are based on fundamental human rights and freedoms.[33]

Because of this, the common frame of reference of the unified—pan-European—model of healthcare define, in particular, the following main characteristics: the legal nature of medical services as a private and quasi-public good; financing of state-guaranteed healthcare under social insurance rules; general provisions for providing medical services; dualism and/or monism for rendering medical services provided for by national law; the legal status of healthcare providers as subjects of private and public law.

As it was stated above, there is currently no unified legal instrument dealing specifically with the unified legal model of healthcare and general terms of medical services rendering. Fragmentary regulation is provided by both universal and regional international instruments.

However, some applicable rules may be found in the *Charter of Fundamental Rights of the European Union* (2012) (hereinafter—as Charter of EU).

According to Art. 152 of the said Charter, 'The Community shall ensure a high level of healthcare protection, . . .improve healthcare, . . .encourage cooperation with third States and competent international organizations in the field of healthcare.'[34]

These provisions are extremely important. In the absence of explicit powers of the Community in Healthcare, provided for in Art. 152 of the Charter makes it possible to pursue healthcare policy at the Community level, immersing it in all Community

[32] Art. 2 of the Treaty on European Union. The Union is founded on the values of respect for human dignity, freedom, democracy, equality, the rule of law and respect for human rights, including the rights of persons belonging to minorities. These values are common to the Member States in a society in which pluralism, non-discrimination, tolerance, justice, solidarity and equality between women and men prevail.

[33] Fadejkina (2014).

[34] Charter of Fundamental Rights of the European Union (2012). https://eur-lex.europa.eu/legal-content/EN/TXT/?uri=CELEX%3A12012P%2FTXT.

policies. This has played a very important role in determining the directions of the development of the law enforcement practice of the European Court. For example, in the decision of the ECtHR in the case *British American Tobacco (Investments) and Imperial Tobacco* (2002) it is stated that in case of a reference to Art. 95 of the EU Treaty as a legal basis, the legislator cannot exclude that the factor underlying the decision is public health. Also, since the adoption of any action by the Community should ensure a high level of protection of human health, the same level of protection should be assured in the implementation of measures on harmonization.[35]

Basic principles of healthcare reforms for all European countries are envisaged in the Ljubljana Charter oh Healthcare Reform, which was developed under the auspices of the WHO Regional Office for Europe and approved by European member states of the WHO on 19. June 1996. The Ljubljana Charter addresses healthcare reforms taking into account the specific features of the European region and is based on the fact that the most important task of healthcare is to improve the health and quality of life of the population.

The Ljubljana Charter emphasizes that the healthcare systems of the European Region should: be based on the principles of human dignity, equality, solidarity, and professional ethics; aim to improve health; be guided by the needs and expectations of citizens; focus on improving the quality and efficiency of costs; receive sufficient funding for the sustainable provision of medical care to all citizens, which provides for universal coverage of the population and equal access to the necessary care; meet the requirements of comprehensiveness, continuity, and consistency of primary healthcare.

Particular attention is paid to making and the development of healthcare policy, taking into account the views and choices of citizens on key issues, reorganizing the system for providing medical services, changing the nature of human resources use, improving governance mechanisms.[36]

In accordance with the Recommendations of the Committee of Ministers of the Council of Europe on rule-making in the field of healthcare management (CM/Rec (2010) in all Member States:

> I. Laws and regulations on healthcare management should be based on fundamental values and principles.
>
> 1. The legal framework for the healthcare system should be based on the three fundamental values of the Council of Europe: respect of human rights and human dignity; the rule of law; democracy. The right to healthcare should be based on the principles of universality, equality, and solidarity.

[35]Case C-491/01 The Queen v Secretary of State for Health, ex parte British American Tobacco (Investments) Ltd and Imperial Tobacco Ltd. https://eur-lex.europa.eu/legal-content/EN/TXT/HTML/?uri=CELEX:62001CJ0491&from=EN.

[36]The Ljubljana Charter on reforming health care in Europe of 18 June 1996. http://www.euro.who.int/__data/assets/pdf_file/0012/113304/E55363R.pdf?ua=1.

2. Member States are invited to put in place monitoring systems to systematically access the adequacy of governance mechanisms.[37]

Directive N 2011/24//EU of the European Parliament and of the Council of 9 March 2011 on the application of patient's rights to cross-border healthcare provides as follows:

> As defined by the Council in its Conclusions of 1-2 June 2006 on Common Values and Principles in the European Union Health System[38] (hereinafter referred to as the 'Council Conclusions'), there are several operative principles that are common to the healthcare system throughout the Union.
>
> These principles are necessary to ensure patient confidence in cross-border healthcare services, which is necessary to achieve patient mobility, as well as a high level of healthcare. In the same statement, the Council recognized that 'the practical ways of implementing these values and principles differ significantly from one Member State to another. In particular, decisions on the basket of healthcare services to which citizens are entitled and the mechanisms used to finance and provide such healthcare services, such as the extent to which it is appropriate to rely on market mechanisms and competitive pressures to manage healthcare systems should be taken in a national context.[39]

In the context of globalization and harmonization of EU law with the national law of European countries in the field of healthcare, it is expedient to define in various instruments of legal unification, in particular in the European Parliament and the Council, the recommendations of the Committee of Ministers of the Council of Europe decisive characteristics (determinants) of a new comprehensive policy to unify the healthcare model. These determinants include general provisions for providing medical services and other healthcare standards that will take into account the diversity and specificities of healthcare models, national healthcare systems and healthcare policies of the European countries, developed market economies and countries in transition, as well as the decisions and mechanisms, which should be taken in the national context to meet the needs of a market economy and take advantage of the experience and legal framework of the European Union.

[37] Recommendation CM/Rec (2010) 6 of the Committee of Ministers to member states on good governance in health systems. https://search.coe.int/cm/Pages/result_details.aspx?ObjectId=090000168063d340.

[38] Council Conclusions on Common values and principles in European Union Health Systems (2006) C 146/01, OB C 146, p. 1.

[39] Directive 2011/24/EU of the European Parliament and of the Council of 9 March 2011 on the application of patients' rights in cross-border healthcar. *OJ L 88, pp 45–65.* https://eur-lex.europa.eu/legal-content/EN/TXT/?uri=celex%3A32011L0024.

3 Concluding Remarks

The pan-European unified legal model of healthcare is a system of legal norms, which are provided by the instruments of unification of European law and contain principles and decisive characteristics (determinants) of healthcare in the European countries at national and international levels. They combine recognized values and operative principles in the EU with acceptable economic efficiency and growth of the healthcare of European countries, taking into account common and distinctive features of European countries, developed economies and countries in transition.

This unified healthcare model should be the basic healthcare standard, setting a minimum level of healthcare for all European counties, combining universal coverage with public-private hospital and ambulatory care to secure a high level of healthcare provision. It should also provide for equal participation of consumers in the payment of medical services, necessary to avoid excessive use of medical services, other tools of managed competition under tight control and regulation of the state, taking into account European values and principles, financial and institutional ability, mentality and other national traditions of European healthcare systems.

The legal instruments of European unification should provide a common frame of reference for the pan-European unified healthcare model, which will define the basic principles, characteristics (determinants) of the unified model, principles of international policy, the exclusive competence of national law, the interrelation of international and national healthcare policies based on the exclusivity of the competence of national law and the subsidiarity of the norms of the international healthcare law.

The pan-European unified healthcare model is based on the recognition of EU values: universality, access to good quality care and solidarity; and the operative principles of health care which include quality, safety, evidence, and ethics, redress, privacy, and confidentiality in the field of healthcare.

The decisive characteristics (determinants) of the unified European healthcare model include general understanding, conditions of provision, and methods of financing medical services. The basis of the European unified healthcare model of law shall the understanding of the 'good'/'product' of healthcare and the social essence of medical services for society.

The decisive values of the European Union and orientation of Europe towards the formation of a market and social society determine the unacceptability of the concepts of healthcare services as a purely public or private good and the need to understand healthcare services as a private good (the subject of the contract for rendering medical services) and quasi-public good (the subject of authority on medical care), obligations to provide medical services are performed according to the general rules of the fulfillment of obligations under the Civil Code, taking into account the features provided by law.

The general understanding of medical services as a private and quasi-public good and the financing of the latter mainly through budget funds under social insurance rules determine the social insurance type of a unified healthcare model based on public run healthcare insurance and unacceptability for European countries of exclusively public or market (private) healthcare systems.

References

Andersen TM, Holmström B, Honkapohja S et al (2007) The Nordic modell. Embracihg Globalization and sharing risks. Taloustieto Oy, Helsinki. https://economics.mit.edu/files/5726

Case C-491/01 The Queen v Secretary of State for Health, ex parte British American Tobacco (Investments) Ltd and Imperial Tobacco Ltd. https://eur-lex.europa.eu/legal-content/EN/TXT/HTML/?uri=CELEX:62001CJ0491&from=EN

Charter of Fundamental Rights of the European Union (2012) https://eur-lex.europa.eu/legal-content/EN/TXT/?uri=CELEX%3A12012P%2FTXT

Chung M (2017) National Health care reform: learning from other major health care systems. Princeton Public Health Revue. https://pphr.princeton.edu/2017/12/02/unhealthy-health-care-a-cursory-overview-of-major-health-care-systems/

Council Conclusions on Common values and principles in European Union Health Systems (2006) C 146/01. https://eur-lex.europa.eu/LexUriServ/LexUriServ.do?uri=OJ:C:2006:146:0001:0003:EN:PDF

Den Exter A (2002) Health Care Law-making in Central and Eastern Europe (Social Europe Series). Intersentia Publishers file:///C:/Users/Admin/Downloads/020926_Exter,%20Andre%20Pieter%20den.pdf

Directive 2011/24/EU of the European Parliament and of the Council of 9 March 2011 on the application of patients' rights in cross-border healthcar. OJ L 88, pp 45–65. https://eur-lex.europa.eu/legal-content/EN/TXT/?uri=celex%3A32011L0024.

Enthoven A (1993) The history and principles of managed competition. Health Aff 12(suppl. 1): 24–48. https://www.healthaffairs.org/doi/10.1377/hlthaff.12.Suppl_1.24

Fadejkina NV (2014) Peculiarities of Management in the field of Healthcare. Sibirskaya finansovaja shkola 5:22–30. https://www.elibrary.ru/item.asp?id=22561286

Ferrera M (1996) The 'Southern Model' of welfare in social Europe. J Eur Soc Policy. https://doi.org/10.1177/095892879600600102. https://journals.sagepub.com/doi/10.1177/095892879600600102

Tadevosyan G (2000) Cooperation in the field of health care among the BSEC Member States. Doc. GA15/CC14/REP (d) /00/r Fifteenth Plenary Meeting of the General Assembly Committee on Culture, Health and Social Affairs https://www.pabsec.org/depo/documents/reports-and-recommendations/ru-rep-zm640srrze.pdf

Klein E (2007) The Health of Nations: Here's How Canada, France, Britain, Germany, and our Own Veterans Health Administration Manage to Cover Everybody at Less Cost and with Better Care than We Do. American Prospect. https://prospect.org/features/health-nations/

Martis R, Winkhart-Martis M (2014) Arzthaftungs-recht. Fallgruppenkommentar von Ruediger Martis und Martina Winkhart-Martis, 4. Auflage. Verlag Dr. Otto Schmidt, Koeln

Lisac N, Schlette S (2006) Health care reform in Germany: is Bismarck going Beveridge? Eurohealth 12(3):31. https://www.euro.who.int/__data/assets/pdf_file/0009/80478/Eurohealth12_3.pdf

Pronevych OS (2017) Implementation of the basic elements of the European model of relationships 'state-patient-physician' in the national legislation of Ukraine. Forum prava 2:104–111. https://journals.indexcopernicus.com/api/file/viewByFileId/297497.pdf

Recommendation CM/Rec (2010) 6 of the Committee of Ministers to member states on good governance in health systems. https://search.coe.int/cm/Pages/result_details.aspx?ObjectId=090000168063d340

Reform of Healthcare systems in Europe – harmonization of requirements for equity, quality and efficiency: recommendation of the Parliamentary Assembly of the Council of Europe 1626 (2002) http://www.coe.int/T/r/Parliamentary_Assembly/%5bRussian_documents%5d/%5b2003%5d/%5bScpt_2003%5d/Rec%201626%20Rus.asp#TopOfPage

Reid TR (2009) The healing of America: a global quest for better, cheaper, and fairer health care. Am J Pharm Educ 73(7):127. https://www.ncbi.nlm.nih.gov/pmc/articles/PMC2779642/pdf/ajpe127b.pdf

Rodwin VG (2003) The health care system under French national health insurance: lessons for health reform in the United States. Am J Public Health 93(1):31–37. https://pubmed.ncbi.nlm.nih.gov/12511380/. https://doi.org/10.11603/1681-2786.2014.2.3377

Shikha P (2020) Comparing Healthcare models and their role in the Covid-19 response. https://www.peaceinnovation.com/blog/comparing-healthcare-models-and-their-role-in-the-covid-19-response

Summary of International Health Systems (2011) http://caphysiciansalliance.org/wp-content/uploads/2011/11/International-Comparison.pdf

Tanner M (2006) No miracle in Massachusetts: why governor Romney's health care reform won't work. Cato Institute Briefing Paper 97. https://www.cato.org/sites/cato.org/files/pubs/pdf/bp97.pdf

Tanner M (2008) The grass is not always Greener: a look at national health care systems around the world. Policy Anal 613:48. https://doi.org/10.2139/ssrn.1262978

The Ljubljana Charter on reforming health care in Europe of 18 June 1996. http://www.euro.who.int/__data/assets/pdf_file/0012/113304/E55363R.pdf?ua=1

Voronenko YV, Skorohod AV (2014) Introduction of budget insurance model of the healtcare system on principles of public-private partnerships. Visnyk sozialnoji gigieny ta organizazii ohorony Ukrainy 2. https://doi.org/10.11603/1681-2786.2014.2.3377

Wallace LS (2013) A view of health care around the world. Ann Fam Med. 11(1):84. https://www.ncbi.nlm.nih.gov/pmc/articles/PMC3596027/

An Obsolete Health Act and the Rise of a Patients' Rights Act in the Netherlands: Lessons to the Ukraine?

André den Exter

Contents

Abstract Introducing several waves of reforms, the Dutch Health Act 1956 appeared outdated. What remained is a minimalistic piece of legislation defining the supervisory role of the Health Care Inspectorate in the field of public health. One of the lessons learned is to cherish the value of an umbrella Health Act, providing a comprehensive and consistent set of legal norms supplemented by more detailed legislation. Otherwise, the risk of a 'patchwork of statutory laws' with inherent inconsistencies is eminent. At the same time, new understanding on pan-European human rights in health care should be an integral part of modernising patients' rights legislation, irrespective of the nature of such norms (civil or public law). It will thus balance both individual and social rights in health care, while incorporating the public debate in emerging health-related issues as adopted by the Oviedo Convention.

A. den Exter (✉)
Erasmus School of Law, Erasmus University Rotterdam, Rotterdam, The Netherlands
e-mail: denexter@law.eur.nl

© The Author(s), under exclusive license to Springer Nature Switzerland AG 2022
R. Maydanyk et al. (eds.), *Ukrainian Healthcare Law in the Context of European and International Law*, European Union and its Neighbours in a Globalized World 7,
https://doi.org/10.1007/978-3-031-05690-1_2

1 Introduction

Reconsidering its legal framework in health care, Ukraine is discussing the need for updating or revising its basic health care law, the Health Act. Such an 'umbrella Act' regulates the basic structure and organisation of health care services and providers, public health services, the role and competences of state actors, the rights of patients, and the monitoring and enforcement issues. Such an all-encompassing law can be found in many countries in Central and Eastern Europe,[1] as well as in several Western countries (e.g. the UK National Health Services Act 2006,[2] the French *Code de la santé publique*,[3] and to some extent, the Dutch Health Act 1956[4]).

A question that may arise in the reform discussion is whether these foreign experiences are of any relevance for the Ukraine. Are there lessons to be learned, even failures to be avoided when revising—or considering the revision of—such an essential part of the legal framework of health care in a particular country? To answer that question would require a full comparative analysis of the underlying legal systems, which is not realistic within the limited scope of this contribution. Instead, the focus will be on highlighting some experiences in a single country, and its relevance to the Ukraine, limited to this book's underlying topic, patients' rights. This analysis demonstrates the importance of a pan-European approach as emphasized in the previous chapter, as far as patients' rights are concerned. Another important observation is that modernising patient rights' legislation in the Ukraine does not necessarily means that a Health Act has become obsolete. On the contrary, such a basic law contributes to a clear structure and certain consistency in legislation.

2 The Dutch Health Act

2.1 Legal Context

The Dutch health care system has been characterised by a rather permanent state of reforms.[5] This is due to major changes introduced in several 'waves of reforms' since the 1960s, both in terms of the organisation and provision, and financing of health care. These reforms have also affected the legal framework, introducing new concepts in the field of social health insurance, lifting the planning of health institutions, a partial liberalisation of price setting in health care, and the introduction of a Patients' Rights Act in 1995, as well as the introduction of various pieces of

---

[1] Den Exter (2002).

[2] https://www.legislation.gov.uk/, search for: National Health Services Act 2006.

[3] https://www.legifrance.gouv.fr/ search for: *Code de la santé publique*.

[4] In Dutch, the '*Gezondheidswet*' (GZW) Stb (Official Journal) 1956.

[5] Den Exter (2010), pp. 223–233.

legislation.[6] A number of these legal Acts have been evaluated, and have been extensively discussed in the legal literature since.[7]

To understand the Dutch legal system, some explanatory remarks are necessary. Under Article 22(1) of the Dutch Constitution, 'the authorities shall take steps to promote public health'. This provision has been generally interpreted as a 'mere' obligation of the government to be concerned with setting up health facilities and facilitating access to necessary healthcare. This obligation has been effectuated by developing a social health insurance system (Health Insurance Act (Zvw) and the Long-term Care Act (Wlz). Consequently, health insurers will purchase necessary care services from private (not-for-profit) health care entities and individual health professionals. Apart from establishing a health insurance system, Article 22 also includes the obligation to regulate the admission of health care facilities to the market by setting preconditions in the Health Care Institutions Admission Act (WTZi), and simultaneously replacing the hospital planning system. Finally, there is an obligation to regulate the purchaser–provider relationship, by means of the Act on Health Care Market Regulation (Wmg). As such, the statutory framework reflects the core elements of the constitutional right to health.[8]

2.2 *The Health Act 1956*

An interesting detail is that the constitutional provision on health itself was only introduced in 1975. That means that the current statutory legal framework is originally based on the Health Act 1956.[9] This Health Act replaced a former Act (1919), extending the state's competences in public (community) health, as well as introducing new competences concerning the organisation and provision of individual health care. Still, these newly introduced competences respect the crucial role of the private (not-for-profit) sector, responsible for the provision of individual health services. At that time, the Health Act reflected the spirit of the Dutch corporatist health care model, based on consensus between public and private entities, at national and regional level.[10]

In the following decades the government introduced various waves of reforms, stripping the relevance of the Health Act as an organic law. What remains are two key institutions: a Health Care Inspectorate (supervision and enforcement) and a Health Council (advisory role). In particular, the Health Inspectorate performs a key role in monitoring and safeguarding quality of care as provided by health professionals and health institutions (hospitals, rehabilitation centres, nursing homes,

---

[6] Den Exter and Guy (2014), pp. 255–273.

[7] Dute (2000), KNMG (2004), ZonMw (2009), KPMG Plexus (2014).

[8] In more detail, Den Exter and Guy (2014), pp. 255–273.

[9] In Dutch *Gezondheidswet* (GZW) Stb 1956, 51.

[10] Helderman (2005), pp. 189–210.

ambulance services, private clinics, pharmaceutical companies, etc.). Its supervisory and enforcement competencies have been enacted in various statutory acts and to a certain extent harmonised, including access to health facilities, patient data, examining patient safety issues and public health risks, enforcing ministerial orders and issuing administrative penalties.

The monitoring and supervision of health care providers' duty to provide 'good care' ('*goede zorg*') is the general norm reviewed by the Health Care Inspectorate. Compliance to 'good care' has been defined as 'safe, effective, efficient, patient-oriented, provided in time and tuned to the real patient needs', as well as 'in line with the professional standards, and respecting the rights of patients'.[11]

3 The Patients' Rights Act

The 'good care' norm corresponds with the quality standard as covered by the Law on Patients' Rights (Medical Contract Treatment Act, Art. 7:453 CC), the 'care of a good professional' standard (*goed hulpverlenerschap*). The 'care of a good professional' norm implies the care is provided by 'a reasonable, qualified health professional'. Both standards ('good care' and 'good professional care') are dynamic, and evolve in time due to new professional understandings and medical technological developments. Since the professional standards have been set by the health professionals themselves, they are binding to all professionals. Deviation is not allowed, unless motivated by substantive reasons. Thus, despite its binding character the professional standards respect the doctor's professional autonomy. This has been confirmed by the court.[12]

The question that may arise is what is considered a professional standard? Without doubt, standards on treatment options for, let's say, chronic pain or diabetes[13] are generally considered as professional standards, defined by the professionals themselves. But what about organisational standards—how to organise and run a private practice? Those kind of standards are not necessarily aimed at, or affect the medical-technical performance of health care, and are thus always binding without reservation since they are set by those other than health professionals (e.g. a hospital management board). The same concerns patients' rights standards, set by law and therefore binding without exception. A good example is the latest standard or so-called Covid-19 triage guideline admission for critical care beds, drafted by the Dutch Medical Doctors Association which has age cut-offs that exclude the elderly.[14] This is a highly controversial issue due to its potential discriminatory

[11] Art. 2 Wkkgz.

[12] ECLI:NL:HR:2001:AB0377; ECLI:NL:PHR:2005:AS6006.

[13] As registered in the quality standards register (in Dutch): https://www.zorginzicht.nl/kwaliteitsinstrumenten.

[14] Covid-19 triage guideline admission (2020).

impact.[15] Since it is such a controversial issue individual doctors have argued they will not apply the standard, claiming their professional autonomy (the 'admission based on medical need' argument). That approach seems to deny the organisational nature of the ICU admission standard applicable in exceptional circumstances such as shortages of ICU beds and staff. In extreme situations as described, medical criteria are insufficient and non-medical criteria are then decisive. Triggering the Covid guideline requires ministerial approval, and is subject to parliamentary review. This, and the fact that the guidelines directly affect the rights of patients (health care access), requires doctors to respect the guideline without any reservation. Any other position would make their actions subject to medical disciplinary and judicial review.

Apart from the 'good professional standard', the Medical Contract Treatment Act covers a wide range of patients' rights and professional duties, including the right to be—or not to be—informed about the recommended treatment, alternative treatment options and the patient's health status; the patient's consent requirement; the duty for keeping and maintaining the patient's medical record, as well as access to the patient's medical record; the right to change and erase data from the medical record; and confidentiality and privacy clauses.[16] Patient's consent based on adequate information ('informed consent') is based on the constitutional value of human integrity, a prerequisite for any procedure and treatment, and generally accepted in both medical practice and the legal doctrine. Also accepted is the latest development: the shift from informed consent to 'shared decision-making' (SDM).[17] SDM promotes the involvement of patients in medical decision-making by discussing treatment options and *agreeing* on treatment decisions in partnership. That new approach is based on reaching consensus *with* the patient about the most appropriate treatment option.

Also generally accepted is the right of access to medical records, which is practically without clauses. Access may be denied only if the granting would result in injuring the privacy of a third party (Art. 456 CC). The right of access to medical records is of major importance whenever a patient considers taking legal action against a doctor or an institution.

On several occasions however, the law accepts exceptions and restrictions of certain patients' rights, either by law (the so-called therapeutic exception and the information clause), or based on professional standards ('conflict of interests' and consent), and subject to judicial review.

A new phenomenon introduced in the law is the notion of 'central liability' of the hospital, which then may be held liable 'as if it were a party to the contract'.[18] This central liability alleviates the patient's burden of proof in medical malpractice cases. Besides the hospital, the doctor remains liable for their own actions, all the same.

---

[15] Den Exter (2020), pp. 495–498.

[16] Markestein (1995), pp. 33–44.

[17] Introduced from 1 January 2020, *Official State J* (*Stb.* 2019, 224).

[18] Art. 462 s. 1.

Given the civil law nature, the physician's liability is in tort law. Here, the basis for medical injury compensation is negligence, which requires the breach of a duty of care based on fault (i.e. an unacceptable act by the health provider that no reasonable practitioner would have done under these circumstances) and the establishing of a causal link between the action and the damages. This remains the basis of an action, even when ADR is available.

Evaluating the law's effectiveness (2000), it was concluded that the law indeed contributed to strengthening the role of the patients, and was recognised by health professions as well.[19] In a way, the law confirmed the understanding and practice at that time (codification). The so-called fear of 'juridification' of the patient–doctor relationship was not justified.[20] Since then, the law has remained largely unchanged with some minor amendments, such as extending the period of keeping medical records from 15 to 20 years (January 2020).

Although the Medical Contract Treatment Act functions as a framework law establishing the general rights of patients, in addition, separate legislation may restrict patients' rights and/or provide additional guarantees, as in case of mental health (consent, mandatory admission and treatment, appeal, etc.), mentally retarded people (guardianship, complaints and appeal), organ donation (rights of the donor), and medical research on human beings (information and consent of participants). Still, the general norms remain valid when consistent with the more specific norms.

Derived from the original Health Act, the Medical Contract Treatment Act confirms the principles of patients' rights as expressed in numerous human rights treaties, including the Oviedo Convention of the Council of Europe, and thus confirms the pan-European notion of human rights in health care. Paradoxally, this confirmation is no reason for the Dutch government to ratify the Oviedo Treaty. This can be explained by the disagreement on the legal nature and policy implications of a key provision, the right to access to health care (Article 3 Oviedo Convention). That discussion is also relevant for other member states, including the Ukrainian healthcare system, about which more later.

4 Some Reflections on the Dutch Approach and Lessons to the Ukraine

As explained before, the patient–health provider relationship in the Netherlands is dominated by civil law contracts. Upholding patients' rights and providers' obligations is largely based on civil law standards such as what parties have agreed upon, and professional standards. These obligations and standards particularly address the so-called *individual* rights and freedoms (information, consent, privacy and medical confidentiality) and less on social rights issues such as access to health care services

[19] Dute (2000).

[20] Dute (2000).

and goods, waiting times and choice of provider. Instead, the right to health care has been realised by social health insurance legislation (e.g. the Health Insurance Act, Zvw). Since human rights are interrelated, indivisible and interdependent, it may be argued that a more balanced approach to patients' rights would require an explicit reference to, or incorporating the right to health care into the Patients' Rights Act itself—even more, given the differences in legal regimes (civil vs. social insurance law). Although the professional standards have been interpreted as incorporating health care accessibility issues (concluding and terminating medical contracts, waiting times, etc.), that is far from complete. In that respect, the Convention on Human Rights and Biomedicine (Oviedo Convention) and its additional protocols include a more integrated approach to patients' rights. Unfortunately, the Dutch government decided not to ratify the Oviedo Convention. Withdrawal from Oviedo is however based on several misconceptions such as the direct effect of Article 3 of the Convention (equal access) and the maximum number of reservations, as explained in the government's letter to parliament.[21] Although withdrawal should not be interpreted as disrespecting patients' rights, that position seems difficult to uphold particularly since the government feared the financial implications of Article 3 claims on necessary health care services. The assumed direct effect of Article 3 might cause an unprecedented burden to the health care system in case of unjustified denial of medical care.[22]

What does this mean for Ukraine, and for the health care reforms in particular? Well, it emphasises the relevance of an integral approach to the revision of a healthcare system. Reforming the organisation of health care, whether or not combined with financing reforms, is inextricably linked to guaranteeing patients' rights. Hence the need to ratify the Oviedo Treaty. This requires Member States to take social and individual patients' rights seriously, without any particular ranking of rights. That affirmation does not affect the design of the legal system. Thus, in addition to a so-called 'framework law', different frameworks may exist that cover separate aspects (financing, organisation, patients' rights, etc.). As long as those legal frameworks are aligned with each other and respect international standards (Oviedo Treaty).

Another issue concerns the use of open norms in legislation, including 'good care' and 'care of good professional standard', translated into, among other things, professional standards as formulated by the medical professions and Health Inspectorate. The advantage of such open norms is their flexible nature. After all, professional norms and standards may change over time, partly as a result of new understandings and technologies. From this perspective, the use of open standards protects legislators from frequent changes in the law strengthening the "tenability" of legislation. The legislator thus relies heavily on professional groups and supervisory authorities, including the Health Inspectorate. Such coordination in the Ukraine is therefore crucial. If successful, it is up to the court to confirm such open standards

[21] Parliamentary proceedings (2015).

[22] Parliamentary papers (2015), as argued by the Council of State in its Advisory Opinion.

and their interpretation by the professional groups. An additional advantage of open standards is the exchange of so-called 'best practices' at the international level. Ultimately, universal medical-ethical standards determine the content of good care and care of good professional standard. The interpretation of these standards at country level enables comparison, and can thus contribute to better acceptance of best practices in good care at the European level.

Another phenomenon is the absence of a social debate on health care rationing, and not only in the Netherlands. Given the expected rise in costs of health care in the coming years,[23] choices have to be made. In concrete terms, this means that certain facilities, therapies and medicines will be excluded from reimbursement. These are painful choices that ultimately have to be made at a political level. But that requires a public debate. For instance, on the application and reimbursement of new medical technologies, in accordance with Article 28 of the Oviedo Convention. The Convention prompts States to create greater public awareness on societal problems with new health technologies, such as rare diseases and access to excessively priced medicines (e.g., personalised immunotherapies); or, in the Covid-19 context, triggering a public debate on the need for age-based triage of hospital intensive care admission in the Covid-19 worst-case scenario.[24] Since these developments directly affect the rights of individual patients and society, the underlying ethical questions and dilemmas require a transparent and inclusive debate, weighing and reflecting on preferences, values and interests of the issue concerned. This kind of 'democratic deliberation' can be expected on other controversial medical innovations too, such as CRISPR gene editing and new reproductive technologies. Despite its recognition by international law, such kind of patient participation in health-related matters remains largely absent in the Netherlands.[25] Similar to the Netherlands, such technologies are also under discussion in the Ukraine and put pressure on the limited healthcare budget. In order to guarantee accessibility to necessary healthcare facilities in the long term, this country too will not escape the need for rationing and the social debate.

5 Conclusions

This contribution described some key characteristics of the Dutch legal framework on patients' rights. Originally covered by the Health Act 1956, this Act appeared outdated when reforming the health care system by liberalising the planning, financing and provision of health care services. What remained is a minimalistic piece of legislation defining the supervisory role of the Health Care Inspectorate in the field of public health. This is not necessarily problematic when replaced by a coherent and

[23] https://stats.oecd.org/Index.aspx?DataSetCode=SHA.

[24] Den Exter (2020).

[25] CESC (2000), par. 54.

comprehensive set of statutory laws. Focusing on patients' rights only, the Medical Treatment Contract Act functions indeed as a framework law, supplemented by more specific legislation on mental health and other topics. As observed, some omissions are not covered by this framework law such as the focus on individual patients' rights while ignoring the social right to health care and related issues, as well as the absence of a public debate on health-related issues, discussions and consultations in public decision-making on innovations in health care or medical-ethical controversial issues.

One of the lessons learned is to cherish the value of a Health Act, providing a comprehensive and consistent set of legal norms supplemented by more detailed legislation. Otherwise, the risk of a 'patchwork of statutory laws' with inherent inconsistencies is eminent.

Simultaneously, new understanding on human rights in health care should be an integral part of modernising patients' rights legislation, irrespective of the nature of such norms (civil or public law). It will thus balance both individual and social rights in health care, while incorporating the public debate in emerging health-related issues as adopted by the Oviedo Convention.

References

Committee on Economic, Social and Cultural Rights, CESC (2000) General Comment on Health, no 14, The Right to the Highest Attainable Standard of Health (Art. 12), 11 August 2000, E/C.12/2000/4, par. 54

Covid-19 triage guideline admission (in Dutch: Draaiboek Triage op basis van niet-medische overwegingen voor opname ten tijde van fase 3 in de COVID-19 pandemie, 24 November 2020, https://www.rijksoverheid.nl/documenten/rapporten/2020/11/24/draaiboek-triage-op-basis-van-niet-medische-overwegingen-voor-ic-opname-ten-tijde-van-fase-3-in-de-covid-19-pandemie

Den Exter A (2002) Health care law-making in Central and Eastern Europe. Review of a Legal-Theoretical Model, Intersentia

Den Exter A (2010) Health system reforms in The Netherlands: from public to private and its effects on equal access to health care. Eur J Health Law 3:223–233

Den Exter A (2020) View. The Dutch critical care triage guideline on Covid-19: not necessarily discriminatory. Eur J Health Law 5:495–498

Den Exter A, Guy M (2014) Market competition in health care markets in the Netherlands: some lessons for England? Med Law Rev 2:255–273

Dute JCJ, Friele RD, Gevers JKM, Hubben JH, Legemaate J et al. (2000) Evaluatie Wet op de Geneeskundige Behandelingsovereenkomst. Deel 1: De evaluatie. Deel 2: het patiëntenperspectief. Den Haag: ZorgOnderzoek Nederland, 2000

Helderman JK et al (2005) Market-oriented health care reforms and policy learning in the Netherlands. J Health Polit Policy Law 1–2:189–210

KNMG (2004) Van Wet naar Praktijk. Implementatie van de WGBO

KPMG Plexus (2014) Evaluatie Zorgverzekeringswet Eindrapportage, Amstelveen

Markestein LF (1995) The codification in the Netherlands of the principal rights of patients: a critical review. Eur J Health Law 2:33–44

Parliamentary proceedings (Kamerstukken II) 34000 XVI no. 106 (2014–2015), 26 March 2015
Supreme Court 1 April 2005, ECLI:NL:PHR:2005:AS6006 (Protocol I and II cases)
Supreme Court (SC) 12 February 2002, ECLI:NL:HR:2001:AB0377
ZonMw (2009) Zorgverzekeringswet en op de zorgtoeslag. Den Haag

Child Health Empowerment in Family Law of Central and Eastern Europe

Olha Rozghon

Contents

Abstract The health of the child is an ultimate value for any European state, therefore the first and foremost tasks of the present rule of law are both protection and defense. The purpose of the study is to analyze and establish the features of the right implementation to health of the child in family law, to determine the state of legislation on child health in Central and Eastern Europe, to clarify the ECHR legal positions in health care related to the child removal at an imminent threat to his life or

This paper is prepared on the basis of the report for the Conference 'Private Healthcare Law: Challenges and Prospects'.

O. Rozghon (✉)
Scientific Research Institute Legal Support of Innovative Development, National Academy of Legal Sciences of Ukraine, Kharkiv, Ukraine
e-mail: rozghon.o@ndipzir.org.ua

© The Author(s), under exclusive license to Springer Nature Switzerland AG 2022
R. Maydanyk et al. (eds.), *Ukrainian Healthcare Law in the Context of European and International Law*, European Union and its Neighbours in a Globalized World 7,
https://doi.org/10.1007/978-3-031-05690-1_3

health, to demonstrate the most vulnerable provisions of the legislation of these states on the right violation to child health. A comprehensive comparative legal analysis of the studied European countries' legislation in the field of health care led to the conclusion that the legislator highlights the child's right to family upbringing, which also includes the child's right to health care. A comparison of the current Ukrainian family legislation, regulating personal non-property relations in the field of health care, with the modern legislation of these states, allows us to conclude about the progressive experience of legal regulation of children's health rights in these states. However, due to the numerous ECHR practices in the field of health care in these countries, the legislation in this area should be corrected to ensure both proper security and protection of a child's right to health.

1 Introduction: Background and Objectives of the Study

The relevance of regulating family relations in the field of health care is stipulated by the realization that the right to health is one of the basic human rights in society.

The creation by the state of conditions for the exercise of the human right to health is a guarantee of development in family legal relations as well. The issue of realizing the right to health of the child in family law is an urgent problem, since children should be assigned to a special group of subjects, to which the principle of the best interests should be applied when resolving disputes regarding violations of their rights.

The novelty of the work is to establish the author's features of the right to health of the child in Central and Eastern Europe and to clarify the practice of the ECHR in the field of health care, which is associated with the removal of the child at an imminent threat to his life or health.

The degree of scientific development of the problem of regulation of personal rights, which includes the right to health, is quite high, as evidenced by a great number of publications of both theoretical and practical nature.

It is important to note a rather perfunctory study in the scientific literature of the problems that arise in the regulation of family law on the rights to the health of the child, while studying in detail the rights that ensure natural human existence, including the right to life, health, safe for life, health and social well-being of the environment, and their legal nature.

However, it is disputable and insufficiently developed to clarify the legal positions of the ECHR in the field of health care, being related to the removal of a child at an imminent threat to his life or health, to demonstrate the most vulnerable provisions in Central and Eastern Europe regarding the violation of the child's right to health.

The experience of legal regulation of the right to child health in Central and Eastern Europe will make it possible to adopt the experience and introduce legal norms into Ukrainian legislation in the field of health, using the comparative legal method.

In this study, we aim to explore the value of the child's right to health as enshrined in international and domestic health legislation in Central and Eastern Europe. Analyzing the practice of the ECHR in the framework of this scientific work, we will consider the problematic issues of realization of the child's right to health and the shortcomings of the legislation of Central and Eastern Europe in the field of health care.

The argument is discussed that guaranteeing the preservation of family relations between the child and his parents, the use of alternative measures to help families with children in difficult living conditions can be used to interpret the right to the highest attainable standard of a child's health. Ensuring social security and providing social services to families with children in need of support is one of the crucial objectives of social policy, an important factor in the successful development of any European state. Such security is a state of protection of the child's interests from both internal and external threats, indicating the degree of ensuring the quality and standard of living of the child, and compliance of national legislation with international human rights standards. European experience determines that there cannot be an effective, socially oriented market economy and the effectiveness of ensuring the country's social security without an active state regulatory role. Thereby, it is important to carry out an analysis of European experience in the provision of social services, social support for families with children being in difficult life circumstances, and the practice of the ECHR on these issues.

2 Features of the Legal Regulation of the Right to Health in International Acts

2.1 The Concept of the Right to Health as a Personal Right

In Europe, *human rights* are an expression of the moral and legal values of civil society and are recognized as the highest value. Universal human rights standards are established, for example, in the Convention on Human Rights and Fundamental Freedoms of 04 November 1950,[1] which has a 'statutory character', where one of the categories of rights and freedoms is *personal rights* (for example, the right to health), defined in chapter I 'Rights and freedoms'.

In the theory of law, *personal rights in a broad sense* are distinguished—any (all) subjective rights of the individual, and in a narrow (special)—a special group of rights other than socioeconomic and political.[2]

[1]European Convention on Human Rights (1950).

[2]Matuzov (1987), p. 94.

Note that the category of '*personal rights*' does not apply in all Central and Eastern European countries. For example, the analogue of *personal non-property rights in Germany* is 'individual rights', or absolute subjective rights that belong to everyone as an individual. Absolute rights are protected under § 823 of the German Civil Code ('the Bürgerliches Gesetzbuch' (BGB)[3] and by a special law.

Later in this study, analyzing the right to health, which is a personal non-property right under Ukrainian law, we will call it a 'personal right' that belongs to an individual.

The interpretation of the term 'health' is contained in the preamble to the Statute of the World Health Organization of 22 July 1946. Thus, *health* should be understood as a state of complete physical, mental and social well-being, not just the absence of disease and physical defects.[4]

The right to health is a principal human right enshrined in *international law*. The right to health is recognized in the International Covenant on Economic, Social and Economic Rights and Cultural Rights (ICESCR)[5] and in a number of other international human rights treaties. The right to health has also been included in the regional agreement on human rights in Europe.[6]

The main international legal document, which proclaimed to be a principle of human rights' protection, is the Universal Declaration of Human Rights in 1948.[7] In this document, legal provisions enshrine *declarative norms* of direct rules of conduct, norms that do not contain specific rules of conduct legal norms. Declarative norms can be enshrined, for example, in constitutions, declarations.

Analyzing Article 25.1 of the Universal Declaration of Human Rights, note that the standard of living is crucial for the realization of the right to health. That is, everyone has the right to a standard of living adequate for the health and well-being of themselves and their families, including food, clothing, housing and medical care and the necessary *social services*.

Thus, *the right to health provided for in international health acts* covers both the right to health care and the right to a wide range of factors that can help to lead a healthy lifestyle; key determinants of health, such as the right to safe and potable water, adequate nutrition, sanitation, housing, healthy working and environmental conditions, and health education and information.[8]

Various international acts or domestic health legislation of the studied countries use a great deal of various health care definitions: the right to medical care; the right to a healthy environment; the right to a level of physical and mental health, etc.

---

[3] German Civil Code (1896).

[4] The WHO Constitution was adopted by the International Health Conference (1946).

[5] International Covenant on Economic, Social and Cultural Rights (1976).

[6] Council of Europe, European Social Charter (revised) ETS 163 (1999), Article 11.

[7] Universal Declaration of Human Rights. (1948).

[8] WHO Factsheet No. 31 on the Right to Health, Office of the United Nations High Commissioner for Human Rights, Geneva (2008), p. 1.

In numerous analyzed countries, the right to health is taken into account as part of *general health legislation*.

The *constitutions of these states usually extend basic human rights*, including the right to health, which recognizes the right to health care, the right to life, the right to safe living conditions, and so on. The most commonly used is the right to health care.

Analyzing the *legislation in the field of health care of the CIS countries* and some European countries, we note that the *right to health care* is regulated primarily in their constitutions. Examples of the constitution, which regulates the *human right to health care* in sufficient detail, are, in particular, the Constitution of Ukraine (Articles 27, 29, 49), the Constitution of the Russian Federation (Articles 20, 41). Constitution of the Republic of Moldova (Article 36), Constitution of the Republic of Belarus (Article 45). In other *states*, the Constitution also guarantees the right to health care, in particular, in Art. 40 of the Constitution of Slovakia. A similar rule is established in Art. 31 of the Constitution of the Czech Republic, Art. 33 of the Constitution of Romania, Art. 51 of the Constitution of Slovenia, Art. 41 of the Swiss Constitution, Art. 70 D. 1) of the Constitution of the Republic of Hungary, Art. 52 of the Constitution of Bulgaria.[9]

In Germany, although *the right to health* is included in the constitutions of several Bundeslanders, it is not part of the Federal Constitution. The closest provision is the 'right to life and physical integrity' (Article 2 (Personal Freedoms) of the German Constitution).[10] The Austrian Federal Constitutional Law[11] also does not contain a section on human rights, as they are contained in various laws.

Thus, the approach that guarantees a person the right to health protection prevails in almost all constitutions of the studied states.

2.2 *The Right to Health of the Child*

If we consider that *the right to health belongs to any person*, then, distinguishing depending on the subject, it can be divided into the right to health of the child, maternal, including reproductive, persons with disabilities, the elderly, etc. . Accordingly, this broad right to health can be divided into specific rights to the health of individuals, in particular *a child's right to health.*

The right to health of the child is set out in Art. 24 of the *Convention on the Rights of the Child* (CRC).[12]

---

[9]Constitution of Ukraine (1996); Constitution of the Russian Federation (1993); Constitution of the Republic of Moldova (1994); Constitution of the Republic of Belarus (1994); Constitution of the Slovak Republic (1992); Constitution of the Czech Republic (1992); Romanian Constitution (2003); Constitution of the Republic of Slovenia (1991); Constitution of the Swiss Confederation (1999); Hungary's Constitution (2011); Constitution of the Republic of Bulgaria (1991).

[10]Basic Law for the Federal Republic of Germany (1949).

[11]Federal Constitutional Law: Austrian act (1920).

[12]Convention on the Rights of the Child (1989).

In addition, Art. Article 41 of the CRC provides that nothing in this Convention shall affect any provisions promoting the realization of the rights of the child and which may be contained in (a) the law of a State Party; or (b) applicable international law for that State'. At the same time, Articles 24 and 41 of the CRC provide an opportunity to develop the right to the highest attainable standard of health of the child by reviewing legal documents other than those relating to the rights of the children.[13]

CRC *has not created the principle of best interests*, but in Art. 18 states that 'the best interests of the child are the primary concern of the parents.' Thus, in *applying the best interests of the child* to all actions', the CRC highlights the symbiotic relationship between both civil and political rights and the economic, social and cultural rights of children, and does not dispute that the words 'all actions' clearly include social justice from the document on the child's right—*the Declaration of the Rights of the Child* of 1924[14]—the rights of social justice were a strong component of children's rights.[15]

Accordingly, the main declarative act of the rights of the child is the Declaration of the Rights of the Child, which provides for 10 basic principles of the rights of the child, i.e. certain normative and value guidelines of behavior, *but no mechanism for realization these rights, including a child's right to health.*

There are reasons to believe that children should be placed in a special group to which *the principle of the best interests* should be applied and which requires health exceptional care and protection, and this should be a priority for any state.

Legislators in most of the countries studied *have regulated human rights, including of the child, in the health sector* at the international, European and national levels. As we can see, there is a certain commonality of legislative approaches to the regulation of these rights. In our opinion, this is due to the fact th*at European countries are developing their own legislation* in the field of healthcare in the afterlight of enhanced protection of the rights of the child, as children are included in special groups that need special attention.

[13] Spronk (2012).

[14] Declaration of the Rights of the Child (1924).

[15] In the Preamble, 'mankind owes to the child the best it has to give' and see arts. 1,2,3 and 4 of the five's article Declaration reproduced in Geraldine Van Bueren, International Documents on Children.

3 Legal Regulation of Family Upbringing in a Child's Right to Health Care Implementation

3.1 Bilateral Nature of Relations in the Field of Health Care with the Participation of Parents and Children

The general health standards in the European Union are among the highest in the world. In Art. 2-1 of the World Health Organization states that one of the key functions of the WHO is to 'promote maternal and child health and well-being and to ensure the ability to live harmoniously in a changing environment'.[16]

Having analyzed General Comment 14 of the ECOSOC, we found that the *implementation of a child's right to health* requires states to take *concrete steps* to ensure the availability and accessibility of health and health care services, especially for a special group—children. In order to *an imminent threat* to the life or health of a child, the government of each European country must fulfill its positive obligations to parents and children in the form of counseling or assistance to enable them to improve their situation. This should be seen as a commitment to immediate action, i.e. a commitment to take 'thoughtful, concrete and targeted' steps towards the full realization of *the right to health*[17] and to adopt and implement a national health strategy and action plan based on the specific needs of children health care.

In the previous paragraph, we recognized that *the right to health* is part of the legislation of the countries studied, which is primarily included in the ECHR. Accordingly, in violation of this fundamental right, a person may seek protection from the ECHR.

In the field of *health care,* the ECHR practice has been developed, in particular with regard to violations of the following articles of the ECHR: Art.2 (right to life), Art. 3 (prohibition of torture), Art. 5 (right to liberty and security of person), Art. 6 (right to a fair trial), Art. 8 (right to respect for private and family life), Art. 10 (right to inviolability of home, freedom of expression). Nevertheless, in our opinion, these are 'purely medical cases. 'In this study, we will try to consider cases of violation of the *child's right to health in the family law in the case of improper upbringing* of the child, when there is an immediate threat to the child's health, entrailing the child removal or parental rights' deprivation.

As noted above, the right to the health of the child is the personal right of the child or the right of the child as an individual. The complex of personal and property rights of the child in the analyzed states is usually enshrined in the *Family Code.*

The personal rights of the child are always opposed to the responsibility of the mother, father or other person who replaces them. The right of parents *to upbringing is specific* because it *is also their responsibility*. Since each parent must participate in

[16]The WHO Constitution was adopted by the International Health Conference (1946).

[17]United Nations Economic and Social Council, General Comment No 14: The right to the highest attainable standard of health. United Nations document E/C.12/2000/4 (2000): paras 53–8.

the upbringing and maintenance of the child (cash and (or) in kind), *the financial maintenance of the child* is aimed *at caring for the child's health, his physical, spiritual, moral development.*

3.2 Immediate Removal of the Child from the Parents in Case of Imminent Threat to the Life or Health of the Child as a Guarantee of Protection of his Rights

Note that the *doctrine of family law* of each state determines its typology of parental rights and responsibilities and personal rights of the child, including care for his health and physical, emotional, intellectual and moral development, as well as the right to be raised in a family that entails cohabitation, parental care and, consequently, *protection and care of the child's health.*

Article 150 of the Family Code of Ukraine[18] establishes the responsibilities of parents for *the upbringing and development of a child.* These responsibilities are opposed by the child's right to a *proper parental upbringing*, which appears from birth and is realized, accordingly, in the family. By implementing the right to a proper parental upbringing, *a child can receive care for his or her health, physical, spiritual and moral development.*[19]

In Art. 77 of the Code of the Republic of Belarus on Marriage and Family[20] is determined that parents raise their children, take care of them and their property. Upbringing means *caring* for the physical, spiritual and moral development of children, their health, education and preparation for independent living in society. For part 1 of Art. 85 of this Code in exceptional cases in case of *imminent threat to the life or health of the child,* the guardianship authority has the right to decide on the immediate removal of the child from the parents or other persons in whose upbringing he is actually. And Art. 85-1 regulates the case of 'recognition of a child as in need of *state protection* through the removal of the child from the parents'.

A similar rule is set out in paragraph 1 of Art. 63 Family Code of the Russian Federation.[21] Parents have the right and obligation to raise their children. Parents are responsible for the upbringing and development of their children. They have a responsibility *to care for the health, physical, mental, spiritual and moral development of their children*. Article 77 stipulates that in the event of *an imminent threat to the life and health of a child*, the guardianship authority has the right to *immediately take it away from the parents (one of them*).

We believe that parents have the right and obligation to raise a child, and the child has the right to family upbringing, which also includes the child's right to health

[18] Family Code of Ukraine (2002).

[19] Krasytska (2015), p. 219.

[20] Code of the Republic of Belarus on Marriage and Family (1999).

[21] Family Code of the Russian Federation (1995).

care, the right to physical, mental, spiritual and moral development, the right to care, maintenance and moral welfare. Accordingly, parents, in exercising the right to raise a child, *have no right to harm the child's physical and mental health.*

The Czech Republic has an interesting experience in regulating family upbringing in giving *a child the right to health care.* In Art. 31 The Czech Charter of Fundamental Rights and Freedoms[22] guarantees parents the right to care for their children and the right to raise them. Accordingly, under Czech law, it is the responsibility of the parents to care for the child, including the child's health, as well as physical, emotional, cognitive and moral development (upbringing). If the life and health of the *child is endangered*, the child can be removed from the custody of the parents, being taken away.

In Poland, the provisions governing the legal institution, being defined as "parental authority", are of decisive importance when it comes to the rules of legal relations between parents and children. This concept includes, inter alia, the obligations and rights of parents to take care of the child and the child's property, as well as *the right to the upbringing of the child* (Sec. 95 § 1 Polish Family and Guardianship Code) and supervision (Sec. 96, sentence 1 Guardianship Code). The obligation to provide the child with the necessary medical care is included in the obligation to *take care of the child's physical developm*ent (Sec. 96, sentence 2 Polish Family and Guardianship Code).[23]

Thus Article. 112-3 The Polish Family and Guardianship Code determines that the placement of a child in a foster family may take place only if other measures are provided for in Art. 109 § 2 para. 1–4, and the forms of assistance to the child's parents specified in the rules on the support of the foster family and the family did not eliminate the situation, the consequences of which may violate the best interests of the child, except when the need providing an alternative to custody of a child stems *from a serious threat to the best interests of the child, in particular a threat to his or her life or health.*[24]

Parental responsibilities are set out in the Swiss Civil Code[25] as the right and obligation to raise a child, i.e. to provide care and education for a child. Parents must raise the child, encourage and protect his or her physical, mental and moral development (Art. 302-1 Swiss Civil Code). If the best interests of the child are at stake and the parents are unwilling or unable to remedy the situation, the child protection authority must *take all appropriate measures* to protect the child (Art. 307-1 Swiss Civil Code).

Article 1666 of the BGB provides that the guardianship courts are required to take the necessary measures if the child's well-being is threatened (Gefährdung de

[22] Czech Charter of Fundamental Rights and Freedoms Resolution of the Presidium of the Czech National Council (1992) on the declaration of the Charter of Fundamental Rights and Freedoms as a part of the constitutional order of the Czech Republic Constitutional act No. 2/1993.

[23] The Family and Guardianship Code (1964).

[24] Ibid.

[25] Swiss Civil Code (1907).

Kindeswohls). The first sub-paragraph of Article 1666a provides that measures aimed at separating the child from the family are permissible only if the authorities are unable to take any other measures if the child's well-being is at stake. The second subparagraph of Article 1666a provides that full [parental] responsibility may be waived only if other measures have proved ineffective or should be considered insufficient to eliminate the danger.[26]

The Austrian legislature authorizes the court to revoke or limit custody of a child depending on the behavior of the parents. Therefore, if the child's well-being is threatened, it is necessary to completely remove him/her from the previous environment against the will of the legal guardian and placement with relatives, according to section 176a of the General Civil Code of Austria (hereinafter—Allgemeines Bürgerliches Gesetzbuch).

As we can see, the analysis gives the right to conclude that in the *analyzed regulations* for the implementation of the child's personal rights in the field of health care at the legislative level assigned to parents' responsibilities of care for the child, his health, physical, emotional, intellectual and moral development. If the actions of the parents regarding the upbringing of the child have a destructive impact on the child's health, it is first advisable to take alternative measures from the state before applying for the removal of the child from the parents or other persons in whose care he or she is actually involved. And in the event of a *serious threat to the life or health* of a child, the child protection authority eliminates that threat in the best interests of the child through *immediate removal from the parents.*

4 ECHR Legal Positions in the Field of Health Care Related to the Removal of a Child at Imminent Threat to his Life or Health

4.1 Apply Sanctions in the Event of an Imminent Threat to the Life or Health of a Child

Failure to comply with parental responsibilities may result in evasion of them and is grounds for parents' avoidance of the responsibility established by law. Accordingly, parents may *be deprived of parental rights* with the *removal of the child.* However, would the removal of a child be a guarantee that his or her rights and interests are protected, and is it proportionate to the proper implementation of parental rights?

Independence of parents' choice of forms and methods of upbringing, lack of regulation and specific instructions in the legislation on upbringing can lead to their *ambiguous interpretation and the situation when children's rights to health care,*

[26] German Civil Code (1896).

physical development are violated due to non-fulfillment or improper fulfillment of obligations by parents. In particular, situations where a child finds himself in difficult living conditions, which may result in the child's *health deteriorating* or leading to his or her death, and so on.

Failure to perform parental responsibilities can be the outcome of both the impossibility of such performance and the lack of self-confidence and carelessness.

In Ukraine, the court may decide *to take the child away from the parents or one of them, without depriving them of parental rights*, in the cases provided for in paragraphs 2–5 of Part 1 of Art. 164 of the Family Code of Ukraine, as well as in other cases, if leaving a child with them *is dangerous for his life, health and moral upbringing*. In this case, the child is transferred to the other parent, grandparents, other relatives (at their request) or the body of guardianship and care. In exceptional cases, when there is an instant danger to life or health of the child, the guardianship authority or the prosecutor has the right to decide on the immediate removal of the child from his parents (Part 2 of Art. 170 of the Criminal Code of Ukraine).

Comparison of items 2–5 part 1 of Art. 164 of the Family Code of Ukraine and Part 2 of Art. 170 of the Family Code of Ukraine certifies that there are two situations in which a child may find himself if the parents do *not create appropriate conditions* for his life: danger to life, health and moral upbringing of the child; imminent threat to the life or health of the child. The way of distinguishing these situations is not established by law.

Assume that *an imminent threat to a child's life or health* will mean a situation where there is no continuity of conditions or circumstances, i.e. the permanence of the child's inappropriate living conditions, which inevitably results in harm to the child's life or health.

An example of the application of a sanction in order of *an imminent threat to the life or health of a child* is also Art. 77 of the Family Code of the Russian Federation. In addition, *the Regulation* on the removal of children from families in the event of an imminent threat to the life or health of a child or in the case of child abuse,[27] provides that both guardianship and trusteeship authority are obliged to immediately remove the child in the presence of an imminent threat to life or health in accordance with Art. 77 Family Code of the Russian Federation.

The legal analysis of the draft of these Regulations establishes that the 'immediate threat to the life and health of the child' was defined at least as 'a situation in which there is no doubt about the inevitability of negative consequences in the form of death, bodily injuries that harm the child's health, persistent disorders of the child's body. In all other cases that do not fall under this definition, *there can not and should not be an imminent threat to the life and health of the child.*

This example of the Russian Federation prompts the proposal to amend Part 2 of Art. 170 of the Family Code of Ukraine in the following wording: 'Imminent threat to the life and health of a child is defined as a situation in which leaving a child with

[27] Reglament otobranija detej iz semej pri neposredstvennoj ugroze zhizni rebenka ili ego zdorov'ju ili v sluchae zhestokogo obrashhenija s rebenkom (2017).

parents (persons replacing them) has negative consequences in the form of injuries that harm health, persistent dysfunction or death of the child.

4.2 Recourse to the ECHR as a Guarantee of Protection of a Child in the Event of an Imminent Threat to his Life or Health

Given the fact that the *child* cannot 'exhaust domestic remedies' on his or her own, and the child's legal representatives are sometimes violators of his or her rights, the issue of protecting children's rights is particularly relevant in the case law of the ECHR. Therefore, it is worth giving examples of the case law of the ECHR, as its feature is that when making appropriate decisions regarding the observance of the rights of the child, new standards of justice are established, as well as the interpretation of the rules of the ECHR.

It should be noted that the case law of the European Court of Human Rights, which affects the right to health care of the child, tends to the principle of preserving the family relationship between the child and his parents.

Here is the first example of the ECHR's activity, which affects the child's right to health and concerns the observance of the right of families with children to social protection (Case).[28]

According to the case file, the children were taken from their parents on the grounds of '*inadequate health of the children.*' The Court concluded that, despite the relevance of the arguments used by the domestic authorities to justify their decision to take the children away from their parents, those arguments were not sufficient to justify such a serious interference with the applicants' family life.

Thus, Art. 8 of the Convention on Human Rights and Fundamental Freedoms was violated. At the same time, this article imposes on the state positive obligations regarding proper 'respect' for private and family life. That is, the removal of the child from the parents is a state interference in the private and family life of the applicants (parents).

In this particular case, the specific findings (that the children were deprived of adequate food, dressed inappropriately and often stayed at home alone) were based *solely on information* from the municipal authorities obtained from their occasional inspections of the applicants' homes. No other evidence supporting these findings, such as the children's own views, their medical records, the views of their pediatricians, or the testimony of neighbors, has been studied. The only evidence to support the inadequate state of health of the children on which the court based its decision was a one-year-old medical certificate confirming the registration of two of the seven children in connection with the initial stage of anemia, the accuracy of which the applicants did not dispute.

[28] See: Case 29948/06, *Saviny v. Ukraine* (Judgment 18 December 2008).

That is, evidence must be provided of the applicants' conduct or the living conditions of the children, which would give reason to believe that leaving them in the care of the applicants would endanger their lives and health.

Thus, the basis for the ECHR decision on the violation of the rights of the child to protect the child's right to health will be the establishment of the fact that the child can be placed in a more favorable environment for him if there is a need to protect the child from danger to his life, physical or mental health. However, the existence of such a hazard must indeed be established.

4.3 *Child Health as a Priority of Social State Policy*

Priority areas of state policy to improve the situation of children are health care and promotion of healthy lifestyles, providing quality education and upbringing of children, improving the economic living conditions of children, improving the efficiency of the state support system for children in particularly difficult life circumstances.[29]

The *system of social protection of families* (individuals) who are in difficult life circumstances is one of the institutions of socio-economic policy, the purpose of which is to ensure social stability and development of society. An effective social protection mechanism is vital for achieving this goal.[30]

Parents (applicants-defendants) in the case 'Saviny v. Ukraine'[31] claimed that their inability to provide better conditions for their children was due only to the fact that the applicants were blind. They argued that they had been discriminated against as disabled people and stressed that instead of taking away their children, the authorities had to provide their families with the *necessary assistance* (within the meaning of social assistance).

Changes from 03.09.2015, Art. 164 of the Family Code of Ukraine is supplemented by a new part 4, which stipulates that when making a decision on deprivation of parental rights, *the court takes into account information* about social support of the family (person) in the case of such support. Thus, at the time of the case 'Saviny v. Ukraine' (ECHR decision of 18.12.2008)[32] *did not yet exist in Part 4 of Art. 164 of the* Family Code of Ukraine and direct instructions on taking into account the court information on the implementation of social support.

Therefore, state intervention in both private and family life of parents and children in such cases can be evident in the fact that:

---

[29] Kozlova (2005), p. 25.

[30] Liubetska (2018), pp. 109–116.

[31] See: Case 29948/06, *Saviny v. Ukraine* (Judgment 18 December 2008).

[32] *Saviny v. Ukraine* (2008).

- first, *state intervention* must have a legitimate aim—to protect the interests of the child from danger to his life, health and moral education and the immediate *threat to his life or health,* it must be justified by an urgent *social need*. The ECHR must assess in the context of the examination of all the circumstances of the case: whether the threat to the child's health has been established as a fact, whether the State's intervention was justified, necessary and sufficient for the purposes of Article 2 § 2. 8 of the Convention on Human Rights and Fundamental Freedoms, so that the decision was fair and able to ensure adequate protection of the interests of children and parents, as required by Art. 8 of the Convention on Human Rights and Fundamental Freedoms.

According to the case 'Y. I. v. Russia'[33] the applicant applied a complaint against the automatic deprivation of parental rights. The applicant alleged that the domestic courts had automatically applied Art. 69 of the Family Code of the Russian Federation only on the grounds that she was a drug addict, and therefore, there was a threat to the *life or health of children*. They did not assess the need and appropriateness of such a strict measure as deprivation of parental rights. Moreover, the domestic authorities had never considered providing *social assistance and support to the applicant and her family*.

The national courts also failed to strike a *fair balance between the interests* in question and to determine the 'appropriate and sufficient' reasons for the decision to deprive the applicant of her parental rights. In fact, the courts linked the risk to the *health and development of the children* only to the fact that the applicant had used drugs that were available and sold in her apartment. As for the above mentioned, the ECHR considers that the reasons relied on by the domestic courts were *insufficient t*o justify the applicant's deprivation of parental rights over her three children and the transfer of the two youngest children to *state custody*. Thus, despite the domestic authorities' freedom of action, the interference with the applicant's family life was disproportionate to the legitimate aim pursued. Respectively, there was a violation of Art. 8 of the Convention on Human Rights and Fundamental Freedoms;

- secondly, *state intervention* is implemented as proportional between the interests of children and parents, i.e. the criterion of proportionality is used. In the Case 'Wallová and Walla v. the Czech Republic' № 23848/04[34] five of the applicants' children were temporarily placed in state child protection facilities.

The applicants (respondent parents) insisted that the placement of the children in *public institutions* was justified only by their financial difficulties and that the authorities had failed to fulfill their positive obligations to them in the form of counseling or assistance to enable them to improve their situation.

The Government acknowledged that the domestic measure contested by the applicants in the present case constituted an interference with their right to respect

---

[33] See: Case 68868/14, *Y. I. v. Russia* (Judgment 25 February 2020).

[34] See: Case 23848/04, *Wallová and Walla* v. the Czech republic (Judgment 26 October 2006).

for family life, as guaranteed by Article 1 § 1. 8 of the Convention on Human Rights and Fundamental Freedoms, but the decision to establish *institutional custody of children* was based on the provisions of § 46 (1) of the Family Institutional Education Act (Zákon o rodině ústavní výchovu) of the Czech Republic and was taken in the interests of protecting children's health and morals and their rights and freedoms. According to the court, such an extremely strict measure as the separation of children from their parents was applied, and *social workers* could provide the applicants with specific advice on how to improve their living conditions keeping out of danger the *child's health*. But such alternative measures were not taken.

According to § 1 of the Family Institutional Education Act, the purpose of institutional or protective education is to provide a minor, usually between 3 and 18 years of age, or an adult under 19 years of age, with *alternative educational* assistance in the interests of his healthy development, proper upbringing and education on the basis of a judicial decisions or decisions about *institutional or protective* education.

This law allows for *'preventive measure - alternative educational assistance* in the interests of its healthy development, proper upbringing and education' for the child, and not just '*placement of children in institutional custody*', and, in our opinion, this is a very *good European experience* as *legislative leadership for Ukraine;*

- third, *state intervention* should not restrict the right of parents to visit their children when they are placed in orphanages. Thus, cohabitation is a key element of family life for parents and children (case 'Kutzner v. Germany'[35]), and measures taken at the domestic level to prevent this are interference with the exercise of the right guaranteed by Art. 8 of the Convention on Human Rights and Fundamental Freedoms. Such an intervention violates Art. 8 of the of the Convention on Human Rights and Fundamental Freedoms, except where it is provided by law, has a legitimate purpose in terms of paragraph 2 of Art. 8 and is necessary in a democratic society to achieve it.

Note that Germany is one of the countries with the highest level of social development. The normative basis for the provision of social services in Germany is the *German Social Code.*[36]

§ 2 of the Eighth Book of the German Social Code sets out the tasks of the Institute for Assistance to Families and Youth, which are divided into 'social services' and 'other tasks' to assist young people and their families.

Social services to assist in the implementation of social support for families (persons) in difficult life circumstances include: professional counseling on all issues of marital relations and family cohabitation, especially in conflict or crisis situations; support for single parents; assistance in the birth of illegitimate children; counseling and support for the child's contact with both parents and other family members;

[35] See: Case 46544/99, *Kutzner v. Germany* (Judgment 26 February 2002).

[36] See: German Social Code (VIII) (1990), Article 1.

providing, if necessary, single mothers raising a child under 6 years of age, a place in the so-called institutions of mother and child (form of cohabitation under supervision); patronage and assistance to a child being in strife.[37]

Assistance to families (individuals) who find themselves in difficult life circumstances is characterized by special preconditions. According to § 27, these social services are provided only when 'there is no upbringing that corresponds to the well-being of the child or young person, i.e. there are not enough socializing conditions to guarantee the proper development of the minor. *Assistance in solving* family problems provides qualified support to families and their individual members in difficult life situations. Access to these services is usually provided through the General Social Service of the Youth Affairs Department, which itself offers some kind of assistance in resolving difficult life circumstances;[38]

- fourth, *state intervention* is based on the fact that the danger to the life and health of the child is proven and the consequences of the situation when the parents and the child are separated will be less traumatic.

In the case 'Kutzner v. Germany'[39] the local Juvenile Service applied to the Guardianship Court for an order depriving the applicants of parental rights in respect of their daughters. The court issued an interim injunction depriving the applicants of the right to decide where their children should live or what medical care should be provided to them, citing the order mainly because the applicants did not have the necessary mental capacity to raise their daughters. The children were placed in an orphanage.

The ECHR has determined that the transfer of a child to public care as a measure cannot be authorized without prior consideration of possible alternative measures and should be assessed in the context of the State's positive obligation to take balanced and consistent measures to promote the reunification of children with their biological parents to this end, to enable them to maintain regular contact with each other and, if possible, to prevent the divorce of siblings.

National courts should consider, for example, whether a child will suffer (*mental health problems*) due to lack of care, poor upbringing and lack of emotional support, or whether state custody of a child is justified by his or her *physical or mental health.*

The ECHR is guided by the *principle of the best child* interests when deciding whether to violate or not violate Art. 8 of the Convention on Human Rights and Fundamental Freedoms, taking into account the harm that can be caused to a child in terms of not only physical but also *mental health.* As a rule, the ECHR strives to take into account the child views as much as possible when resolving conflict situations, not losing sight of the principles of 'health and morality' and *'the right to family life*';

[37] Giffey (2009), p. 129.

[38] Seithe (2007), p. 571.

[39] *Kutzner v. Germany* (2002).

- fifth, *state intervention* is based on more favorable conditions for both upbringing and care of the child. A child can be placed in conditions that are more favorable for his or her upbringing and *health care*, in particular, in public care facilities.

But the establishment of children state custody can also be justified solely by reference to the *unreliability of the situation*, as such problems can be solved by less radical means, without resorting to family separation, for example, by providing targeted financial support and social counseling (case 'Moser v. Austria'[40]).

Considering the case 'Moser v. Austria[41], the ECHR, in order to determine whether the impugned measures were 'necessary in a democratic society' and, taking into account the whole case, we must assess whether the reasons given for justifying such measures were appropriate and sufficient for the purposes of Article 2 § 2. 8 of the Convention on Human Rights and Fundamental Freedoms.

Having analyzed this case, it is relevant to apply to the Austrian experience. *General social services* have been designed to help people in an emergency under the Vienna Law on Social Services (Wiener Kinder- und Jugendhilfegesetz).[42]

Parents can also use such services. If the best interests of the child concerning care and upbringing of the parents or other persons entrusted with the care and upbringing are not guaranteed, then they should be provided with *educational assistance by social institutions*. Under § 32 (1) of this Act, if parents or other persons entrusted with the care and upbringing of children do not agree with the necessary educational assistance, the Agency for the Protection of Children and Youth has the necessary judicial grounds for filing an application, such as deprivation of custody or part of custody (§ 181 of the Austrian General Civil Code (ABGB) In the event of instant danger, both child and youth protection agency must immediately provide the necessary educational assistance and apply to the court (§ 211 ABGB).

The ECHR case law, which also affects *the right to the health* of the child, demonstrates the most unprotected legislation positions of the analyzed states and violations in human rights practice, indicating the need to bring the *legislation of these states* in line with international norms.

Thus, the study (analysis) confirms that for the effective protection of children's health rights, the legislation of certain studied states, which regulates public relations in the field of health care and social services, requires changes to reform the management system in the field of social services related to social support of families (persons) being in difficult life circumstances.

We consider that the successful European experience on the example of Austria *on the previous measure of alternative educational assistance* in the interests of the child and Germany on assistance to families with children in *difficult life circumstances* should be implemented in Ukrainian legislation.

---

[40] See: Case 12643/02, *Moser v. Austria*. (Judgment 21 September 2006).

[41] *Moser v. Austria* (2006).

[42] See: Entire legal regulation for the Vienna Child and Youth Welfare Act of 1 May 2013.

5 Concluding Remarks

Adaptation of Ukrainian legislation to EU legislation is a priority component of the process of Ukraine's integration into the European Union, which, in turn, is a priority of Ukrainian foreign policy, in particular in the field of both health and human life to the Community acquis.

The ECHR is an effective body for the effective protection of children's rights, but the realization of children's health rights requires reforming or introducing domestic child health legislation in Central and Eastern European countries that is in line with international human rights law.

Processes related to the reform or implementation of new child health laws are crucial to the rule of law. The government of each European country must take concrete steps to reform child health legislation: revise, develop and amend child health laws. In connection with the ECHR's practice of respect for private and family life, which is in line with national decisions on the removal of a child and affects the right to health of the child, the Government of these States' protection of the child's health in accordance with international standards of the rights of this special group of persons.

First and foremost, state intervention in both private and family life of parents, must have a legitimate purpose—to protect the interests of the child from danger to his life, health and moral education and the immediate threat to his life or health, in addition to the existence of such danger must really be established as a fact by the court; for another thing, it must be proportionate to the interests of parents and children; in the third place, deprivation of parental rights with the removal of a child is a radical measure and the court, when considering cases of removal of children, must thoroughly examine all the circumstances of the case to determine whether parents can change their attitude and behavior to raise a child to avoid imminent threat to the child life or health, and take alternative measures to help families with children in difficult circumstances.

References

Franziska Giffey (2009) Bundesministerium fur Familien, Senioren, Frauen und Jugend. Kinder— und Jugendhilfe. Achtes Buch Sozialgesetz Buch. Berlin, p 129

Kozlova TV (2005) Prava rebenka v sem'e i otvetstvennost' roditelej za zdorovoe razvitie detej [The rights of the child in the family and the responsibility of parents for the healthy development of children]: Metodicheskoe posobie. Samara, 45 s. https://www.samregion.ru/uncategorized/prava-rebenka-v-seme-i-otvetstvennost-roditelej-zazdorovoe-razvitie-detej/

Krasytska LV (2015) Problemy zdiisnennia ta zakhystu osobystykh ta mainovykh prav batkiv i ditei: thesis. [Problems of implementation and protection of personal and property rights of parents and children: thesis]. Kyiv, 496 p

Liubetska MM (2018) Analiz zarubizhnoho dosvidu nadannia sotsialnykh posluh, zdiisnennia sotsialnoho suprovodu simei (osib), yaki perebuvaiut u skladnykh zhyttievykh obstavynakh. [Analysis of foreign experience in providing social services, providing social support to families (persons) who are in difficult life circumstances]. Investytsii: praktyka ta dosvid. Kyiv 19:109–116

Matuzov NI (1987) Pravovaja sistema i lichnost' [Legal system and personality]. Iz-vo Saratov. un-ta, Saratov, p 94

Seithe M (2007) Hilfen zur Erziehung. Handbuch Familie in Ecarius J. VS Verlag fur Sozialwissenschaften, Weinheim, p 571

Spronk SI (2012) The Right to Health of the Child in International Health and Human Rights Law. https://ssrn.com/abstract=2080018

Prevention of Occupational Morbidity as a Component of Public Health

Iryna Sakharuk, Oleksandra Pohorielova, and Svitlana Batychenko

Contents

Abstract This chapter is devoted to the study of occupational morbidity in Ukraine in the context of improving public health, taking into account international labour standards, ILO practices and practices of individual European countries. Statistical information on the number of insured events causing harm to life or health of employees (in the dynamics of the last 20 years) and the dynamics of major occupational diseases in Ukraine, the level of occupational injuries in some European countries was analysed. The current risks, connected to safety and health of employees (including those caused by the Covid-19 pandemic) and the new challenges on creating a safe and healthy work environment have been explored. The relationship between reforming labour protection, sustainable development and the concept of decent work has been identified. The need to develop and periodically review national policy in the field of labour protection, increasing attention to

This scientific research has been performed within the framework of the state budget project No 0119U100306 'Socio – Legal Principles of Preservation and Development of Labour Potential of Ukraine', being funded from the Ministry of Education and Science of Ukraine.

I. Sakharuk (✉) · S. Batychenko
Law School, Taras Shevchenko National University of Kyiv, Kyiv, Ukraine
e-mail: sakharuk_iryna@knu.ua

O. Pohorielova
Department of Labour Law and Social Security Law at the Law School, Taras Shevchenko National University of Kyiv, Kyiv, Ukraine

© The Author(s), under exclusive license to Springer Nature Switzerland AG 2022
R. Maydanyk et al. (eds.), *Ukrainian Healthcare Law in the Context of European and International Law*, European Union and its Neighbours in a Globalized World 7,
https://doi.org/10.1007/978-3-031-05690-1_4

building a national culture of prevention in the field of labour protection are distinguished between the current trends in the creation of safe and healthy working conditions. The role of compulsory state social insurance in the prevention of occupational diseases has been analysed, the experience of some European countries in this field has been studied. Suggestions on reforming social insurance institutions against occupational morbidity as well as occupational health and safety management have been made. They are aimed at implementing the principles of public health, preventing morbidity and early detection of health disorders.

1 Introduction

Health and life of the human are recognized as the highest social value in the world and in Ukraine, and accordingly, the preservation of health should be a priority in all spheres of human life. It is the task of each country to take all necessary measures to preserve and restore human health. The WHO Charter states that the national health of all countries of the world is a key factor in achieving peace and security, and that governments should be responsible for the health of their peoples,[1] and that health should be one of the main activities of the country. Only if there is a healthy population, a balanced health policy, it is possible to take the necessary measures to preserve and develop labour potential, which is the basis for the development and sustainable development of any country in the world. Given that Ukraine has set a course for European development, European social values and directions of political development should be taken into account when defining health policy.

The cornerstone of European health policy is the Strategy 'Health 2020', adopted in 2012 by the European Regional Bureau of the World Health Organization, which aims to improve the health and well-being of the population. One of the points of this Strategy is the need to strengthen the public health system as a system for the prevention and prophylaxis of infectious and non-infectious diseases. The implementation of measures to promote health and prevent morbidity involves significant economic benefits in the future,[2] as only a healthy person can provide for herself/himself economically and carry out socially useful activities for the development of the country. In addition, public health is one of the national security guarantees, and reveals 'such a section of human health that allows a person to survive in a certain biological and social reality and to feel self-sufficient through a certain social choice—professional, career and personal'.[3]

[1] Constitution of the World Health Organization (1946).

[2] World Health Organization Regional Office for Europe (2013) Health 2020: a European policy framework and strategy for the twenty-first century.

[3] Klantsa (2018), pp. 107–113.

One of the main goals of public health is to ensure the protection of health in all spheres of human life, including work. Therefore, it is crucially important to stipulate in the legislation the needs of health in all state policies,[4] the necessity of public health development in Ukraine, in particular, ensuring safe and healthy working conditions for employees, as the sphere of work occupies one of the key places in human social life.

One of the legal institutions that provides life and health protection of employees in the process of work is the compulsory state social insurance against accidents at work and occupational morbidity that have caused disability.[5] Under current conditions, this institution needs to be reformed, in particular, in order to implement the principles of public health, prevent morbidity and early detection of health disorders. Also, it is impossible to imagine the implementation of public health ideas without proper legal regulation of labour protection legal institute which is responsible for creating safe and healthy working conditions. At the same time, under current conditions the institute of labour protection needs to be reformed focusing on the prevention of human health deterioration both in the process of work and in the future.

The issues of labour protection management, the improvement of compulsory state social insurance have been studied by such national scientists as Y.I. Kundiev,[6] A.M. Nahorna,[7] S.V. Nesterenko,[8] O.V. Orekhova, O.I. Pavlenko,[9] I.V. Senyk,[10] M.A. Sereda,[11] Y.M. Tkachenko,[12] H.A. Trunova,[13] O.I. Tulai[14] etc. At the same time, the question of occupational diseases prevention is not sufficiently studied in the national legal doctrine and is mainly not considered through the prism of public health. In addition, the dynamic development of labour field, the introduction of new risks to life and health of employees in the workplace (including the Covid-19 pandemic) necessitates the updating of research related to occupational diseases prevention.

Practical measures for occupational health and safety management, aimed, among others, at assessing occupational risks, building a national culture of prevention in the field of occupational safety, etc., are being actively developed by the ILO. In this respect, ILO reports, manuals and recommendations are taken as the basis of this study. The works of foreign researchers, in particular J.-Ch.Le Coze, L. Godderis,

[4] Tkachenko (2019).

[5] The Law of Ukraine 'On Compulsory State Social Insurance' (1999).

[6] Kundiev et al. (2011).

[7] Nahorna (2016), Nahorna (2018).

[8] Tretiakov and Nesterenko (2016).

[9] Orekhova and Pavlenko (2014).

[10] Senyk (2020).

[11] Sereda (2020).

[12] Tkachenko (2019).

[13] Trunova (2017).

[14] Tulai (2016).

M.-Cl. Lambrechts, K. De Meester, P. Swuste[15] have also contributed to the theoretical background of the study. The empirical basis of the study is data on occupational accidents and occupational diseases, including the ILO Department of Statistics and the Social Insurance Fund of Ukraine.

The aim of this study is to determine the state of occupational morbidity in Ukraine and European countries, provide the comparative and legal analysis and make suggestions on reforming the institutes of social insurance against accidents and occupational morbidity and labour protection tools for preventing occupational morbidity.

2 The State of Occupational Morbidity in Ukraine and Some European Countries

Occupational morbidity in Ukraine is a complex socio-economic and hygienic problem. In different periods of socio-economic development of the country, the attention given to this problem by scientists, practitioners in the field of health care, society, was not the same as a whole. During the years of independence, Ukraine has developed a legal framework, which can demonstrate positive results in prevention of occupational morbidity. However, the legal regulation of socio-economic relations at work has not yet yielded positive results, as it is not a prerequisite for ensuring safe working conditions and guarantees for the preservation of life and health of employees.[16]

Statistic data on occupational morbidity is essential to fully understand the state of ensuring the right to decent work in the country, as the ILO defines decent work as safe work.[17] Thus, the occupational injuries rate is even included in the list of indicators for assessing progress towards the UN Sustainable Development Goals (within Goal 8 indicator 8.8.1. 'Fatal and non-fatal occupational injuries per 100,000 workers, by sex and migrant status').[18]

Statistical information on the number of insured events of employee's personal injuries (accidents at work and occupational diseases) in Ukraine is summarized and analysed by the Social Insurance Fund of Ukraine. However, official statistics, especially on occupational diseases, cannot be considered complete for a number of reasons, in particular: the complex procedure for establishing cause-and-effect relationships between the disease and the factors of the work environment that caused it; concealing the facts of occupational diseases either by employees or employers (because of fear to lose the job); the formal approach to periodic medical

[15] ILO (2019a) Safety and Health and the Future of Work: A Compilation of Think Pieces.

[16] Kundiev et al. (2011), p. 46.

[17] ILO (2019) ILO Centenary Declaration for the Future of Work.

[18] United Nations Statistics Division (2020) Global indicator framework for the Sustainable Development Goals and targets of the 2030 Agenda for Sustainable Development.

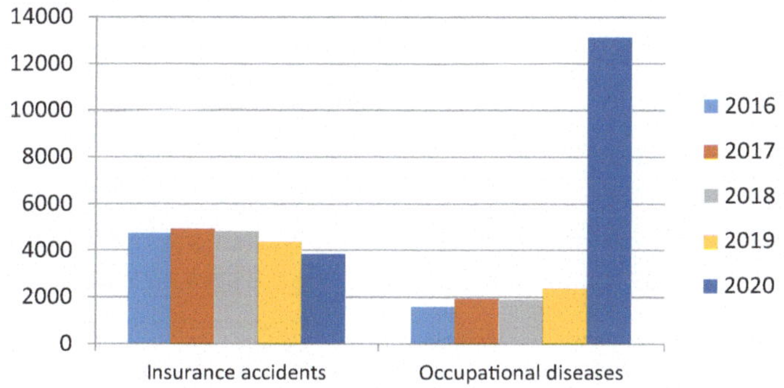

Fig. 1 Dynamics of insurance accidents and occupational diseases (including acute), 2016–2020 (data for January-September for the year 2020 are taken into account). Made by the authors on the basis of annual reports of the Social Insurance Fund of Ukraine for 2017–2020 (Social Insurance Fund of Ukraine: official site (2017–2019). Social Insurance Fund of Ukraine (2020) Prevention of occupational injuries and occupational diseases during 9 months of 2020: statistical data)

examinations; the significant percentage of off-the-books employment. Among the factors indicating the inconsistency of occupational morbidity statistics with the true state of affairs some authors also mention the poor quality of periodic medical examinations due to the insufficient training of doctors in the field of occupational pathology and poor logistics of health care facilities, which hampers full medical examinations. Also, the elimination of the sanitary service, which makes it difficult to obtain sanitary characteristics from the place of work is of great importance.[19] According to the ILO Department of Statistics (ILOSTAT) 'under-reporting is thought to be present in countries at all levels of development, but may be particularly problematic in developing countries'.[20] Such a situation is also typical for Ukraine. At the same time, it should be noted, that the Social Insurance Fund of Ukraine indicates in its statistical information the number of reported accidents and occupational diseases, thus, it cannot take into account cases of occupational diseases in the informal economy and cases that have not been reported by the employer to the Fund.

Analysing the dynamics of occupational morbidity over the past 5 years, we can note a gradual decrease in the number of accidents at work and a slight increase in the number of occupational diseases (Fig. 1).

At the same time, there is a sharp increase in the number of occupational diseases caused by the spread of the Covid-19 pandemic during 9 months of 2020. Thus, according to the Social Insurance Fund of Ukraine, compared to 9 months of 2019, the number of accidents reports/acute occupational diseases (poisoning) reports for the same period in 2020 has increased by 3.7 times (from 4427 to 16,286), the number of reports about fatal accidents has increased by 4.4% (from 908 to 948).

[19] Nahorna (2016), p. 5.

[20] ILO Statistics (2020) Indicator description: Occupational injuries.

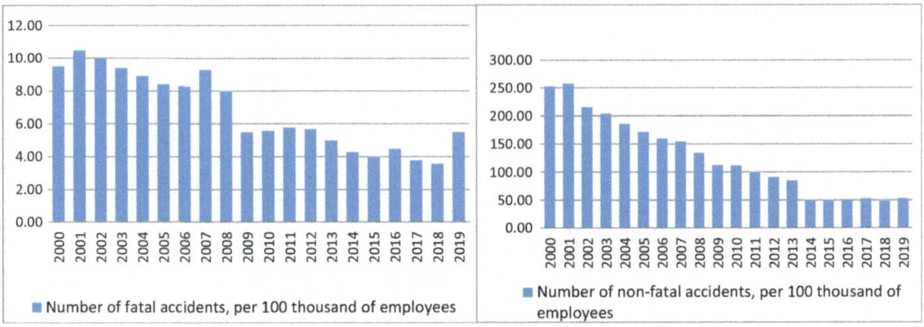

Fig. 2 Dynamics of accidents in Ukraine per 100 thousand of employees, 2000–2019. Made by authors according to the data of the ILO Statistics (ILO Data Explorer (2020) Fatal occupational injuries per 100,000 workers by sex and migrant status)

This is due to cases of infection of medical and other workers with COVID-19, whose work is related to the performance of professional duties in conditions of increased risk of infection, and which are investigated as cases of acute occupational disease. 11,591 reports of such cases were registered during 9 months of 2020, which is 71.2% of their total number.[21]

At the same time, the analysis of only quantitative indicators of occupational morbidity does not allow to draw unambiguous conclusions about the positive or negative dynamics of accidents and occupational diseases in Ukraine. In our opinion, the analysis of the relevant indicators per 100,000 employees gathered within the framework of UN Sustainable Development Goals occupational injury indicators analysis is more significant. Thus, according to ILOSTAT, we can see the dynamics of periodic decrease and increase in the number of fatal accidents and in general the positive dynamics in the decrease in the number of non-fatal accidents for the last 20 years (Fig. 2).

As for occupational injuries, socio-cultural sphere and trade were recognized as the most traumatic in 2019 in Ukraine—924 injured persons. Among other top-five industries are: coal industry—690 injured persons; agro-industrial complex – 517 injured persons; transport industry—293 injured persons; machine-building—270 injured persons. However, the number of fatal injuries is not decreasing: 422 deaths in 2019. The agro-industrial complex has the highest level of fatal injuries—80 dead people, followed by transport industry—75 dead people; socio-cultural sphere and trade—63 dead people; construction industry—61 dead people; coal industry—20 dead people; energy industry—20 dead people; machine-building—20 dead people; housing and economic—20 dead people.[22]

A relatively low level of occupational injuries compared to European countries is typical for Ukraine. According to this indicator, Ukraine is at the level of Belarus and

[21] Social Insurance Fund of Ukraine (2020) Prevention of occupational injuries and occupational diseases during 9 months of 2020: statistical data.

[22] Sereda (2020).

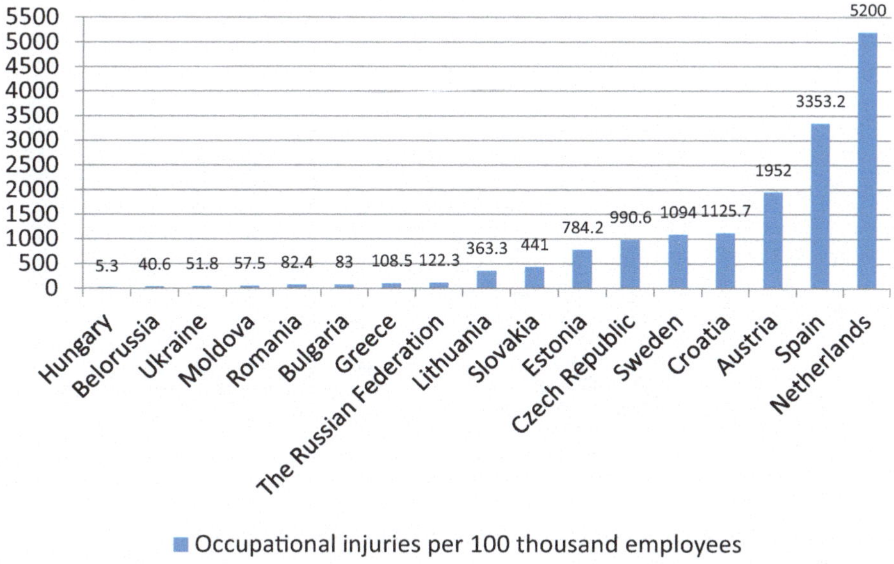

Fig. 3 The level of occupational injuries in European countries, 2016. Made by authors according to the data of the ILO Statistics (ILO Statistics: Data Explorer (2020) Cases of fatal occupational injury by sex and migrant status)

Moldova. The highest level of injuries in European countries is observed in the Netherlands, which is 100 times higher than in Ukraine (Fig. 3).

As for fatal cases of occupational injuries, we can see the opposite situation. Ukraine is characterized by high values of the mortality rate of occupational injuries among European countries. According to this indicator, the country is at the level of such post-Soviet countries as Estonia, Lithuania, Moldova and the Russian Federation. The best situation with the mortality rate of occupational injuries is typical for Sweden, where this rate is 4.5 times lower than in Ukraine (Fig. 4).

With the positive dynamics, the share of employees working in harmful conditions is decreasing by 1–2% every year. The highest percentage of employees working in conditions harmful to their health live in Donetsk, Dnipropetrovsk, Zaporizhzhia and Luhansk regions (35–47%). And the lowest share of employees working in such conditions is typical for Transcarpathian region, Chernivtsi, Kherson and Chernihiv regions (less than 20%) (Fig. 5).

Regarding the geographical distribution of occupational diseases of the population, the maximum values of this indicator are typical for Dnipropetrovsk (36.8%), Lviv (17.9%) and Donetsk regions (16.4%). The number of victims of occupational diseases in these areas is 73% of the total number of victims in Ukraine who have occupational diseases.

In the structure of occupational diseases, the first place belongs to respiratory diseases, the second place—to diseases of the musculoskeletal system (radiculopathy, osteochondrosis, arthritis, osteoarthritis), the third place—to hearing

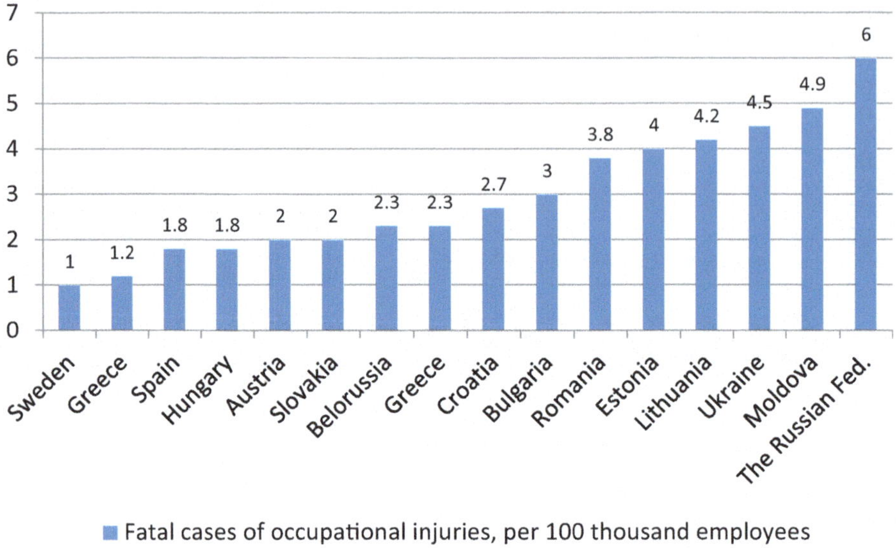

Fig. 4 Fatal cases of occupational injuries per 100 thousand employees, 2016. Made by authors according to the data of the ILO Statistics (ILO: Data Explorer (2020) Cases of fatal occupational injury by sex and migrant status)

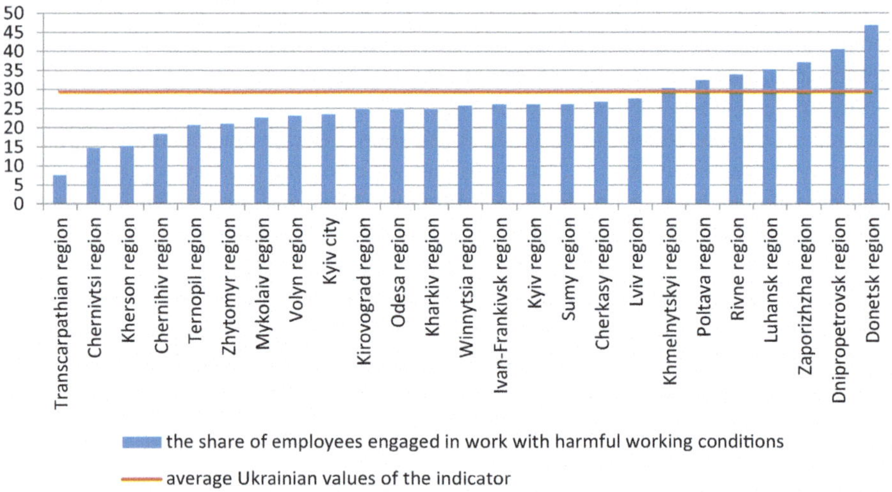

Fig. 5 Percentage of employees employed in harmful working conditions in the regions of Ukraine in 2019. Made by authors according to the data (Senyk (2020), p. 198)

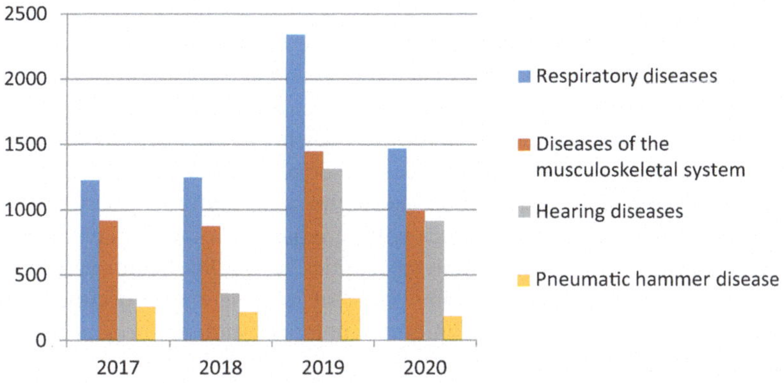

Fig. 6 Dynamics of the main types of occupational diseases in Ukraine, 2017–2020 (data for January-September of 2020 are taken into account). Made by authors according to the data of annual reports of the Social Insurance Fund of Ukraine (Social Insurance Fund of Ukraine (2020))

diseases, the fourth—for pneumatic hammer disease (Fig. 6). Of concern is the growing proportion of patients with neoplasms and tuberculosis caused by occupational factors, although their share in the structure of occupational diseases is insignificant.

The distribution of occupational diseases of the musculoskeletal system and peripheral nervous system according to manufacturing fields allows to state the largest number of victims in the coal industry (45–54% of the total number in the country, mainly due to radiculopathies, osteoarthritis). The remaining 46–55% are distributed among employees in the metallurgical industry, agriculture and other economic activities.[23] Hygienic imperfection of equipment, machines and mechanisms that generate high levels of noise and vibration, continue to be the cause of the formation of vibrating-noise pathology in employees.[24] Occupational disease of employees with pulmonary tuberculosis is registered among employees of the following sectors of economic activity: health care (94.3% of all cases), in mining (0.3%), processing industry (1.7%), construction (0.1%); agriculture (1.1%); other industries (2.4%).[25]

The highest rate of occupational diseases over the past four years are recorded in the sectoral structure of the economy, namely in the mining industry and quarrying (2017–82.6%, 2018–84.1%, 2019–84.6%, 9 months of 2020–85.5%). The next places in terms of the number of occupational diseases are occupied by the metallurgical industry and mechanical engineering.

Such activities as uranium and thorium ore mining do not account for a large number of cases compared to the leading industries in Ukraine, but it should be noted

[23] Nahorna (2018), p. 10.
[24] Nahorna (2016), p. 11.
[25] Nahorna (2018), p. 7.

that it forms the largest rate of oncological pathology of occupational origin. As well as a high incidence of cancer diseases are peculiar to employees when performing welding work in machine-building, metallurgical and chemical industries.[26]

It should be noted that the concealment of accidents and occupational diseases has certain negative consequences: first, workers who suffer health injuries because of work are treated as opportunities to receive social benefits, compensation for the restoration of health functions, and secondly, the opportunity to assess objectively the need for what preventive processes will be required in the workplace is lost.[27] Only real statistics will allow authorized entities to predict health problems and ensure appropriate prevention measures. Lack of information on occupational diseases does not allow to properly inform employers and develop public policy measures that would be aimed at preventing occupational diseases.

3 National Politics of Labour Protection Strategy as the Principle of Ensuring the Safety and Health of Employees

Art. 43 of the Constitution of Ukraine regulates the right of everyone to adequate, safe and healthy labour conditions that proceeds from the provision that, among other things, recognition of human life and health, immunity and safety is the highest social value (Art. 3). The right to healthy and safe labour conditions is recognized in Art. 3 of the European Social Charter (revised) (ratified by Ukraine) and Art. 2 of the Labour Code of Ukraine.[28] In the context of the implementation of this right, according to Art. 3 of Part II of the Charter, countries undertake to develop, implement and periodically review consistent national policies in the field of labour protection, occupational hygiene and the occupational environment. The purpose of such policy is to improve labour protection, as well as to prevent accidents and injuries resulting from work-related activities that take place in the process of its implementation.[29]

Ensuring healthy and safe working conditions is among the goals defined by the UN Sustainable Development Goals by 2030: 'Develop the capacity of all countries, especially developing countries, in the field of early warning, risk reduction and management of national and global health risks' (p. 3.); 'Protect labour rights and promote reliable and safe labour conditions for all employees...' (p. 8.8).[30] The last subgoal is specified in the National Report for 2017 'Sustainable Development Goals: Ukraine': to promote the provision of reliable and safe labour conditions

[26] Nahorna (2016), pp. 12–13.

[27] Tjalvin (2020).

[28] Labour Code of Ukraine (1971) with amendments.

[29] Council of Europe (1996) European Social Charter (Revised) ETS 163.

[30] UN Ukraine (2020) Sustainable Development Goals.

for all employees, in particular through the use of innovative technologies in the field of labour protection and industrial safety (p. 8.5). At the same time, indicators for monitoring progress in its achievement are expressed in: (a) the number of victims of occupational accidents; (b) the number of deaths from occupational accidents; (c) the share of employees engaged in work with harmful working conditions.[31] Relevant indicators (analysed in detail in Section 1) should be the basis for improving Ukraine's national policy in the field of labour protection in order to minimize occupational injuries and occupational diseases.

Protection of life and health of the employee in labour process is one of the key standards, also in law-making activities of the ILO. Thus, in the preamble of the charter of the ILO for year 1919, the protection of employees from disease, occupational diseases and accidents at work are distinguished among the tasks of the Organization,[32] and according to point g of the Art. III of Philadelphian Declaration for year 1944,[33] the ILO is obliged to facilitate the adoption of programs by Member States aimed at ensuring the necessary protection of the lives and health of employees of all professions.

During the 100-year history of the ILO, a large number of conventions, recommendations and other instruments (Codes of Practice, reports) have been adopted, which set standards in the field of protection of life and health of employees at work.

ILO conventions in the field of occupational safety and health can be conditionally classified as: (1) universal, defining the general principles of occupational safety and management in this area (Convention No.155 on occupational safety and health and the labour environment of 1981, Convention No. 187 on the foundations for occupational safety and health of 2006); (2) on labour protection management (Convention No. 81 on labour inspection in industry and trade of 1947, Convention No. 161 on Occupational Health Services of 1985); (3) associated with specific risks (ionizing radiation, asbestos, occupational cancer, chemicals, etc.); (4) related to specific fields of work (agriculture, construction, etc.).[34]

At the same time, a comprehensive analysis of the main ILO conventions allows us to determine the main objectives of national policy in the field of labour protection: (1) the need to create a management system for labour protection at the state level and individual employers; (2) establishing responsibility for labour protection for all subjects of social partnership—the state, employers and employees.

The protection of workers' health and safety enshrined in the EU Charter of Fundamental Rights is one of the key elements of an EU economy that works for people. The right to a healthy and safe workplace is reflected in principle 10 of the European Pillar of Social Rights. In European Union the key role for regulation in the field of occupational safety and health belongs to the European Framework

---

[31] Ministry of Economic Development and Trade of Ukraine (2017) Sustainable Development Goals: Ukraine. Baseline National Report.

[32] Charter of the ILO (1962).

[33] Declaration concerning the aims and purposes of the ILO (1944).

[34] Sakharuk (2019), p.167.

Directive on Safety and Health at Work (Directive 89/391 EEC). It is of fundamental importance as it the basic safety and health legal act which lays down general principles concerning the prevention and protection of workers against occupational accidents and diseases. The Directive introduces as a key element the principle of risk assessment and defines its main elements (e.g. hazard identification, participation of workers, introduction of adequate measures with the priority of eliminating risk at source, documentation and periodical re-assessment of workplace hazards). On the basis of the Directive 89/391 EEC were adopted 24 specific directives that address particular risks, groups and settings.

EU Strategic Framework on Health and Safety at Work 2014–2020 emphasized the need to improve the prevention of work-related diseases by tackling existing, new and emerging risks. It has been underscored, that new technologies and innovations in work organisation have substantially improved well-being at work and working conditions, but effective prevention of work-related diseases requires anticipating potential negative effects of new technologies on workers' health and safety. In addition, specific attention should be given to addressing the impact of changes in work organization in terms of physical and mental health.

EU Strategic Framework on Health and Safety at Work 2021–2027 focuses in particular on such priorities as (1) anticipating and managing change in the context of green, digital and demographic transitions (2) improving the prevention of work-related accidents and diseases, and striving towards a Vision Zero approach to work-related deaths. The document emphasizes that the Covid-19 pandemic has shown how crucial OSH is for protecting workers' health, for the functioning of our society, and for the continuity of critical economic and social activities. Therefore, the road to recovery and reactivation of productivity must also include the renewed commitment to keep occupational safety and health at the forefront and to improve the synergies between OSH and public health policies.

The EU-Ukraine Association Agreement[35] regulates the need to strengthen dialogue and cooperation to ensure, in particular, safe and healthy labour conditions (Art. 419) to achieve such goals as: improving the quality of human life; improving the quality of jobs with decent labour conditions; improving the level of health care and safe labour conditions, in particular, by promoting the implementation of preventive measures, exchange of best practices and research results in this area (Art. 420). According to Art. 424 and Supplement XL to Chapter 21 of the Agreement, Ukraine needs to ensure gradual approximation to EU standards, including on occupational safety and health. At the same time, the section 'Health and Safety of the Nation' of the Supplement XL[36] provides for the need to implement 27 Directives in the field of labour protection (the largest number among the Directives on labour relations).

---

[35] Association Agreement between the European Union and its Member States, of the one part, and Ukraine, of the other part (2014).

[36] UA-EU Association Agreement (2014) Annex XL to Chapter 21 'Cooperation in the field of employment, social policy and equal opportunities.'

Despite the existence of a detailed system of international labour standards, the ILO emphasizes that labour protection instruments are often not ratified or put into practice to address persistent risks to the safety and health of employees.[37] Therefore, it is important to ensure proper and healthy labour conditions in the process of work, along with the implementation of international labour standards in the field of occupational safety, *the development of national tools to minimize occupational diseases.* At the same time, according to the provisions of the European Social Charter (revised), such measures must be implemented comprehensively and be reflected in national labour protection policy. According to Art. 4 of the Law of Ukraine 'On Labour Protection' as of October 14, 1992, the state policy in the field of labour protection is determined by the Verkhovna Rada of Ukraine and is aimed at creating appropriate, safe and healthy working conditions, prevention of accidents and occupational diseases. One of the key principles of this state policy, according to the Law, is the priority of life and health of employees and full responsibility of the employer for the creation of appropriate, safe and healthy labour conditions.[38]

In 2013, the National Social Program for Improving Safety, Occupational Health and the Occupational Environment for 2014–2018 was adopted,[39] which defined a wide range of public policy objectives, including the adaptation of national legislation to international and EU legislation, improving the efficiency of labour security management systems, prevention of risks of occupational injuries and occupational diseases, economic incentives to improve labour protection, increase the level of occupational safety culture, etc. At the same time, after 2018 the Verkhovna Rada hasn't adopted any new documents that would define the state policy in the field of labour protection, although the relevant obligation is determined by the ESC.

The National Profile on Occupational Safety and Health of Ukraine 2018[40] (developed within the ILO Project 'Strengthening Labour Administration to Improve Working Conditions and Overcome of Undeclared Work') identifies the current state of occupational safety and health in Ukraine and gives recommendations that can improve this situation and promote the adaptation of national labour legislation to international and European labour standards and best practices of foreign countries. One of the key problems identified in the Profile (noted in Section 1 of the study) is the lack of a system for collecting statistical information on occupational accidents and occupational diseases. Accordingly, we agree with the recommendation to introduce an effective national system to ensure proper registration, report and investigation of occupational accidents, occupational diseases, and the collection, analysis and publication of statistics on them in accordance with the ILO Code of Practice for Reporting on Occupational Accidents and Occupational

[37] ILO (2019a) Safety and health at the heart of the future of work. Building on 100 years of experience.

[38] The Law of Ukraine No 2694-XII 'On Labour Protection' (1992).

[39] The Law of Ukraine No 178-VII 'National social program to improve safety, occupational health and the working environment for 2014-2018' (2013) Vidomosti Verkhovnoi Rady 10, Art. 112.

[40] ILO (2018) National Profile on Occupational Safety and Health of Ukraine.

Diseases and their registration.[41] At the same time, it is necessary to harmonize the Ukrainian criteria and methods of collection, classification and registration of data on occupational accidents with the European statistics of occupational accidents of the Statistical Office of the European Communities.[42]

The next topical issue in the field of labour protection management both at the level of the enterprise/organization/institution and at the national level is the lack of focus on the prevention of occupational diseases. Thus, the Concept of reforming the management system of labour protection in Ukraine in 2018 rightly notes that today the management of labour protection is formed following the principle of 'corrective action', i.e. responding to dangerous cases and situations, and not by the principle of 'preventive action', i.e. prevention of dangerous cases and situations.[43]

Among the principles of labour protection state policy (Art. 4 of the Law of Ukraine 'On labour protection') preventive measures to preclude occupational accidents and diseases are not distinguished. At the same time, an important trend in the development of international standards for ensuring safe and healthy labour conditions is the *shift of emphasis in the management of labour protection to the preventive mechanism*. The ILO Global Strategy for Occupational Safety emphasizes the need to build and maintain a national culture of occupational safety and health (national preventative safety and health culture).[44] Such culture is defined by the ILO as a culture in which the right to a safe and healthy occupational environment is respected at all levels, when governments, employers and employees are actively involved in ensuring a safe and healthy occupational environment through a system of established rights, responsibilities and obligations and when the principles of prevention are given the highest priority (Art. 1 of the ILO Convention No. 187.)[45]

The need to introduce a preventive culture in the field of labour protection is emphasized in the ILO Guidelines on Occupational Safety and Health Management Systems (ILO-OSH 2001[46]), in the EU-Ukraine Association Agreement (Art. 13.3).[47] EU Framework Directive on Safety and Health at Work focuses on a risk-prevention culture and lays down employers' obligations on: (1) risk assessments; (2) preventive measures; (3) giving OSH information to workers; (4) training; (5) consultation; (6) balanced participation. Encouraging a culture of safety and prevention through the effective exchange of knowledge about tools and the best

[41] ILO (2018) National Profile on Occupational Safety and Health of Ukraine, p. 198.

[42] Eurostat (2001) European Statistics on Accidents at Work (ESAW)—Methodology.

[43] The Order of the Cabinet of Ministers of Ukraine No. 989-p (2018) The concept of reforming the management system of labour protection in Ukraine. Official gazette of Ukraine 100, Art. 3338.

[44] ILO (2003) Global Strategy on Occupational Safety and Health. Conclusions adopted by the International Labour Conference at its 91st Session.

[45] ILO (2006) Promotional Framework for Occupational Safety and Health Convention—C187.

[46] ILO (2001) Guidelines on occupational safety and health management systems.

[47] Association Agreement between the European Union and its Member States, of the one part, and Ukraine, of the other part (2014).

practices in the field of occupational safety and health was also provided by the ILO Decent Work Agenda for Ukraine for 2016–2019.[48]

Prevention of occupational injuries and diseases is important not only to minimize risks to the lives and health of employees, but also to the economic development of employers. Thus, K. De Meester observed that taking calculated risks is part of being successful in business. Prevention is the most rational means to protect against risk. Prevention allows the elimination or reduction of uncertainties, although it cannot guarantee total safety or zero harm.[49]

In this aspect, the implementation of the Concept for year 2018 of a national system of occupational risk prevention based on the principles of hazard elimination, assessment, risk control and management, which will include a coherent general policy of occupational risk prevention (covering technology, work organization, working conditions, social relations and the impact of factors related to the working environment) would be a significant positive step.[50] A similar approach is provided for in Directive №89/391/EEC.[51] Among the expected results of the implementation of the national system of prevention of industrial risks, the Concept rightly defines the formation of a culture of occupational safety and health, which corresponds to the provisions of the ILO Convention No. 187. At the same time, we support the recommendations set by the National Profile for Occupational Safety and Health Ukraine on: (1) introduction of a high-level proactive approach to occupational safety and health, based on encouraging the improvement of occupational safety and health at enterprises, accurate and continuous risk assessment and risk prevention; (2) enshrining the regulatory obligation of the employer (without transferring this obligation to others) to provide employees with safe and healthy conditions, applying all necessary preventive measures.[52]

The next challenge that should be considered when developing a national health and safety policy is the ***emergence of new risks to the safety and health of employees.*** Anticipation of such risks is extremely important in connection with the emergence of new technologies in the work process organization, demographic change, different employment models. In addition, as the ILO emphasizes, this is the most important first step for effective risk management and building a preventive culture of occupational safety in a continually changing world.[53] The ILO Global Strategy for Occupational Safety and Health in 2003 analyses all available (at the time of adoption) ILO instruments on occupational safety and health with an

---

[48] ILO (2016) Decent Work Country Programme for Ukraine 2016–2019.

[49] ILO (2019a) Safety and Health at the Heart of the Future of Work: A Compilation of Think Pieces.

[50] The Order of the Cabinet of Ministers of Ukraine No. 989-p (2018) The concept of reforming the management system of labour protection in Ukraine. Official gazette of Ukraine 100, Art. 3338.

[51] European Agency for Safety and Health at Work (1989) Council Directive 89/391/EEC on the introduction of measures to improve the safety and health of employees at work.

[52] ILO (2018) National Profile on Occupational Safety and Health of Ukraine, p. 164.

[53] ILO (2019a) Safety and health at the heart of the future of work. Building on 100 years of experience, p. 55.

indication of their relevance or need for revision.[54] At the same time, since the adoption of the Strategy, new challenges have arisen in the field of legal regulation of labour, which require a response and the development of additional tools of influence. Thus, the report of the ILO Global Commission 'Work for a Brighter Future' of 2019 emphasizes that it is time to recognize that occupational safety and health is one of the fundamental principles and rights in the field of labour in the world where nearly 3 million employees continue to die each year as a result of occupational accidents and occupational diseases.[55] The need to increase investment in labour market institutions, including occupational safety and health is provided in report among the key areas of labour legal regulation development.

They also need radical changes in the system of labour protection management, as today they often create excessive bureaucracy due to the tendencies towards standardization, which root from the regimes of certification and self-regulation.[56]

That is why the ILO Convention No. 187 regulates that the national system of occupational safety and health should include, in particular: (1) information and advisory services on occupational safety and health; (2) research work in the field of occupational safety and health (Art. 4).[57] At the same time, conduction of researches to determine the most effective methods of occupational safety management and prevention of occupational diseases is the basis for the development of national policies in the field of occupational safety and health. As P. Swuste, J.-Ch.Le Coze emphasized rightly, although there is a growing consensus on the structure and elements of safety management systems, its scientific basis is still very small.[58] For example, L. Godderis, M.-Cl. Lambrechts noticed that digital revolution has led to an increase in the amount of research into electronic health (eHealth) and mobile health (mHealth), so we need to use the new e-health technologies as an opportunity.[59]

The need to review the strategies of national policies in the field of labour protection was stressed in 2020 in view of the Covid-19 pandemic. At the same time, the pandemic showed both the need to improve the management of labour protection (including the prevention of occupational diseases) and the direct connection between the state of labour protection and the situation in the health care system. First, in 2020 we observe the dynamics of growth in the number of occupational diseases by more than 4 times (Fig. 1, Section 1) given Covid-19 as an occupational disease of medical staff. Secondly, in addition to physicians, the risk

[54] ILO (2003) Global Strategy on Occupational Safety and Health. Conclusions adopted by the International Labour Conference at its 91st Session.

[55] ILO (2019b) Work for a Brighter Future: report of the Global Commission on the Future of Work, p. 39.

[56] ILO (2019a) Safety and Health and the Future of Work: A Compilation of Think Pieces, p. 47.

[57] ILO (2007) Convention No187 on the Fundamentals of Occupational Safety and Health of 15.06.2006. Occupational safety newsletter 1.

[58] ILO (2019a) Safety and Health and the Future of Work: A Compilation of Think Pieces, p. 47.

[59] ILO (2019a) Safety and Health and the Future of Work: A Compilation of Think Pieces, p. 21, 22.

of transmission is also a very high for a number of other employees, which necessitates an increase of occupational safety measures application (medical examinations, briefings, ventilation, etc.), proper performance of duties to provide workers with individual protection. Also, as the ILO emphasizes, risk management measures should be specifically tailored to the needs of employees at particular risk for Covid-19 infection.[60] Third, under conditions of pandemic, people, efforts and the supply of medical products—all this is refocused on the implementation of emergency response measures. This often leads to neglection of basic and conventional medical services.[61] Moreover, health facilities, especially emergency rooms, can become foci of infection transmission if proper prevention and control measures are not ensured.[62]

At the same time, health and safety policies can have a positive impact on public health and can help to improve epidemical situation under the conditions of Covid-19. The ILO notes that experience gained during outbreaks of severe acute respiratory syndrome (SARS), influenza A (H1N1) and Ebola in recent years has highlighted the importance of focusing not only on risk groups identifying but also on implementing successful control and prevention measures. Enterprises are effective platforms where employers and employees can jointly disseminate information and discuss safety and health issues, in particular on preventive and protective measures aimed at reducing the spread of infectious diseases.[63]

Building and maintaining a national culture of prevention in the field of labour protection also involves *educational activities* to increase the level of knowledge of employees about the occupational dangers and risks (physical, psychosocial, etc.) and ways to prevent them. According to Global Strategy on Occupational Safety and Health, although occupational accidents and occupational diseases cause great suffering and loss to humanity, their outcomes have high economic value, the level of awareness of employees on health and safety is usually low and does not receive proper priority.[64] That is why the ILO pays special attention to educational work in the field of labour protection. For example, since April 28, 2003, the ILO has celebrated World Day for Safety and Health at Work to promote a global culture of prevention in occupational safety and health.[65] ILO prepares on a regular basis reports, summaries and manuals on topical issues of labour protection. For example, more than 10 practical documents have been developed to respond to the crisis caused by Covid-19, including 'An employers' guide on managing your workplace

---

[60] ILO (2020) In the face of a pandemic: Ensuring Safety and Health at Work, p. 15.

[61] ILO (2020) In the face of a pandemic: Ensuring Safety and Health at Work, p. 14.

[62] World Health Organization (2018).

[63] ILO (2020) In the face of a pandemic: Ensuring Safety and Health at Work, p. 9.

[64] ILO (2003) Global Strategy on Occupational Safety and Health. Conclusions adopted by the International Labour Conference at its 91st Session.

[65] ILO (2019a) Safety and health at the heart of the future of work. Building on 100 years of experience, p. 24.

during COVID-19', 'Principles of Effective Remote Work in a COVID-19 Pandemic', 'Prevention and Mitigation of Covid-19 in the workplace' etc.[66]

With the purpose to intensify educational work in the field of labour protection in Ukraine, it is appropriate to recommend: (1) inclusion of OSH materials in the curricula of educational institutions at different levels of educational system in order to form a culture of occupational risk prevention during preparation for work; (2) the inclusion of OSH materials in vocational education and training initiatives in order to promote the acquisition of knowledge and skills to prevent occupational accidents and occupational diseases; (3) organization and implementation of training and information initiatives aimed at employers and employees, as well as awareness-raising activities on OSH issues for the population.[67]

Development of national policy in the field of labour protection requires an integrated approach and consideration of all elements of labour protection management. Thus, K. De Meester noticed, that the challenge is to mainstream OSH in all segments of economic activity from conception, to planning, to execution and delivery of goods and services. We have to put the people and their work at the centre of our OSH policy. OSH should not be a separate measure, service or discipline. It's not OSH; it's all elements from the overarching world of work.[68] The company is better prepared to develop prompt, coordinated and effective response measures adapted to the specific situation in which it faces due to the employer's comprehensive risk management plan, emergency preparedness (including epidemics).[69] However, in order to implement such activities under Covid-19, employers need to liaise with occupational safety and health services, local health authorities and other partners for information, materials and technical advice.[70]

An integrated approach to health and safety policy is reflected in ILO programs. For example, Safety + Health for All is a flagship programme of the ILO that aims at improving the safety and health of employees throughout the world. The programme deploys necessary standards (e.g. directly supports member states in implementing key ILO Conventions), disseminates actionable information, and implements innovative approaches to improve the safety and health of employees by reducing the incidence of occupational injury, disease and fatalities. It will seek to reach this overall objective by: (1) building knowledge on OSH issues; (2) creating conducive national frameworks for improved OSH conditions; (3) strengthening national capacities to improve compliance with OSH standards; (4) promoting demand for safe and healthy workplaces.[71]

---

[66] ILO (2020) In the face of a pandemic: Ensuring Safety and Health at Work, pp. 38–45.

[67] ILO (2018) National Profile on Occupational Safety and Health of Ukraine, p. 180.

[68] ILO (2019a) Safety and Health at the Heart of the Future of Work: A Compilation of Think Pieces, p. 6.

[69] ILO (2020) In the face of a pandemic: Ensuring Safety and Health at Work, p. 10.

[70] ILO (2020) Prevention and Mitigation of COVID-19 at Work. Action checklist.

[71] ILO (2015) Flagship Programme Strategy, p. 1, 3.

The opportunity of transferring some of the activities and functions that are currently performed by the state (such as training, medical examinations, certification of workplaces and equipment) to private entities or cooperatives that have the technical capacity to implement OSH activities with leaving for the state its main powers and supervisory role in such issues should also be considered.[72]

4 Preventive Measures of Occupational Morbidity in the System of Social Insurance

The ILO names chronic diseases in its study as a hidden epidemic and emphasizes the importance of preventive measures of occupational morbidity using labour protection systems. It also notes that prevention is the key to success because it is not only a guarantee of employee's safety, but also a guarantee of economic and social development.[73]

The European Regional Bureau of the WHOstates in its action plan for capacity-building and public health services that disease prevention consists of several levels: (1) primary preventive measures, which aim to prevent the disease; (2) secondary preventive measures, which involve the detection of the disease at an early stage; (3) tertiary preventive measure, which should be aimed at restoring health in the presence of the disease; (4) and the last fourth stage, which aims to mitigate or prevent health consequences after treatment.[74]

The system of social insurance against occupational accidents and diseases is designed to provide the WHO levels of prevention of morbidity in the professional environment. In Ukraine, the institute of social insurance against occupational accidents and occupational diseases is now perceived as compensation for injuries to employees.

The Law of Ukraine 'On Compulsory state social insurance' stipulates that social insurance is a system of rights, obligations and guarantees, which provides material support, insurance payments and provision of social services to insured persons at the expense of the Social Insurance Fund in Ukraine,[75] that is, the legislator already in the definition does not aim to take preventive measures at social insurance level. Most of the expenditures of the budget of the Social Insurance Fund are already directed to the treatment of chronic diseases, and the provisions of Art. 12 of this Law on the need to finance preventive measures from the budget of the Social Insurance Fund are not actually applied. For example, the report of the Social

[72] ILO (2018) National Profile on Occupational Safety and Health of Ukraine, p. 167.

[73] ILO (2013) The Prevention Occupational Diseases. World Day for safety and health at work, p. 4–5.

[74] ILO (2012) European Action Plan for Strengthening Public Health Capacities and Services. Regional Committee for EuropeSixty-second session, p. 17.

[75] The Law of Ukraine 'On Compulsory State Social Insurance' (1999).

Insurance Fund of Ukraine for 2019 states that only 11,301 UAH was provided to be used for preventive measures, however, at the end of the year, the report stated that the Fund did not incur insurance costs.[76]

However, today it is important to emphasize that the social insurance system should be an important institution for preventing damage to the health of employees. The ILO emphasizes in its report on strengthening the role of insurance programs and prevention of occupational accidents and diseases the need to provide preventive measures before the payment of compensation, i.e. before the moment of damage to health,[77] which in turn is guaranteed to improve health, reduce costs on social benefits and corresponds to the concept of public health.

H.A. Trunova emphasizes that the creation of a preventive insurance program in Ukraine should be the main trend in the legal regulation of social protection against occupational accidents and occupational diseases. One of the areas of such regulation should be the implementation of regulatory measures by including labour protection in social insurance programs against occupational accidents and diseases.[78] Unlike in Ukraine, foreign countries already fund preventive measures to avoid occupational accidents and occupational diseases. Thus, Austria allocates 5% of the budget of insurance programs for preventive measures, Germany—6.9, Switzerland—6.5, Poland—0.07, etc.[79] The lack of provisions in the labour legislation on the need to finance preventive measures of occupational diseases at the expense of the Social Insurance Fund is a significant shortcoming of the legislation.[80] Increasing of preventive measures financing will help to reduce the number of victims and to preserve human potential. It is necessary to create such conditions in the country that it is profitable for employers to invest in human development and occupational safety and health, and for employees to take care of their health and be responsible in the event of an occupational accident and occupational disease.[81]

The Social Insurance Fund should establish a service of insurance experts on labour protection, prevention of occupational accidents and occupational diseases in order to implement measures to prevent occupational accidents and occupational diseases. The Resolution of the Board of the Social Insurance Fund as of December 20, 2011 No. 63 approved the responsibilities of the Social Insurance Fund for prevention measures that are carried out by insurance experts.[82] The main

[76] Resolution of the Board of the Social Insurance Fund of Ukraine No 21 (2020) 'On approval of the Report on the implementation of the budget of the Social Insurance Fund of Ukraine for 2019'.

[77] ILO (2013) Strengthening the Role of Employment Injury Schemes to Help Prevent Occupational Accidents and Diseases.

[78] Trunova (2017), p. 85.

[79] ILO (2016) Strengthening the role of employment injury schemes to help prevent occupational accidents and diseases, p. 23.

[80] Tretiakov and Nesterenko (2016), p. 43.

[81] Tulai (2016), pp. 151–155.

[82] The Board of the Social Insurance Fund against Accidents at Work and Occupational Diseases (2011) Resolution No 63 'On Approval of the Regulations on the Service of Insurance Experts on Occupational Safety, Prevention of Accidents at Work and Occupational Diseases'.

responsibilities of insurance experts include assistance to employers in implementing an effective occupational health and safety management system; inspection of preventive work and labour protection; checking the knowledge of officials in labour protection; informing employers about the effectiveness of preventive work and about positive experiences in the field of labour protection; control over the implementation of measures to eliminate the causes of health damage, assistance in the development of internal documents in the field of labour protection, inspections of compliance with prevention requirements at enterprises, etc.

The Social Insurance Fund in its report for 2020 (January-September) reports on the work done at enterprises by insurance experts. Thus, during 9 months of 2020, 2571 inspections on the state of preventive work at enterprises were carried out, during inspections 19,264 violations of labour protection legislation were revealed. Insurance experts of the Social Insurance Fund held 2449 seminars, round tables, competitions, published 2551 articles on the prevention of insurance cases, as well as work on the implementation of occupational health and safety management systems at 3958 enterprises.[83]

The Social Insurance Fund also emphasizes the importance of preventive work in the investigation of occupational accidents and occupational diseases. By identifying the causes of occupational accidents and occupational diseases, it is possible to carry out further preventive work to eliminate them. During 9 months of 2020, experts of the Social Insurance Fund took part in the work of 10,580 acute occupational diseases investigation commissions; a large number of cases of occupational diseases this year occurred due to infection of doctors with COVID-19.[84]

International Social Security Association (ISSA) determined that social security and insurance against occupational accidents and occupational diseases during the pandemic play an important role in ensuring and protecting citizens, stressed the importance of preventive measures, as only prevention can ensure the health of the population in this case.[85] Today, the question of preventive measures of COVID-19 is very relevant, in particular, among medical staff, which is recognized as an occupational disease of such employees. Under the pandemic conditions, social funds play a special role in ensuring both prevention and compensation. In order to classify a disease as an occupational, it is important to establish a cause-and-effect relationship between the disease and labour conditions when the disease occurs. At the same time, the National Lists of Occupational Diseases and the procedure for establishing a link between work and disease play a significant role in establishing an occupational disease.

In the social insurance system, it is important to establish the criteria by which the disease is determined as occupational. There are cases when an occupational disease

---

[83] Social Insurance Fund of Ukraine (2020) Prevention of occupational injuries and occupational diseases during 9 months of 2020: statistical data.

[84] Social Insurance Fund of Ukraine (2020) Prevention of occupational injuries and occupational diseases during 9 months of 2020: statistical data.

[85] ISSA (2020) COVID-19: Safety and health at work can save lives.

is difficult to diagnose due to the long development of occupational morbidity, and it is difficult to identify which factors may have caused the disease, especially among those employees who changed areas of activity and were exposed to harmful factors many years ago.

Convention of the ILO No. 121 'On assistance in cases of occupational injuries' identified the need for each Member State to approve a list of occupational diseases.[86] The ILO emphasizes the need to constantly review the list of occupational diseases, and to take into account recent researches of the ILO in this field.[87] In 2010, the ILO approved a new list of occupational diseases.[88] O.V. Oriekhova and O.I. Pavlenko note that the mentioned list of the ILO 'reflects the current state of the problem of linking diseases to the profession worldwide and is the latest global agreement on diseases that are internationally recognized as diseases caused by occupational factors'.[89]

In Ukraine, the list of occupational diseases adopted in 2000 has not been significantly updated. Thus, in 2017 tuberculosis was included in the list of occupational diseases of the employees of the State Penitentiary Service in places of detention where patients with tuberculosis are[90] and in 2020 COVID-19 was included in the list as an occupational disease of medical staff.[91] Today there are new factors constantly appearing in the world which negatively affect the health of employees and which belong to the factors of occupational diseases, including nanotechnology, the emergence of new chemical, biological and physiological factors. A large number of occupational diseases are beginning to arise due to the increasing prevalence of computer work, the development of the IT industry, new psychosocial risks associated with the increasing use of remote work. However, in Ukraine, the list of diseases does not include new production factors that harm the health of employees, so there is an urgent need to update such lists, taking into account the requirements of the ILO.

The absence of one disease or another in the list significantly complicates the procedure for employees to recognize the disease as occupational and may result in failure to recognize the disease as an occupational. This state of affairs can also have a negative impact on statistics, as a result of which occupational risks will not be subject to preventive measures. It should also be emphasized that scientific achievements of the Institute of Occupational Medicine, which studies modern factors that

[86] ILO (1964) Convention 121 on Assistance in Cases of Industrial Injuries.

[87] ILO (2013) The Prevention Occupational Diseases. World Day for safety and health at work, p. 14.

[88] ILO (2010) List of occupational diseases (revised 2010). Identification and recognition of occupational diseases: Criteria for incorporating diseases in the ILO list of occupational diseases.

[89] Orekhova and Pavlenko (2014), pp. 73–82.

[90] The Cabinet of Ministers of Ukraine (2017) Resolution No 294 'On making changes and recognizing as invalid some resolutions of the Cabinet of Ministers of Ukraine'.

[91] The Cabinet of Ministers of Ukraine (2020) Resolution No 394 On amending the list of occupational diseases.

lead to damage to health should be taken into account during development of a list of occupational diseases.

As data in Section 1 illustrates, the probability of occupational disease depends on the type of economic activity of the enterprise and the measures taken to prevent adverse health effects. However, in 2016, Ukraine introduced a system whereby employers pay a single social contribution regardless of the type of activity, which is 22% of the minimum wage. This contribution is the same for all companies regardless of the risk of occupational accidents and occupational diseases at enterprise. It was calculated depending on the occupational risk class of the enterprise and prior changes to the system of payment of the single social contribution in 2016. The occupational risk class depended on the level of occupational injuries and occupational diseases. Itwas determined by the ratio of the total cost of insurance to the size of the payroll, which accrued insurance premiums for compulsory social insurance against occupational accidents and diseases for the previous calendar year. That is, the magnitude of the occupational risk of the enterprise depended on the quality and safety of all its employees to perform their duties, i.e. on the magnitude of the individual occupational risk of employees. With Resolution of the Cabinet of Ministers of Ukraine 'On approval of the procedure for determining insurance rates for enterprises, institutions and organizations for compulsory state social insurance against occupational accidents and occupational diseases (currently not valid)[92] only 67 occupational risk classes of enterprises that depended on types of economic activity of the enterprise were established.

However, this system did not take into account the possibility of transition from one occupational risk to another while improving labour conditions and implementing preventive measures, which actually indicated a lack of incentives for employers to increase measures to prevent occupational diseases and improve labour conditions.

There are supporters of building such a system according to occupational risk classes in the world, as well as opponents who say that building a system of occupational risk assessment will help to hide occupational accidents and occupational diseases and not pay contributions.[93] However, we believe that such a system of payment of social contributions, based on occupational risks, should be combined with economic incentives for employers. It is noted in the scientific literature that the lack of interest of employers in improving labour conditions leads to an increase in harmful labour conditions and occupational diseases, which should be addressed by introducing differentiated contributions depending on labour conditions and the number of occupational accidents and occupational diseases.

[92] The Cabinet of Ministers of Ukraine (2000) Resolution of No 1423 'Procedure for determining insurance rates for enterprises, institutions and organizations for compulsory state social insurance against accidents at work and occupational diseases'.

[93] ILO (2016) Strengthening the role of employment injury schemes to help prevent occupational accidents and diseases, p. 23.

The International Social Security Association (ISSA) has defined guidelines for occupational risk prevention. One of the first principles is the need to establish economic incentives for employers to create safe labour conditions.[94] At the same time, economic incentives for employers to improve labour conditions can be established both by the state by reducing the tax burden and by the Social Insurance Fund of Ukraine by reducing the amount of insurance premiums. For example, companies with a low level of occupational accidents and occupational diseases may pay lower insurance premiums, and, accordingly, companies with a high incidence have to pay higher rates.

In Germany, measures of financial incentives and penalties have been used for many years. This means that sectoral insurance companies have the power to determine the amount of insurance premiums for individual companies based on the number and scale of consequences of accidents. Conscientious treatment of employers is encouraged even in high-risk industries, and unfair practices are punishable by fines.[95]

We see the need for transition of Ukraine to a system of paying contributions according to classes of occupational risks, which should be determined, among others by statistics, as well as to establish a real opportunity for companies to move from one class to another with a smaller insurance premium. This shift should be tied to the estimated value of occupational and industrial risk and should be provided on the basis of an annual audit of occupational and industrial risk at enterprises, institutions and organizations (may be conducted on the basis of inspections by insurance experts of the Social Insurance Fund).

5 Conclusions

Statistics on occupational accidents and occupational diseases are important for determining the dynamics of occupational injuries and, accordingly, for improving the system of measures for occupational safety management and planning of preventive measures. At the same time, information on the fields that are most traumatic, the types of occupational diseases that predominate are indicators that allow to identify the most vulnerable areas in which appropriate measures should be taken first. It is important to systematize the collection of statistical information, the availability of analysis by type of economic activity in order to determine occupations and types of high-risk employment.

Based on the analysis of the main international standards in the field of labour protection management, it can be concluded that the states should develop, implement and revise national policies taking into account current risks and challenges to life and health of employees in order to ensure safe working conditions. In Ukraine,

[94] ISSA (2016) Guidelines on Prevention of Occupational Risks.

[95] Trunova (2017), p. 85.

the state policy in the field of labour protection must be approved by the Verkhovna Rada of Ukraine in accordance with the Law of Ukraine 'On labour protection', but there is no current program to improve occupational safety.

The issue of labour protection is considered at the level of the ILO not as a separate institution of labour law, but as part of a comprehensive strategy to reform the system of labour relations within the framework of decent work and achieving the Sustainable Development Goals. An important trend in the development of international labour protection standards is to shift the emphasis in occupational safety management to the preventive mechanism and determine the need to build a national culture of prevention in the field of safety and hygiene. Building and maintaining such a culture allows both research to identify new risks and challenges in the field of health and safety and educational activities to increase employees' knowledge of occupational hazards and risks and ways to prevent them.

The system of social insurance against accidents and occupational diseases is an effective mechanism in the world of prevention and compensation of occupational diseases. However, today the Social Insurance Fund mainly takes measures to compensate for occupational diseases that have already occurred and are chronic, so there is a need to reorient to the preventive direction. In addition, in Ukraine there is a problem of insufficient allocation of funds to finance preventive measures by the Social Insurance Fund, which should be carried out by insurance experts. Based on the experience of European countries, prevention measures should bring more cost-effective results than compensation payments.

The implementation of proper prevention of occupational diseases can be available only with the most realistic indicators of statistical data on occupational diseases, where one of the main factors is the definition of a disease in the national list of diseases. In Ukraine, such a list needs to be urgently updated to include current risk factors for employees' health. In addition, real statistics are important for identifying occupational risks in the context of employer contributions. In our opinion, the differentiation of contributions depending on the number of occupational accidents and occupational diseases (risk classes) with the combination of the system of providing benefits to employers in the payment of contributions, is the most effective mechanism to motivate employers to create the safest occupational conditions.

References

ILO (2013) The prevention occupational diseases. World Day for safety and health at work. http://bit.ly/2LPdIIc

ILO (2016) Strengthening the role of employment injury schemes to help prevent occupational accidents and diseases. http://bit.ly/3987yeM

ILO (2019a) Safety and Health and the Future of Work: A Compilation of Think Pieces, 104 p. ISBN: 978-92-2-133718-8

ILO (2019b) Work for a Brighter Future: report of the Global Commission on the Future of Work. ISBN978-92-2-132796-7

ILO (2020) In the face of a pandemic: Ensuring Safety and Health at Work. https://bit.ly/3sNogIh
ILO Statistics (2020) Indicator description: Occupational injuries. http://bit.ly/39SphGm
Klantsa AI (2018) Hromadske Zdorovia Yak Umova Natsionalnoi Bezpeky Derzhavy (Public health as a condition of national security) Bulletin of the National Academy of Public Administration under the President of Ukraine. Series. Public Adm 1:107–113. https://bit.ly/3pccDIN
Kundiev YI, Nahorna AM, Sokolova MP et al (2011) Dynamika Profesiinoi Zakhvoriuvanosti V Ukraini Ta Dosvid Instytutu Medytsyny Pratsi NAMN Ukrainy (Dynamics of occupational morbidity in Ukraine and the experience of the Institute of Occupational Medicine of the National Academy of Medical Sciences of Ukraine). Ukrainian J Occupat Med Iss 1(25):46–52
Nahorna AM (2016) Stan Profesiinoi Zakhvoriuvanosti V Period Zakonodavchykh Zmin V Ukraini (The state of occupational morbidity during the legislative changes in Ukraine). In: Nahorna AM, Sokolova MP, Vitte IH et al. Ukrainian J Occupat Med Iss 1:3–17
Nahorna AM (2018) Epidemiolohichni Doslidzhennia Profesiinoho Zdorovia V Ukraini (Epidemiological studies of occupational health in Ukraine). Ukrainian J Occupat Med Iss 14(57):3–20
Orekhova OV, Pavlenko OI (2014) Problems of occupational health and occupational pathology in connotations and recommendations from the International Labour Organization. Ukrainian J Occupat Med 3(40):73–82. http://oplib.org.ua/3263/1/Ujpmp_2014_3_10.pdf
Sakharuk IS (2019) Pravovi Osnovy Zabezpechennia Bezpechnykh Ta Zdorovykh Umov Pratsi Zghidno Standartiv MOP u XXI Stolitti (Legal basis for ensuring safe and healthy working conditions according to ILO standards in the XXI century). J Kyiv Univ Law 3:167
Senyk IV (2020) Statystychnyi Zbirnyk ‘Pratsia Ukrainy 2019’ (Statistical collection ‘Labour of Ukraine 2019’) State Statistics Service of Ukraine, Kyiv
Sereda MA (2020) The state of occupational injuries in 2019. In: Labour protection service (official site). https://bit.ly/2LNVyXf
Tjalvin G (2020) Work-related and occupational diseases. http://bit.ly/3sP3GY6
Tkachenko YM (2019) Current state and problems of legal regulation of public health in Ukraine. Current public health issues in today’s world (Suchasnyi Stan I Problemy Pravovoho Rehuliuvannia Okhorony Hromadskoho Zdorovia V Ukraini. Aktualni Pytannia Hromadskoho Zdorovia V Umovakh Suchasnosti). In: Volkova MA, Harbel RT, Bazyka EL (eds) Abstract of scientific conference, Mykolaiv. https://bit.ly/3iEuUvH
Tretiakov OV, Nesterenko SV (2016) Systema Strakhuvannia Vid Neshchasnykh Vypadkiv – Diievyi Vazhil Upravlinnia Bezpekoiu Pratsi V Ukraini (The accident insurance system is an effective lever for occupational safety management in Ukraine) construction, materials science. Series: Safety of life 93(201):43
Trunova HA (2017) Sotsialne Strakhuvannia Vid Neshchasnoho Vypadku Na Vyrobnytstvi Ta Profesiinoho Zakhvoriuvannia Tendentsii Rozvytku Pravovoho Rehuliuvannia (Social insurance against accidents at work and occupational diseases: trends in legal regulation). Law Innov 3(19):85
Tulai OI (2016) Suspilna Rol Sotsialnoho Strakhuvannia Vid Neshchasnykh Vypadkiv Na Vyrobnytstvvi Ta Profesiinykh Zakhvoriuvan (The social role of social insurance against accidents at work and occupational diseases) Bulletin of Odessa National University. Series: Economics 21(7)2:151–155.
World Health Organization (2018) Managing epidemics: key facts about major deadly diseases. WHO, Luxembourg
World Health Organization Regional Office for Europe (2013) Health 2020: a European policy framework and strategy for the 21st century. https://bit.ly/3o8M99O

Part II
Human Autonomy. Circulation of the Deceased's Organs

Human Autonomy in the Field of Medical Care: National Regulations, Foreign Experience and Case Law

Iryna Senyuta

Contents

Abstract Human autonomy in the field of healthcare as one of the fundamental principles in medical practice, the value of legal medicine and a tool for the formation of a human-centered healthcare system has been researched. Medical sorting and autonomy in decision-making have been considered, clinical and priority triage has been allocated, key principles of priority sorting have been proposed. It has been found out that the principle of autonomy in priority medical sorting is subject to significant restrictions, which negatively affect the observance of human rights in the field of healthcare. It has been noted that ensuring the individual mobility of persons with disabilities with the maximum possible degree of their autonomy, independence from outside assistance will guarantee the constitutional principle of equality of all people in their rights and freedoms. It has been emphasized that the 'legitimate expectation' enshrined in the caselaw of the ECtHR and the Constitutional Court of Ukraine should serve as a guide for legislators and a starting point for justice in order to respect human rights, in particular in the field of healthcare. The experience of foreign countries, which is important for borrowing

This paper is prepared on the basis of the report for the Conference 'Private Healthcare Law: Challenges and Prospects'.

I. Senyuta (✉)
Department of Medical Law at the Faculty of Post-Graduate Education of Danylo Halytskyi Lviv National Medical University, Lviv, Ukraine

© The Author(s), under exclusive license to Springer Nature Switzerland AG 2022

R. Maydanyk et al. (eds.), *Ukrainian Healthcare Law in the Context of European and International Law*, European Union and its Neighbours in a Globalized World 7,
https://doi.org/10.1007/978-3-031-05690-1_5

best practices of human rights and their implementation in the national legal framework, has been analyzed.

1 Introduction

The principle of independence is usually associated with the activities of a particular professional community, in particular, attorneys, judges, doctors, who, with the use of this principle as a tool, ensure human rights, based on the peculiarities of the profession. What does it mean for a person to 'not' depend in the field of medicine and from whom or what exactly?

European Court of Human Rights (hereinafter—ECtHR), through the prism of taken decisions, adheres to the position that although Art. 8 of the Convention for the Protection of Human Rights and Fundamental Freedoms (hereinafter—the Convention) does not expressly mention the right to autonomy or self-determination, nor does it address the issue of consent to medical care, but protects these rights.

Autonomy became legally binding on health-care decisions through the requirement to consent to medical care and the corresponding legal recognition of the right to refuse medical care, as well as through the search of the balance between protecting patients' right to life and protecting their right to respect for private and family life and personal autonomy. Exemplary, in particular, are such the ECtHR judgement as "Lambert and others v. France", "Charles Gard and Others v. the United Kingdom".

The right to refuse medical care based on personal autonomy, allowing a person to protect his or her physical integrity. As a rule, the competent patient must give free and informed consent before any medical intervention. Every medical intervention, even a minor one, that is not consistent with these requirements, is an interference in his personal life and will violate Art. 8 of the Convention, if this cannot be justified in terms of Part 2 of Art. 8 of the Convention.

Certain aspects of human autonomy, revealed through the prism of law and jurisprudence, illustrate freedom and personal autonomy in the maximum spectrum. Autonomy is a value of human-centered medicine, where human rights and freedoms in the field of health care are protected, relations between the parties are based on respect, mutual observance for rights and responsibilities, actions in the best interests of the patient, in confidence with the doctor.

2 Medical Sorting (Triage) and the Independence in Decision-Making

The COVID-19 pandemic has raised difficult issues for discussion around the world, including those in the field of triage when it comes to making vital decisions, especially how to bring benefit to the majority of people and be fair and transparent in the sorting process.

Ukraine, like other countries in the world, is on the verge of triage, and this will happen for the first time from the start of the pandemic. Ukraine has developed a plan to combat COVID-19 in accordance with four levels of danger. At the fourth level, when the resources of the health care system are exhausted, a medical sorting protocol with the priority of providing medical care will be put into effect. Before the COVID-19 pandemic in Ukraine, the term 'medical sorting' was out of use, and nowadays triage sounds like a sentence, because some people may not receive medical care.

The concept of sorting has historically come from Napoleon's battlefields. The chief surgeon of the French military leader, Baron Dominique Jean Larrey, came to the conclusion that physicians should first and foremost care for the most dangerous of injuries, regardless of rank or distinction. Subsequently, doctors added other criteria for selecting the wounded, including the likelihood of survival during treatment, or the time required to care for the patient.

The analyzed legal construction is familiar for the legislation of Ukraine, it was introduced at the European Football Championship 2012 carrying out in Ukraine. According to item 2 of section 1 of the General requirements concerning carrying out medical sorting of victims and patients at a pre-hospital stage and in reception departments (departments of emergency medical care) of health care institutions, including at hospitalization of victims of an emergency situation during preparation and carrying out in Ukraine of the final part of the European Football Championship 2012, approved by the Ministry of Health of Ukraine Order[1] (hereinafter—the MOH Order No 366), medical sorting is the division of victims and patients (hereinafter—victims) into categories with homogeneous treatment and prophylactic and, evacuation measures in accordance with medical indications, volumes of medical care provided at each stage of medical evacuation and evacuation procedure. Medical sorting is carried out taking into account the need for specific treatment measures: reducing the consequences of injuries (diseases) that threaten the lives of victims; prevention of complications, reduction of their severity; preparation and conduct of evacuation.

---

[1] General requirements for medical sorting of victims and patients at the pre-hospital stage and in admission departments (emergency departments) of health care institutions, including hospitalization of victims of emergencies during the preparation and holding of the final part of the European Championship 2012 in Ukraine on football: Ministry of Health of Ukraine Order (2012) No 366 https://zakon.rada.gov.ua/laws/show/z0884-12#Text.

According to report of an assessment project co-ordinated by the World Health Organization 'Emergency Medical Services Systems in the European Union', triage can be defined as the sorting of patients into priority groups according to their needs and the resources available.[2] This standard procedure ensures the efficient use of available resources e.g. personnel, supplies, equipment, means of transportation and medical facilities; and thus affects the extent and quality of care delivered by the Emergency Medical Services system.

In addition, Ukrainian legislation contains the Guidelines for Battlefield Sorting of Wounded Patients. Annex 5 to the New Clinical Protocol 'Emergency medical care: pre-hospital stage', approved by the MOH Order 'On approval and implementation of medical and technological documents for standardization of emergency medical care'.[3]

The legal act intended to regulate medical sorting in Ukraine in the conditions of COVID-19, concerning the priority of medical care, is currently under development.

However, nowadays, medical sorting (triage) is regulated by the MOH Order 'Organization of medical care for patients with coronavirus disease (COVID-19)'[4] (hereinafter—the MOH Order No 722). In particular, Standard 3 'Inpatient treatment of patients with COVID-19' states that when a patient is admitted to a health care facility, medical sorting has to be performed, namely: (1) early recognition of patients with severe acute respiratory syndrome associated with COVID-19; (2) assessment of the severity of the disease; (3) initiation of medical care measures n accordance with the Protocol 'Provision of medical care for the treatment of coronavirus disease (COVID-19)', if necessary.

Nevertheless, the MOH Order No 722 refers to clinical sorting, in order, in particular, to properly provide timely medical care, control patient flows, ensure early detection and control of the source of infection.

Clinical medical sorting will no longer be an issue at the fourth level of danger, there shall be determined who will have access to medical care in conditions of limited resources, primarily human resources, i.e., priority medical sorting.

WHO has developed an Algorithm for COVID-19 sorting and routing. Medical sorting and referral of patients with limited resources,[5] which provides general guidelines for the sorting and referral of patients with COVID-19 symptoms,

---

[2] Emergency Medical Services Systems in the European Union: Report of an assessment project co-ordinated by the World Health Organization, 2008. https://www.euro.who.int/__data/assets/pdf_file/0016/114406/E92038.pdf.

[3] New clinical protocol 'Emergency medical care: pre-hospital stage': Ministry of Health of Ukraine Order 'On approval and implementation of medical and technological documents for standardization of emergency medical care' (2019) No 1269. https://zakon.rada.gov.ua/rada/show/v1269282-19#Text.

[4] Organization of medical care for patients with coronavirus disease (COVID-19): Ministry of Health of Ukraine Order (2020) No 722 https://ips.ligazakon.net/document/MOZ32008.

[5] Algorithm WHO for COVID-19 triage and referral. Patient triage and referral for resource-limited settings during community transmission. https://apps.who.int/iris/bitstream/handle/10665/331915/COVID-19-algorithm-referral-triage-eng.pdf?sequence=1&isAllowed=y.

provides a general framework that needs to be adapted to local health systems in countries. The document states that effective sorting of patients with COVID-19 at all levels of health care facilities (primary, secondary and tertiary) will help the national planning, response and case management system to cope with the influx of patients, direct the necessary medical resources to effectively support critically ill and protect safety of medical workers.

A lot of issues, not only those of a legal nature, will arise in course of formation of a national legal act, because each regulation will have an ethical color, which requires special clarity and certainty of the provisions on the basis of which decisions are to be made.

The attention shall be drawn to the Regulation on Medical Ethics in Disaster Conditions (WMA, September 1994), which states that sorting is the first ethical issue arising from the limited availability of immediately available medical resources and the large number of victims with various health conditions. Sorting is a medical activity based on predominant treatment and care based on diagnosis and prognosis. Patient survival depends on sorting. It should be carried out quickly, taking into account medical needs, opportunities for medical intervention and available resources.

It is unethical for a doctor to persistently support the life of a hopeless patient at any cost, thus wasting the scarce resources needed elsewhere. However, the physician shall show compassion and respect for the dignity of the privacy of their patients, for example, by separating them from others and prescribing appropriate analgesics and sedatives. The physician has to act in accordance with their conscience, taking into account the available resources. He or she should try to establish a treatment order that will save the maximum number of critically ill patients who have a chance of recovery and minimize the incidence, taking into account, at the same time, limits imposed by certain circumstances.[6]

With priority medical sorting, a physician's professional independence will be embedded in the legal framework of choice and, of course, this will affect the social role of the profession, create conscientious objection among physicians who will have to make decisions outside the independence principle, and call into question the patient's 'legitimate expectations' for their constitutional right to medical care. There will be more than one duality on the scales: 'conscientious objection and public interest', 'individual and public health', 'trust in the profession and death'.

Dr. Frederick M. Burkle Jr., a former military doctor during the Vietnam War, outlined the treatment of victims of a large-scale bioterrorist event.[7] After the SARS outbreak in Toronto hospitals in 2003, a number of his ideas were suggested by Canadian doctors, and they were included in many US plans after the H1N1 pandemic in 2009. The physician was concerned that the protocols often contained strict criteria for disconnection from pulmonary ventilation or even refusal of

[6] WMA Statement on medical ethics in the event of disasters (1994). https://www.wma.net/policies-post/wma-statement-on-medical-ethics-in-the-event-of-disasters/.

[7] Fink (2020).

hospitalization. Some have used age as a basis for exclusion or pre-diagnosed diseases, such as progressive oncology, renal failure, or a serious neurological disorder. Dr. Burkle, however, stressed the importance of reassessing the level of resources, sometimes on a daily or hourly basis, in an attempt to minimize the need to refuse treatment.

In addition, plans may fail to achieve their survival goals. For example, most called for a reassignment of the ventilator after a few days if the patient did not recover, allowing it to be given to another patient. However, the rapid relocation of ventilators may not give anyone enough chance to improve. When COVID-19 causes severe pneumonia, doctors find that patients need treatment for several weeks.

Guidelines for medical sorting exist in almost all European countries, both formal and informal. Most of them coincide in the aspect that only patients with a severe form of the disease could be treated in certain hospitals, while patients with a mild course of the disease should be observed in makeshift public facilities or at home.[8]

The issue with the regulation of priority medical sorting is that COVID-19 is still poorly studied, that is why it is not easy to be sure that the medical criteria are being considered correctly. The experience of foreign countries in this matter is also spectral. Age is often one of the key criteria for priority medical sorting. The Italian guidelines state that it may still be necessary to set an age limit for intensive care. The Swiss guidelines also stipulate that in the event of an absolute shortage of intensive care (where there are no free intensive care beds), the elderly should not be hospitalized for intensive care. The priority of younger patients over elderly patients is described in the guidelines of Australia/New Zealand, South Africa and Canada.

First came, the first served (waiting list) is considered an option in Belgium, but is not recommended by other countries. No guideline sets priorities based on the basis of achievement or social status. There are no clear recommendations in German guidelines for sorting patients with the same prognosis.[9]

Almost all EU Member States (24 out of 27) use triage protocols in their hospitals, while in 21 countries, the ambulance service also uses triage. However, only 19 countries assert that triage protocols are used by dispatch centres.

In the Netherlands, for example, the so-called ‘fair innings’ principle, which is also mainly related to the patient’s age and life expectancy after overcoming the disease, is applied. Andre den Exter emphasizes that in this case, triage must be compatible with the right to non-discrimination.[10]

Admission of patients in health care facilities in Poland is carried out according to the division into certain areas: red (for patients with suspected coronavirus or confirmed disease) and green (for all other patients). There is also an orange area in health care facilities for medical staff to change protective clothing. Medical

[8]Han et al. (2020).

[9]Jöbges et al. (2020).

[10]Den Exter (2020).

sorting of patients in this case is carried out in mobile tents before the health care facility entrance.[11]

Experiences from Norwegian general practitioners participating in prehospital emergency situations show that the general practitioners downgrade 42% and upgrade 11% of the patients when triaging them on the scene compared to the initial Emergency medical communication centre dispatch. Acute abdominal cases were at highest risk of initial under-triage.[12]

However, there is a problem of balancing over-triage and under-triage is vital with regards to resource allocation. The Italian study found that these calls were predominantly made by next of kin reporting no life-threatening symptoms, but they were also shorter than other emergency calls and characterized by inadequate collection of vital information by the operators.[13] The Danish under-triage study found that 152 (0.16% of the low-acuity) patients died the same day as the 112 call, and 12% of these were considered potentially preventable if the call had been assessed as acute.[14]

The key principles of priority medical sorting include, in particular: (1) inadmissibility of discrimination, i.e., unjustified unequal treatment taking into account such characteristics as, in particular, age, nationality, sexual orientation, disability or socio-economic status; (2) lack of age as a single criterion for the decision on sorting, it needs to be correlated with comorbidities and survival prognosis (short-term and long-term perspective), despite its objectivity; (3) avoiding individual decisions in sorting: it is better to involve multidisciplinary councils/teams; (4) formation of fair and clear system of decision-making, documentation and the possibility of their appeal; (5) application of sorting only when providing care in intensive care units and only in the absence, not a limited number, of resources (for example, equipment); (6) provision of palliative care to patients whose treatment has been canceled or whose treatment has been denied; (7) provision of psychological support to medical workers, taking into account excessive physical and emotional overload during sorting; (8) provision of psychological support to patients and members of their families in priority medical sorting; (9) formation of 'sorting system' in which the sorting regulations (state level) and the availability of the necessary resources (local level, hospital level) will be dynamically and permanently revised; (10) taking into account the will of the patient/legal representative, which, if possible, should be respected.

[11] Coronavirus: All hospitals in Poland on duty. https://healthcaremarketexperts.com/en/news/coronavirus-all-hospitals-in-poland-on-duty/.

[12] Norwegian Index for Emergency Medical Assistance. https://bora.uib.no/bora-xmlui/handle/1956/16736.

[13] Palma et al. (2014), pp. 476–483.

[14] Andersen et al. (2014).

Under Part 5 of Art. 284 of the CC of Ukraine,[15] Part 2 of Art. 43 of the Law of Ukraine 'Fundamentals of the legislation of Ukraine on health care'[16] (Fundamentals), in urgent cases, in the presence of a real threat to the life of an individual, medical care is provided without the consent of the individual or their parents (adoptive parents). According to Part 1 of Art. 52 of the Fundamentals, healthcare professionals are required to provide full medical care to a patient who is in an emergency. Active measures to support the patient's life are terminated if the person's condition is defined as irreversible death. Therefore, in terms of priority sorting, it is important to remember: (1) the patient is in a state in which there is a direct threat to life, and the doctor is obliged to provide full medical care, even without their consent; (2) in Ukraine the institute of 'preliminary order' is gradually introduced, in particular in item 4.4. of the New clinical protocol 'Emergency medical care: pre-hospital stage', approved by the MOH Order 'On approval and implementation of medical and technological documents for standardization of emergency medical care' dated 05 June 2019 №1269. This Order requires a document that describes the procedures allowed in certain medical conditions, including all or only some of the following: what to do with cardiac arrest, whether artificial nutrition is allowed, the desire to be a donor or not, dialysis, and other parameters. This preliminary injunction may often not apply to urgent or transient medical conditions. Due to the fact that this institution, introduced by a bylaw, does not correlate with the statutory professional duty of a medical worker in Art. 52 of the Fundamentals, the expression of will in the conditions of sorting will be an additional argument in the decision-making of persons responsible for such adoption.

The attention shall be drawn to Part 2 of Art. 64 of the Constitution of Ukraine,[17] which ensures that in conditions of martial law or state of emergency, certain restrictions on rights and freedoms may be established, indicating the term of these restrictions. Therefore, the constitutional right to health care, medical assistance and medical insurance foreseen in Art. 49 of the Basic Law of the state, can be limited only in the conditions of introduction of a state of emergency. Additionally, of course, it is worth remembering that only laws (not bylaws) determine the rights and freedoms of human and citizen, safeguards of these rights and freedoms (Art. 92 of the Constitution of Ukraine).

A similar position is set out in the Constitutional Court of Ukraine Judgement,[18] where the Court noted: according to Art. 64 of the Constitution of Ukraine, the

[15] Civil Code of Ukraine (2003). https://zakon.rada.gov.ua/laws/show/435-15#Text.

[16] The Law of Ukraine 'Fundamentals of the legislation of Ukraine on health care' (1992). https://zakon.rada.gov.ua/laws/show/2801-12#Text.

[17] Constitution of Ukraine (1996). https://zakon.rada.gov.ua/laws/show/254%D0%BA/96-%D0%B2%D1%80#Text.

[18] Constitutional Court of Ukraine judgment in the case on the constitutional petition of the Supreme Court on the constitutionality of certain provisions of the resolution of the Cabinet of Ministers of Ukraine 'On quarantine to prevent the spread of acute respiratory disease COVID-19 caused by coronavirus 2-SARS-Co and stages of mitigation of anti-epidemic measures', the provisions of parts one, three of Art. 29 of the Law of Ukraine 'On the state budget of Ukraine for 2020', the ninth

constitutional rights and freedoms of human and citizen may not be restricted, except in cases provided by the Constitution of Ukraine; in conditions of martial law or state of emergency, certain restrictions on rights and freedoms may be established, indicating the term of these restrictions; the rights and freedoms provided for in Arts. 24, 25, 27, 28, 29, 40, 47, 51, 52, 55, 56, 57, 58, 59, 60, 61, 62, 63 of the Constitution of Ukraine may not be restricted. The Constitutional Court of Ukraine emphasizes that the restriction of constitutional rights and freedoms of human and citizen is possible in cases specified by the Constitution of Ukraine. Such a restriction may be established only by law—an act adopted by the Verkhovna Rada of Ukraine as the only legislative body in Ukraine. Establishing such a restriction by a bylaw contradicts Arts. 1, 3, 6, 8, 19, 64 of the Constitution of Ukraine.

In addition, it should be noted that failure to provide medical care in terms of priority medical sorting may violate the constitutional right to respect for dignity (Art. 28), which is not limited even in a state of emergency. Art. 3 The 'Prohibition of torture' of the ECHR guarantees that no one may be subjected to torture or to inhuman or degrading treatment or punishment. The ECtHR has established in its case law that failure to provide adequate treatment shall be deemed as conduct that degrades human dignity and, therefore, is a violation of Art. 3 of the Convention (for example, the judgment in Nevmerzhitsky v. Ukraine[19]).

Thus, the principle of autonomy in priority medical sorting is subject to significant limitations in terms of both the professional freedom of the doctor and the expression of the patient's will, which negatively affects the observance of human rights in the field of medical care.

3 Persons with Disabilities and Autonomy

Federal Constitutional Court of Germany in its judgment[20] noted that the prohibition to put a person with a disability at a disadvantage also covers situations where such a disadvantage is not an intention but an accidental consequence of a neutral ban (e.g., prohibition of access to dogs to the clinic). Requiring the applicant to leave the guide dog outside the clinic and become dependent on strangers is incompatible with the purpose and fundamental concept of an independent person.

The applicant was treated by a physiotherapist, who could be reached via a public steel lattice staircase. The floor could also be accessed through the premises of the orthopedic clinic. Both methods were equipped with pointers. The applicant

subparagraph of paragraph 2 of section II 'Final provisions' of the Law of Ukraine 'On amendments to the Law of Ukraine 'On state budget of Ukraine for 2020' (2020) No 10-p/2020. https://zakon.rada.gov.ua/laws/show/v010p710-20#Text.

[19] *Nevmerzhitsky v. Ukraine* (2005).

[20] Judgment of the Federal Constitutional Court of Germany (2020) (case 2 BvR 1005/18). https://www.bundesverfassungsgericht.de/SharedDocs/Entscheidungen/EN/2020/01/rk20200130_2bvr100518en.html.

repeatedly went through the clinic with her guide dog. Twice, the clinic's doctors denied her access to the room with the guide dog and asked her to use the stairs. The applicant brought an action in court requesting that the orthopedic clinic allow her access through their premises with a guide dog. She said her dog was unable to use the ladder because it had previously been injured when its claws got stuck in a steel lattice and therefore was afraid to use the ladder. The claim was dismissed.

The Federal Constitutional Court upheld the constitutional complaint, finding it manifestly well-founded, and referred the case to the Supreme Regional Court for a new judgment. The ban on passing through the clinic was found disproportionate, and the inconvenience caused by it—incompatible with the Constitution. The impugned decisions violate the applicant's right set out in the second sentence of Art. 3.3 of the Basic Law, according to which no one may be subjected to unequal treatment due to disability; the possibility of putting people with disabilities in a negative position is allowed only for good reasons (measures that worsen the situation of persons due to their disability).

According to Art. 20 of the UN Convention on the Rights of Persons with Disabilities,[21] 2006 (ratified by Ukraine in 2009), States Parties shall take effective measures to ensure the individual mobility of persons with disabilities to the fullest extent possible, in particular by facilitating access for persons with disabilities to mobility aids of good quality, devices, assistive technologies and services of assistants and intermediaries.

The preamble of the Law of Ukraine 'On the fundamentals of social protection of persons with disabilities in Ukraine'[22] guarantees persons with disabilities equal opportunities with all other citizens to participate in economic, political and social fields of society, creating the necessary conditions to enable persons with disabilities to effectively exercise their rights and freedoms of human and citizen and to lead a full life in accordance with individual capabilities, abilities and interests. Art. 26 of this Law stipulates that persons with disabilities are guaranteed by enterprises, institutions and organizations to create conditions for unimpeded access to objects of the physical environment, including persons with disabilities who use means of transportation and guide dogs. Item 1.2 'Functional needs' of the MOH Order 'Emergency medical care: pre-hospital stage. New Clinical Protocol' dated 05 June 2019 No 1269 stipulates that assistant animals do not fall under the classification of pets and therefore should always be close to the owner. An exception in the regulations may be when: (a) the animal is out of control or the owner cannot take effective measures to control it; (b) the animal is not trained to maintain cleanliness.

The bylaw has defined exceptions that are not contained in the law, which are evaluative and may serve as a violation of human rights. The analyzed judgment of the Federal Constitutional Court, for example, regarding cleanliness, stated that a

[21] *Convention on the Rights of Persons with Disabilities (2006).*

[22] The Law of Ukraine 'On the basics of social protection of persons with disabilities in Ukraine' No 875-XII (1991).

dog that periodically passes through the waiting area is unlikely to significantly affect hygiene. Given that the applicant relied on her guide dog and that other patients could take it easy, there was no reason to conclude that such actions would lead other patients to suspect a lack of hygiene.

The constant search for a balance in value-oriented issues is a difficult task for every member of society and the state as a whole, which is simply solved by understanding the essence of human dignity as a manifestation of the greatest respect for human and the rule of law. Dignity, in accordance with constitutional safeguards, is recognized as the highest social value (Art. 3), and no one has the right to encroach on it. The Constitutional Court of Ukraine emphasizes that human dignity must be interpreted as a right guaranteed by Art. 28 of the Constitution of Ukraine, and as a constitutional value that fills the meaning of human existence, is the foundation for all other constitutional rights, a measure of determining their essence and a criterion for the admissibility of possible restrictions on such rights. This is indirectly confirmed by the unique importance of human dignity in the Constitution of Ukraine, according to which, in particular, a person's life and health, honor and dignity are recognized in Ukraine as the highest social value (Part 1 of Art. 3); all human beings are free and equal in dignity and rights (Art. 21); everyone is obliged to strictly abide by the Constitution of Ukraine and the laws of Ukraine, not to encroach on the rights and freedoms, honor and dignity of other people (Part 1 of Art. 68).[23]

The legal conclusion of the Constitutional Court of Ukraine provided in the judgment dated 29 December, 1999 No 11-рп/1999[24] states: 'The above gives grounds for the conclusion that the inalienable right of every person to life is inextricably linked with his right to human dignity. As fundamental human rights, they determine the possibility of exercising all other human and civil rights and freedoms and can neither be restricted nor abolished.'

[23] Grand Chamber of the Constitutional Court of Ukraine judgment in the case on the constitutional petition of 49 public deputies of Ukraine on the constitutionality of paragraph 12 of Section I of the Law of Ukraine 'On amendments and repeal of certain legislative acts of Ukraine' (2018) No 5-p/2018. https://zakon.rada.gov.ua/laws/show/v005p710-18.

[24] Constitutional Court of Ukraine judgment in the case on the constitutional petition of 51 public deputies of Ukraine on the constitutionality *provisions of the Articles 24, 58, 59, 60, 93, 190-1 of the Criminal Code of Ukraine in the part that provides for the death penalty as a form of punishment (the death penalty) (1999)* No 11-рп/1999. https://zakon.rada.gov.ua/laws/show/v011p710-99#Text.

4 Independence from the Possibilities of Public Budgets and the Human Right to 'Legitimate Expectations'

Lack of public funds in the field of health care is a 'perpetual motion machine' for the authorities, which are constantly looking for a way out to ensure the constitutional right to health care, medical care and health insurance, which is guaranteed in Art. 49 of the Basic Law of Ukraine. Changing financial algorithms from direct budget funding to guaranteed funding for health services has not particularly solved the problem, as there is a dependence on funds in public budgets. Should a person suffer in such a state 'dependence' and depend on the capacity of public budgets?!

The Declaration of Independence and Professional Freedom of Physicians[25] (WMA, October 1986) states that a physician must have professional independence in presenting and protecting the patient's medical needs in front of anyone who wishes to deprive or facilitate the provision of necessary care to the sick and injured. A physician should not be expected to be guided by governmental and social priorities in the course of professional activities and health care provision in the allocation of insufficient health care resources. Such a situation would create a conflict with the physician's responsibilities to the patient and would significantly undermine the professional independence of the physician on which the patient relies.

The attention shall be drawn to the ECtHR judgment in the case of Fedulov v. Russia (application No. 53068/08), in which the ECtHR found a violation of Art. 1 of Protocol No 1 to the Convention. The applicant complained that the authorities had failed to provide him with the free medicines he was entitled to in connection with his cancer treatment. He was entitled to Bicalutamide, which he needed for 8–12 months. However, the pharmacy, which was intended to give him the medicine free of charge, provided it only once on these terms. In the following months, he paid 1400 euros for treatment. He complained to the authorities and the courts about the lack of free medicines and sought reimbursement, but in February 2008 the district court dismissed his claim in full. He found that the authorities involved, the St. Petersburg Health Insurance Fund and the St. Petersburg Health Committee had complied with the law. The applicant complained that he had not been provided with the medicines to which he was entitled under the law free of charge and that the authorities had not reimbursed him after he had had to purchase the necessary medicines at his own expense, grounding his position on Art. 1 of Protocol № 1 (protection of property). The ECtHR stated in its assessment that the parties did not deny that four times out of five the applicant had not been able to obtain the medication needed to treat his illness due to the lack of this medicine for distribution free of charge. Given that the applicant had a 'legitimate expectation' that he would

[25] WMA Declaration on physician independence and professional freedom (1986). https://www.wma.net/policies-post/wma-declaration-on-physician-independence-and-professional-freedom/.

receive preferential assistance, the ECtHR concluded that there had been an interference with the applicant's right under Art. 1 of the Protocol No 1.[26]

In the present case, the ECtHR notes that, although the applicant's right to the benefit was never in doubt, the domestic courts had, in fact, justified the refusal on the ground that it lacked the budget allocated to the St. Petersburg authorities for this purpose, which entitles the residents of this city to free medicine. At the same time, they did not invoke any legislative provision which would stipulate the refusal to provide the relevant benefit by any restrictions on budget funds, which provided for any discretion on the part of the executive authorities to reduce or deny this right after reaching the budget allocation limit or any similar provision that could provide a legal basis for such a conclusion. In this regard, subsequent court rulings in similar claims have made it clear that the existing legal framework establishes the right of those entitled to the necessary medicines not only free of charge but also without any restrictions, and the fact that the maximum number of specific medicines per person or insufficient budget funding allocated to a particular region cannot be grounds for refusing to provide interested persons with medicines that are important for their lives.

The 'legitimate expectation' that arises in a person in the presence of regulatory safeguards is under conventional protection, as illustrated in the ECtHR judgments, and to change the paradigm requires a transformation of legislation. The principle of the rule of law is guarded so that dissonance does not deepen and the 'legitimate expectation' through a guaranteed right does not depend on the lack of public funds. The Constitutional Court of Ukraine considers the right of a person to rely on reasonable and predictable stability of existing legislation and the ability to predict the consequences of the application of legal regulation, I.e., legitimate expectations, as part of legal certainty (paragraph 4.1 of the Constitutional Court of Ukraine judgment dated 28 August, 2020 No 10-p/2020).

Legal certainty implies that the legislator must strive for clarity and intelligibility in the wording of the law. Depending on the circumstances, each person should be able to find out which rule of law applies in a particular case and have a clear understanding of the specific legal consequences in the relevant legal relationship given the reasonable and foreseeable stability of the rule of law.[27]

In this way, the right of a person guaranteed by law will be ensured by dependence on public resources, different legal understandings depending on the law enforcement agency, will promote proper law enforcement and, if necessary, will serve to effectively protect human rights.

The highlighted segments of independence testify to the versatility of the principle in the field of medical care, reveal the full spectrum of freedom, autonomy of

[26] *Fedulov v. Russia* (2020).

[27] Grand Chamber of the Constitutional Court of Ukraine judgment in the case on the constitutional petition of 49 public deputies of Ukraine on the constitutionality of certain provisions of Section I, Clause 2 of Section III 'Final provisions' of the Law of Ukraine 'On amendments to certain legislative Acts of Ukraine concerning pension provision' (2020) No 1-p/2020. https://zakon.rada.gov.ua/laws/show/v001p710-20#Text.

human from any dependence and the full scope and essence of their rights in this area. Each such fragment of autonomy is built into a single legal mosaic, which is the key to the rule of law, in which the foundation is the rule of law, and the crown—human and their goods.

5 Conclusions

1. A pro-human "autonomous" standard formulated through the prism of the Convention and the case law of the ECtHR, in particular the judgment in "Jehovah's Witnesses of Moscow and Others v. Russia",[28] is based on the following axioms: (1) respect for human dignity and human freedom is the essence of the Convention; self-determination and personal autonomy are important principles underlying the interpretation of guarantees of it observance; (2) in the case of refusal of medical care, even in cases where a particular method of treatment may lead to lethal consequences, compulsory treatment, without consent of a legally capable and adult patient is an interference with his or her right to personal inviolability and an encroachment on the rights guaranteed by Art. 8 of the Convention; (3) the freedom to agree or disagree with a particular treatment or to choose an alternative treatment is of primary importance for the principles of self-determination and personal autonomy; (4) although the state's interests in protecting the patient's life and health are undoubtedly legitimate and significant, priority should be given to the patient's even more significant interests in determining his or her life path. Thus, the balance of private and public interests will be dominated by private; (5) freedom of choice and self-determination are fundamental components of life, and in the absence of any indication of the need to ensure the protection of third parties, for example by compulsory vaccination of the population during an epidemic, the state should abstain from interfering with citizens' freedom of choice on health issues, as such interference can only reduce rather than increase life values.
2. Priority medical sorting will limit the principle of autonomy in medical practice, as follows: (1) doctors will be obliged to make decisions within the sorting protocol, taking into account health resources; (2) doctors will have 'immunity' from the obligation to provide full medical care to a patient who is in an emergency, as they will select only priority patients; (3) professional freedom will have normative limits of sorting when making clinical and ethical decisions about the patient; (4) the patient's will will be of secondary importance, although it may be taken into account by persons responsible for making the decision.
3. A mandatory component of human dignity is human access to the minimum social benefits that can provide them with a sufficient and decent standard of

[28] *Jehovah's Witnesses of Moscow and Others v. Russia*. http://hudoc.echr.coe.int/eng?i=001-145420.

living. Ensuring the individual mobility of persons with disabilities with the maximum possible degree of their autonomy, independence from outside assistance will guarantee the constitutional principle of equality of all people in their rights and freedoms to exercise those.
4. Legislative changes, difficult financial and economic situation, the need to ensure the balance of the State Budget of Ukraine, lack of public resources should not lead to a violation of human dignity, which belongs to the fundamental conventional and constitutional values.
5. The 'legitimate expectation' enshrined in the case law of the ECtHR and the Constitutional Court of Ukraine should serve as a guide for legislators and a starting point for justice in order to respect human rights, in particular in the field of medical care.
6. Human autonomy in the field of medical care is one of the fundamental principles in medical practice, the value of legal medicine and a tool for the formation of a human-centered health care system, and thus a powerful state.

References

Algorithm WHO for COVID-19 triage and referral. Patient triage and referral for resource-limited settings during community transmission. https://apps.who.int/iris/bitstream/handle/10665/331915/COVID-19-algorithm-referral-triage-eng.pdf?sequence=1&isAllowed=y

Andersen MS, Johnsen SP, Hansen AE, Skjaerseth E, Hansen CM, Sørensen JN et al (2014) Preventable deaths following emergency medical dispatch – An audit study. Scand J Trauma Resusc Emerg Med

Coronavirus: All hospitals in Poland on duty. https://healthcaremarketexperts.com/en/news/coronavirus-all-hospitals-in-poland-on-duty/

Den Exter A (2020) View. The dutch critical care triage guideline on Covid-19: not necessarily discriminatory. Eur J Health Law 27:495–498

Emergency Medical Services Systems in the European Union: Report of an assessment project co-ordinated by the World Health Organization, 2008. https://www.euro.who.int/__data/assets/pdf_file/0016/114406/E92038.pdf

Fink Sh (2020) The Hardest Questions Doctors May Face: Who Will Be Saved? Who Won't? https://www.nytimes.com/2020/03/21/us/coronavirus-medical-rationing.html

Han E, Tan M, Turk E, Sridhar D, Leung G, Shibuya K, Asgari N, Oh J, Garcia-Basteiro A, Hanefeld J, Cook A, Hsu L, Teo Y, Heymann D, Clark H, McKee M, Legido-Quigley H (2020) Lessons learnt from easing COVID-19 restrictions: an analysis of countries and regions in Asia Pacific and Europe. https://www.thelancet.com/action/showPdf?pii=S0140-6736%2820%2932007-9

Jöbges S, Vinay R, Luyckx VA, Biller-Andorno N (2020) Recommendations on COVID-19 triage: international comparison and ethical analysis. Bioethics 00:1–12

Norwegian Index for Emergency Medical Assistance. https://bora.uib.no/bora-xmlui/handle/1956/16736

Palma E, Antonaci D, Colì A, Cicolini G (2014) Analysis of emergency medical services triage and dispatch errors by registered nurses in Italy. J Emerg Nurs 40:476–483

The Doctrine of the Patient's Personal Autonomy in Absolute Legal Relations: Directions of Improvement of the Legislation of Ukraine

Galyna Myronova

Contents

Abstract This chapter is devoted to the analysis of the provisions of the legislation of Ukraine on the autonomy of the patient regarding the withdrawal from medical intervention. Modern factors of actualization of the declared topic are features of modern medical technologies and shift of ethical paradigm of relations in the field of medical care. During just a few decades, there have been significant changes in both the public consciousness and doctrinal approaches to the legal regulation of health care. The paternalistic approach was replaced by a contractual concept based on the principle of personal autonomy, and these objective processes need their scientific justification. The medical field is extremely sensitive to existing technological, ethical changes, because medicine directly affects the most intimate and vulnerable things that a modern person has: body, mind, feelings, beliefs, abilities, desires. Thus, medicine directly affects the physical and moral autonomy and inviolability of man, which are the highest values. Legal interpretation of the patient's personal autonomy in medical care is based on the principle of informed voluntary consent. This fundamental principle is introduced into the legal plane through the system of special legal means—absolute rights that legally ensure self-determination and moral autonomy of the patient in private law relations in the field of medical care.

G. Myronova (✉)
Academician F. H. Burchak Scientific Research Institute of Private Law and Entrepreneurship of the National Academy of Legal Science of Ukraine, Kyiv, Ukraine

© The Author(s), under exclusive license to Springer Nature Switzerland AG 2022

R. Maydanyk et al. (eds.), *Ukrainian Healthcare Law in the Context of European and International Law*, European Union and its Neighbours in a Globalized World 7,
https://doi.org/10.1007/978-3-031-05690-1_6

1 Introduction: Background and Objectives of the Study

The legal significance of personal autonomy in the field of medical care is becoming increasingly important. This is due to the objective processes taking place in the global space of civilization. In particular, the modern era has been marked by the final realization of the fact that medical activities involve the application of standard medical technologies to individual patients who are not identical in their physiological data and their culture, worldview and values. Moreover, this entailed ethical and legal recognition of patients' personal autonomy. Until recently, the patient actually acted as a passive object of medical manipulation. However, according to the modern contractual doctrine, the health care provider has the right to use its capabilities depending on the personal choice of the patient, who makes his own conscious and responsible decisions, on the basis of professional opinions and advice of the doctor. Despite the fact that the patient usually does not have special education and the necessary knowledge, he is the owner of his own body and only he has the right to decide what is good or bad for him, considering his own ideas and common sense

These social trends are crucial for self-identification of the community, which aims to be modern. Therefore, Ukraine's success on the path of European choice will largely depend on the ability to assimilate and institutionalize values of the Western European legal tradition. In particular, such values include the value of personal autonomy of a person, which in Ukraine, despite declarative recognition, is not provided with appropriate institutional means including: legislative regulation, law enforcement mechanisms and legal consciousness of both political elites and the majority of the population. Given the above, the urgent task for the science of private law is to analyze the personal autonomy of the patient as a special social and individual value and a personal intangible asset. This should be provided at the level of both legal doctrine and legal means of implementation of medical care.

2 Interpretations of Personal Autonomy of the Patient in the European Legal Tradition

The significance of the phenomenon of personal autonomy in the coordinate system of the global European space is beyond doubt. However, recognition does not mean that all derivative problems of institutionalization and limits of realization are automatically solved. On the contrary, the legal legitimacy of value phenomena has difficulties, because of their interpretive elusiveness.

The legal interpretation of value concepts depends on the chosen system of sociohumanistic coordinates. Included in the certain cultural context, they acquire a certain semantic meaning and then serve as a guide for lawmaking and choosing the appropriate set of remedies. When it comes to the fundamental social values of modernity including: dignity, integrity, inviolability and personal autonomy, we are interested in the context of the Western European humanistic tradition and their normative interpretation.

A particularly important contribution to the substantiation of the ontology and axiology of personal autonomy is the principle of Kant's philosophy on the autonomous, that is 'self-legitimate' will of the individual. In his work 'Fundamentals of Metaphysics of Morality' (1785) I. Kant wrote that: "Autonomy of the will is such a property of the will, thanks to which it is the law for itself".[1] In the modern philosophy of law, personal autonomy is concretized as "the ability to make choices in conditions of self-restraint and self-control".[2] Here there is the very essence of personal autonomy is that it is a manifestation of the defining natural freedom of a person, which is manifested in his initiative and responsible decisions on various aspects of life.

All of the above also applies to such a social segment as the field of medical care. After all, the participants in these relations are individuals with all their inherent characteristics, including their worldview and set of values. Values form the inner essence of a person which is manifested in personal lifestyle choices (in particular, in terms of hygiene, nutrition, care, treatment). Medicine, in general, is more sensitive to individual characteristics, as it touches the internal, intimate aspects of human life. The universal idea of personal autonomy covers a wide range of manifestations of each person's personal choice, including the ability to dispose of the body. However, this was not always obvious, much less recognized at the level of law.

The legal doctrine of personal autonomy of the patient has existed for about a hundred years, it was gradually formed in the last century as a result of the global human rights movement and the adoption of important court decisions and legal acts recognizing the right of patients to participate directly in medical decisions. As a result of these processes, a fundamentally new ethical approach was introduced in clinical and experimental medicine. This approach is called the 'informed consent principle', which is based on two fundamental provisions: every patient has the right to know about his state of health; medical care should be provided only on the basis of voluntary consent.

The concept of 'informed consent' as an element of the human rights system was formed during the work of the US military tribunal in Germany in 1947, which, along with the verdict in the 'medics' case, prepared a document called the Nuremberg Code. In 1981, the World Medical Association, an independent professional organization of physicians around the world, adopted the Lisbon Declaration of the Rights of Patients, which proclaimed a minimum international standard of patients' rights to freely choose a doctor and obtain adequate and complete health information. The foundations of the European concept of patients' rights were laid in 1994, when the European Consultative Meeting of the WHOon Patients' Rights adopted the Declaration on the Promotion of Patients' Rights in Europe. The aim was to define the principles and strategies to promote patients' rights in the context of the

---

[1] Kant (1965), p. 283.

[2] Maksimov (2002), p. 276.

health care reform process within in most countries. The document declares the following human rights and values in healthcare: 1.1 Everyone has the right to respect for his or her person as a human being. 1.2 Everyone has the right to self-determination. 1.3 Everyone has the right to physical and mental integrity and to security of his or her person.[3]

A significant step towards the formation and implementation of European legal standards for patients' rights was the conclusion of the Oviedo Convention. The adoption of the document was a testament to the recognition of the patient's legal status as a subject of the right to choose in a European jurisdiction. Accordingly, the rights of the patient have acquired the status of a legal obligation for states to ensure and protect them. The general rule of consent enshrined in Art. 5 has been recognized as the legal basis, which provides the basis for lawful medical intervention: "An intervention in the health field may only be carried out after the person concerned has given free and informed consent to it. This person shall beforehand be given appropriate information about the purpose and nature of the intervention, as well as its consequences and risks. The person concerned may freely withdraw consent at any time".[4]

This chapter deals with consent and affirms at the international level an already well established rule that no one may be forced to undergo an intervention without his or her consent. Human beings must therefore be able to give or refuse their consent to any intervention concerning their persons. This rule makes clear patients' autonomy in the relationship with health care professionals and restrains the paternalist approaches which might ignore the will of the patient.

3 The Doctrine of Personal Autonomy of the Patient in Absolute Legal Relations

Particular importance for the formation of the doctrine of personal autonomy of the patient has the legal interpretation of the ECtHR. Given the powers of the court and the ECHR, to which Ukraine is a party, the content and argumentation of the legal positions of the ECHR on understanding personal autonomy in medical care are important.

It should be noted that the ECHR, adhering to egalitarian liberal values, in its practice systematically operates with the category of personal autonomy as a fundamental value and principle of law. This is explained by the fact that the achievement of effective legal protection of human rights and freedoms enshrined in the ECHR

---

[3]WMA Declaration of Lisbon on the Rights of the Patient, September/October (1981). http://zakon2.rada.gov.ua/laws/show/990_016/.

[4]Convention for the protection of Human Rights and dignity of the human being with regard to the application of biology and medicine: Convention on Human Rights and Biomedicine Oviedo (1997) https://www.coe.int/en/web/conventions/full-list/-/conventions/treaty/164.

requires the legal recognition and defense of the individuality, personality, autonomy of a person as a subject of fundamental rights.

In the decisions of the ECtHR, personal autonomy appears as freedom from coercion, freedom of self-determination, in particular, in matters of identity and choice of legal means to pursue one's own interests. Thus, from the standpoint of the court, each person is recognized to have their own ideals, values, goals, meaning of life, needs, worldview, conscience and legal awareness. To be guided by them in everyday life means to live by one's own rules, to be an autonomous person. The personal autonomy of a person in those forms that do not harm the rights and interests of others must be protected from any external, even state, interference.

The main legal principle of the ECHR, in which the Court directly refers to the value of personal autonomy in the provision of medical care, relate mainly to cases under Arts. 2, 3, 8 of the ECHR. In the case of Jehovahs Witnesses of Moscow v. Russia it is stated: The very essence of the Convention is respect for human dignity and human freedom and the notions of self-determination and personal autonomy are important principles underlying the interpretation of its guarantees. In the sphere of medical assistance, even where the refusal to accept a particular treatment might lead to a fatal outcome, the imposition of medical treatment without the consent of a mentally competent adult patient would interfere with his or her right to physical integrity and impinge on the rights protected by Art. 8 of the Convention. In the case of Arska v. Ukraine, the court argued that personal autonomy stated that a person could determine his or her treatment from those offered by doctors and choose the conditions in which his or her life would end. In the case of Lambert and others v. France, the ECHR ruled that even after loss of consciousness, the patient's personal autonomy in the choice of treatment offered by specialists is taken into account retrospectively.

In the case of Nevmerzhitsky v. Ukraine, the ECtHR has recognized the forced feeding of the starvining prisoner to be a violation of the prohibition of torture, taking into account the requirement for physicians to respect personal autonomy, the dignity of the patient, fulfilling their duty to save his life. In the case of V.C. v. Slovakia, the ECHR equated sterilization without the patient's consent with torture, after all, when using coercion, the state must avoid the task of unnecessary suffering and respect the personal autonomy of the individual. In the case of Laskey, Jaggard and Brown v. the United Kingdom, the ECHR pointed out that in cases where physical harm is inflicted on a person with his consent, the level of tolerable damage should be determined on the basis of the need to protect personal autonomy, public health, law and order.

The ECHR's legal principles concerning the human right to refuse the treatment, even in cases when doctors consider it vital, are set out in such provisions. The freedom to accept or refuse specified medical treatment, or to select an alternative form of treatment is vital to the principles of self-determination and personal autonomy. A competent adult patient is free to decide, for instance, whether or not to undergo surgery or treatment. Free choice and self-determination are fundamental constituents of life and with absence of any indication of the need to protect third parties. For example, mandatory vaccination during an epidemic, the State must abstain from interfering with the individual freedom of choice in the sphere of health care, for such interference can only lessen and not enhance the value of life.

The state undoubtedly has a strong interest in protecting and preserving the lives and health of its citizens. There clearly are circumstances where this interest may override the individual's right to self-determination. For example, the state may, in certain cases, require that citizens submit to medical procedures in order to eliminate a health threat to the community.

The state's interest in preserving the life or health of a competent patient must generally give way to the patient's stronger interest in directing the course of her own life. There is no law prohibiting the patient to decline necessary treatment. When the individual's conduct threatens injury to others, the State's interest is manifest and the State can generally be expected to intervene. But the State rarely acts to protect individuals from themselves, indicating that the State's interest is less substantial when there is little or no risk of direct injury to the public. This is consistent with the primary function of the State to preserve and promote liberty and the personal autonomy of the individual. The State will intervene to prevent suicide, but merely declining medical care, even essential treatment, is not considered a suicidal act or indication of incompetence.

Thus, taking into account the principles of the ECHR, the Oviedo Convention and the interpretation of the ECHR of the principles of self-determination and personal autonomy of the patient, it is possible to make a conclusion: the right of an adult competent patient to knowingly consent (and refuse) to medical care is a natural and fundamental human right. This right is absolute, as the right of the subject is opposed by an indefinite number of persons who are obliged not to violate it. However, of course, that any subjective right has certain limits, such as a certain positive corridor of permitted powers for the subject of law. Such boundaries are formed by the public interest in public health and the private interests of others. When human behavior poses a threat to others, the state intervention is appropriate.

Concerning emergencies burdened with loss of consciousness, in such situations, special regulation is applied, based on the principles of Arts, 8 and 9 of the Oviedo Convention. Art. 8: If because of an emergency the appropriate consent cannot be obtained, any medically necessary intervention may be carried out immediately for the benefit of the health of the individual concerned. The hypothesis of the Art. covers all clinical cases where a person is in danger of losing his life or significant damage to health without urgent medical intervention.

Additional legal features of emergencies in which the provisions of this article apply are the inability to obtain consent from the patient or his legal representatives, including through legally valid documents from previous orders. The last condition is contained in Art. 9 of the Oviedo Convention: The previously expressed wishes relating to a medical intervention by a patient, who at the time of the intervention is not in a state to express his or her wishes shall be taken into account. The article therefore covers not only the emergencies referred to in Art. 8, but also situations where individuals have foreseen that they might be unable to give their valid consent, for example, in the case of a progressive disease, such as senile dementia.

A similar mechanism is proposed in the DCFR. Art. IV. C. – 8:108 contains the following rules: Obligation not to treat without consent (1) The treatment provider must not carry out treatment unless the patient has given prior informed consent to it. (2) The patient may revoke consent at any time. (3) In so far as the patient is incapable of giving consent, the treatment provider must not carry out treatment unless: (a) informed consent has been obtained from a person or institution legally entitled to take decisions regarding the treatment on behalf of the patient; or (b) any rules or procedures enabling treatment to be lawfully given without such consent have been complied with; or (c) the treatment must be provided in an emergency. (4) In the situation described in paragraph (3), the treatment provider must not carry out treatment without considering, so far as possible, the opinion of the incapable patient with regard to the treatment and any such opinion expressed by the patient before becoming incapable. (5) In the situation described in paragraph (3), the treatment provider may carry out only such treatment as is intended to improve the health condition of the patient. (6) In the situation described in paragraph (2) of IV. C.—8:106 (Obligation to inform in case of unnecessary or experimental treatment), consent must be given in an express and specific way. (7) The parties may not, to the detriment of the patient, exclude the application of this article or derogate from or vary its effects.[5]

Thus, personal autonomy is a key category of the European doctrine of patients' rights, around which special legislation is formed to ensure the implementation of appropriate legal remedies. At the legal level, the recognition of personal autonomy means the patient has the right to determine the method of his treatment from those proposed by the doctor, to choose the conditions of care and has the right to choose a decent end to life. At the same time, the principle of personal autonomy is extended to the situation of the patient's loss of part of competence and even loss of consciousness. After all, in such clinical conditions, doctors have a duty to retrospectively take into account the will and personal preferences of the patient regarding the methods of medical intervention. This approach, legally enshrined in the Oviedo Convention, is gradually being introduced into the legislation of European countries.

At the same time, some countries choose different ways in which legal remedies are introduced into the legislation, which ensure the patient's autonomy in choosing the methods of medical intervention and obtaining medical information. Some jurisdictions have enacted special legislation governing patient rights, while others have incorporated special rules into general civil law. The author analyzes the legislation of some countries on the legal regulation of patient autonomy in the monograph.[6] In this section, as an illustration of possible approaches to the legislative consolidation of norms on patient autonomy in absolute legal relations, it is advisable to give the following examples.

[5]Principles, Definitions and Model Rules of European Private Law Draft Common Frame of Reference (DCFR) Outline Edition (2009), p. 246.

[6]Myronova (2015), pp. 223–244.

Of interest is the special legislation of the United Kingdom in terms of extending the autonomy of the patient in the event of loss of part of his/her competence. In the jurisdictions of England and Wales, certain matters relating to the autonomy and prior orders of the patient are governed by the Mental Capacity Act of 2005,[7] which entered into force on 1 October 2007. This Act allows every competent adult to make decisions regarding medical treatment in advance. In particular, the Act allows for perpetual powers of attorney to make decisions about personal well-being: Art.11. (7) If a long-term power of attorney authorizes the donee (or, if more than one, any of them) to make decisions about the donor's personal well-being, powers—(c) extend to the granting or refusal of consent to the provision or continuation of treatment by a person providing medical care for a donor". The Mental Capacity Act also regulates the mechanism of Advance decisions to refuse treatment (Art. 24, 25).

In Austria issues concerning autonomy and prior patient orders are governed by the 55th Federal Act on Living Wills,[8] which entered into force on 1 July 2006. This act regulates the requirements and effectiveness of living wills. The validity of a living will does not contradict the fact that it contains further remarks of the patient, in particular the appointment of a specific proxy, refusal to contact a specific person or the obligation to notify a specific person (§ 11). Preliminary expression of the patient's will is mandatory for physicians under certain conditions. However, by means of the previous directive the patient cannot limit the duties imposed on him by special legislative provisions concerning treatment (§ 13).

4 Personal Autonomy of the Patient in Absolute Legal Relations in the Law of Ukraine

The development of private law and civil legislation of Ukraine took place in accordance with the pan-European trend of returning to humanistic values. In the latest legislation of Ukraine, a person and his inviolable rights have taken precedence in the hierarchy of social priorities. The Constitution of Ukraine of 1996, like the ECHR, embodies the doctrine of natural law and the concept of natural human rights based on it. The new civil law is based on a new understanding of belonging. The new civil legislation is based on a new understanding of belonging of basic human values (life, health, honor, dignity), above all, to personal interests and personal disposal. That is why the legal relations, which is based on these values, is quite appropriately classified as personal non-property relations. Personal non-property relations are effectively regulated and protected by civil law tools, which are based on the principles of free will, personal autonomy and dispositiveness.

[7]Mental Capacity Act of 2005. (UK Public General Acts). https://www.legislation.gov.uk/ukpga/2005/9/contents.

[8]Bundesgesetz über Patientenverfügungen (Patientenverfügungs-Gesetz – PatVG) https://www.ris.bka.gv.at/GeltendeFassung.wxe?Abfrage=Bundesnormen&Gesetzesnummer=20004723.

Private legal relations in the field of medical care are classified in the CC of Ukraine to the group of personal non-property relations. They are governed by the rules of Chapter 21 Personal Non-Property Rights Providing Natural Existence of an Individual. Arts. 284, 285, 286 of the CC of Ukraine and Arts. 38, 39, 43 of the Law of Ukraine 'Fundamentals of the legislation of Ukraine on health care' contain a legal model of personal autonomy of the patient, which is realized through a number of subjective civil rights of an individual, and the conditions of their implementation. Basic rights of the patient: the right to seek medical care, the right to choose a doctor and a medical institution; the right to choose treatment methods; the right to consent to medical intervention; the right to refuse medical intervention.

So, in accordance to Art. 284 of the CC of Ukraine, a person, who reached the age of fourteen and applied for medical aid, shall have the right to choose a doctor and the methods of treatment recommended by a doctor. Medical aid for a person who reached the age of fourteen shall be provided upon his/her consent. A capable person of age who is aware of his/her actions and can control himself shall have the right to abandon treatment.[9] Also, in Art. 43 of the Law of Ukraine 'Fundamentals of the legislation of Ukraine on health care' are provided that the consent of the informed patient is required for the application of methods of diagnosis, prevention and treatment; a patient who has acquired full civil capacity and is aware of the significance of his actions and can manage himself, has the right to refuse treatment. Formally, according to the law, in all cases without exception, the patient must provide informed voluntary consent.[10]

However, both the legislation and the doctrine of Ukraine allow for the possibility of deviating from the rule of voluntary informed consent of the patient in certain cases. In Art. 284 (part 5) of the CC of Ukraine it is providing for the following legal norms: "In the emergency upon a real threat to the life of a person, the medical aid is provided without consent of a person or his/her parents (adoptive parents), a guardian, a tutor". Regarding the interpretation of this norm in the domestic legal opinion, the prevailing position is that the legislation allows in urgent cases to provide medical care and medical intervention without the consent of the patient. The legal nature of such a derogation is explained by scholars as an exception to the general rule or as a legal restriction on the patient's rights.

For example, Bedenko E.A, Seregin A. Y. consider: 'If according to the subjective assessment of the doctor refusal of carrying out manipulation or hospitalization threatens the life of the patient, they should be carried out'[11] (without the patient's consent—G.M.). O. Kokhanovska, referring to the provisions of the Declaration of the Promotion of Patients' Rights in Europe regarding the right to abandon treatment, believes that 'such a provision is debatable in its content and premature for its

---

[9] Tsyvilnyi kodeks Ukrainy No 435 IV (2003) Vidomosti Verkhovnoi Rady Ukrainy No 40–44. Art. 356.

[10] Zakon Ukrainy "Osnovy zakonodavstva Ukrainy pro okhoronu zdorovia" (1992) Vidomosti Verkhovnoi Rady Ukrainy 1993 No 4. Art. 19.

[11] Bedenko and Seregin (2007), pp. 142–143.

inclusion in the CC of Ukraine. The absence of this right is quite justified'.[12] R. Stefanchuk holds the same opinion: 'Free disposal of one's health does not take place in all cases, so the legislator imposes certain restrictions on the free refusal of treatment. So in urgent cases, in the presence of a real threat to the life of an individual the consent of the patient or his legal representatives is not required'.[13]

This is how these legal norms are applied in judicial practice, as stated in the motivating part of the Decision on the civil case № 581/625/18 Lipovodolinsky district court of Sumy region: 'The refusal of an individual from medical intervention has certain legislative exceptions that are established in order to preserve and protect human life from arbitrary encroachments by third parties or to eliminate the risk of disease, severe deterioration of health, which can lead to death. This exclusion is imperative and cannot be limited either judicially or administratively, as it is the implementation of the state's obligation to protect the health of its citizens and others. (Art. 3, Part 3 of Art. 49 of the Constitution of Ukraine)'.[14]

The vague formulation of the provision part 5 of Art. 284 of the CC of Ukraine leads to the understanding that "any medical intervention aimed at saving lives is justified, even when there is no consent of the patient who is able to express it. Or if the patient deliberately opposed the medical intervention".[15] Summarizing this understanding of part 5 of Art. 284 O. Krylova rightly notes: 'A literal understanding of the content of this rule allows us to conclude that a doctor has the right (or even obligation) to conduct a compulsory medical intervention'.[16]

Authors of the publication 'Human Rights in Health Care: A Practical Guide' also interpret this rule of Art. 284 of the CC of Ukraine in terms of the doctor's right to provide medical care without the patient's consent and the patient's obligation to receive such medical care. In this publication, among the responsibilities of the patient is called '6.2.5. Responsibility to receive medical assistance without one's own consent or consent of one's own representative in emergency situations when there is a real threat to one's life'. This responsibility, according to the authors, from the direct instruction of the legislator in Art. 284 (part 5) of the CC of Ukraine and in Art. 43 (part 2) of the Law of Ukraine 'Fundamentals of the legislation of Ukraine on health care'. 'This responsibility of the patient corresponds to the right of a health care practitioner to perform a medical intervention without the consent of a patient and/or his/her legal representatives'.[17] Accordingly, among the rights of a medical worker is called '7.1.9 Right to Conduct Medical Intervention Without Consent of a Patient and/or His/Her Legal Representatives'.[18]

---

[12] Naukovo-praktychnyi komentar Tsyvilnoho kodeksu Ukrainy (2005), p. 472.

[13] Tsyvilnyi kodeks Ukrainy: naukovo-praktychnyi komentar (2004), p. 385.

[14] Rishennia Lypovodolynskoho raionnoho sudu Sumskoi oblasti vid 14.11.2018 r. (Sprava No 581/625/18). http://www.reyestr.court.gov.ua/Review/77899139.

[15] Dvornichenko (2014), p. 34.

[16] Krylova (2007), p. 88.

[17] Byrne et al. (2012), p. 297.

[18] Byrne et al. (2012), p. 347.

This is a completely unacceptable situation. The Explanatory Report to the Oviedo Convention clarifies the conditions for the application of Art. 8: In emergencies, doctors may be faced with a conflict of duties between their obligations to provide care and seek the patient's consent. This article allows the practitioner to act immediately in such situations without waiting until the consent of the patient or the authorisation of the legal representative can be given. As it departs from the general rule laid down in Arts. 5 and 6, it is accompanied by conditions. Firstly, this possibility is restricted to emergencies, which prevent the practitioner from obtaining the appropriate consent. The article applies both to persons who are capable and persons who are unable either de jure or de facto to give consent. An example that might be put forward is a patient in coma, who is unable to give his consent, or a doctor who is unable to contact an incapacitated person's legal representative, who would normally have to authorise an urgent intervention.

However, even in emergencies health care professionals must make every reasonable effort to determine what the patient would want. Secondly, the possibility is limited solely to medically necessary interventions, which can not be delayed. Interventions for which a delay is acceptable are excluded. However, this possibility is not reserved for life-saving interventions.[19]

So, the provisions of this article are applied for the sole purpose of protecting the interests of the patient. However, the context of Arts. 6 and 9 of the Oviedo Convention indicates the obligation of medical staff, even in such limited circumstances, to make every reasonable effort to ascertain the patient's wishes.

Therefore, the doctor has a duty to provide medical care, this duty is related to the voluntary informed consent of the patient. Similarly, the obligation of medical staff to provide emergency medical care with absence of will arises from the patient's right to receive such care. So, from the right or legal requirement of the patient to receive medical care arises the corresponding duty of the medical worker. No specific right of a physician is subject to such an obligation, nor can there be any obligation on the part of the patient to receive medical care against his or her will.

The norm of part 5 of Art. 284 of the CC of Ukraine gives grounds to expect that the existing (or imaginary) threat to life can serve as an excuse for medical intervention, irrespective to the will of the patient. So, the legislation of Ukraine allows the restriction of the absolute rights of the patient in the case of an existing threat to his life and health. These restrictions are currently the most controversial for reasons of their incompatibility with the fundamental principles of modern civilized law, fundamental human rights, which are declared in the Constitution of Ukraine. Therefore, this position is erroneous.

[19] Explanatory Report to the Convention for the protection of Human Rights and Dignity of the Human Being with regard to the Application of Biology and Medicine: Convention on Human Rights and Biomedicine (1997). https://rm.coe.int/16800ccde5.

5 Directions for Improving the Ukrainian Legal Model of Personal Autonomy of the Patient

Against this background, an inconspicuous but very important steps forward were the changes to Art. 43 of the Law of Ukraine 'Principles of Ukrainian Health Care Legislation'. Just a few added words have radically changed not only the formula of the article, but also the concept of legislation on the rights of patients who find themselves in a situation of emergency. Art. 43, as amended, is worded as follows: "The consent of the patient or his legal representative to the medical intervention is not required only in the presence of signs of direct threat to the patient's life, *provided that it is impossible for objective reasons to obtain consent for such intervention from the patient or his legal representatives*'(italics mine—G. M.). This new formula of the article has brought Ukraine closer to the modern civilized world, which recognizes the priority of the patient's will even in the case of the need to immediate intervention. However, this legislative novelty, as a whole, remained invisible to both the medical and legal community. For example, changes to the article of the special law were not duplicated in the Central Committee of Ukraine, as it is required by the rules of legislative technique.

The patient's inability to express his will (temporary, prolonged or irreversible) regarding the forms and methods of medical intervention is a specific problem of medicine that needs a legal solution in Ukraine. In fact, Ukrainian legislation is not adapted for situations when the patient is unable to give consent due to temporary or prolonged incapacity caused by illness, there are no legal mechanisms for the implementation of the patient's preliminary choice in case of loss of capacity. In Ukraine, at the legislative level, it is not defined who will decide on the issue of conducting medical intervention for the benefit of a person in such conditions. However, an appropriate mechanism for making legal decisions in such clinical situations significantly narrows the scope of arbitrariness and inadequate decisions that are contrary to the will of the incapacitated patient.

In clinical cases, when a patient can not make an informed choice, paternalistic decisions should not be made, ignoring the patient's known wishes. It is for such cases, that the institute of preliminary expression of will for treatment and care is appointed, which is, in fact, unknown in Ukraine. After all, as a general rule, the principle of tacit consent of the patient applies. However, such a special legal institution is an important civil law mean of making medical decisions in urgent cases, burdened by the loss of consciousness of a patient. In the light of modern European standards regarding the autonomy, dignity and individuality of the patient, premature wishes are an important tools for protecting the rights of incompetent patients. Advance directives are conceptualised as a means of increasing 'patient autonomy', as they enforce individuals' power of choice over a post-competence process. The agreed position on this issue is fixed in the norms of Art. 9 of the Oviedo Convention.

Private law regulation of personal non-property relations in the field of medical care can be effective and can fulfill the social demand in the case of adequate understanding of the current needs of social development. In Ukraine, this is a vector of Western European development. The legal direction of Ukraine's European integration development includes bringing domestic legislation in line with the provisions of international agreements with Ukraine. Ratification of the Oviedo Convention signed by Ukraine on March 22, 2002 is currently on the agenda. The urgency of this event is confirmed by the Resolution of the Verkhovna Rada of Ukraine 'On the plan of bill work of the Verkhovna Rada of Ukraine for 2020' dated 16.06.2020 No 689-IX, which provides for the development of the draft Law of Ukraine 'On Ratification of the Convention on the Protection of Human Rights and Dignity of the World with regard to the Application of Biology and Medicine'.[20]

Ratification of international treaties of Ukraine is carried out in accordance to the Law of Ukraine 'On International Treaties of Ukraine' No 1906-IV of June 29, 2004 and goes through several mandatory stages. If an international agreement is submitted for ratification, the implementation of which requires the adoption of new or amendments to existing laws of Ukraine, the drafts of such laws shall be submitted to the Verkhovna Rada of Ukraine along with the draft law on ratification. Both laws are adopted simultaneously.

As an example, the new version of the Civil Code of the Republic of Moldova[21] deserves attention in the post-Soviet space. Part 4 'Measures of contractual and judicial protection' of the CC of the Republic of Moldova contains new rules that regulate special means of protection of rights, interests, well-being of individuals and promote the realization of their autonomy. If person needs protection only in the form of the help in decision making, it can sign the contract on assistance with person which expressed desire to give such help (assistant). Person can have one or several assistants (Art. 74.1).

Also, the person which reached age of majority or found other legal way full legal capacity (principal), can authorize one or several attorneys to represent its interests in situation when owing to mental disease or physical, intellectual or psychological violation it is not able to understand fully value of the actions or to express the will (Art.76.1). The Order about protection in the future can provide: (a) the right of the attorney to accompany the principal everywhere where it is necessary, and to help it with decision making, connected with his health; (b) power of the attorney to agree on behalf of the principal to physical examinations and interventions (Art.79.2).

The civil legislation of Ukraine does not contain such a participant in private relations as a representative of an adult competent patient, so in practice no person (even spouses, adult children, other relatives) can agree (or refuse) medical intervention or hospitalization; sign any documents on behalf of the patient. However, the order of the Ministry of Health of Ukraine 'On approval of the Procedure for choosing a doctor who provides primary care and the form of declaration on the

[20]The Verkhovna Rada Ukrainy 'Pro Plan zakonoproektnoi roboty Verkhovnoi Rady Ukrainy na 2020 rik' (2020) No 689-IX https://zakon.rada.gov.ua/laws/show/689-20#Text.

[21]Civil Code of the Republic of Moldova of June 6, 2002 No. 1107-XV. https://cis-legislation.com/document.fwx?rgn=3244.

choice of a doctor who provides primary care' from 03/19/2018 № 503[22] granted legal status to the patient's proxy for notification in case the onset of an emergency with the patient.

In addition, the order of the Ministry of Health 'On approval and implementation of medical and technological documents for standardization of emergency care' from 05.06.2019 № 1269[23] approved a new clinical protocol 'Emergency care: prehospital stage', which introduced into the legal system of Ukraine preliminary patient orders, in particular, transactions 'Do not resuscitate'.

In the conditions of recodification of the civil legislation which proceeds in Ukraine, there is a unique opportunity to fill legal gaps and to state new norms in the updated CC of Ukraine. Given the above, the author proposed to set out part 5 of Art. 284 of the CC of Ukraine in the following wording: '5. In urgent cases, in the presence of a real threat to the life of an adult competent person, medical care is provided without the consent procedure if it is impossible to obtain a person's consent or his/ her authorized persons' consent for objective reasons, or because of the absence of documents of previous orders'. Similar changes are proposed to part 2 of Art. 43 of the Law of Ukraine 'Fundamentals of the legislation of Ukraine on health care': 'The consent of an adult competent patient is not required only in the presence of signs of imminent threat to life, if it is impossible to obtain consent from the person or his/her authorized persons for objective reasons, or because of the absence of documents of patient's previous orders'.

The introduction of special norms into the updated civil legislation, which regulate the relations concerning the contractual representation of the patient and previous orders, will promote the autonomy of the patient in Ukraine.

6 Concluding Remarks

Personal autonomy is a key value and legal principle of modern civilized and democratic countries. This fundamental principle is introduced to the legal plane through a system of special legal means—absolute rights that legally ensure self-determination and moral autonomy of the patient in private law relations in the field of medical care.

The legislation and doctrine of Ukraine give the possibility of ignoring the voluntary informed consent of a patient to medical intervention in all emergencies that threaten the life and health of a patient. However, in urgent cases burdened with

[22]Nakaz Ministerstva okhorony zdorov"ya Ukrayiny 'Pro zatverdzhennya Poryadku vyboru likarya, yakyy nadaye pervynnu medychnu dopomohu, ta formy deklaratsiyi pro vybir likarya, yakyy nadaye pervynnu medychnu dopomohu' vid 19.03.2018 r. № 503. https://zakon.rada.gov.ua/laws/show/z0347-18#Text.

[23]Nakaz Ministerstva okhorony zdorov"ya Ukrayiny 'Pro zatverdzhennya ta vprovadzhennya medyky-tekhnolohichnykh dokumentiv zi standartyzatsiyi ekstrenoyi medychnoyi dopomohy' vid 05.06.2019 № 1269. https://zakon.rada.gov.ua/rada/show/v1269282-19#Text.

loss of consciousness, additional means are needed to protect the patient's personal autonomy. Such a modern tool, provided by the Oviedo Convention, is to take into account the previously expressed wishes of the patient. Advance directives are conceptualised as a means of increasing patient autonomy.

Based on the analysis, the author concluded that it is necessary to supplement the civil legislation of Ukraine with new legal instruments: preliminary orders for future medical care, voluntary representation of the patient, the patient's trustee. It is also necessary to adapt civil law institutions of legal capacity, representation, and power of attorney to the needs of private law regulation of personal non-property relations in the field of medical care.

References

Bedenko EA, Seregin AY (2007) Pravovoye regulirovaniye okazaniya pomoshchi patsiyentam, kotoryye nakhodyatsya v ugrozhayushchikh zhizni sostoyaniyakh. Meditsina neotlozhnykh sostoyaniy 3:142–143

Byrne I, Ezer T, Cohen J, Overall J, Senyuta I (2012) Human rights in patient care: a practitioner guide. LOBF Publishing House Medicine and Law, L'viv

Dvornichenko A S (2014) Osoblyvosti medychnoho vtruchannia bez informovanoi zghody patsiienta Naukovyi visnyk Mizhnarodnoho humanitarnoho universytetu Seriia: Yurysprudentsiia 12(2):33–37

Explanatory Report to the Convention for the protection of Human Rights and Dignity of the Human Being with regard to the Application of Biology and Medicine: Convention on Human Rights and Biomedicine Oviedo (1997). https://rm.coe.int/16800ccde5

Kant I (1965) Osnovy metafiziki nravstvennosti. In: Kant I. Sochineniya v shesti tomakh Vol 4 Part 1 Mysl, Moskwa, pp 219–310

Krylova OV (2007) Predstavnytstvo interesiv patsiienta v dohovori pro nadannia medychnoi dopomohy Aktualni problemy derzhavy i prava Issue No 31:85–92

Maksimov SI (2002) Pravovaya realnost: opyt filosofskogo osmysleniya: monografiya. Pravo, Kharkov

Myronova GA (2015) Pryvatnopravove rehulyuvannya osobystykh nemaynovykh vidnosyn u sferi nadannya medychnoyi dopomohy: monografiya. Naukovo-doslidnyy instytut pryvatnoho prava i pizhpryyemnytstva imeni akademika F. H. Burchaka NAPrUkrayin, Kyyiv

Naukovo-praktychnyi komentar Tsyvilnoho kodeksu Ukrainy U 2-kh t. Vol. 1. (2005) Yurinkom Inter, Kyiv

Principles, Definitions and Model Rules of European Private Law Draft Common Frame of Reference (DCFR) Outline Edition (2009) European Law Publishers GmbH, Munich

Tsyvilnyi kodeks Ukrainy: naukovo-praktychnyi komentar U 2-kh. ch. Part 1 (2004) Kontsern "Vydavnychyi Dim In Yure", Kyiv

Civil Circulation of the Deceased's Organs in the Countries of Eastern Europe

Sviatoslav Slipchenko and Oleksandr Shyshka

Contents

Abstract Based on the analysis of the legislation of some Eastern European countries, the authors have studied the ability of the deceased's organs to be involved in civil circulation. To answer this question, the authors of the study set a number of tasks, namely: to determine the legal status of the body of the deceased and his organs; to establish the presence or absence of the features of natural and civil circulability of the removed organs from the deceased body and methods of civil circulation. The conducted study by the authors allowed us to make the following conclusions. Organs removed from the deceased body have a dual nature, that is they contain both personal non-property and property value. In the latter case, they are things. Organs removed from the deceased body, being things, are not only freely transferable (have natural and civil circulability), but are also actively involved into civil circulation. At the same time, they are not in free circulation and are limited things in civil circulation, and the circulations are usually non-commercial.

This paper is prepared on the basis of the report for the Conference 'Private Healthcare Law: Challenges and Prospects'.

S. Slipchenko · O. Shyshka (✉)
Department of Civil Disciplines, Kharkiv National University of Internal Affairs, Kharkiv, Ukraine

© The Author(s), under exclusive license to Springer Nature Switzerland AG 2022
R. Maydanyk et al. (eds.), *Ukrainian Healthcare Law in the Context of European and International Law*, European Union and its Neighbours in a Globalized World 7,
https://doi.org/10.1007/978-3-031-05690-1_7

1 Introduction

The dynamics of the development of public relations requires new scientific research and constant improvement of civil law. Their intensification gradually but inevitably affects the general worldview of people.[1] It is due to the fact that a wide range of different goods currently circulates as objects. That includes not only things, but also the results of intellectual, creative activity (works of science, literature and art, inventions, utility models, etc.), means of individualization (brand names, trademarks, etc.), as well as services, work results, information, other benefits. As a result, previously unknown groups of relationships arise or already known relationships receive unusual development in new conditions.[2] Those that arise in connection with the removed human organs (human anatomical materials) are of great importance among them.

An important aspect of practical and theoretical orientation is the legal certainty regarding the regulation of such relations. In fact, it depends on the legal norms that regulate them (public or private; if private, what kind of regime should be applied to such relations, the one that regulates property or non-property relations) and how such legal norms can enable a person to determine not only the behavior, but also the consequences of their application to the relevant legal relations.

There is no doubt that the removed human organs are now objects of civil rights. Considering the fact that such objects are subject-matter of the material world, then there is an important question with regard to their ability to participate in civil circulation. In this regard, V. A. Bielov quite rightly notes: 'It is important for a specialist in civil law to know whether any subject-matter (substrate) is the object of civil rights (legal relations), but whether it is the object of civil circulation. The first is necessary to determine the content of legal relations that could be developed in relation to the relevant object; the second is necessary to determine the range of factual circumstances that are the grounds for the dynamics (movement) of such legal relations'.[3]

Problems of cadaveric donation, including the legal regime of the deceased organs and their circulation, have been the subject of research by many scholars, in particular: M. Gunnarson, J. De Jong, S. Lundin, L. van Balen, Z. Orr, I. Byström, S. Berglund, U. Essen, M. Gunnarson, M. Idvall, M. Liljefors, S. Lundin, E. Malmqvist, A. Putnina, S. Schicktanz, M. Schweda, F. Svenaeus, C. Waldby, and others. However, we believe that this issue is not exhausted. As a matter of fact, the world jurisprudence faces the task of developing certain standards of legal regulation of relations in the field of medicine in the general and donation and

[1] Kuznetsova (2011), p. 47.
[2] Slipchenko (2013a), p. 10.
[3] Belov (2007), p. 70.

transplantation—in particular. It will allow both to develop a single international legal array, and to create guidelines while forming and reforming national legislation of those countries that are moving towards the universalization of a single legal field.[4]

Unification of legal regulation of cadaveric donation in Eastern European countries is very relevant in this regard. In fact, most of them had a common or similar history, their legislation mostly provided the routine removal of organs, and the perception of legal reality was based (is based) on similar theoretical developments.

2 Terms Used in the Research

Civil circulation is the lawful alienation or transition of objects of civil law from one person to another.[5] It contains three key points.

1. Alienation or transition indicate the dynamics of the objects of civil law and are methods of civil circulation.
2. Legality indicates the dynamics of rights in relation to objects of civil law (objects of civil circulation). It is a legal registration (form) of the dynamics of objects and is carried out by succession or legal establishment.
3. The dynamics of objects and the dynamics of rights to them are so inextricably related to each other that the absence of one of these elements destroys the structure of civil circulation in the whole.[6]

Objects of civil circulation are objects of civil law that are capable of being in civil circulation. This ability depends on two groups of conditions of circulability: (a) severability or non-severability from the subject; (b) presence or absence of a direct indication of the law on their withdrawal from civil circulation. The first ones indicate the natural properties of the good[7] which influence on the potential ability (inability) to circulation. Severability creates the conditions for natural tradability. Others indicate that the object is admitted to civil circulation by the current legislation, i.e. is not withdrawn from circulation. Admission to civil circulation is a condition of civil circulability.[8] This understanding of circulability allows us to divide the benefits into those that are able and unable to civil circulation due to their natural circulability (severability or non-severability). The objective law can

[4] Slipchenko et al. (2018).
[5] Slipchenko (2017).
[6] Slipchenko (2019).
[7] Bajbak (2005).
[8] Slipchenko (2011), p. 71.

establish the degree of civil circulability (admission to free circulation, restriction and withdrawal from the circulation) only for those objects that have the features of natural circulability.

3 The Dead Body and Removed Organs as Objects of Civil Law, Their Legal Regime

It is no doubt that both the body as the whole and any its part cannot be considered as an object of law during a person's lifetime. It is due not only to the legal provisions, but also to the fact that the understanding of the object is always provided through the opposition to its subject, through the manifestation of the external nature of the first one, in relation to the second one. The human body during the lifetime is its biological component. In fact, it is the subject. And the subject, as well as its any part cannot be considered as the object of legal relations.

From the moment of death of an individual, his legal capacity is terminated and the subject of civil legal relations disappears, and the body (both in the whole and any part) acquires the characteristics of the object of law.

There is a point of view in the legal literature that the fate of a dead body is currently determined by the special legislation, which does not belong to the field of civil law, but is the norms of administrative law (for example, establishing the burial place, sanitation norms, etc.) and criminal law (for example, establishing the liability for abuse of bodies and burial places, etc.).[9] However, it should be noted that the body of a deceased person is also the object of civil law. The same is equally applied to the organs removed from it.

This conclusion is based on the analysis of the national legislation of certain Eastern European countries and their theoretical heritage. In particular, it is obvious that civil law regulates civil relations. The application of a positivist (normative) approach to understanding the law indicates that civil relations are those that are regulated by civil law. And the existence of such regulation in relation to the organs and body of the deceased is beyond doubt.

For example, the Art. 298 of the CC of Ukraine states that everyone is obliged to respect the body of a person who has died. The right to demand such treatment belongs to the family members and close relatives. And in case of violation of this right, such persons may demand compensation for property and moral damage. Thus, as we can see, the norms of civil law establish certain rules of conduct (regulate the relations) in regard to the body of a person who has died. The Art. 289 of the CC of Ukraine provides the possibility of an individual to dispose of the transfer of the organs and other anatomical materials of his body after the death to scientific, medical or educational institutions; the Art. 1240 of the CC of Ukraine indicates the right of the testator to impose the obligation to take actions to determine

[9] Mayfat and Lisachenko (2017).

the place and form of burial ritual on the heir; the Art. 290 of the CC of Ukraine establishes the right to give consent to the donation of the organs and other anatomical materials in case of the death or to prohibit the removal of the organs and other anatomical materials from the body after the death; the Arts. 749, 1201, 1232 of the CC of Ukraine establish the obligation for certain persons to bury the deceased and to distribute burial expenses; the Art. 21 of the Law of Ukraine 'On the Use of Transplantation of Anatomical Materials to Humans' provides the exchange of the organs, and until 2019 also the sales.

A similar approach is observed in the legislation of other Eastern European countries. For example, § 92 of the Civil Code of the Czech Republic stipulates that the human body is under legal protection even after the person's death. It is forbidden to dispose of human remains and human relics in a form unworthy of the deceased. If human remains are not in a public burial place, the person authorized by the person before his or her death has the right to issue them; otherwise, alternately one of the spouses, the child or the parents, and if neither of them is present or if they refuse to take the remains, they are received by the heir. Also, § 113 stipulates that a person has the right to decide how his body will be treated after his death. The thanatopsy or use of a human body after the person's death without the consent of the deceased may be carried out only in cases if it is provided by another law. Herewith, § 114 is normalized and a person has the right to decide how he will be buried. And, if a person has not made a decision before his death, the decision will be made by one of the spouses of the deceased, if there is no spouses, then the children of the deceased; if there are no children, the decision will be made by the parents, and in their absence by the brothers or sisters of the deceased; if they are dead, the decision will be made by their children, and if they do not exist, then by someone among close relatives; if none of these persons is present, the decision will be made by the municipality where the person died. Besides, it is worth noting the provisions of § 493 which stipulate that the human body and its parts, although separated from the body, are not things.

The Civil Code of Moldova also contains norms regulating relations, the object of which is the body of the deceased person or his organs. For example, such Code stipulates that every individual has the right to respect for his body after his death (Part 1 of the Art. 43 of the Civil Code of Moldova), and the body of the deceased is given respect (Part 1 of the Art. 49 of the Civil Code of Moldova). In this case, any person can determine the type of his burial and can dispose of own body after the death; if there is no the expressed will of the deceased, then we take into account the will of one of the spouses, parents, descendants, relatives in the lateral line up to the fourth degree of kinship, heirs or orders of the mayor of the village (commune), city or municipality where the death occurred (Part 2 and Part 3 of the Art. 49 of the Civil Code of Moldova).

This approach is fully in line with the provisions of Directive 2010/45/EU of the European Parliament and of the Council of 7 July 2010 on standards of quality and safety of human organs intended for transplantation.

The existence of civil and legal norms regulating the relationship to the body of the deceased or the removed organs, allows not only to conclude that such relationships are civil, but also to assert the emergence of civil legal relations. And as we know, mandatory elements of the structure of the latter are the objects of civil law.

The views of researchers who consider the body of the deceased person and its parts (organs) as objects of civil law can be divided into several groups.[10] Some consider the human body and the organs as property (quasi-property). Others proceed from the fact that 'there is no property in the human body', and the correlation between a person and his body is considered as bodily autonomy, personal (physical) inviolability, donation, respect for the body of the deceased, etc.

Analysis of these points of view allows us to agree that the body of the deceased person, as well as its separate parts (organs) have personal non-property value.[11] In this case, they are tangible but non-property benefits.[12] And this is not surprising, because certain religious, cultural, philosophical views give the body of the deceased (its separate parts), above all, spiritual (moral) significance,[13] and the law norms enshrine this possibility, determine the appropriate pattern of behavior.

At the same time, there is no doubt that the body of the deceased person and the organs removed from the body have a personal non-property value, i.e. are non-property goods, it is believed that they can be considered as property goods. Thus, based on the classical understanding of the objects for the countries of the Eastern European legal system, there is every reason to believe that the removed organ and the body of the deceased completely fall under the concept of things, where things are objects of the material world external to a man, available for possession and able to meet the needs of the participants of civil legal relations.

Similar elements of the characteristics of the organ removed from the human body are stated in the Art. 3 Directive 2010/45/EU of the European Parliament and of the Council of 7 July 2010 on standards of quality and safety of human organs intended for transplantation.

In fact, the body after the death of a person, like any part, is no longer a part of a man. They are objects of the material world. The body (removed organ) of the deceased person in relation to other people is the subject matter of the material world external to a man. They are available for possession. As for the useful properties of the body (removed organs) of a person who has died, the analysis of empirical material suggests that such a feature is inherent in this object. The term of "organ characteristics" is used to denote this property in the Directive 2010/45/EU of the European Parliament and of the Council of 7 July 2010 on standards of quality and safety of human organs intended for transplantation. It is revealed as information about the properties of the organs that are necessary to assess their suitability and to optimize the results of the usage. They can be considered as carriers of information about the cause and method of death. Therefore, it represents a certain value

[10] Ondrúš (2016), p. 27.

[11] Fiala et al. (2009), p. 64.

[12] Slipchenko (2013b); Shyshka (2019).

[13] See: Slipchenko et al. (2020), pp. 119–133.

(usefulness) for the forensic expert, pre-trial investigation agencies, and other interested persons. Anatomical materials for transplantation and (or) production of bioimplants can be taken from the body of the deceased, genetic material can be used for reproduction technologies (artificial insemination, surrogacy, etc.). It is obvious that recipients and those who perform transplantation, consumers and producers of bioimplants, institutions where reproductive technologies are implemented, etc. are interested in this. Considering the fact that organs and other anatomical materials of the human body can be used in research, biomedical research, and the educational process, they are of some value to scientific, medical, or educational institutions. There are other ways to use the body of the deceased or its part. In particular, as an object of worship (for example, the relics of saints or embalmed bodies of Pirohov, Kotovskyi, Lenin, Mao Zedong, etc.), as museum exhibits (for example, mummies of Egyptian pharaohs, Princess Ukok of Altai, etc.). Centers, where the corpse, at the patient's request, is frozen a few minutes after clinical death and then stored at low temperature in a hermetically sealed cylinder filled with liquid nitrogen have emerged since the mid-60's of the XX century in the United States, Great Britain, France, Russia and other countries. It is done in order to wait until medicine is able to overcome the disease that caused the death.[14]

Moreover, such types of activities as transporting and storing the body of the deceased and/or organs removed from it related to transplantation also indicate that such objects are considered by law to be things. Such an approach is logically reflected both in international law, in particular in the Directive 2010/45/EU of the European Parliament and of the Council of 7 July 2010 on standards of quality and safety of human organs intended for transplantation, and in the national legislation of a number of Eastern European countries. According to the storage agreement, one party (custodian) undertakes to store the thing transferred to it by the other party (bailor) and safely return it to the bailor (the Art. 936 of the CC of Ukraine, the Art. 1537 of the Civil Code of the Republic of Moldova, the Art. 776 of the Civil Code of the Republic of Belarus, the Art. 86 of the Civil Code of the Russian Federation, the Art. 835 of the Civil Code of the Republic of Poland, etc.), and under the contract of carriage—the carrier undertakes to deliver the goods entrusted to it by the sender and bring it to the destination and to handle it to the recipient, where the goods are also a thing or set of things (the Art. 908 of the CC of Ukraine, the Art. 1411 of the Civil Code of the Republic of Moldova, the Art. 739 of the Civil Code of the Republic of Belarus, the Art. 785 of the Civil Code of the Russian Federation, the Art. 835 of the Civil Code of the Republic of Poland, etc.). The experience of settling relations regarding the body of the deceased and the organs removed from it in the Czech Republic is very interesting in this regard. Despite the fact that the domestic legislation of the country also provides that the objects of storage and transportation are only things (§ 2402, 2555 of the Civil Code of the Czech Republic), nevertheless § 493 of the Czech Civil Code clearly states that parts separated from the human body are not things. This should raise some logical questions. For example, what is

[14] Slipchenko (2016); Shyshka (2011).

stored or transported then? If personal non-property good (tangible and non-property), then how can the property benefits regime be applied to it, in particular the constructions of storage and transportation contracts? In case of improper fulfillment of the terms of these contracts, will the property damage related to the loss or damage of an organ removed from a human body be reimbursed? It is obvious that this position of the Czech legislator creates a certain uncertainty in the law, which, incidentally, the Czech researchers themselves pay attention to.[15] In fact, on the one hand, the organs removed from the body, including the deceased, are not recognized as things, and on the other hand, the relations arising in relation to such goods are regulated similarly to those that arise in relation to things.

Another confirmation that organs removed from the human body are a kind of property can be found in court decisions in such categories of cases as theft of these objects. Although the given example of the decision does not directly relate to the countries of Eastern Europe, but it seems that it can be considered within the framework of the raised issue within the framework of unification and universalization of legal approaches in order to illustrate global tendencies and taken into account while improving domestic civil legislation of certain countries.

The case concerned the theft of body parts (35 to 40 parts) of the deceased at the Royal College of Surgeons, which were used in educational activities. In order to admit the secret seizure of the organs of the deceased as a theft, it was necessary to establish in the legal sense that such organs are property. In fact, theft, according to the court, is the misappropriation of someone else's property. Property includes tangible property (things). In order to admit the theft, it was necessary to establish that the seized human organs were property belonging to a certain person who lawfully owned or controlled it, had property rights to it or interests. If there was a secret seizure of body parts of the deceased, but such parts were not property, then there was no theft. In the course of the case the court recognized that there was a theft, which meant that the court considered the stolen parts to be property.

Thus, the body of a person who has died and the organs removed from it have all the features of things,[16] and things are known to be a kind of property. In turn, property is a good that can be valued in money's worth. And the presence of such ability can be confirmed as follows.

It is known that there is an exchange of organs at the level of international cooperation. Such an exchange is provided in most Eastern European countries (for example, in the Czech Republic, Moldova, Belarus, Russia, Poland, Ukraine, etc.) and at the level of international law. The exchange of organs between EU Member States is also regulated in the Directive 2010/45/EU of the European Parliament and of the Council of 7 July 2010 on standards of quality and safety of human organs intended for transplantation. And it can be equivalent or non-equivalent, but the exchanged goods must be valued within universal equivalent and money is such an equivalent. Moreover, Ukraine could even enter into sales

[15] Ondrúš (2016), p. 27.

[16] Maleina (2003), p. 13.

contracts until 2019 within the framework of international cooperation and receive or pay a fair price for them. Iran, although still the only country, has an officially regulated domestic system of kidney sales, and the practicc of buying and selling organs was banned only in 1994 in India. It can also be a confirmation of the potential ability of these benefits to be valued in money or in another equivalent. Another proof is the data of the World Health Organization, according to which more than 10,000 operations on selling human organ are carried out on the black market every year. And although such trade is illegal, the organs have a clearly defined price at the black market.

Thus, the body of a deceased person and the organs removed from it are the objects of civil law. Moreover, as rightly emphasized in the legal literature, they have a dual nature[17]—non-property and property one.[18] We believe that the first one (non-property) complicates the perception of the latter (property). Nevertheless, the body of the deceased person and the removed organs acquire the regime of things, property benefits. The fact that in most countries of the world they cannot be the object of sales or other transactions does not change their dual nature.

4 The Natural Circulability of Removed Organs of the Deceased

As mentioned before, the severability of objects from an individual or a legal entity indicates their natural circulability. Things, due to natural qualities are endowed with such natural circulability. Having spatial boundaries, they are able to move from one person to another or to be alienated.[19] Given that the organs removed from the deceased body have all the features of things, as it was established, it is logical to conclude that they are also inherent in the natural circulability. Severability (separation) indicates the natural property of such goods to change their owner.

The presence of the natural circulability of the deceased body and the organs removed from it is recognized by the legislation of the countries of Eastern Europe. For example, the Art. 21 of the Law of Ukraine 'On the Use of Transplantation of Anatomical Materials to Humans' provides the exchange of organs within the framework of international cooperation. Obviously, such an exchange is based on a contract of exchange. In turn, each party under the contract of exchange is obliged to transfer one benefit in exchange for another to the other party. And such a transfer is possible only in case of severability of the object of exchange from the subject. Similar norms exist in Belarus (the Art. 4 of the Law of the Republic of Belarus 'On Transplantation of Human Organs and Tissues'), Moldova (Arts. 4, 5 of the Law of the Republic of Moldova 'On Transplantation of Human Organs, Tissues and

[17] Gruzinskaja et al. (2019), p. 33.

[18] Slipchenko (2019).

[19] Slipchenko (2018).

Cells'), Czech Republic (§ 26 of the Law of Czech Republic 'On Transplantation'), etc.

Thus, if the legislation provides the exchange of organs removed from the human body, and such an exchange takes place by the transfer, then the legislator recognizes the natural circulability of these objects.

Confirmation of the natural circulability of the removed organs, as unusual it may seem, is the ban on concluding contracts for the sales of human anatomical materials (removed organs) (the Art. 5 of the Law of the Republic of Belarus 'On Transplantation of Human Organs and Tissues', the Art. 20 of the Law of Ukraine 'On the Use of Transplantation of Anatomical Materials to Humans', the Art. 44 of the Law of the Republic of Poland 'On the Collection, Storage and Transplantation of Cells, Tissues and Organs', § 28 of the Law of Czech Republic 'On Transplantation'). In fact, this prohibition is really a restriction of civil circulation, and the degree of admission to circulation (free, limited) or its prohibition is set only for objects having a natural tradability. If the good would be inseverable from the person, due to its natural properties, it can not be alienated or can not be transferred to another person, and therefore it is generally impractical to raise the question on its withdrawal from circulation, on the restriction or non-restriction within the circulation.[20] Thus, the establishment of any degree of civil tradability (free or limited circulation, withdrawal from the circulation) indicates that the object, in respect of which a degree is established, has a natural ability (has natural properties) to civil circulations. Otherwise, such an establishment would be illogical.

5 The Civil Circulability

Civil circulability indicates the admission of certain goods that have natural circulability to civil circulation by the objective law. In fact, it is normative and legal establishment of the limits for the freedom of alienation or movement of objects between the participants in civil circulation. Such establishment can be of three types: free circulation, limited circulation and withdrawal from circulation.

Considering the above mentioned, the organs removed from the deceased body, as well as the body of the deceased, are limited in circulation. Moreover, this limitation may be changed, it is dynamic. For example, Ukraine until 2019 had the opportunity to carry out an equivalent exchange or sales of removed organs, within the framework of international cooperation in the field of applying transplantation of anatomical materials to humans. And from 2019 had the opportunity only to carry out an exchange. Another example. The conclusion of agreements providing the sales of human anatomical materials for transplantation is prohibited in Ukraine (the Art. 20 of the Law of Ukraine 'On the Use of Transplantation of Anatomical Materials to Humans'). Thus, the conclusion of contracts of lease and lifetime

[20] Slipchenko (2011), p. 72.

maintenance, gift is not formally prohibited in accordance with the dispositive principles of private law (everything is allowed that is not directly prohibited by law). Similar norms are contained in the legislation of Moldova (the Art. 28 of the Law of the Republic of Moldova 'On Transplantation of Human Organs, Tissues and Cells') and Russia (Arts. 1, 15 of the Law of the Russian Federation 'On Transplantation of Human Organs and/or Tissues'). At the same time, Belarus prohibits the conclusion of any payment transactions for human organs and (or) tissues (the Art. 5 of the Law of the Republic of Belarus 'On Transplantation of Human Organs and Tissues').

The following restrictions are also set:

- according to the subject composition, for example, subjects of international cooperation in the field of applying transplantation of anatomical materials to humans or business entities that are legally entitled to carry out activities related to transplantation;
- if necessary, obtaining a special permit for the civil circulation of these objects, for example, health care facilities that have the license to conduct business in medical practice, which stipulates the right to provide medical care with the application of transplantation;
- according to the types of transactions that may (may not) be made with these objects, for example, it is prohibited to conclude contracts involving the sales of human anatomical materials.

6 Methods of Civil Circulation of the Deceased's Removed Organs

The organs removed from the deceased body have natural and civil circulability that allows to involve them into civil circulation. Moreover, we believe that the activities associated with organs removed from the human body without it, including for transplantation, or in other cases specified by law would be impossible or at least significantly complicated.

Perceiving the civil circulation as a lawful alienation or transfer of objects of civil law from one person to another, the preliminary statement can be illustrated as follows.

It is obvious that the activity related to transplantation is the activity of subjects who have the right to: remove organs, including from the deceased body; prepare them for transportation; transportation; storage; transplantation of the organ to a recipient; manufacture of bioimplants, etc. And if we assume that each of the activities associated with transplantation (removal, preparation, transportation, storage, manufacture, transplantation, etc.) is carried out by various specialized entities, such activities would be impossible without civil circulation. For example, a health care facility that has removed an organ must transfer it to another entity to prepare for transportation. The entity that received and prepared the body for transportation is subsequently transferring it to the carrier. The latter, in turn, transfers to the institution of the biobank for storage, etc.

The analysis of the simulated situation gives grounds for the following considerations. The organ, immediately after removal from the body of the deceased, is in the health care facility that removed it. It means that this object of the material world is in the possession of the facility—and it is the fact. With the lawful removal of the organ, it is in the lawful possession. After the transfer of the removed organ for preparation to transportation, it is in the possession of the entity that has to prepare it. And such possession is legitimate, which indicates the legitimacy of the transfer of this object from one person to another. During transportation, the organ prepared for this is in the possession of the carrier. It is obvious that the carrier owns it lawfully. From the moment of transfer of the delivered organ for storage to the institution of the biobank, there is lawful possession of the latter, which in turn indicates the legitimacy of the transfer of the object. And such a circulation can be continued, for example, in the opposite direction for transplantation of an organ to the recipient or while transferring it to the subject for production of bioimplants.

As one can see, the illustration clearly shows the transition of organs removed from the deceased body from one person to another. Such dynamics of the object is not based on sales contracts, since it is legitimate, because it does not violate the established prohibition. And returning to the defined terms at the beginning of the article, the lawful transfer of objects of civil law from one person to another is the civil circulation. The absence of counter-payment for the provided (received) organs indicates only their non-commercial circulation.

It is also obvious that the exchange of organs, in the framework of international cooperation—in the field of transplantation of anatomical materials to humans, is also the civil circulation. Its analysis gives grounds for the following considerations. As a result of such exchange, one person transfers to another the removed organ, mutually received from him. Upon the transfer, the object is alienated in favor of the purchaser. After all, the alienation itself, as the method of civil circulation, allows the purchaser to use the removed organ provided to him, including by the way of transplantation. He becomes the owner of the acquired.

Thus, as a result of the exchange, there is a lawful alienation of objects of civil law (organs removed from the human body) from one person to another. And such alienation is the method of the civil circulation. Moreover, such circulation is non-commercial, but it can be conditionally attributed to the one based on free of charge basis, as sometimes stated in the national legislation of some Eastern European countries (the Art. 4 of the Law of the Republic of Belarus 'On Transplantation of Human Organs and Tissues'). In fact, the alienator receives a countergrant from the purchaser in the form of similar or other organs or anatomical materials. And such a provision, in fact, is a payment for the provided object.

Activities related to transplantation are not the only ones where there is the civil circulation of the body of the deceased and the organs removed from it. It can be activities related to education, research, medical development, etc. It also involves the transfer of the body of the deceased and the organs removed from it. For example, the body of the subject for the removal of an organ, the removed organ (body) to a scientific institution, and the scientific institution—to an educational or other scientific institution, etc. Obviously, such a circulation will be different from the civil circulation associated with transplantation. Since, the legal requirements, prohibitions and restrictions imposed on transplantation do not cover other activities, unless otherwise expressly provided by law.

Judges of the Supreme Court of California first paid attention to the peculiarity of this circulation in the case of John Moore v. the University of California (No. S006987 dated from July 9, 1990).[21] Although California is not part of the Eastern European region, first of all, this case clearly illustrates the formation of global tendencies in the perception of human body parts as objects of civil circulation, and secondly, in our opinion, it both recognizes the possibility of involving human body parts to civil circulation and, under certain conditions, to the stream of commerce. We believe that this case was the impetus for the development of modern perception of separated human organs as objects of civil circulation, including in the Eastern European countries.

One of the issues for the Court was whether John Moore's removed spleen, which was subsequently used by researchers at the University of California to create a pharmaceutical drug without the patient's consent, was reimbursable. Notwithstanding the defendants' argument, the purchase and sale of organs removed from the human body is prohibited under the US law, and therefore cannot be the subject of property benefits. The court concluded that such a ban was applied only to organs removed for further transplantation. There are no such prohibitions for transferring them for research, scientific, educational activities. Therefore, it was concluded that the sale of removed organs for non-therapeutic purposes (not for transplantation) was allowed. It means that J. Moore had the right to receive property benefits for the spleen removed and used later in the research.[22]

The analysis of the national legislation of the countries of Eastern Europe leads to a similar conclusion in most cases. For example, Part 4 of the Art. 289 of the CC of Ukraine, the Art. 6 of the Law of Ukraine 'On Burial and Funeral Affairs', the Art. 68 of the Law of the Russian Federation 'On the Basics of Public Health in the Russian Federation', the Art. 47 of the Law of the Republic of Belarus 'On Health Care' provide the transfer and use of the body or anatomical materials (organs, tissues) of the deceased aimed at achieving medical, scientific and educational purposes. However, special legislation does not directly prohibit the payment of such a transfer. The latter is intended only for activities related to transplantation and production of biomaterials. Therefore, based on the dispositive principles of private law (everything is allowed that is not expressly prohibited by law), it is logical to conclude that the transfer to scientific, medical or educational institutions of the body

[21] See in particular Case No. S006987, Moore vs. University of California regents (1990). https://caselaw.findlaw.com/ca-supreme-court/1774382.html.

[22] See in particular Case No. S006987, Moore vs. University of California regents (1990). https://caselaw.findlaw.com/ca-supreme-court/1774382.html.

of the deceased and/or organs removed from it for the use in medical, scientific and educational purposes, can be both paid and free of charge.

Regarding the methods of such a circulation, it can be both transition and alienation. In particular, alienation will take place during the transfer of the body (removed organs) to scientific, medical, educational institutions or from one institution to another. The transition will take place if transferred to a carrier, custodian, from one institution to another, for example, to demonstrate to students, interns, etc.

The civil circulation of human organs also occurs during the public and legal activities of the relevant state agencies. For example, the seizure of parts of a human body by the relevant state law enforcement agencies that have been illegally separated from a living person (including the body of a deceased person) or illegally sold (purchased), creates lawful possession for such law enforcement agencies. Subsequent transfer of the removed human organs to the institution for forensic examination, including for their storage, also gives rise their legal possession for such an entity. Although this transfer takes place within the framework of criminal procedure, but it should be noted that there is a lawful transition (alienation) of these parts of the deceased body within this procedure. In fact, the law norms allow the relevant persons to lawfully own such objects of the material world, limited use and disposal in the manner and within the limits prescribed by law. The above allows us to conclude that there is the civil circulation of objects with limited circulability even in this case. Herewith, the circulation is civil despite the fact that the transition (alienation) takes place within the criminal procedure. The activities of the officials of law enforcement agencies, experts or other persons would be impossible without this. And this activity depends on the lawful possession and lawful transfer of the removed organs of the human body by one subject to another.

The above allows us to state that two groups of norms are applied within the criminal procedure. On the one hand, these are norms that are intended to bring to criminal liability for certain crimes (for example, forced donation, violation of the statutory procedure for transplantation of human anatomical materials, abuse of the body of the deceased, illegal trade in human anatomical materials, etc.), including the procedural ones. On the other hand, these are norms that are designed to establish the civil and legal regime and the procedure of civil circulation of illegally removed human organs in cases and in the manner prescribed by law.

With regard to such a method of circulation of human organs as alienation, it may take place during their destruction[23] or during the transfer of the removed organs to scientific, medical, educational institutions in the manner prescribed by national law.

---

[23] In particular, we talk about those cases, when there is a need to address the issue about the fate of organs separated from the human body, due to the exhaustion of public and legal procedures, which determine the receipt of important information about the circumstances relevant to criminal proceedings. If the person designated by the law has not expressed or has expressed his desire to leave the organs of the deceased in the institution where they are stored as material evidence, their fate is determined in accordance with national law. For example, fate may concern the decision to destroy them. Since the destruction of organs separated from the human body can be carried out by an entity that is different from the one who alienates them, and given the fact that the transfer of such organs

In this case, such a circulation, as we see, is non-commercial.

7 Conclusions

Thus, the analysis of the legislation of Eastern European countries and a number of scientific studies concerning this issue allows us to state the following. The organs removed from the corpse have a dual nature, i.e. they contain both personal non-property and property value. In the latter case, they are things. The organs removed from the deceased body as things, they are both freely transferable (have natural and civil circulability), and are actively involved into civil circulation. Moreover, those types of activities related to transplantation, biomaterial production, a number of scientific studies, medical education, investigation of crimes related to human trafficking, etc. would be impossible without the latter. It is the lawful alienation and transfer of organs removed from the deceased body, or their transfer from one person to another ensures the achievement of the goal of the relevant activity.

However, they are not in free circulation and are things limited in civil circulation. Such restrictions may be set in accordance with the subject composition, with the need to obtain a special permit, with the types of that transactions may (may not) be made with these objects. Depending on the type of activity, where the civil circulation takes place, its restrictions may relate to the counter-provision of property, purpose of use (transplantation, production of biomaterials, scientific research, education, etc.) and others. It is non-profit in most cases.

The conclusions indicate the need to rethink the legal regime of these objects, to establish the boundaries of their circulation, to clarify the nature of those rights (responsibilities) that arise, change, are ceased as a result of alienation or transfer of these benefits, the moment of their occurrence (termination).

References

Bajbak VV (2005) K voprosu ob oborotosposobnosti objazatel'stvennyh trebovanij [On the question of the circulability ability of obligatory requirements]. Arbitrazhnye spory 1(29):101–118

Belov VA (2007) Ob′ekt sub′ektivnogo grazhdanskogo prava, ob′ekt grazhdanskogo pravootnoshenija i ob′ekt grazhdanskogo oborota: soderzhanie i sootnoshenie ponjatij. In: Ob′ekty grazhdanskogo oborota [The Object of Subjective Civil Right, the Object of Civil Legal Relationship and the Object of Civil Turnover: the Content and the Interrelation of Concepts. In: The Objects of Civil Turnover]. Sbornik statej. Moskva: Izdatelstvo 'Statut', 2007

Fiala J, Kindl M et al (2009) Občanské právo hmotné. 2. vyd. Plzeň: Aleše Čeněk, 2009, p. 159, poznámka pod čarou č. 64

is usually carried out through the mechanism of alienation to a person, whose activities are related to waste disposal, then we talk about the civil circulation.

Gruzinskaja EI, Ponomareva MJu, Shugaj AR (2019) Organy i tkani cheloveka kak ob`ekt grazhdansko-pravovyh otnoshenij [Human organs and tissues as an object of civil law relations]. In: Pravovye, jekonomicheskie i gumanitarnye voprosy sovremennogo razvitija obshhestva: teoreticheskie i prikladnye issledovanija. Sbornik nauchnyh trudov 4:33

Kuznetsova NS (2011) Sovershenstvovanye mekhanyzma pravovoho rehulyrovanyya hrazhdanskykh pravootnoshenyy [Perfection of the mechanism of legal regulation of civil-law relations]. In: Aktual'ni problemy tsyvil'noho, simeynoho ta mizhnarodnoho pryvatnoho prava (Matvyeyevs'ki tsyvilistychni chytannya): materialy mizhnar. nauk.-prakt. konf. Kyyiv, 10 lystopada 2011 roku. Kyyiv: Alerta

Maleina MN (2003) Status organov, tkanej, tela cheloveka kak ob`ektov prava sobstvennosti i prava na fizicheskuju neprikosnovennost' [The status of organs, tissues, human body as objects of property rights and the right to physical integrity]. Zakonodatel'stvo 11:13–20

Mayfat AV, Lisachenko AV (2017) Sobstvennost' na telo cheloveka [Ownership on the human body], viewed 17 May 2017. URL: http://www.urallaw.ru/articles/person_2/id_35.html

Ondrúš M (2016) Právní povaha lidského těla a jeho částí: Rigorózní práce [Legal nature of the human body and its parts: Rigorous work]. Brno, p 27

Shyshka OR (2011) Pravo neisnuiuchoho uchasnyka tsyvilnykh pravovidnosyn yak pravova fiktsiia [The right of a non-existent participant in civil relations as a fiction of the right]. Pravo ta upravlinnia: elektronne naukove vydannia 1:489–511

Shyshka OR (2019) Nemainovi vidnosyny z materialnymy blahamy v predmeti tsyvilnoho prava [Non-property relations with material goods in the subject-matter of civil law]. In: Aktualni problemy pryvatnoho prava: materialy XVII nauk.-prakt. konf., prysviach. 97-y richnytsi z dnia narodzh. d-ra yuryd. nauk, prof., chl.-kor. AN URSR V. P. Maslova (Kharkiv, 22 Jul. 2019 r.). Kharkiv: Pravo, pp 255–259

Slipchenko AS (2017) Sutnist ta oznaky tsyvilnoho oborotu [The essence and signs of civil turnover]. In: Visnyk Kharkivskoho natsionalnoho universytetu imeni V. N. Karazina. Seriia Pravo 23:129–132

Slipchenko AS (2018) Otchuzhdenie i perehod ob`ektov grazhdanskogo oborota v Ukraine: sootnoshenie ponjatij [Alienation and transition of objects of civil circulation in Ukraine: correlation of concepts]. Legea şi viaţa 10(2):100–104

Slipchenko AS (2019). Sposoby ta formy tsyvilnoho oborotu rechei: thesis [Ways and forms of civil circulation of things: thesis] Kharkiv, 252 p

Slipchenko SA (2011) Oborotosposobnost' ob'ektov lichnyh neimushhestvennyh prav, obespechivajushhih social'noe bytie fizicheskogo lica: monografija [The circulability ability of objects of personal non-property rights providing social being of an physical person: monograph]. Kharkiv, p 71

Slipchenko SA, Shyshka AR, Buleca SB, Sinegubov OV, Gryn'ko RV (2018) Sostojanie mezhdunarodnogo pravovogo regulirovanija posmertnogo donorstva: na puti k unifikacii (obzor) [The State of International Legal Regulation of Cadaveric Donation: On the Path to Unification (Review)]. Georgian Med News 10:175–179

Slipchenko SA, Shyshka AR, Buleca SB, Shishka NV, Slipchenko AS (2020) Pravovoj rezhim donorskih orgonov v mezhdunarodnom chastnom prave [Legal regime of donor organs in private international law]. Georgian Medical News 7–8:169–177

Slipchenko SO (2013a) Osobysti nemainovi pravovidnosyny shchodo oborotozdatnykh obiektiv [Personal Non-Property Legal Relations Concerning Tradable Objects]. Kharkiv

Slipchenko SO (2013b) Mistse obiektiv osobystykh nemainovykh pravovidnosyn u systemi obiektiv tsyvilnoho prava [The place of objects of personal non-property legal relations in the system of objects of civil law]. Pravo i suspilstvo 6-2:87–92

Slipchenko SO (2016) Tilo liudyny, yaka pomerla, yak obiekt tsyvilnoho prava [The body of a deceased person as an object of civil law]. In: Problemy tsyvilnoho prava ta protsesu: materialy nauk.-prakt. konf., prysviach. svitlii pamiati O. A. Pushkina, 27 trav. 2016 r. Kharkiv: KhNUVS. pp 34–37

Part III
Protection of Rights and Medical Dispute Resolution

Protection of Personal Non-Property Rights of Individuals, Biological Materials and Personal Data of Whose Are Subject to Research as a Part of Biobanks in Ukraine: Comparison with the EU Recommendation CM/Rec(2016)6

Nataliia Kvit

Contents

Abstract The European integration process in Ukraine requires the harmonization of legislation regulating the lawful and safe use of human biological material and data as parts of biobanks, in accordance with European standards. The legislation currently in force in Ukraine only partially regulates these relations and is characterized by fragmentation and absence of a special law that would establish a general framework for the permissibility of scientific and clinical research involving human subjects, and using research biobanks and future scientific use of biological materials and data obtained initially with non-research purpose. This study concludes that there is a need to adopt a special law "On the legal regulation of research activities involving human subjects and using biobanks", the task of which will be: to establish permissible limits of such research; to promote the quality, competence and transparency of clinical research in humans, and its aim will be the protection of human dignity, privacy and health in the process of carrying out research in humans. A general concept has been formulated for legal regulation of legal guarantees of

N. Kvit (✉)
Department of Civil Law and Procedure, Ivan Franko National University of Lviv, Lviv, Ukraine

© The Author(s), under exclusive license to Springer Nature Switzerland AG 2022

R. Maydanyk et al. (eds.), *Ukrainian Healthcare Law in the Context of European and International Law*, European Union and its Neighbours in a Globalized World 7,
https://doi.org/10.1007/978-3-031-05690-1_8

probants non-property rights, balancing them with interests of science and freedom of scientific research activities. The probants legal status has been determined, which is bound up to the legal status of a researcher (a biobank manager or its users) and is disclosed through the right of a probant to self-determination. The ways to protect personal data of a probant have been identified, in the form of pseudonymization and anonymization.

1 Introduction

Management of biobanks, i.e., their use can and should be limited by both national and international legislation, but requires a well-structured approach by the legislator to this issue. In particular, there is a need through the use of legal norms, on the one hand, to protect the rights and interests of probants and, on the other hand, to establish a reasonable framework for use of research biobanks, at the same time, not restricting the freedom of scientific activity and adversely impacting on the development of science.

The global pandemic of COVID-19 has a great consequences for the use of human biospecimens stored in biobanks, there are risks associated with the collection and processing of human biospecimens with unknown status in relation to SARS-CoV-2, whether for diagnostic, therapeutic or research purposes, which should be considered.[1] This situation led to necessity to provide a list of resources that researchers working against COVID-19 can access via the BBMRI-ERIC network.[2] But the main idea was on the one hand to support researchers of the new disease and at the same time to guarantee safe handling, processing, storage and shipment of biospecimens to reduce health risks to biobank staff.[3] Of a great importance is also the WHO laboratory biosafety guidance related to COVID-19.[4] That is why we agree with the idea, that the only possible way to prevent consequences of the SARS-CoV-2 pandemic on the future use of materials from biobanks for research activities is for biobanks to separately store all human samples collected during the COVID-19 outbreak.[5]

[1] Hofman et al. (2020), p. 809.

[2] COVID-19 Research | BBMRI-ERIC: making new treatments possible. https://www.bbmri-eric.eu/covid-19/.; (2020) BBMRI-ERIC response to COVID-19. Resources from biobanks across Europe available for research on SARS-CoV-2 and COVID-19. https://www.bbmri-eric.eu/wp-content/uploads/BBMRI-ERIC-response-to-COVID-2.10.pdf.

[3] Biobanking best practices for COVID-19 specimens and the role of LIMS. https://cloudlims.com/blog/biobanking-best-practices-for-covid-19-specimens.html.

[4] Vaught (2020), pp. 153–154. https://doi.org/10.1089/bio.2020.29069.jjv.

[5] Hofman et al. (2020), p. 810.

The analyzes of the biobanking market in Ukraine shows, that Ukrainian collections of human biological materials are often subject for scientific usage by foreign researchers including those from EU. This and also the fact, that Ukraine is on the path to integration with the EU means that there is a need to bring legislation in the field of research use of materials of human origin in line with European standards. That is why it is important to compare the current Ukrainian legislation with the requirements of EU. The most important current European regulation in this field is to be found in the Recommendation CM/Rec (2016)6 of the Committee of Ministers of the Council of Europe to member States on research on biological materials of human origin[6] adopted on 11 May 2016. This Recommendation is a revision of the previous one (Recommendation (2006)4) and takes into account new developments in the field of biobanking, such as the increasingly diverse origin of biological materials stored in collections, the difficulty to guarantee non-identifiability of such samples, the increasing amount of research involving materials coming from different collections, and the importance of research on biomaterials removed from persons not able to consent.

It should be noted that the legal status of probants as subjects transferring their biological materials/data for scientific research, including clinical trails of tissue and cell transplants, is insufficiently regulated in the Ukrainian legislation, and therefore requires special attention of lawyers and analysis of foreign experience in this field in order to fill existing gaps. The legal status of researchers, although partially regulated, is, in particular, mainly in the context of clinical research of tissue and cell transplants, but still has no systematic conceptual character. Therefore, considering the fact that the legal status of probants and researchers are closely interrelated, in particular their corresponding rights and duties, a system of mutual rights and duties should be well-defined within a special law. Thus, on the one hand, we will guarantee the protection of the rights of probants and, on the other hand, we will create conditions for freedom of scientific activity of researchers, who, in good faith, act for the benefit of public interests, as they care about the development of science and medicine. The issue of legal regulation of the limits of use of research biobanks has not previously been studied in Ukraine.

[6]Recommendation CM/Rec(2016)6 of the Committee of Ministers of the Council of Europe to member States on research on biological materials of human origin adopted on 11 May 2016. https://search.coe.int/cm/Pages/result_details.aspx?ObjectId=090000168064e8ff.

2 Defining the Limits of Permissibility of Research, Including the Use of Research Biobanks: Comparison with the Recommendation CM/Rec (2016)6

In view of the existence of such a significant gap in the Ukrainian legislation and absence of a systematic special act regulating all research areas involving humans, we consider it necessary to adopt a special law 'On the legal regulation of research activities involving human subjects and using biobanks', the task of which will be: to establish limits to the permissibility of such research; to promote the high quality, competence and transparency of clinical research in humans, and its aim will be the protection of human dignity, privacy and health in the process of carrying out research in humans.

2.1 Types of Research Involving a Human Subject

One of the Ukrainian legislation problems is the absence of a unified terminology refer to subjects involved in research, namely different terms are used: "subjects of research", "research participants", "researched", "tested' persons" and others. This diversity of terminology requires carrying out systemization and determination of differentiation of the legal status of various subjects involved in research and medical experiments.

In the context of this study, it is necessary to establish a boundary and to emphasize that when it comes to so-called clinical research on humans such research is always linked to testing of new drugs or new therapies directly on humans, who are referred to as research participants or the researched, and who can be both sick and healthy individuals (volunteers), depending on the purpose and methods of the research. Clinical researchers are always doctors, and these clinical trials must always be subject to prior doctors' evaluation and approval by the ethics committee.

On the other hand, research of biological materials and associated personal data mostly does not have clinical signs, as human subjects from whom the biological material is taken (probants) are not directly/physically involved in the research itself, such research is mostly conducted in laboratories using information technology tools (e.g., DNA sequencing) and researchers are mostly not doctors, biologists, geneticists, mathematicians or statists. It is also important to note that the purpose of these studies, as opposed to clinical ones, is mainly to investigate the links between biological properties, namely heredity, environmental factors and certain diseases occurrence. In this case, the question is about fundamental research that serves to expand knowledge, which is also of great practical importance for medicine, especially for the diagnosis and prevention of certain diseases, while clinical research is mainly the basis for the development of therapeutic medicine, that is to say, with the aim of improving its therapeutic direction. Thus, these two types of research involving human subjects differ significantly, particularly with regard to their subject matter and purpose.

In the context of the current Ukrainian legislation, we can illustrate the difference in the subject matter of these two types of research, using the example of the Procedure for clinical trials of tissue and cell transplants and expertise of clinical research materials.[7] In the case of probants, as those who transfer their tissues and cells for research, and whom the regulation refers to donors of tissues and cells, they need to be separated from individuals who are the direct subjects of clinical trials, research (e.g., participants in clinical trials of tissue and cell transplants), as, in the case of probants, their biological material is examined, previously separated from their body on the grounds of their informed consent, directly for the purpose of the research or with another one (therapeutic/diagnostic), but then, on the grounds of their informed consent, they are transferred for research (for example, their biological materials, from which tissue or cell transplants have been made—donors of tissues and cells) and the participants in the research (whom, in the given example, these transplants are introduced in the process of tissue or cell transplantation and the effect of such transplantation is studied) are individuals on whom new treatment methods or new drugs are directly tested in clinical trials.

It is also worth noting that in the context of biobanking activities subjects, transferring their biological materials for research (probants), also differ from the participants in the research as the process of transferring of biological materials to a biobank is not always accompanied by medical intervention but, if accompanied, it is first of all one-time intervention (with the aim of obtaining biological material), secondly, there is a significantly lower risk to the health of a probant, but such transferring is always a certain interference with a probant's privacy, since the biological material also contains personal data and confidential information, except cases of anonymization (anonymisation of personal data).

Considering the risk levels of different research types, it is important to emphasize, that first among general provisions contained in Chapter II of the Recommendation CM/Rec (2016)6 are the risks and benefits in relation to research activities. This means, that it is one of the most important basic questions, which must be evaluated and it also means, that the researcher must minimize all physical risks arising from removal of biological materials for storage for future research and the other risks, in particular for private life, related to the obtaining, storing and use of biological materials. The requirement to minimise the risks implies that, whenever possible, biological materials should be stored and used in a non-identifiable form. However, rendering the biological materials non-identifiable may be incompatible with the scientific requirements of the research projects or be contrary to the interests of the persons concerned. And all these risks should not be disproportionate to the potential benefit of the research activities.

[7] Procedure for carrying out clinical trials of tissue and cell transplants and expertise of clinical trials materials affirmed by the Ministry of Healthcare of Ukraine (2007) No 630 https://zakon.rada.gov.ua/laws/show/z1206-07#Text.

Thus, the difference between these subjects lies mainly in the level of risk they are exposed to as a result of such research. Obviously, participants of the research are more vulnerable and therefore require greater public protection, in particular by regulating the proceeding of such clinical trials. However, it is mainly regulated at the level of non-legislative acts and only on a partially, namely, regarding clinical trials of medicinal products as well as trails of tissue/cell transplants. At the same time, the legal status of probants as subjects transferring their biological materials and related information on the grounds of the informed consent to a research biobank or for research purposes of individual researchers (scientists) require the attention of a legislator to safeguard their generalized regulation in order to guarantee the protection of their personal rights, even though the risks to the probants are much lawer than the participants of clinical research.

In our point of view, these two categories of subjects that are directly (researched) or indirectly (probants) involved in various trails can be described as varieties of individuals involved in the research, and the criteria for their definition will be risk profile and level of their involvement in such research. Therefore, with a view to systematizing and unifying the terminology in the field of biomedical research, we propose to use the term "individuals involved in the research", as a generic term that includes two types of these subjects, namely researched and probants. We therefore propose to define this concept in the framework of a special law as follows: 'An individual involved in the research is the individual taking direct part in the research (researched) or an individual, whose biological material and/or health-related personal data is the object of the research (probant)'.

2.2 *Legal Status of a Probant*

Unfortunately, scientific-research use of biological materials is excluded from the scope of the Law of Ukraine 'On the application of transplantation of anatomical materials to a human'[8] (hereinafter referred to as the Law on Transplantation). In particular, the new version of the law, unlike the previous one, contains an innovation in Art. 3, where among the types of relations excluded from the scope of the law, the 'retrieval of anatomical materials for diagnostic and scientific research' is also indicated. Therefore, it is necessary to create a special law, which will regulate these relations to guarantee the protection of probants rights and help researchers to conduct their work in the legal field.

[8]The Law of Ukraine 'On application of transplantation of anatomical materials to a human' No. 2427-19 (2018) https://zakon.rada.gov.ua/laws/show/2427-19#Text.

2.2.1 The Right of a Probant to Self-Determination

As it is stated in the Art.1 of the Recommendation CM/Rec (2016)6, Member States should protect the dignity and identity of all human beings and guarantee everyone, without discrimination, respect for their integrity, the right to respect for private life and other rights and fundamental freedoms with regard to any research activity governed by this recommendation. And this must be the basis for the further regulation development in the field of research on biological materials of human origin. Such basic guarantees can be concluded from the Constitution of Ukraine, as well as from the Fundamentals of the Law of Ukraine on Healthcare No. 2801-12 (1992).

Forming the legal status of a probant we mostly concentrate on the list of rights, but it is important to emphasize, that rights are preceded by duties. And we must agree with the position of Onora O'Neill, who said, that you cannot claim anyone's rights, without stating who has the duty to fulfill these rights. She supposes, that a better approach to securing sound ethical standards and the rights of the individual is to focus on obligations because "(. . .) a right that nobody is required to respect is simply not a right".[9]

To specify the probants legal status, the first and most certainly one of the fundamental rights is the probant's right to self-determination, which is exercised in several stages and requires its affirmation by establishing, firstly, right-related duty of a biobank manager to explain to a probant the purpose of the collection and use of his biological material and personal data and possible results of such research, and provide adequate information on all risks, resulting from his involvement in such research.

According to Art.10 of the Recommendation . . . prior to consent to or authorisation for the storage of biological materials for future research, the person concerned (meant probant or other authorized person if the probant is unable to concent) should be provided with comprehensible information that is as precise as possible with regard to: the nature of any envisaged research use and the possible choices that he or she could exercise; the conditions applicable to the storage of the materials, including access and possible transfer policies; and any relevant conditions governing the use of the materials, including re-contact and feedback. The person must be also informed about the right to refuse consent or authorisation and to withdraw consent or authorisation at any time. Also if the removal of biological materials for storage for future research is taking place the person concerned should be provided with additional information specific to the intervention carried out to remove the materials. Important also is, that even if the probant is unable to consent, nevertheless he/she should be informed in a manner compatible with their understanding.

Therefore, we consider it expedient, to enshrine in a special law the fundamental rights and duties of probants and a biobank manager in order to establish a clear regulation of their legal status. In particular, we propose in the section 'Conditions

[9] O'Neill (2002), p. 78.

for the Establishment and Use of a Biobank' of the special law 'On the legal regulation of research activities involving human subjects and using biobanks' in a separate article to enshrine the duty of a biobank manager to explain all the information to the probant and/or authorized person prior to transfer his biological material and personal data to the biobank and shall be revised as follows:

> The duty of a biobank manager is to provide a future probant with the necessary information regarding the consent.
>
> The person responsible for the establishment and use of the biobank (the manager) is obliged to report and explain to the future probant all circumstances, which are essential for his decision-making and informed consent to the transfer of his biological material and health-related personal data to the biobank, in particular to provide full and reliable information on:
> - the purpose of the collection and use (including research) of biological material;
> - risks of retrieval of biological material (if a special retrieval is made);
> - other efforts and obligations of a probant resulting from his participation in such research projects;
> - possible additional results of the research;
> - obligations to report on expected and unexpected results of the research and the right of a probant to refuse to provide him with such information;
> - ways of processing and protecting personal data;
> - the right to refuse or withdraw previously given consent at any time without giving reasons;
> - consequences of the withdrawal of consent by a probant for future use of the collected materials and data;
> - arrangements to cover any unforeseen losses associated with the research project, including procedure for compensation of damage, caused by the research to the probant;
> - main sources of funding for the research project;
> - other rights of the probant which can arise after his given informed consent.
>
> The explanation should be understandable to the probant, i.e., done in such a way that he can make a decision consciously and voluntary on whether to give informed consent or not. The probant should also be given enough time to make such a decision. The probant must be provided with written documents verifying carrying out the explanation, and which testify the will of the probant, signed by himself, except cases when the probant is physically unable to sign the documents himself, in this case a person authorized by the probant may do it in the presence of two witnesses.
>
> Explanation is not required only in exceptional cases, in particular when the probant has already been previously informed, and has given the informed general consent for future research of his biological and health-related personal data or if he refused to be provided with an explanation in writing.
>
> In case informed consent is given by an authorized person, not by the probant himself, in accordance with the requirements of the law, if no written instructions of the probant considering his refusal or agreement to the research of his biological materials were previously given, the explanation must be given to this authorized person in accordance with the requirements of Paragraph 1–3 of this Article.
>
> If the probant is unable to give informed consent by himself because of his age or state of health (minors, disabled persons), he must also be given an explanation of the essential circumstances, in accordance with Paragraph 1 of this Article, in an understandable form, if he is able to perceive any information.

The consent for processing probants personal data, including health and genetic data must be given in written form sepratly and in accordance to the Personal data protecting Law.

Imposing such requirements at the legislative level to the duty of a biobank manager to conduct the explaination to the probant with a view to obtaining his informed consent, including the manner in which the procedure is to be carried out for minors and disabled persons, could ensure conditioning for receiving the informed consent of the probant, in compliance with all European and international standards, ensuring the proper protection of their rights. It is also important to emphasize, that CTR generally require that clinical trial participants provide their informed consent to participate in a clinical trial.[10] But at the same time the Q&A confirms that consent under the GDPR (protecting privacy) should be distinguished from clinical trial informed consent (protecting ethics), and that consent is generally not the appropriate justification under the GDPR.[11] The last paragraph of the suggested article creates a rule, which emphasizes the difference between these two types of probants consent.

2.2.2 Informed Consent as a Component of the Probant's Right to Self-Determination

The next component of the right to self-determination of a probant and his autonomy support is his right to express the will, that is, to give informed consent to the transfer of his biological material and personal data to a biobank.

Informed consent, as a condition for the retrieval of biological material, is an important legal fact without which, in most cases, relationships for the establishment and use of a biobank could not emerge. Such retrieval may take place in a number of ways that also dictate the specific legal framework for getting such consent.

In particular, biological material may be taken in the course of carrying out diagnostic or therapy measures. Such person has the status of a patient and in this case consent to the intervention is given in accordance with the norms of Art. 42–45 of the Fundamentals of the Law of Ukraine on Health care.[12] The consent to biological material transfer to a biobank in this case may be granted by a person before medical treatment, at the same time with consent to diagnostic and/or therapeutic intervention or after such removal, if before intervention such transfer was not foreseen. Part 10 of Art.14 of the Law on Transplantation can be executed to

[10] Regulation (EU) 536/2014 of the European Parliament and of the Council of 16 April 2014 on clinical trials on medicinal products for human use, and repealing Directive 2001/20/EC (referred hereafter as 'Regulation (EU) 536/2014).

[11] Regulation (EU) 2016/679 of the European Parliament and of the Council of 27 April 2016 on the protection of natural persons with regard to the processing of personal data and on the free movement of such data, and repealing Directive 95/46/EC (General Data Protection Regulation or GDPR).

[12] Fundamentals of the Law of Ukraine on Healthcare No. 2801-12 (1992) https://zakon.rada.gov.ua/laws/show/2801-12#Text.

regulate this issue, however, its scope is limited as it applies only to the consent to the use of such biological material for bio-implants manufacturing.

But according to Art.11 Par. 2 of the Recommendation CM/Rec (2016)6, biological materials previously removed for another purpose should only be stored for future research with the consent of the person concerned, as provided for by law. Whenever possible, consent should be requested before biological materials are removed. Which means, that there must be a legal request before each intervention, which foresees the removal of biological materials of the patient to ask for patiens' consent for tits farther storing and scientific usage. Unfortunately Ukrainian legislation does not contain such a rule, which creates a gap and doesn't help in guaranteeing patients rights.

At the same time, the consent of a person to the retrieval of biological material for the primary and single purpose to transfer it to a biobank is quite different and regulated by other norms.

In particular, in the case of the retrieval of biological material for the purpose to realize the personal non-property right of a person to donation and, consequently, for transplantation or manufacturing of bio-implants, the procedure for such retrieval, including the procedure for receiving donors informed consent, is regulated by the Law on Transplantation, namely Section 3.

Legal regulation of the conditions and procedure for the transfer of biological material to a research biobank is currently absent in Ukraine. In this case, it is only possible to apply the general norms of the Fundamentals of the Law of Ukraine on Healthcare concerning the conditions for permissibility of medical intervention. The same applies to the procedure for the removal of biological material for personal storage and use. In our view, however, the issue of giving informed consent in these cases, namely the transfer of biological material to a biobank, requires special legal regulation, which should be included in a special law.

This question is regulated in Art. 11 Par. 1 of the Recommendation CM/Rec (2016)6, which containes the rule that free, express and documented consent of the person concerned should be obtained before biological materials are removed for storage for future research. This consent should be specific to the intervention carried out to remove the materials and be as precise as possible with regard to the research use envisaged.

So, giving informed consent is a key principle in bioethics, and can be applied not only in scientific and medical experiments but also in all health interventions, thus, it is logical to apply it in the relationship between a probant and researchers, since the activities of the researcher have direct signs of probant's health intervention. Thus, this right also requires that its legitimization in a separate article, which, in our view, shall be revised as follows:

> Procedure for giving the informed consent by a probant/authorized person.
>
> Informed consent of a probant/authorized person is obtained before the biological material and personal data are transferred to the biobank. The probant has a right to give the general informed consent to the use of all his biological materials and personal data in future research, which releases the biobank manager from the obligation to obtain the probant's

> informed consent before each particular research, carrying out of which could not be foreseen.
>
> If the probant does not have sufficient legal capacity (the disabled, minors), the informed consent to the transfer and use of his biological material and personal data is given by the authorized person, except the case when there is a written document of the disabled probant, signed by him prior to recognition of his disability, about his agreement or refusal to participate in such research in the future (so-called medical will).
>
> For person, who is unable to give informed consent, his samples of biological material for scientific research may be taken only if such probant has been previously informed in a form understandable to him and in the presence of his legal representative about all the essential circumstances provided in Paragraph 1 of the previous article, subsequently he has clearly not refused to be a probant and it must be confirmed in writing by the legal representative.
>
> Collection of biological material, which requires operative intervention in a minor or disabled probant, may be carried out only in his or her direct interest.
>
> Collection of biological material in a minor or disabled probant, which takes place without physical or minimal intervention (blood test, etc.) or involves the use of biological material obtained by diagnostic and/or therapeutic measures, is also permitted in cases of research without the expected direct benefit, if there are no other alternative methods for carrying out such research, and only with the consent of the legal representative.
>
> The informed consent of a probant concerned or, to the extent permitted by law, the person authorized to do so is valid only if the biobank manager fulfils the obligation of explanation, as required by the previous article and in Part 1 of this article, provided it complied with its written form.[13]

Such norm-formulation meets the requirements for the consent to medical intervention provided for in Part 1, Art.43 of the Fundamentals of the Ukrainian legislation on healthcare, including the specifics of giving informed consent by legal representatives of minors and the disabled. The special feature of the proposed norm is that the probant is not always a patient at the same time, since it is also possible to research biological materials of healthy persons, and transfer of biological materials for research is not always accompanied by medical intervention.

Although it should be noted that it is in the case of minors and disabled persons (with no legal capacity) research can be carried out only for the benefit of such persons (for the purpose of diagnosis or treatment of certain diseases—i.e. direct benefit) that excludes the possibility of carrying out research on biological materials of healthy minors or disabled persons, and hence the peculiarity of this category of probants is that they will always be patients by legal status at the same time.

The peculiarity of the proposed wording as compared to the above-mentioned norm of Art.43 of the Fundamentals of the Law of Ukraine on Healthcare is that we consider it necessary, with reference to Art.12 of the Recommendation CM/Rec (2016)6, to explain not only to the legal representative but also to the person whom he represents in an understandable to him form to avoid the possibility of carrying out such research and retrieving biological material against the will of such persons, i.e. forcibly, while at the same time ensuring respect for their dignity.

[13] Kvit (2020), p. 172.

The proposed wording also emphasizes the dual legal nature of a biobank as a combination of biological material and personal data of the probant. This means that informed consent of the probant must also include his consent to the processing of his personal data by a biobank manager, which presupposes that the text of the consent must specify the way the data are processed and its consequences, specifically, in the case of pseudonymization of the data of the probant, his personal relationship to the biological material is preserved and it is possible for the researcher to provide feedback to him, for example in the case of presentation of research results or reveal of important additional unexpected results. It is also possible for the probant to exercise his right to refusal of previously given informed consent in whole or in part, while anonymization of the probant's personal data means discontinuation of the personal relation with the probant's biological material, it means that it is impossible for the probant to exercise the above-mentioned rights. Therefore, it is important to provide this information in informed consent, which will ensure that the probant is completely informed and that the biobank manager is able to refer, in the case of a conflict with the probant, to the text of the informed consent given to him as written evidence.

In the context of peculiarities of the processing of personal data, based on the content of this norm, namely that the biological materials of minors and disabled persons may be researched only in their direct interest, it may be concluded that the personal data of such persons cannot be anonymized, whereas the interests of such persons cannot be protected in such case, since it is impossible to provide feedback and the results of such research. It is therefore quite understandable that for this category of probants only pseudonymization is a possible way of processing personal data.

It is also important to note that, from the point of view of ensuring the freedom of scientific and research activities, the possibility of the probant to give so-called general consent for the use of his biological materials in future studies is important and enshrined in Part 1 of this article; in turn, it relieves the researcher of the relatively onerous obligation to obtain a new informed consent of the probant, while examining samples for the purpose, which at the time of obtaining consent could not be foreseen.

It is understandable that science is developing and new research is constantly becoming necessary, and if possibilities for giving general consent were not provided for in legislation, this would automatically mean that a biobank, established with a specific purpose, once achieved it, would be subject to destruction or would require the consent of all the probants for future research, which would substantially restrict future scientific activity. However, it is worth noting here that when such general consent is given to future research by the probant, he does not forfeit the right to withdraw such consent at any time without explanation of the reasons except as provided by the law. Consequently, this norm is one of the balancing elements that aim to balance the right to self-determination of the probant with the freedom of scientific and research activity.

2.2.3 Other Information Rights of a Probant, Included in his Right to Self-Determination

The next important element of the probants right to self-determination is guaranteeing his other information rights, which we believe should be enshrined in the information duties of the biobank manager.

These information rights flow out of the principle of individual feedback, which is regulated in the Art. 17 of the Recommendation CM/Rec (2016)6. Namely, in paragraph 1 it is stated that findings that are relevant for the health of the persons resulting from the use of their biological materials, including persons who, according to law, are not able to consent must be subject for a feedback. In line with Art. 10, par.1, of this Recommendation, the issue of feedback on potential health-related findings should be addressed when consent or authorisation is requested. More specifically, the persons concerned should be informed about whether, and if so, how, feedback on potential health-related findings will be provided. In the context of this Article the principles concerning biomedical research contained in Chapter VIII "Confidentiality and right to information" of the Additional Protocol must be also applied. Art.17 par. 2 also sets out that, where feedback is provided, this should take place within a framework of appropriate health care or counselling.

It is also important to emphasize, that the right to know "goes hand in hand" with respect for the wish of an individual not to be informed about findings that are relevant to their health. The right not to know can also be exercised in the different way, namely to exercise their right to know under certain circumstances and such wishes should also be respected. The right to know or respect for the wish not to be informed may be restricted in the individual's own interest or else on the basis of Art. 26, par. 1 of the Convention on Human Rights and Biomedicine, for example, in order to protect the rights of another person (e.g. where the information would allow preventive or curative action relating to the health of a minor) or when necessary in a democratic society in the interest of public safety, for the prevention of crime or for the protection of public health. Additionally, the last paragraph of Art. 10 of the Convention sets out that in exceptional cases national law may place restrictions on the right to know or respect for the wish not to be informed in the interests of the individual's health.

Taking into consideration the abovementioned recommendations, we propose that other information duties of a biobank manager should be regulated in a separate article of the special law as follows:

> Other information duties of a biobank manager.
>
> The biobank manager is obliged to report immediately a probant or authorized person, who gave the informed consent, on the results of the research, including the unforeseen abnormalities or diseases detected in the research if the person has already given consent and did not refuse to be provided with such information.
>
> If research has been carried out by an authorized user of a biobank, the information specified in Part 1 of this article is given to a probant or authorized person by the biobank manager.

> If an unforeseen abnormality or disease is detected, which gives reason to believe that the person/persons, genetically related to the probant, may also have a detected disease or an abnormality which can be preventable or treated, such information has to be reported in accordance with Part 1 of this Article.

Legislative recognition of the duty of a biobank manager to inform a probant or authorized person giving informed consent in the interest of the probant about the results of the research, including unforeseen findings, i.e., additional findings, is of great importance because it is intended to protect the interests of the probant as well as genetically related persons by enabling him to respond in a timely manner and to seek help from specialists in order to prevent or treat the detected disease or abnormality.

It is also worth noting that use of the evaluative concept "immediately" concerning the duty to report results of the research or additional findings is not accidental and provides for transfer of mentioned information without deliberate delay by the biobank manager. Such formulation should ensure that the essential information is provided promptly for the timely organization of preventive or curative measures.

It is also important to note that only a legally capable probant, who personally signed the informed consent, may refuse to provide such information, as the refusal to provide such information, done by the authorized person in the informed consent will be insignificant, since such actions clearly do not correspond to the interests of a minor or disabled (legally incapable) probant, as we have mentioned before, the research on the biological materials of such persons may only be carried out only in their interests.

2.2.4 The Right of a Probant to Consent Withdrawal

Another important element of the probant's right to self-determination is his right to consent withdrawal. This particular right is to be found in Art.13 of the Recommendation CM/Rec (2016)6, which in the first paragraph provides that a person who has provided consent to storage of identifiable biological materials for future research purposes should, without being subject to any form of discrimination, in particular regarding the right to medical care, retain the right to withdraw consent at any time. This provision reaffirms the principle introduced in Article 5 of the Convention on Human Rights and Biomedicine that freedom of consent implies an unconditional right to withdraw consent at any time and without specification of reason. When the person has withdrawn his or her consent, the Article provides that he or she should have the right to have, in the manner foreseen by national law, the biological materials and associated data either destroyed or rendered non-identifiable. Certain flexibility is therefore left for national systems to choose between these possibilities. The person who is considering withdrawing consent should be made aware of any limitations on withdrawal of his or her biological materials, which is one more information duty of the biobank manager. The Recommendation also emphasises that it is best practice to, where possible, offer any person who has provided consent to storage of identifiable biological materials for future research the possibility to alter the scope of that consent.

It is also very important to specify such a right in the situation where the biological materials stored for future research have been removed from a person who, according to law, was not able to consent, which is done in Art13 par.2. It provides that the representative, authority, person or body provided for by law having given authorisation for storage for future research of the identifiable biological materials should, without any form of discrimination for the person from whom the materials have been removed, in particular regarding the right to medical care, retain the right to withdraw authorisation at any time, and where possible should also be able to alter the scope of that authorisation. Where the person from whom biological materials have been removed attains or regains the capacity to consent, he or she should have the rights set out in par. 1. In particular the basis for this provision is Art.26 of the Convention on Human Rights and Biomedicine. It should be noted that, in a similar manner, no restrictions should be placed on the exercise of the rights and protective provisions contained in this Recommendation other than such as are prescribed by law and are necessary in a democratic society in the interest of public safety, for the protection of public health, or for the protection of the rights and freedoms of others.

It is important to emphasize here, that as any biobank consists not only of biological materials but also of the personal data of a probant, accordingly, withdrawal of the consent may relate to withdrawal of the consent to use both biological materials and personal data of the sample for research purposes, which entails the destruction of both the probes/samples and the data of a probant, and can also be manifested in requirement of a probant to anonymise his personal data, which automatically means allowing a biobank manager to handle the biological material of the probant on his own, since, as a result of the anonymization of personal data, the probant loses personal connection with the biological material and its further use is possible without probant's consent and is done by a biobank manager at his sole discretion.

Thus, it is also necessary to regulate in detail the right of a probant to withdraw the consent, which we propose to enshrine in a separate article of a special law and to reformulate it as follows:

> The right of a probant/authorized person to withdraw the consent.
>
> A probant or authorized person may at any time, considering the future, withdraw the informed consent given previously to the biobank manager in whole or in part in writing or orally. If the withdrawal of consent has been made orally, the biobank manager is obliged to document this fact immediately.
>
> The biobank manager is obliged to notify the researcher about the withdrawal of the consent if possible.
>
> The biobank manager is obliged to inform the probant and/or the authorized person about the possibility and consequences of withdrawal of the consent.
>
> If the probant or authorized person has withdrawn the consent in whole, the biological material of the probant has to be destroyed or handed over to the probant or authorized

> person (with his/her consent) but personal data of the probant which were held in the biobank have to be erased. In the case if the research of the samples and data of the probe is ongoing at the time when the consent has been withdrawn, the researcher could continued using them only if the competent ethics committee has agreed and if the researcher can prove, that the withdrawal of the consent would make it impossible to carry out the research, which has already been launched, and to achieve the purpose, which has previously been agreed with the probant.
>
> In the case when the probant withdraws his consent in a part of the processing of his personal data, i.e. the probant's requirement to anonymize his personal data, his data are be anonymized and his biological materials, transferred him to the biobank manager for research, are to be used at his discretion, as a result of which the probant loses personal connection with the biological material and control over his further fate.

This article enshrines not only the right of the probant to withdraw consent, but also sets out clearly defined duties of a biobank manager, which are closely related to him. In particular, there is an established duty to inform the probant and/or the authorized person about possibilities and consequences of such withdrawal of the consent, and a duty, in the case of the oral withdrawal of the consent, to document it, in the end, such withdrawal must always be reduced in writing. Also, there is an established duty of a biobank manager to notify the user about withdrawal of the consent if possible, which means that the biobank manager, having the connection to the user, must provide him with the information about withdrawal of the probant's consent and the need to destroy samples and data. However, if, due to reasons independent of a biobank manager, he is unable to contact the user (for example, if the foreign subject, died (the individual researcher) was liquidated or reorganized (if the legal person) and it is impossible to find him or his successor), it is logical that in this case the biobank manager is relieved from such obligation because of the objective impossibility of its realization.

It is also important that this article gives clear instructions on the actions of the biobank manager, and depending on the extent of such withdrawal it determines its legal consequences. Also, in order to ensure the freedom of scientific activity and to avoid creating too narrow framework for researchers by ensuring the unrestricted right to self-determination of a probant, this article contains an exception to the rule, which restricts a little the right of a probant to withdraw consent, but sets a clear framework and conditions for such restriction.

In particular, part four of this article establishes the exceptional possibility to keep using samples and/or data of the probant despite his withdrawal, but only if such withdrawal would make it totally impossible to achieve the purpose of the research, previously agreed with the probant. It means that the researcher would then have to prove to the ethics commission that the withdrawal of consent and, as a consequence, the destruction of samples and/or data would make it totally impossible to carry out the on-going research and thus achieve its purpose, previously agreed with the probant. If these facts are proved, the ethics committee has to issue the approval. In our view, this norm will establish balance between the rights of the probants and the rights of researchers and ensure their balanced implementation in practice.

2.3 Legal Regulation of Future Use of Biological Material/Data, Initially Collected for Research Purposes in Connection with Data Protection

Future use of biological materials and health-related personal data for research purposes, which in our opinion, is also an important issue in the context of regulating the legal status of biobanks and probants and must be regulated by a separate part of a special law.

2.3.1 Types of Personal Data of a Probant

The issue of the protection of personal data and technologies used to do so, namely coding, is bound up with the previous issue. In order to ensure the correct interpretation of the proposed norms, it is obvious to include in a special law such definitions of the terms:

Health-related personal data are considered to be information on health, diseases, including genetic data of a person, enabling to identify this person.

Genetic data is information on human heredity received in genetic research.

Anonymized biological materials and personal data are biological and health-related personal data, their connection to a particular person cannot be established or their definition requires excessive effort.

2.3.2 Ways of Protection of Personal Data as a Tool to Ensure the Rights of a Probant in the Case of Future Use of his Biological Material and Data

Firstly, it is important to establish a framework for the future use of biological material and genetic data because of their particular sensitivity.

The data protection duty is based on the Art.7 of the Recommendation CM/Rec (2016)6, which reaffirms in Par. 1 the principle of confidentiality of information of a personal nature collected in the field of research on biological materials, thereby reaffirming the principle introduced in Art. 8 of the European Convention on Human Rights and reiterated in the Convention for the Protection of Individuals with regard to Automatic Processing of Personal Data. It should be also pointed out that, under Art. 6 of the latter Convention, personal data concerning health constitute a special category of data and are as such subject to special regulation. This principle was also reiterated in Art.10 of the Convention on Human Rights and Biomedicine. The Art.7 Par.2 of the Recommendation CM/Rec (2016)6 also requires that biological materials should only be obtained, stored, transferred and used in such conditions as to ensure the confidential nature of the data which may be associated or may be obtained from them. The main aim of this provision is to avoid against unauthorised access or use.

In this context there is a need to mention, that the Recommendation CM/Rec (2016)6 in Art.11 Par.3 states, that biological materials previously removed for another purpose and already non-identifiable may be stored for future research subject to authorisation provided for by law. This norm means, that if there are some non-identifiable samples removed and stored for some other purpose, they can be used for research but only after proper authorization. This provision also proves, how important it is, also, when there is no more recognizable connection of the sample with the person, to protect it from an unauthorized usage, because almost all samples carry with it the genetic information, which means, that its full anonymization is impossible. And even when the biological material is non-identifiable it must be protected by law, because it cannot be used in any way, by anyone and for any purpose.

So, the most complicated question, which arises when we evaluate the protection of personal data in biobanking is that not only the data itself must be protected, but also some types of biobanking substances can be also qualified as personal data. This question was subject for the research of Dara Hallinan and she suggested that the concept of personal data can be usefully broken down into two aspects of any processing operation. First, the substance being processed: to qualify as personal data, a substance must be able to fulfil three criteria. A substance must be 'information', it must 'relate to' a specific person, and that person must be a 'natural person'. In the biobanking context, health, lifestyle, and biographical information, sequenced genomic data, and individual research results certainly fulfil these criteria. Second, the link between the substance and a specific individual: to qualify as personal data, a substance must relate to an individual who is 'identified or identifiable'. All biobanking substances processed in either linked or pseudonymised form will certainly qualify as 'identified or identifiable'.[14]

In particular, it should be formalized in a separate article that biological material and genetic data, coded and not coded, may be transferred for future use for the research purposes if the person from whom it originates, and, in cases prescribed by law, their legal representatives or close relatives give their consent after being properly informed. Such consent may be withdrawn by the subject who has given it at any time without giving reasons. At the same time, biological material and genetic data in an anonymised form may be transferred for further use for the research purposes if the person from whom they originate, legal representatives or close relatives have been properly informed and have given their written consent. The withdrawal of such consent after the anonymization procedure is impossible.

The use of non-genetic and health-related personal data, which should be regulated in a separate article of a special law, is also given certain specifics. In particular, such data, not coded and coded, may be transferred for future use for research purposes if the person concerned, and, in cases prescribed by law, his legal representatives or close relatives, have given consent, after being properly informed. Such consent may be withdrawn at any time by the person who has given it, without

[14] Hallinan (2021).

giving reasons. The procedure for receiving such consent is subject to the general requirements established by a special law.

In addition, within this part, a separate article should deal with the legal consequences of absence of consent and information provided for in the previous articles, namely, that in such cases objects 'may be used for further scientific research only if:

- the proper information is provided and consent or prohibition cannot be received or require excessive efforts;
- there is no documented withdrawal of the person from whom the biological material and data originate;
- destruction of such research object due to the impossibility of receiving consent may make it impossible to continue such research and may significantly impair the expected benefits of such research for persons suffering from severe and incurable diseases;
- all the above mentioned conditions are confirmed and approved by the competent ethics committee'.

It is also proposed that the requirements and procedure for correct and safe anonymisation and coding of such personal data of probants, as well as the grounds and conditions for decoding are clearly defined in Law of Ukraine "On Protection of Personal Data".[15]

3 Conclusions

As the result of the analysis of the EU regulation and recommendations on the research use of human biological materials and related data we have concluded the absence of the proper regulation in the national law and the need for adopting a special law "On legal regulation of research activities involving human subjects and using biobanks", aimed at: setting limits to the permissibility of such research; to promote the quality, competence and transparency of research carrying out, and to protect dignity, inviolability and health of a person in the course of carrying out research activities regarding him.

A general concept has been defined for the regulation of the legal guarantees of the non-property rights of probants, balancing them with the interests of science and freedom of scientific/research activity.

The legal status of probants has been determined, which is bound up to the legal status of the researcher (a biobank manager or its users) and is disclosed through the right of a probant to self-determination, which is exercised in several stages and needs to be consolidated by establishing: firstly, the duties of a biobank manager, corresponding to this right, to explain to the participant the purpose of the collection

[15]The Law of Ukraine 'On protection of personal data' (2010) No 2297-17 https://zakon.rada.gov.ua/laws/show/2297-17#Text.

and use of his biological material and personal data and possible results of such research, and to provide adequate information on all risks of his involvement in such research, secondly, an integral part of the right to self-determination of a probant and his autonomy security is his right to express his will, that is, to give informed consent for transfer of his biological material and personal data to a biobank, the right of a probant to withdraw his consent and possible ways of its legal restriction in the interests of scientific progress, as well as other information rights of a probant.

A classification of human research types has been carried out, and ways have been identified to protect the personal data of a probant, in the form of pseudonymization and anonymization. The conditions for the permissibility of transferring the parts of a biobank for both research and non-research purposes, as well as the possibility of further using the biomaterial and data obtained initially for a diagnostic or therapeutic purpose, have been proposed.

References

BBMRI-ERIC response to COVID-19 (2020) Resources from biobanks across Europe available for research on SARS-CoV-2 and COVID-19. https://www.bbmri-eric.eu/wp-content/uploads/BBMRI-ERIC-response-to-COVID-2.10.pdf

Biobanking best practices for COVID-19 specimens and the role of LIMS. https://cloudlims.com/blog/biobanking-best-practices-for-covid-19-specimens.html

COVID-19 Research BBMRI-ERIC: making new treatments possible. https://www.bbmri-eric.eu/covid-19/.

Hallinan D (2021) Protecting genetic privacy in biobanking though data protection law https://oxford.universitypressscholarship.com/view/10.1093/oso/9780192896476.001.0001/oso-9780192896476. https://doi.org/10.1093/oso/9780192896476.001.0001.

Hofman P, Puchois P, Brest P et al (2020) Possible consequences of the COVID-19 pandemic on the use of biospecimens from cancer biobanks for research in academia and bioindustry. Nat Med 26:809–810. https://doi.org/10.1038/s41591-020-0890-8

Kvit N (2020) Informed consent in Biobank-Donor relations: proper regulation for Ukraine needed. Int J Supremance Law 1:167–174

O'Neill OA (2002) Question of trust: the Bbc Reith lectures 2002. Cambridge University Press

Recommendation CM/Rec(2016)6 of the Committee of Ministers of the Council of Europe to member States on research on biological materials of human origin adopted on 11 May 2016. https://search.coe.int/cm/Pages/result_details.aspx?ObjectId=090000168064e8ff

Vaught J (2020) Biobanking during the COVID-19 pandemic. Biopreserv Biobank 18:153–154. https://doi.org/10.1089/bio.2020.29069.jjv

Towards Effective Medical Disputes Resolution in Ukraine and Lithuania: Comparing Analyses, Challenges and Perspectives

Iryna Izarova and Vigita Vėbraitė

Contents

Abstract Health law as well as medical law are new branches of law in the modern world which cannot be attributed to such traditional areas as civil and labour; at the same time, they are gradually gaining their place in the legal system of each state. Ensuring the proper exercise of a person's right to health care is an important duty on the path to the sustainable development of society, while disputes arising in the field of health care, medical services and medical care are among the most difficult in judicial practice. This leads to a new area of regulation evolving to find the most effective ways to protect the rights of medical relations between patients and doctors. The coronavirus pandemic revealed problems that exist in the health care system and prompted more active comparative legal research on the ways to resolve health disputes. The Lithuanian experience in medical dispute resolution was chosen due to the new provisions of law, according to which, since 1 January 2020, the no-fault

This chapter was prepared in the frame of the scientific project " Strengthening of alternative dispute resolution in Lithuania and Ukraine: Finding the cross-border solution" Project No. (2019) 7263870-25/11/2019.

I. Izarova (✉)
School of Law, Taras Shevchenko National University of Kyiv, Kyiv, Ukraine
e-mail: irina.izarova@knu.ua

V. Vėbraitė
Faculty of Law, Vilnius University, Vilnius, Lithuania
e-mail: vigita.vebraite@tf.vu.lt

© The Author(s), under exclusive license to Springer Nature Switzerland AG 2022
R. Maydanyk et al. (eds.), *Ukrainian Healthcare Law in the Context of European and International Law*, European Union and its Neighbours in a Globalized World 7,
https://doi.org/10.1007/978-3-031-05690-1_9

compensation model is implemented. In this article we propose to explore the notion of medical disputes through the definition of medical law in Ukrainian and Lithuanian law doctrine. Analysis of national case law in the health care field allows for the identification of advantages and disadvantages in terms of ensuring effective protection of the rights of persons involved. In the concluding remarks we propose a comprehensive application of special alternative methods to settle medical disputes which takes into account specifics and ensures the effective protection of an individual's right to adequate medical care.

1 Introduction: Background and Objectives of the Study

The Universal Declaration of Human Rights declared the right of every person to a standard of living adequate for the health and well-being of oneself and one's family, including medical care.[1] Since then, attention to the realization of an individual's right to health and medical care has increased significantly, while there is yet no unity of views on its nature and essence.

Some degree of health law harmonization was arrived at in the EU, where health legislation was adopted under the Treaty on the Functioning of the European Union, article 168, which is related to public health protection, as well as article 153 on social policy. In particular, the EU health law includes patients' rights in such areas as cross-border health care, pharmaceuticals and medical devices, serious cross border health threats, tobacco, organs, blood, tissues and cells.[2]

In the meantime, as it was rightly noted, the result, in general, is not a united EU policy but "a complex system of partial overlapping national and EU competences that at various points both come into conflict and complement each other."[3]

Health law, in the EU, is a complex discipline which is difficult to define due to its varying rates of development in different states, as well as differing widely used terms like health care law or medical law.[4] The most appropriate notion is definitely 'health', as this was chosen by the WHO. According to Hervey and McHale, health law is the best term due to its recognition by national societies and programs, as well as by academic press, which witnesses matters for the academic and practitioners' communities. Nevertheless, some details below prove that using the proper title follows the national doctrine and legislation.

---

[1] The United Nations (1948).

[2] An official website of the European Union (2020) EU Health Policy https://ec.europa.eu/health/policies/overview_en; European Commission (2020) The EU Health Policy Platform https://webgate.ec.europa.eu/hpf/.

[3] Guy and Sauter (2016).

[4] Hervey and McHale (2015), pp. 30–70.

Medical law is considered as a branch of law which covers the relations of medical professionals and their patients. Among the branches of medical law there are the law of torts (medical malpractice), criminal offences, medical ethics, as well as health law and regulation.

In contrast, health law means the field of law that regulates relations between providers, payers and vendors of the health care industry and patients, by means of the delivery of health care services.[5]

The differences between these definitions in many cases also depend on the specifics of how the national health care system is organized, as well as health care standards, and so on. Among the differences between health law and medical law, which stand out in science, there is a concern with individual human rights, professional liability, access to and practicing health care and regulating health care institutions, funding and organization of health system, public health and regulation of human material in a health context. At the same time, it should be recognized that national approaches to the doctrinal definition of the field of law are a priority.

In Ukraine, health care law and medical law is formed gradually. The implementation of the right to medical care and health care, enshrined in the Constitution of Ukraine, has become a proper basis for this. At the same time, the term 'health law' is not used, therefore, the determining factor for the development of this legal category is the stage of its development in national law and legislation.

In recent decades, the concept of medical law in Ukraine has been established primarily on the basis of practical needs, because everyone throughout life inevitably becomes a subject of relations regarding the provision of medical care, so there is a need for an effective legal mechanism to ensure human rights to medical care.[6]

At the same time, national legislation does not provide a comprehensive answer, not only to questions concerning medical law or health care law, but also to other central institutions. In particular, the Constitution of Ukraine enshrines the right of a person to health care, medical assistance and health insurance, and health care is provided by state funding of relevant programs; the state provides conditions for effective and affordable medical care (Article 49).[7] But the concept of medical care is not disclosed in the Constitution of Ukraine, and it was absent in the Fundamentals of Health Care Legislation and other regulations.[8]

Only in 2011 and 2017 were the relevant laws amended to define the concepts of 'health care' and 'medical care' (Article 3). The established notion of health care

---

[5] It is noteworthy, that the Journal of Medicine and Law, published by Bril, was replaced by the European Journal of Health Law in 1994, the official journal of the European Association of Health Law.

[6] Bolotina (1999), pp. 116–121; Bolotina (2005).

[7] The Constitution of Ukraine (1996).

[8] See in particular the decision of the CCU from 25.11.1998 No 15-rp/98 in the case on the constitutional petition of 66 people's deputies of Ukraine on compliance with the Constitution of Ukraine (constitutionality) of the Resolution of the Cabinet of Ministers of Ukraine "On approval of the list of paid services provided in state health care facilities and higher medical educational institutions" (case on paid medical services).

covers all entities that can carry out economic activities in medical practice to preserve and restore physiological and psychological functions, optimal performance and social activity. According to the law, medical care is the activity of professionally trained medical workers aimed at prevention, diagnosis, treatment and rehabilitation in connection with diseases, injuries, poisonings and pathological conditions, as well as in connection with pregnancy and childbirth.

The definition of medical service is limited to the indication of special requirements for the subject of service provision, namely licensing of business activities in medical practice, without defining the features of these services.

On the other hand, Ukraine has been trying, since 1998, to develop and implement legislation on compulsory state social insurance. In particular, in accordance with the current legislation (though, not implemented in practice), the compulsory state social insurance provides health insurance, including diagnosis and outpatient treatment; inpatient treatment; provision of medicine and medical devices; preventive and educational measures; and the provision of medical rehabilitation for persons who have undergone particularly difficult operations or have chronic diseases. The scope of services provided at the expense of compulsory health insurance is determined by the basic and territorial programs of compulsory health insurance, which are approved in the manner prescribed by law.[9]

However, this has influenced the formation of doctrinal approaches to the definition of medical or health law. The relationship that arises between physician and patient is considered central to medical law.[10] At the same time, there are definitions of medical law as a complex branch of law that regulate relations in the field of health care, in particular, the provision of medical care, in order to ensure human rights in the field of health care;[11] it is also seen as an institution of social security law.

The most reasonable position is that medical law is a comprehensive branch of law,[12] where it is necessary to distinguish between public and private relations. The latter includes the obligation to provide medical services (in accordance with relevant agreement), a unilateral promise or actions in the interests of a third party without a power of attorney. Such relations are characterized by equality of the parties, so they are subject to the relevant rules of civil law, which gives us reason to distinguish the relevant categories of cases considered in civil proceedings—these are cases arising from the relationship between medical services. Public relations include those that secure the right to compulsory state social insurance and health insurance as its part.

[9]Osnovy Zakonodavstva Ukrainy Pro Zahalnooboviazkove Derzhavne Sotsialne Strakhuvannia (1998) (Fundamentals of the legislation of Ukraine on compulsory state social insurance) with amendments https://zakon.rada.gov.ua/laws/show/16/98-вр#Text.

[10]Hubskyi et al. (2007); Klymenko (2012), pp. 107–109.

[11]Encyclopedia of Modern Ukraine (2018) Medychne Pravo (Medical Law). http://esu.com.ua/search_articles.php?id=66077.

[12]Maydanyk (2010), pp. 52–66. See also Buletsa (2016), Gerts (2016), p. 14.

Accordingly, the definition of Ukrainian medical law allows for the identification of a number of conflicts that arise from these legal relations and are specific to this branch of law. At the same time, some uncertainty in the relationship covered and governed by medical or health law creates uncertainty about the application of complex rules to dispute resolution and protection of rights.

On the other hand, in Lithuania there is no exact definition of medical law. Different law areas regulate specific issues. Medical services provided by the State are regulated by public law; rights of the patients are regulated by public and private law; emerging challenges in the healthcare field, arising out of the development of medical technologies and biotechnologies are also regulated by intellectual property rules; also, some questions in the medical field are regulated by EU law.

Thus, in our article we will try to outline the main features of medical disputes, analyse ways to resolve them and determine the extent of how effective the protection of a person's rights is in such conflicts. The comparative component of our study will help to determine the features of the effective resolution of such disputes within the national justice system. It has been chosen to compare Ukraine and Lithuanian systems because of the cultural and institutional similarities. In both countries public medical services are much more developed than private funded medical services, also the Lithuanian experience in medical dispute resolution was chosen due to the new provisions of law, according to which, since 1 January 2020, the no-fault compensation model is implemented.

2 The Notion of Medical Disputes

Disputes arise from relations, as without them there can be no conflicts. Therefore, almost all types and forms of social relations may cause conflicts between their parties, which are on either side of the conflict. As we may define the relations covered by medical law or health law, we may define the disputes, which arise from these relations.

Relations related to medical services, as well as health care relations, may be the proper ground for various types of disputes.

Almost all types and forms of social relations can potentially become the basis of conflicts between their participants. As we can identify relations in the sphere of medical or health care law, we can identify disputes that arise from such relations. At the same time, the lack of specificity of these cases gives rise to their ambiguous nature, as they also belong to more traditional categories of cases (consumer protection disputes, contractual disputes, insurance contracts disputes, etc.).

Relations in the sphere of health services, as well as relations within health care can be a valid basis for all sorts of disputes, from breach of obligations under a health care contract to malpractice. At the same time, referring individual disputes to the category of medical, one should focus on those of them that relate to the concepts of medical law, not those related to violations of other obligations (i.e., the violation of the payment procedure under the contract for medical services should be classified as a contractual dispute rather than a medical one, because the specifics of the dispute are not related to the complex nature of medical legal relations arising between its parties).

It is usually recognized that medical disputes belong to a highly specialised legal area involving a complex intertwining of law and medicine. The topic of medical disputes, i.e., disputes between patients and healthcare institutions, whether they are resolved before the courts or behind closed doors, has been scarcely explored in Lithuania. Neither specific statistical information on such disputes is collected, nor specific data on how long the resolution of such disputes takes is available. In Lithuanian law, an issue of compensation for damage suffered by patients is generally analysed through a general assessment of the scope of delictual liability, which is a pre-condition for that liability, and through an analysis of the civil liability of the doctor.

Among the diversity of national judicial practice and based on medical law definition in Ukrainian law doctrine, we can classify several categories of cases as medical ones considered in civil proceedings:

(1) disputes over contracts for medical services
    a. on compensation of damage,[13]
    b. on invalidation of agreements;[14]
(2) disputes regarding compensation for damages caused by illegal actions by doctors.[15]

Similar in nature and subject to contractual relations are the categories of disputes arising from health insurance contracts with insurance companies (3), in particular, regarding the reimbursement of medical expenses.[16]

The lion's share of cases, concerning the protection of a person's right to health care and proper medical care, contain claims for damages. The basis for compensation for damage caused to a person is either contractual liability, i.e., determined by the contract for medical services concluded between the parties, or tortious, i.e., which occurs for causing harm to a person, in particular, due to the actions of medical workers. This is regulated by the Central Committee of Ukraine and is determined at the discretion of the person applying to the court for protection. The

[13] See, for example: The Resolution of the Supreme Court of Ukraine (2019) in the case No 643/4417/16-ц. https://reyestr.court.gov.ua/Review/83925606.

[14] See: The Decision of Pischanskyi Raion Court in Vinnytsia Oblast (2019) in the case No 134/845/18. https://reyestr.court.gov.ua/Review/81402504; The Resolution of the Supreme Court of Ukraine (2020) in the case No 134/845/18. https://reyestr.court.gov.ua/Review/87640383.

[15] The Decision of the Suvorovskyi Raion Court in the city of Odessa (2018) in the case No 523/12321/15-ц. https://reyestr.court.gov.ua/Review/72583382. See also The Decision of the Terebovlia Raion Court (2019) in the case No 606/2209/17. https://reyestr.court.gov.ua/Review/86020339.

[16] See, among others the Resolution of the Supreme Court of Ukraine (2020) in the case No 761/19072/18. https://reyestr.court.gov.ua/Review/92315161.

onset of tort liability for damage to health requires the following conditions: illegal behaviour of the person who caused the damage, the presence of damage, the causal link between wrongful conduct and damage, and the presence of guilt. At the same time, in these cases there is a presumption of guilt of the perpetrator, who must prove the absence of guilt.[17] The victim proves the facts of the damage with the participation of the defendant, the amount of damage, as well as the fact that the defendant is the causer of the damage. At the same time, many cases in national jurisdiction can be attributed to the so-called meritless cases where the plaintiff is denied satisfaction of the claim as declared without grounds or without evidence of causation.

Fact finding of a person's wrongful conduct causing the damage, the presence of damage as well as the causal link between wrongful conduct and damage in such specific disputes as medical is based on forensic examination, which greatly complicates the trial and resolution of such cases. In particular, attention should be paid to the conditions in which such an examination of a patient suffering from improperly provided medical care may be carried out, as well as the temporal boundaries and the likelihood of unambiguous conclusions. What will also significantly affect the terms of consideration of such a case is that according to the current Ukrainian civil procedural legislation, cases that require examination are considered, in general, claim proceedings.

The most widely known medical dispute is medical malpractice, which is a legal cause that occurs when medical or health services deviate from standards, causing injury to the patient. Medical malpractice is a common term used widely, but not in Ukraine.

Medical negligence or carelessness in Ukraine qualifies as a crime under Article 140 of the Criminal Code of Ukraine, namely a failure or improper performance, by a medical or pharmaceutical worker, of professional duties due to negligent or dishonest treatment, if this then causes serious consequences for the patient.

This necessitates the establishment of liability of the employee in criminal proceedings, and only then is it possible to apply for damages compensation in civil proceedings.

At the same time, it should be noted that since 2016, Ukraine has introduced regulations for the clinical expert commissions of the Ministry of Health, which is an advisory body operating on a permanent or temporary basis, formed for the peer review of appeals on quality assessment of provision of medical services.[18] The decision of such commissions on the improper quality of the provided medical services concerns the administrative activity of specially authorized subjects concerned with the right method to check the quality of the medical service provided

[17] See: The Supreme Court of Ukraine (2014) The decision in the case № 3-51rc14 from August 19, 2014. https://protocol.ua/ua/postanova_vsu_vid_19_08_2014_roku_u_spravi_3_51gs14/. The Supreme Court of Ukraine (2019) The decision in the case № 643/4417/16- ц from 28 August 2019. https://reyestr.court.gov.ua/Review/83925606. See also Gerts (2016), p. 14.

[18] Ministry of Health of Ukraine (2016) Order No 69 of 05.02.2016 "On the organization of clinical and expert assessment of the quality of medical care and medical care". https://zakon.rada.gov.ua/laws/show/z0286-16#Text.

by the executor and received by the consumer. These cases are considered in administrative proceedings, while disputes concerning the protection of the right to health care should be considered in civil proceedings.[19]

In view of the abovementioned, analysing the categorical nature of private law medical disputes, we include, in the latter, those disputes arising from contracts for the provision of medical services or insurance, as well as those that deal with compensation for damage caused to the patient during the non-contractual provision of medical services.

It has been argued that two models of compensation for damage are prominent in developed countries when dealing with the issues of compensation for harm suffered due to the health care: the judicial claim model and the no-fault compensation for damage (the administrative model).[20] The main feature of the judicial claim model is that it is based on the imposition of civil liability for injury caused to a liable person. In that case the dispute is held between the patient and the healthcare institution (the healthcare specialist), where conditions of civil liability must be established and the functions of compensation for damage and prevention are exercised through the application of civil liability. In Lithuania, it was only the judicial compensation model that was applied before 1 January 2020, where only a court could have awarded compensation for damage. Compensation for damage was awarded based on the binding pretrial procedure for the resolution of disputes by referring to the commission for an evaluation of damage inflicted upon the health of patients under the Ministry of Health. In case of disagreement with the decision made, the issue of compensation for damage could have been resolved before courts where the conditions of civil liability were to be established in all cases when seeking the compensation of damage.

In 2020, the amendments to the Republic of Lithuania Law on the Rights of Patients and Compensation of the Damage to their Health came into force[21] whereby the model of no-fault compensation for damage came into force as well. This model serves as an alternative for the judicial resolution of medical disputes. The establishment of this model eliminates the duty to assess the doctor's fault, as this model is based on the evaluation of the suitability of a certain specific case in terms of receiving compensation for damage and that damage is awarded from a specific fund during the administrative proceedings. According to that system, the compensation shall be awarded where the commission for an evaluation of damage inflicted upon the health of patients establishes that damage was inflicted upon the health of the patient when providing the healthcare services to that person and that it was not the imminent damage. This decision shall be made without taking account of the fault of the healthcare institution and healthcare specialist who inflicted that damage. The

[19] Kharkiv District Administrative Court (2019) Decision in the case No 82943794 of 11.07.2019. https://youcontrol.com.ua/catalog/court-document/82943794/.

[20] Morkūnaitė (2017), p. 115.

[21] Register of Legal Acts (2019) The amendments to the Republic of Lithuania Law on the Rights of Patients and Compensation of the Damage to their Health No 2019-12799.

persons who disagree with the decision adopted by the commission for an evaluation of damage inflicted upon the health of patients shall have the right to bring an action before the ordinary court following the procedure established by the Code of Civil Procedure with regard to the examination of the compensation for damage inflicted upon the health of the patient on the merits. The court is ordered to follow Article 24 of the Law on the Rights of Patients and Compensation of the Damage to their Health whereby it is entitled to award a higher or lower amount of compensation.

This officially provided system is defined as the binding pretrial procedure which must be employed by the patient or another person seeking compensation for damage following the procedure laid down in the Code of Civil Procedure.[22] Thus, it is not perceived as an alternative, voluntary system based on a free choice of the entity.

It must be noted that the commission for an evaluation of damage inflicted upon the health of patients, when considering the compensation for damage, must follow the amounts of non-material damage to be compensated for referred to in the description. It could be, therefore, stated that it is only the court that is fully entitled to compensate for damage in Lithuania.

We would assume that the current legal regulation is not sufficiently defined as it is not clear if full protection of the interests of the patients is ensured. The said regulation and the compensation system also suggest that the role of the courts in this process further remains fundamental. These disputes, to a large extent, are probably further resolved before the courts, and the issues arising out of the resolution of the disputes before the courts, for the regulation in question, are neither mentioned nor resolved.

Although the time limit for making a decision on the compensation for damage by the commission for an evaluation of damage inflicted upon the health of patients is set (at 20 working days from the receipt of the complaint by the healthcare institution), no other amendments to the legal regulation are proposed in parallel. There are no suggestions or considerations on the peculiarities of judicial proceedings in such disputes and how to assure shorter duration of court proceedings. Moreover, the surveys conducted by the Seimas Ombudsmen's Office revealed that the commission for an evaluation of damage inflicted upon the health of patients does not always follow the time limits set for the dispute resolution.[23]

---

[22] Official Gazette (2002) *Valstybės žinios* No 36-1340 with its successive amendments.

[23] For more information see: The Seimas Ombudsmen's Office of the Republic of Lithuania (2020) http://www.lrski.lt/naujausi-tyrimai/578-seimo-kontrolierius-konstatavo-kad-pacientu-sveikatai-padarytos-zalos-nustatymo-komisija-nepagristai-vilkino-pareiskimo-nagrinejima.html.

3 To Protect the Right to Health Care: Finding the Most Effective Way to Resolve Malpractice Disputes

The nuances of the realization that a person has the right to health care, proper medical care and medical services have led to an increase in the number of disputes arising over the provision of this right. The application of the judicial form of protection of these rights seems excessively formalized and costly, both in terms of time and money for both parties of such disputes. In itself, the nature of medical services is specific due to its temporal feature, i.e., the protection of rights must be carried out in a timely manner. At the same time, their cost is usually not high, and their number is large, so patients are not inclined, in the vast majority of cases, to go to court, but rather to change the doctor or medical institution.

Given the fact that patients and consumers of medical services can reasonably be attributed to weaker parties in the process[24] and in contractual relations,[25] ensuring the equal rights of each party in litigation is not easy.

Among the main problems of judicial settlement of so-called medical disputes are also: highly formalized judicial proceedings,[26] a determination of rights protection methods (the issue of the separation of contractual and tortious liability),[27] the need for forensic examinations[28] and other questions of evidence in such cases, such as the incorrect definition of the defendant in case,[29] etc.

At the same time, it is worth noting the growing attention and widespread use of alternative methods of resolving medical disputes as a faster and less costly settlement. In particular, even in China, research proves the effectiveness of mediation in medical disputes.[30] We can fully agree with the view that the performance of mediation mechanisms helps to resolve medical disputes and reduce the need for initiating litigation and may ultimately increase satisfaction with the healthcare system.[31]

Interest in an alternative solution of medical malpractice disputes arose in the late 1980s and early 1990s. The proliferation of out-of-court dispute resolution has logically led to the interest and desire to find more effective ways to protect people's rights to health care.

The advantages of using alternative dispute resolution (ADR) in medical malpractice disputes include decision making that is more qualified, medical professionals who are directly involved, a reduction in litigation cost and in the trauma of

---

[24] Lazic (2014).

[25] Škarka (2018).

[26] Šustek and Holčapek (2017), pp. 233–242.

[27] Seniuta (2011), pp. 11–18.

[28] Seniuta (2011), pp. 11–18.

[29] Melitopol district court of Zaporizhzha oblast (2018) Decision in the case № 320/5911/17 of 24.01.2018. https://reyestr.court.gov.ua/Review/72055166.

[30] Wang et al. (2020).

[31] Wang et al. (2020).

malpractice litigation, an improvement in the quality of expert witnesses, the handling of small cases, and dealing with frivolous litigation.[32]

Among the various schemes of ADR, used in dealing with medical malpractice, we have to mention the following:

(1) Risk management is created by hospitals to monitor and improve the quality of care, to avoid arising conflicts or the prompt identification of injuries that occurred.[33]
(2) Negotiation is the most informal form of ADR,[34] particularly when combined with early disclosure and apology programs, (e.g., "I am sorry" legislation), which allows physicians to offer confidential and inadmissible apologies, which may facilitate the resolving of disputes,[35] principally by reducing costs.
(3) Arbitration, where parties agree to use an arbitrator, a privately retained person,[36] and which is more formal and binding parties.[37] One of the popular forms is a pre-treatment arbitration agreement.[38] It was even proposed to establish permanent specialized arbitration courts for medical negligence disputes.[39]
(4) Mediation as a way to facilitate the parties' understanding of the nature of the dispute and finding the best solution, which does not require the applicable substantiated law principles.[40] The mediator may be an attorney or a retired judge, but the most successful are part of institutionalized mediation programs.[41] Mediation ordered by a court seems less effective.[42] Some think that facilitative mediation, evaluative mediation and transformative mediation are most important due to the specifics of each particular case.[43]
(5) Screening panels, for special litigation procedures in malpractice cases, commonly called 'pretrial screening panels', require a plaintiff to submit their claims to a special panel, which includes a physician, an attorney and a lay member.[44] Early Neutral Evaluation, as a court sponsored program, by an experienced neutral attorney, is the basis of brief presentations by the parties.[45] The other

---

[32] Metzloff (1992).

[33] Metzloff (1992).

[34] Sohn and Sonny Bal (2012), pp. 1370–1378.

[35] Sohn and Sonny Bal (2012), pp. 1370–1378. See also Šustek and Holčapek (2017), pp. 233–242.

[36] Metzloff (1992).

[37] Sohn and Sonny Bal (2012), pp. 1370–1378.

[38] Sohn and Sonny Bal (2012), pp. 1370–1378.

[39] Šustek and Holčapek (2017), pp. 233–242.

[40] Metzloff (1992).

[41] Sohn and Sonny Bal (2012), pp. 1370–1378.

[42] Sohn and Sonny Bal (2012), pp. 1370–1378.

[43] Šustek and Holčapek (2017), pp. 233–242.

[44] Metzloff (1992).

[45] Metzloff (1992).

term used for this form of ADR is 'pretrial screenings,'[46] which allows for an assessment of the relative strengths of a case before going to trial. This is followed due to the high numbers of meritless cases.[47]

(6) Court-Ordered Arbitration is a process of channelling to a non-binding arbitration process following the completion of a designated period of discovery.[48]

At the same time, the use of any alternative methods for the resolution of medical disputes should be duly justified and appropriate, taking into account the specifics of the relationship between the parties to medical disputes, and the legal regulation of medical relations and health care in the country. In particular, for example, mediation resolves the dispute and preserves the trust in the doctor-patient relationship, but according to some, it will only be effective under the current court-annexed system with a modification where the parties may choose mediation at any time upon the registration of the case and without the need to wait for the pretrial case management stage.[49]

Undoubtedly, the advantage of using mediation is its preventive function,[50] which is to respond to the conflict in a timely manner and with a confidential attempt to find a compromise, at the expense of the interests of both parties, which will preserve the relationship between institution and patient. Analysis of conducted mediations is a source of feedback for healthcare staff and health institutions. It would greatly contribute to prevent possible damage and medical conflicts, specially within the specialties with the most complaints. But we believe that risk management, created by hospitals and medical institutions, will provide much more useful information for research as well as a timely response by the institution itself to prevent conflicts, or resolve them quickly, and their interest in retaining the patient for future relations, under usual conditions.

A serious challenge on the way to the introduction of mediation in medical disputes in Ukraine is the lack of legislative regulation of this method of dispute resolution. Given the specifics of medical disputes, the development of mediation in medical disputes seems to be intensified only after the adoption of this law.

At the same time, it should be noted that ADR in health care disputes leads to a significant increase in the number of specialists involved in resolving such disputes.[51] However, there are only a few training programs for lawyers in Ukraine, among them are those that provide training in the subject 'Medical Law' for law students (the National University Kyiv-Mohyla Academy,[52] the Educational and

---

[46] Sohn and Sonny Bal (2012), pp. 1370–1378.

[47] Sohn and Sonny Bal (2012), pp. 1370–1378.

[48] Metzloff (1992).

[49] Khan et al. (2020), pp. 2309–2323.

[50] Tissie and Bravo (2020), pp. 211–215.

[51] Boserup et al. (2015).

[52] KMA Law (2020) Medical Law. https://law.ukma.edu.ua/courses/medychne-pravo/.

Scientific Institute of Law of Sumy State University,[53] Dnieper Medical Academy,[54] Donetsk State University of Management,[55] V.N. Karazin Kharkiv National University);[56] Ivan Franko Lviv National University has the subject 'Social Medical Law'.[57] Separate departments of medical law have been established in some universities of Ukraine.[58] At the same time, there are only a few training programs for specialists in medical law, in particular, the certified program 'Medical Law' at Yaroslav the Wise NSU.[59] Taras Shevchenko National University of Kyiv has a 'Health Care Law' program, and in 2020, the department of medical law was established. It should be noted that the Institute of Medical and Pharmaceutical Law and Bioethics has been established at the Academy of Advocacy of Ukraine.[60]

Several specific examples of different ADR models are found in the literature, in particular the Rush Model, the VA Model, and the University of Michigan Model.[61] These models combine several factors of success, which in our opinion, were decisive, namely the complete disclosure of the facts, as well as the focus on compromise and maintaining normal relations between the parties to the conflict.

---

[53] International, European and Civil Law Department (2020) Medical Law. https://kmeep.law.sumdu.edu.ua/uk/medychne-pravo.

[54] Dnipropetrovsk Medical Academy (2020) Medical Law. https://101.dsma.dp.ua/studentam/%D0%BC%D0%B5%D0%B4%D0%B8%D1%87%D0%BD%D0%B5-%D0%BF%D1%80%D0%B0%D0%B2%D0%BE.

[55] Donetsk State University of Management (2020) Medical Law. https://dsum.edu.ua/storage/documents/syllabuses%20of%20selective%20disciplines/Medychne%20pravo.pdf.

[56] V. N. Karazin Kharkiv National University: Official Site (2020) Faculties. https://www.univer.kharkov.ua/ua/departments/jurisprudence/chair/civil_law.

[57] Faculty of Law (2020) Information letter on the organization of the educational process at the Faculty of Law. https://law.lnu.edu.ua/en/news.

[58] For example, there is a Department of Forensic Medicine and Medical Law at the O.O. Bogomolets National Medical University (http://nmuofficial.com/zagalni-vidomosti/kafedri/department-forensic-medicine/. at Ivano-Frankivsk National Medical University (https://ifnmu.edu.ua/uk/strukturni-pidrozdili-2/kafedry/kafedra-sudovoi-medytsyny-ta-medychnoho-prava, Department of Medical and Pharmaceutical Law was established at Krok University (https://www.krok.edu.ua/ua/pro-krok/pidrozdili/navchalni/yuridichnij-fakultet. Zaporizhzhya State Medical University has a Department of Management and Economics of Pharmacy, Medical and Pharmaceutical Law (http://zsmu.edu.ua/p_182.html. The Department of Social Medicine, Public Health and Medical Law has been established at Odessa National Medical University (https://onmedu.edu.ua/istorichna-dovidka-pro-kafedru-socialnoi-medicini-gromadskogo-zdorovja-ta-medichnogo-prava/. Department of Medical and Pharmaceutical Law, General and Clinical Pharmacy of Kharkiv Medical Academy of Postgraduate Education (https://med.edu.ua/ukr/structure/view_fakultet/89/, in Lugansk State Medical University there is a medical faculty.

[59] Yaroslaw Mudryi National University of Law (2020). Medical Law. https://nlu.edu.ua/%D1%81%D0%B5%D1%80%D1%82%D0%B8%D1%84%D1%96%D0%BA%D0%B0%D1%82%D0%BD%D1%96-%D0%BE%D1%81%D0%B2%D1%96%D1%82%D0%BD%D1%96-%D0%BF%D1%80%D0%BE%D0%B3%D1%80%D0%B0%D0%BC%D0%B8/%D0%BC%D0%B5%D0%B4%D0%B8%D1%87%D0%BD%D0%B5-%D0%BF%D1%80%D0%B0%D0%B2%D0%BE/.

[60] Academy of Advocacy of Ukraine (2020) Institute of Medical and Pharmaceutical Law and Bioethics. http://aau.edu.ua/ua/medical-law-institute-info/.

[61] Balcerzak and Leonhardt (2008).

The collection and analysis of open information on the work of leading medical institutions in Ukraine[62] showed that, for the most part, dispute resolution is not provided. Only one of them (the Isida Clinic) provides a position of quality control manager who can resolve a dispute between patient and doctor. At the same time, in Ukraine there are no centres for settling medical disputes outside medical institutions, under the Ministry of Health, etc.

Given concerns for litigation independence, we believe that commissions following the example of so-called 'pretrial screening panels' will be more in demand, which can be implemented as pilot projects in national courts to test their effectiveness in medical disputes settlement. Currently, the use of a dispute resolution procedure with the participation of a judge is the only possible option for conciliation in these categories of cases, which should be properly assessed. In particular, during such a procedure, the parties can more realistically assess their chances of winning the case and change their attitude to the existing conflict, using the so-called pretrial screenings.

4 COVID Challenges in Medical Dispute Resolution

Another not less important issue arising during medical disputes consideration is the issue of medical workers social security. To date, the pandemic has made some adjustments to these legal relations, and therefore their legal regulation, although having undergone significant changes, still has controversial issues and the order of their consideration. The potential for disputes over the quality of health care provided, as well as the provision of health care workers, is profound and will increase significantly in the near future.

The year of 2020 will be seen as being exceptional not only because the no-fault compensation model came into force in Lithuania but also because of the outbreak of the COVID-19 pandemic. Thus, it has already led to complaints regarding exposure to the virus in hospitals or inadequately received medical services after the introduction of quarantine. It has been stated that the commission for an evaluation of damage inflicted upon the health of patients had received 10 complaints of this nature. Only 2 complaints were handled and both were dismissed. There has been no information so far on whether the claims were later referred to the court. There is almost no doubt that the number of such disputes will continue to grow. During the second phase of the pandemic a high number of coronavirus cases occurred mainly in the institutions providing medical services.

[62] ISIDA Clinic does not have a center for resolving disputes that may arise between a patient and a doctor, but there is a position of quality control manager who can resolve such a conflict. (See: https://isida.ua/) At the Oberig Hospital (See: https://oberig.ua/ru/) and MEDIKOM (See: https://medikom.ua/ru/) there are call centers for receiving incoming calls, including complaints and suggestions that are forwarded to management, which subsequently resolve such conflicts. The authors are grateful for Polina Sedova's help in finding information.

The normative acts established programs of state guarantees for medical care in 2020,[63] which define, in particular, certain aspects of providing medical services to patients with suspected or established acute respiratory disease (COVID-19) within the program of medical guarantees related to which The National Health Service of Ukraine concludes health contracts for medical care with health protection institutions. In addition, adequate remuneration of medical and other employees who provide medical care to such patients[64] were established, namely up to 300 percent of salary (with increases), taking into account the statutory mandatory surcharges and allowances for a specific list of positions, which is approved by the head of the relevant health care institution.

Several decisions have already dealt with cases[65] where administrative responsibility is identified for violations in the calculation of surcharges to medical workers who provide medical services related to the provision of medical care to patients with acute respiratory disease (COVID-19), who were in self-isolation. It is necessary to equalize their salaries with the salary for a full working month in the amount of up to 300 percent of the salary of the official salary (with increases), taking into account the obligatory surcharges and allowances provided by the legislation.[66]

We believe that the number of such disputes concerning state guarantees of health care, during a coronavirus pandemic, can reach millions, so a well-thought-out strategy for their effective settlement can save a huge amount of funds for the state budget and ensure adequate trust in state and public institutions. In particular, given that there is no legislation in Ukraine on collective or mass lawsuits, as well as the need for timely consideration of their specifics, we believe it is possible, with the help of a national body, for settling collective disputes concerning state guarantees of health care during the coronavirus pandemic. Extensive involvement of representatives of society, associations and unions of medical workers, the protection of patients' rights, as well as representatives of public authorities will provide appropriate guarantees of independence, professionalism and impartiality in the consideration of such a complex catalogue of disputes.

---

[63] Some issues of implementation of the program of state guarantees of medical care in 2020. See: Resolution of the Cabinet of Ministers of Ukraine of February 5, 2020 № 65 (as amended). https://zakon.rada.gov.ua/laws/show/65-2020-%D0%BF.

[64] On urgent measures to provide state financial guarantees for medical care of patients with acute respiratory disease COVID-19 caused by coronavirus SARS-CoV-2, and proper remuneration of medical and other workers who provide medical care to such patients, see: Resolution of the Cabinet of Ministers of Ukraine of April 24 2020 № 331 (with amendments and additions). https://zakon.rada.gov.ua/laws/show/331-2020-%D0%BF#Text.

[65] The decision of the Novozavodsky district court of Chernihiv № 751/5963/20 of 12.10.2020. https://reyestr.court.gov.ua/Review/92188380.

[66] The decision of the Novozavodsky district court of Chernihiv № 751/5963/20 of 12.10.2020. https://reyestr.court.gov.ua/Review/92188380.

5 Concluding Remarks

Each state requires a full and comprehensive state guaranteed strategy for medical dispute resolution, in particular with widely used ADR schemes.

For the Lithuanian example, we may see that from the beginning of 2020 the no-fault compensation model for the damage caused to the patients was introduced. We would assume that such legal regulation is still not sufficiently defined as it is not clear if full protection of the interests of the patients is ensured by it. We believe still the court will play a significant role to compensate for damage in Lithuania.

The judicial method of rights protection in medical disputes will traditionally remain in higher demand in Ukraine too, as the population is more inclined to express coercive justice. Therefore, pretrial screening panels, in our opinion, will be the most successful combination of ADR and judicial form for protection of the rights of individuals in medical disputes, which will lead to the gradual emergence of trust in independent dispute resolution bodies.

Each of the existing ADR schemes has its own characteristics that should be used to resolve specific categories of dispute. Accordingly, a comprehensive approach and the use of different dispute resolution methods to resolve medical disputes or conflicts, from the moment they arise, will make it possible to better protect the rights of individuals to health care and, more importantly, to prevent some of them. The balance of interests of the parties to the contract for the provision of medical services should be ensured by a wide arsenal of such schemes that allow a compromise to be reached and an effective result in any particular case.

In particular, as the analysis showed, medical institutions in Ukraine generally do not develop risk management policies and do not use ADR and preventive procedures to resolve disputes that arise between them and their patients.

At the same time, in our opinion, the wider introduction of risk management and negotiation, combined with the early disclosure and apology programs, will allow for a quick reaction to the conflicts that arise between the clinic and the patient, and this is very important for medical disputes. It also provides necessary information to prevent possible conflicts that the clinic can use. Such a speedy settlement of the dispute will also make it possible to maintain normal relations with clients, which is also an important argument, at the moment.

An important issue, according to our view, is the introduction of programs designed to provide choices that can be made to protect rights, in particular, the choice to apologize to a person who has been harmed by the improper provision of medical services.

Other methods of ADR, in particular, mediation with a professional mediator, an attorney or a retired judge, which are known for specialism in such disputes, will help to overcome doubts about impartiality when considering a dispute with the participation of the clinic and the patient. Mediation could also play a bigger role in medical disputes in Lithuania in order to solve medical disputes in a shorter duration and with an amicable agreement, suited to both parties of the dispute, being found. The introduction of the Law of Ukraine on Mediation should stimulate the development of this method of medical dispute resolution, as the settlement of mediation relations is an important basis for the emergence of confidence in such a method of rights protection.

An important element in the development of a strategy for the effective rights protection of patients and doctors should be state support for medical law programs in higher education or second education programs. The probable potential quantity of participants in medical disputes in Ukraine is equal to the population, because today there is, almost certainly, no person who would not seek medical help for one case or another. This means there is a high probability for an increasing demand for consultations and professional legal assistance in the settlement of medical disputes of various kinds, including out-of-court forms, with the help of specialists.

At the same time, we believe that the events that have taken place in Ukraine in recent years indicate that disputes, related to the health care of persons during the coronavirus pandemic, as well as during the conflict in western Ukraine, have the potential to be considered in courts for years and may not provide effective protection of individuals' rights to health. Both of these events will leave a significant mark on the lives of many people, in particular, through the damage caused by the inadequate provision of medical services and inadequate health care. The potential for such disputes is extremely high, so, in our opinion, in order to prevent their escalation, it is worth considering the need to establish a national commission to resolve disputes to protect the rights of patients and doctors during this coronavirus pandemic. These are disputes concerning the quality of medical services and medical care, as well as the provision of doctors' rights. The involvement of specialists in the field of medical law in the work of this commission will make it possible to resolve disputes faster and better, while ensuring the interests of individuals.

References

Balcerzak GA, Leonhardt KK (2008) Alternative Dispute Resolution in Healthcare. A Prescription for Increasing Disclosure and Improving Patient Safety. Patient Safety & Quality Healthcare https://www.psqh.com/julaug08/resolution.html

Bolotina NB (1999) Medical law in the legal system of Ukraine. Law Ukraine 1:116–121

Bolotina NB (2005) Pravo Sotsialnoho Zakhystu: stanovlennia i rozvytok v Ukraini (The right of social protection: formation and development in Ukraine). Znannia, Kyiv

Boserup V, Parmelee B, Roscoe JP et al. (2015) What Is... ADR in health care disputes? ABA Book Publishing. See also: JAMS Health Care Mediation, Arbitration and ADR Services (2020) Extensive Health Care Industry Knowledge & Efficient, Affordable ADR. https://www.jamsadr.com/healthcare

Buletsa SB (2016) Tsyvilni Pravovidnosyny Shcho Vynykaiut U Sferi Zdiisnennia Medychnoi Diialnosti (Civil relations arising in the field of realization of medical activity: theoretical and practical problems). Dissertation, National University "Odessa Law Academy". http://dspace.onua.edu.ua/bitstream/handle/11300/3307/%D0%91%D1%83%D0%BB%D0%B5%D1%86%D0%B0%20%D0%A1.%D0%91.-%D0%B0%D0%B2%D1%82%D0%BE%D1%80%D0%B5%D1%84%D0%B5%D1%80%D0%B0%D1%82.pdf?sequence=13&isAllowed=y

Encyclopedia of Modern Ukraine (2018) Medychne Pravo (Medical Law). http://esu.com.ua/search_articles.php?id=66077

European Commission (2020) The EU Health Policy Platform. https://webgate.ec.europa.eu/hpf/.
Gerts AA (2016) Contractual obligations in the field of medical services. Dissertation, National Academy of Science of Ukraine: VM Koretskiy Institute of State and Law. http://idpnan.org.ua/files/gerts-a.a.-dogovirni-zobov_yazannya-u-sferi-nadannya-medichnih-poslug-_a_.pdf
Guy M, Sauter W (2016) The history and scope of EU health law and policy. In: Hervey TK, Young CA, Bishop LE (eds) Research handbook on EU health law and policy. Edward Elgar Publishing, Cheltenham, pp 17–35
Hervey TK, McHale JV (2015) What is European Union health law? In: European Union health law: themes and implications, law in context. Cambridge University Press, Cambridge, pp 30–70
Hubskyi YI, Serdiuk VH et al. (2007) Pravove rehuliuvannia nadannia medychnoi dopomohy v Ukraini (Legal Regulation of Medical Care in Ukraine). In: Abstracts of I All-Ukrainian Scientific Conference "Medical Law in Ukraine: problems of formation and development, Lviv, 19–20 April 2007. http://medicallaw.org.ua/uploads/media/01_105_04.pdf
Khan HA, Bastiampillai A, Mon SW (2020) Mediation as a suitable dispute resolution method in medical negligence cases: special reference to the Malaysian position. Pertanika J Soc Sci Human 28(3):2309–2323
Klymenko OV (2012) Istoriia vynyknennia medychnoho prava (The history of medical law emergence). Derzhavne Upravlinnia 5:107–109. http://www.investplan.com.ua/pdf/5_2012/30.pdf
Lazic V (2014) Procedural Justice for 'Weaker Parties' in cross-border litigation under the EU regulatory scheme. Utrecht Law Rev 10(4). URN:NBN:NL:UI:10-1-115844
Maydanyk R (2010) Dohovir pro nadannia medychnykh posluh (Contract for provision of medical services). Med Law 5(1):52–66. http://medicallaw.org.ua/uploads/media/Maydanyk.pdf
Metzloff TB (1992) Alternative dispute resolution strategies in medical malpractice. Alaska Law Rev 9(2) https://scholarship.law.duke.edu/cgi/viewcontent.cgi?article=1295&context=alr
Morkūnaitė M (2017) Teisminis pacientų patirtos žalos atlyginimo modelis. Law 103:115
Seniuta I (2011) Zakhyst Prav Subiektiv Medychnykh Pravovidnosyn Deiaki Teoretyko-pravovi Aspekty (Protection of the rights of subjects of medical legal relations: some theoretical and legal aspects) Bulletin of the Ministry of Justice of Ukraine 4: 11–18. http://medicallaw.org.ua/fileadmin/user_upload/pdf/zaxust_prav_lydunu_y_cferi_ox_zdorovja.pdf
Škarka A (2018) Protection of weaker party in the EU case law. Master's thesis, Masaryk University. https://is.muni.cz/th/p7uyk/Protection-of-weaker-party-in-the-EU-case-law_MT_AdamSkarka_116585.pdf
Sohn DH, Sonny Bal B (2012) Medical malpractice reform: the role of alternative dispute resolution. Clin Orthop Relat Res 470(5):1370–1378. https://www.ncbi.nlm.nih.gov/pmc/articles/PMC3314770/
Šustek P, Holčapek T (2017) Alternative Dispute Resolution in Medical Malpractice Disputes. In: Radic Ze, Roncevic A et al. Economic and Social Development: 22nd International Scientific Conference on Economic and Social Development – "The Legal Challenges of Modern World": Book of proceedings, p 233–242. https://ssrn.com/abstract=3213596 https://papers.ssrn.com/sol3/papers.cfm?abstract_id=3213596
The Constitution of Ukraine (1996) with amendments. https://zakon.rada.gov.ua/laws/show/254к/96-вр#Text
The United Nations (1948) Universal Declaration of Human Rights. https://www.ohchr.org/EN/UDHR/Documents/UDHR_Translations/eng.pdf.
Tissie DL, Bravo L (2020) Mediation in public healthcare: opportunities for improvement. Revista Medica de Chile 148(2):211–215
Wang M, Liu GG, Zhao H et al (2020) The role of mediation in solving medical disputes in China. BMC Health Serv Res 20:225. https://doi.org/10.1186/s12913-020-5044-7

Part IV
Reproductive Rights

Posthumous Reproduction: Comparative Review of Legislation and Court Practice

Kateryna Moskalenko

Contents

Abstract This chapter analyses the provisions of legislation and court practice in cases regarding posthumous reproduction in Ukraine and foreign countries. Legislators in foreign countries regulate the question of posthumous reproduction in different ways. Countries can be divided into three groups, depending upon the adopted rules on post-mortem reproduction. The first group consists of countries where posthumous reproduction is forbidden: France, Germany, Sweden, Hungary, Slovenia; the second group is formed by the countries where posthumous reproduction is allowed: the United Kingdom, New Zealand, Spain, Belgium, Kyrgyz Republic, Portugal, Brazil; the third group combines the countries where posthumous reproduction is not regulated by the law. Such legal vacuum exists in Ukraine, the Russian Federation and other countries. New technical medical possibilities give way to a lot of questions which need to be answered by legal specialists: should the lawmaker allow taking gametes after the death of the donor?; should the donor give consent to taking gametes after his/her death, and if so—what should be the form of such consent?; should the donor be recognized as a legal parent of the child conceived and born post-mortem? Can the child conceived posthumously be a legal heir of the donor? Some of these questions have been analysed in the court

K. Moskalenko (✉)
Civil Law Department at the Law School of Taras Shevchenko National University of Kyiv, Kyiv, Ukraine

© The Author(s), under exclusive license to Springer Nature Switzerland AG 2022

R. Maydanyk et al. (eds.), *Ukrainian Healthcare Law in the Context of European and International Law*, European Union and its Neighbours in a Globalized World 7,
https://doi.org/10.1007/978-3-031-05690-1_10

practice of New Zealand, the USA, France and other countries, which are listed in the article. There are a number of problems in the legal regulation of posthumous reproduction in Ukraine, namely: regarding the possibility of posthumous donorship of sexual reproduction cells, paternity/maternity of the deceased person and the possibility of children conceived and born post-mortem to inherit the property of the biological mother or father. These problems can be solved by adopting a special law on assisted human reproduction.

1 Introduction: Why Is a Proper Regulation of Posthumous Reproduction Needed?

Posthumous reproduction, i.e. conception and birth of the child after the death of one or both of its genetic parents, is no longer a fantasy. Legal and bioethical problems of AHR are thus a subject of a number of scientific discussions. Legal scholars began to actively discuss the necessity of legal regulation of AHR after the airplane crash in Chile in 1983, leading to death of American couple—Mario and Elsa Rios. The Rios couple were receiving AHR treatment in Melbourne, Australia. One of the embryos conceived by the couple was implanted in Ms. Rios' uterus, however she was not able to carry it and give a birth to the child. Remaining embryos were left in Australian clinic. Since the couple had not signed any documents regarding the future fate of the embryos, a public discussion, involving lawyers, doctors and church clerks on the legal status of the remaining embryos and their future started. As a result, in 1984, the Victoria Parliament passed a law, under which the embryos were to be given to a patient with fertility problems.[1]

Today it is common practice to retrieve genetic material from cancer patients before they undergo chemotherapy, allowing the preservation of healthy gametes, that can be further used to give birth to healthy children. In the meantime, in many countries of the world, (e.g. in Israel), military servants often cryopreserve sperm before being called to their military duty. The idea of banking sperm of military servants has been considered by parliaments in some post-soviet countries. In 2016, Members of Parliament of the Republic of Armenia announced such an initiative.[2]

Opponents of postmortem reproduction refer to the potential harm for the future child, indicating that the relatives of the deceased are often guided by personal interests when they make the decision to apply AHR using the genetic material, wishing to numb the pain of having lost a loved one. The relatives normally do not take into account that the absence of one (or both) genetic parents can influence the future child and its development in a negative way. However, these arguments do not prevent the application of posthumous reproduction because a lot of donors, while

[1] Steinbock (2011), p. 212.

[2] Vardanyan (2016), p. 22.

exercising their reproductive rights, choose to document their wish to use their sexual reproduction cells for conception after their death. It's impossible to deny that giving birth and raising a biological child of the deceased will bring joy to the members of his/her family. Even without a legislative framework, there are different options for those who wish to obtain this outcome. Cases of so-called reproductive tourism, i.e. travelling to another country with the sole aim to use AHR with the cells of the deceased, are very wide-spread if such procedure can't be undertaken in the country of residence of the patients.

The issue of post-mortem reproduction was analysed by a number of scholars, both foreign and Ukrainian: G. Anikina, A. Golovaschuk, L. Vardanyan and O. Grygorenko, M. Sabatello, B. Weber, R. Kodama, K. Jarvi, K. Parizer-Krief, N. Pearl, D. Eduardo, V. Raposo, C. Steeb, U. Ahluwalia, M. Alora, J. Robertson, C. Robey and others. Nevertheless, a lot of questions on post-mortem reproduction have not been resolved yet in Ukraine, both in theory and in practice. Therefore, studying the application of AHR after the death of one or both of the genetic parents is in very high demand.

This research aims to study the legal regulation of posthumous reproduction in foreign countries; analysing court decisions in cases involving post-mortem reproduction; studying the legal regulation of AHR in Ukraine and offering amendments to the current Ukrainian legislation.

2 Legal Regulation of Posthumous Reproduction in Foreign Countries

Legislators in foreign countries regulate the question of posthumous reproduction in different ways and it is interesting to compare both European and non-European systems, as in some non-European countries the regulation of posthumous reproduction exists for quite some time and it is interesting to consider such an experience. Also, there is no consensus in Europe towards the regulation of posthumous reproduction, and it is especially interesting to consider different legal norms withing one region.

The countries can be divided into three groups, depending on the adopted rules on post-mortem reproduction.

The first group consists of countries where posthumous reproduction is forbidden: France, Germany, Sweden, Hungary, Slovenia.

In accordance with the French Public Health Code, 'the man and woman forming the couple must be alive and of reproductive age and must have given prior written consent to the embryo transfer or insemination. Obstacles to insemination or embryo transfer are constituted by the death of one of the members of the couple, initiation of divorce or separation proceedings, or cessation of cohabitation, as well as either partner's written revocation of consent, filed with the doctor in charge of proceeding with the medically assisted procreation procedure.'[3] The abolition of conceiving the child after the death of the sperm donor was first mentioned in 1988 after the Braibant Report. The authors of the report mentioned that it was unethical to give birth to a child, that would legally have only one parent.[4] The legislative prohibition of posthumous reproduction was introduced in 1994.

In accordance with Section 4 of the German Act for Protection of Embryos, 'anyone will be punished with up to three years of imprisonment or a fine, who... 3. Knowingly fertilises artificially an egg cell with the sperm of a man after his death'.[5]

According to the Genetic Integrity Act of Sweden, 'eggs or sperm from a donor who is deceased may not be used for fertilization' (Section 6 of Chapter 7).[6]

Following Section 166 of the Act CLIV of 1997 on Health (Hungary), reproductive cells from deceased parties, including from persons who are brain-dead, of from dead fetuses, shall not be used in reproduction procedures.[7]

The future Law on Infertility Treatment and on Biomedically Assisted Procreation in Slovenia does not allow posthumous use of gametes. This prohibition is based on the principle that it's necessary to imitate nature and allowing only such natural conception that nature has deprived these patients from.[8]

The second group is formed by the countries where posthumous reproduction is allowed: the United Kingdom, New Zealand, Spain, Belgium, Kyrgyz Republic, Portugal, Brazil.

In 2003 the Act on Human Fertilisation and Embryology (Deceased Fathers Act) was adopted in the United Kingdom. In accordance with this act, the man, whose sperm was used after his death to conceive a child is recognized as the father of the child. It is necessary to receive the prior written consent of the man 'to the use of his sperm after his death (which brought about the creation of the embryo carried by the woman or (as the case may be) to the placing in the woman after his death of the embryo which was brought about using his sperm before his death), and to being treated ... as the father of any resulting child'. The woman is allowed to register the deceased man as the father of the child for 42 days after the day on which the child was born, given that there is no-one else to be named the father of the child.[9]

The Assisted Reproductive Treatment Act (Australia) as of 2008 allows posthumous use of gametes or an embryo in treatment provided by a registered AHR

[3] Parizer-Krief (2016), p. 92.

[4] Parizer-Krief (2016), p. 98.

[5] Act for Protection of Embryos of 13th December, 1990. https://bilimakademisi.org/wp-content/uploads/2016/04/EmbryoProtectionAct.pdf.

[6] The Genetic Integrity Act (2006:351) issued on May 18, 2006. http://www.smer.se/news/the-genetic-integrity-act-2006351/.

[7] Act No. CLIV of 1997 on health. http://www2.ohchr.org/english/bodies/cescr/docs/E.C.12.HUN.3-Annex10.pdf.

[8] Zupancic et al. (2000).

[9] Human Fertilisation and Embryology (Deceased Fathers) Act dated 2003. http://www.legislation.gov.uk/ukpga/2003/24/introduction.

provider upon the following conditions: the AHR is carried by the deceased person's partner; the deceased person provided written consent for such a procedure; the Patient Review Panel has approved the use of the gametes or embryo and the person who will be receiving the treatment has received counselling.[10] Following the Assisted Reproductive Treatment Regulations (Australia) 2019, during the counselling prior to posthumous use of gametes or embryos, the following matters should be mentioned: the grieving process and the possible impact on the child to be born as a result of the treatment procedure.[11]

Art. 22 of the Law of Portugal 'On Assisted Human Reproduction' forbids to use the gametes after the death of the man, however it allows post-mortem implantation of the embryos if the embryo was conceived while both partners were alive and if enough time has passed from the moment of the partner's death to consider the decision to carry on posthumous reproduction after careful thought.[12]

In case of the deceased person having given written consent to use cryopreserved biomaterial, post-mortem reproduction is allowed in accordance with the Resolution of Federal Council of Medicine of Brazil.[13]

As follows from Art. 9 of the Spanish Law 'On Assisted Reproductive Technologies', reproductive material of the husband can be used by his wife during 12 months from the moment of death in case the deceased husband gave prior written consent. In case the couple participated in an AHR program, the consent of the husband to implant conceived embryos is presumed.[14]

Implantation of embryos after the death of one or both partners is allowed in accordance with Art. 15–17 of the Belgium Law on medically assisted reproduction and the disposition of supernumerary embryos and gametes, adopted in 2007. It is necessary to receive consent of both partners and also ensure that minimum 6 months have passed since the death of the donor. Posthumous reproduction is possible not later than 2 years after the partner's death.[15]

In accordance with the Greek legislation—the Law 'On Medical Assistance in Human Reproduction' and the Law 'On Applying the Methods of Assisted Reproductive Technologies', AHR is possible only if one (or both) partners was (were) suffering from infertility and has (have) given notarized consent to conceive the child using his/her biomaterial after death. As in Belgium, posthumous AHR in

[10] Assisted Reproductive Treatment Act 2008. No. 76 of 2008. https://www.legislation.vic.gov.au/in-force/acts/assisted-reproductive-treatment-act-2008/024.

[11] Assisted Reproductive Treatment Regulations No. 002 of 2019. https://www.legislation.vic.gov.au/search?q=Assisted+Reproductive+Treatment+Act+2008&queryType=title_content&page=1&sort%5B_score%5D=desc&sort%5Btitle_az%5D=asc.

[12] Lei No. 32/2006 de 26 de Julho 'Procriação medicamente assistida'. http://www.fd.unl.pt/docentes_docs/ma/tpb_ma_4022.pdf.

[13] Resolucio CFM No 2.121/2015. http://www.portalmedico.org.br/resolucoes/CFM/2015/2121_2015.pdf.

[14] Ley 14/2006, de 26 de mayo, sobre técnicas de reproducción humana asistida. https://www.boe.es/buscar/act.php?id=BOE-A-2006-9292.

[15] Pennings (2007), p. 257.

Greece is possible not earlier than 6 months from the moment of death of the donor of biomaterials and not later than 2 years after his death.[16]

Due to Part 2 of Art. 2 of the Law of Kyrgyz Republic ‘On Reproduction Rights and the Guarantees of their Exercising’ dated July 4, 2015[17] the right to use gametes of the deceased person with the aim to conceive is vested in the spouse, father, mother, native brothers and sisters.

The draft of the Assisted Human Reproduction Bill is currently widely discussed in Ireland. Post-mortem reproduction is allowed by the mentioned draft under the following specific provisions: ‘the deceased person had specifically consented; only a female surviving partner may use and must carry pregnancy herself; the surviving person receives counselling and consents to treatment; a minimum of one year has passed since the death; if donor gametes are used, the embryo must have been created during the lifetime of the deceased’.[18] The exclusion of the male surviving partner from using posthumous AHR has been widely criticized.[19]

The third group combines the countries where posthumous reproduction is not regulated by law. Such a legal vacuum exists in Ukraine, in the Russian Federation and in other countries.

3 Analysis of Court Practice in the Cases Involving Posthumous Reproduction

Even in countries where special regulations on post-mortem reproduction are implemented, different bioethical problems which arise in the course of AHR application are yet to be solved. New medical technical possibilities invoke a lot of new questions which need to be answered by legal specialists: should the lawmaker allow taking gametes after the death of the donor?; should the donor give consent to taking gametes after his/her death and if yes—what should be the form of such consent?; should the donor be recognized as a legal parent of the child conceived and born post-mortem?; can the child conceived posthumously be a legal heir of the donor? Some of these questions have been analysed in the court practices of foreign countries.

[16] Leon et al. (2011), p. 821.

[17] Zakon Kyrgyskoi Respubliki ‘O Reproduktivhyh Pravah Grazhdan I Garantiyah Ih Realizatsii’ as of July 4th, 2015 No. 148. http://cbd.minjust.gov.kg/act/view/ru-ru/111191.

[18] Report on Pre-Legislative Scrutiny of the General Scheme of the Assisted Human Reproduction Bill of July 2019. P. 26. https://data.oireachtas.ie/ie/oireachtas/committee/dail/32/joint_committee_on_health/reports/2019/2019-07-10_report-on-pre-legislative-scrutiny-of-the-general-scheme-of-the-assisted-human-reproduction-bill_en.pdf.

[19] Ibid.

3.1 *The Court Cases on Retrieving Gametes After the Donor's Death*

Courts have mainly dealt with the issue of taking sperm after the death of the man, but not with the taking of ova's. One of the most cited court cases is the case of Diana Blood, that was heard in the United Kingdom in 1997. Diana and Stephen were a childless married couple. In 2005 Stephen contracted meningitis and then fell into a coma. Diana addressed the medical institution with the request to take a sample of sperm from her husband. Given the mutual desire of the couple to have common children (as Ms. Blood stated) and despite the absence of the written consent of the husband to such a procedure, the sample of biomaterial was taken and then sent for storage to the Infertility Research Trust. During his third day in a coma, Stephen died. After his death Diana addressed a request to use the sperm samples to the Human Fertilisation and Embryology Authority. This request was denied because of absence of written consent of the deceased to post-mortem conceiving children. The court of the first instance supported the decision of the Human Fertilisation and Embryology Authority.[20] The court of appeal, however, granted the request of the widow to obtain the samples. Despite the legal ban to use the gametes after the death of person without the written consent of such person, the court of appeal sympathised with Ms. Blood. By that time, she was able to make use of relevant medical assistance in another country of the European Union—Belgium.[21] Ms. Blood exercised her right, granted by the court decision, and went to Belgium where she gave birth to 2 sons—Liam and Joel. In February 2017, 20 years after she had won the right to use the sperm of her deceased husband, Telegraph published an interview with Diana and her 2 sons, in which the woman proudly shared the achievements of her children and Liam explained that he did not feel that his life was abnormal because of his father's absence.[22]

Similar cases were also heard by the courts in New Zealand. In the matter of Warren Andrew Gray which was decided by the Supreme Court of Queensland, the applicant, being 42 years old, filed a claim to the court to extract the sperm of her husband—Mr. Gray who tragically died when he was 37 years old. The couple had already had a son, but the applicant told the court they had decided on having a second child in the near future. The Supreme Court of Queensland refused the application for several reasons. First of all, the materials of the case did not contain the evidence that written consent of the deceased husband for extracting his sperm was given before his death; secondly, the disclosure of the information on the

---

[20] Sabatello (2014), p. 29.

[21] Court of Appeal, Civil Division. Judgement in the case Human Fertilisation and Embryology Authorty, ex parte Blood. http://www.globalhealthrights.org/wp-content/uploads/2013/03/EWCA-1997-R-v.-Human-Fertilisation-and-Embryology-Authority-ex-parte-Blood.pdf.

[22] Exclusive: Diane Blood on family life 20 years later after she won the right to use her dead husband's sperm. http://www.telegraph.co.uk/women/family/exclusive-diane-blood-family-life-20-years-won-right-use-dead/.

conditions of conceiving and birth could emotionally harm the future child. Moreover, interference with the dead body was recognized as a criminal offence by the Criminal Code.[23]

As follows from the materials of the case Simone Baker v. State of Queensland, that was heard by the Supreme Court of Queensland, Andrew Clark tragically died in 2002. His partner, Simone Baker, filed a claim to the court, requesting to remove his spermatozoa with the aim to further conceive and give birth to a child. Refusing the application, the court noticed that the applicant failed to provide evidence that the deceased agreed to posthumous reproduction. The judge also underlined that the issue of posthumous reproduction should be regulated by law, because only the law-maker can adequately balance the interests of all parties and the community values.[24]

Despite two previous refusals to extract sperm post-mortem, the Supreme Court of Queensland granted the application of Elizabeth Ann Denman to retrieve biomaterial of her husband, Edward Denman, who was killed.[25] The judge mentioned that the child, conceived after the death of biological father, would grow up in an incomplete family. However, children who were born in a family with both parents can also end up being raised without one or both parents. Given the absence of a direct prohibition to extract biomaterial after the death of a person, the judge granted the claim of Ms. Denman.[26]

The courts have also granted the applications to retrieve sperm after a man's death in the USA. Daniel Thomas Christy was seriously injured in a car accident. His fiancé had discussed with his parents the possibility of taking his sperm with the aim to give birth to his biological child. The parents gave their consent to the removal of biological material. As follows from the text of the court decision, the Uniform Anatomical Gift Act, adopted in the USA, allows for any donor to give his/her anatomic material. Such decision could also be made by the parents of the donor, provided that the donor had not expressed the wish to not give his anatomic material after death. During the court consideration, the parents of Daniel submitted the affidavit of the author of the Uniform Anatomical Gift Act, where the author confirmed that it was the intention of the law-maker that the Uniform Anatomical Gift Act regulated also the issues of giving gametes by the donor. The judge granted the claim.[27]

The technology of retrieving ova is more complicated than sperm extraction, therefore there are much less court decisions on the topic of taking oocytes.

---

[23] Supreme Court of Queensland Judgment in the matter of Gray. https://archive.sclqld.org.au/qjudgment/2000/QSC00-390.pdf.

[24] Supreme Court of Queensland Judgment in the matter of Simone Baker. https://archive.sclqld.org.au/qjudgment/2003/QSC03-002.pdf.

[25] Supreme Court of Queensland in the matter of an application by Elizabeth Ann Denman. http://archive.sclqld.org.au/qjudgment/2004/QSC04-070.pdf.

[26] Ibid.

[27] Pushing the dead into the next reproductive frontier: post mortem gamete retrieval under the uniform anatomical gift act. https://pubmed.ncbi.nlm.nih.gov/19493077/.

In 2011 the Israeli court considered the case of Chen Aida Ayash, a 17-years old girl, who died in the hospital after a car accident. Aida's parents requested an extraction of her gametes, their fertilisation and cryopreservation of the embryos conceived. Despite the fact that the court granted only the first demand (on ova retrieval), this decision became revolutionary for Israel.[28]

It can be concluded from the above court cases that taking biomaterial from a deceased person is both possible in the case of previously documented consent and the absence of such consent. It is very difficult to foresee what a Ukrainian court would decide in such a case, as Ukrainian legislation does not contain any regulatory provisions. It is most likely that future legislation will stipulate the necessity of express written consent in these cases.

4 Analysis of Court Practice in the Cases on Using Gametes for Conceiving and Giving Birth to the Child Post-Mortem

A separate issue is the necessity to provide consent by the donor to use his/her biomaterial for posthumous conceiving, leading to childbirth. Express written consent of the man to posthumous conceiving of the child will undoubtedly be the best evidence of his intentions. However, there are court decisions, where post-mortem reproduction was granted without such written consent. In a famous court case, Parpalaix v. CECOS, in France in 1984, the court considered a widow's request to use the gametes of her deceased husband. In accordance with the materials of the case, Alain Parpalaix, suffering from cancer, had cryopreserved his gametes immediately after he found out about his diagnosis and not left any instructions on how to use his genetic material after his death. After Alain's death, his wife and parents applied to the medical institution to receive his biomaterial and use it. The court concluded that the parents and wife of the deceased can give sufficient evidence about the deceased's real intentions with regard to his sperm, given the absence of any written document with his will. The court granted the application, because both the parents and widow of Alain stated the same—Alain wanted to conceive a child with his wife.[29]

Undoubtedly, even when the donor has given express written consent to use his biomaterial, court disputes may arise. One of the first court cases on posthumous reproduction, that was heard in the USA, was the case of William E. Kane (Hecht v. Superior Court). William has stored his reproductive material at the Californian cryobank. He had signed an agreement with the cryobank, under which he authorized the cryobank to allow his sperm to be used by his partner, Deborah E. Hecht.

[28] Israeli Woman's Eggs Can Be harvested And Frozen After Her Death, Court Rules. https://www.huffingtonpost.com/2011/08/08/israeli-woman-eggs-harvested-frozen-death_n_921639.html.

[29] Steeb (2000), pp. 150–151.

Mr. Kane had also left a will, under which his genetic materials was to be given to Ms. Hecht after his death, to enable her to give birth to their child. A part of his property was to be inherited by his adult children, and the other part—by Ms. Hecht. Mr. Kane committed suicide, after which his partner and children signed the agreement on division of his property. Later Ms. Hecht filed the application to the cryobank, requesting to receive the reproductive material. However, she was refused, because the text of the agreement that she and Mr. Kane's children had signed did not contain any provision on the property of Mr. Kane's gametes. The children of Mr. Kane insisted on destruction of the genetic material. The Californian Court of Appeal took into account the position of Kane's children, who objected against giving the sperm to Deborah because the cells were not considered a property and couldn't be inherited. Moreover, they argued that a single woman giving birth to a child would go against public order. Ms. Hecht stated that specific instructions were mentioned in Mr. Kane's will and therefore she was entitled to receive the gametes. According to her, destruction of the sperm cells would violate her right to privacy. The court granted the demands of Ms. Hecht because the donor had left very clear and express consent for the use of his biomaterial by Ms. Hecht.[30]

The question of post-mortem usage of sperm was considered by the ECtHR in the case of Petithory Lanzmann v. France. Following the circumstances of the case, the applicant wanted to transfer her deceased son's sperm abroad to arrange either AHR or gestational surrogacy. Her son was diagnosed with cancer in 2014 and had expressed his wish to become a father even in case the child would be born after his death. Following his death in 2017 the applicant tried to transfer the sperm of her son to Israel, however she was not authorized to do so. The applicant claimed that the refusal of domestic courts to have her son's sperm transferred violated both her son's right to decide how and when to be a parent and her own right to become a grandparent, basing her claims on the Art. 8 of the ECHR. The ECtHR declared both parts of the application inadmissible. As to the violation of the applicant's son's right to become a parent, the ECtHR noted that this right could not be transferrable and the applicant could not claim this on behalf of her son. As to the alleged violation of her right to become a grandparent, the ECtHR decided that 'Art. 8 did not guarantee a right to become a grandparent, however worthy the applicant's personal aspiration to continue the genetic line'.[31]

In some jurisdictions, AHR after the death of the person can be allowed by the donor only in written form (as follows, for example, from the legislation of Australia and the United Kingdom).

The donorship of gametes and embryos in Ukraine is regulated by the Order of the Ministry of Healthcare of Ukraine 'On Adoption of the Order of Application of

[30] Steeb (2000), pp. 152–153.

[31] Press Release issued by the Registrar of the ECtHR. Refusal to allow Claude Lanzmann's widow to export her deceased son's sperm with a view to artificial insemination: inadmissible. https://nostal.ge/wp-content/uploads/2019/12/Decision-Petithory-Lanzmann-v.-France-refusal-to-allow-Claude-Lanzmanns-widow-to-export-her-deceased-sons-sperm.pdf.

Assisted Reproductive Technologies'.[32] The mentioned Order lays down the necessity of a written voluntary consent for such donorship. However, the text of such a consent does not mention the usage of genetic material after the death of the donor. As stated before, written consent of the patient to posthumous reproduction will be the best evidence of intent of the donor to procreate after his death and such clear intent shall be taken into account by Ukrainian law maker. Any disputes arising because of the absence of written consent, shall be decided by the court.

4.1 Post-Mortem Reproduction and the Law of Inheritance

Another issue that must be mentioned is the possibility of succession by the child, conceived and born after the death of the testator. Most scholars are of the opinion that the children conceived posthumously are not entitled to an inheritance from the deceased parent because it is impossible to define when the genetic material of the deceased person would be used. Technically, the conceiving can take place for a long time after the death has occurred.[33] This situation becomes even more complicated when there's other successors involved, who may possibly consider their own rights violated as the direct result of posthumously conceived child. On the other hand, however, not allowing the child to inherit the property of its biological parent is discriminatory, because children can't alter when and under which circumstances they are born.

In the USA, in 2002, the court developed a 4-condition test that should be fulfilled to recognize the right to inheritance of the child conceived post-mortem. As follows from the materials of the case Woodward v. Commissioner of Social Security, after being diagnosed with leukaemia, Warren Woodward decided to cryopreserve his genetic material. He intended to use cryopreserved sperm after chemotherapy, to be able to have healthy children with his wife. However, the medical treatment was not successful and Mr. Woodward died, leaving all of his estate to his widow. 2 years later, Ms. Woodward gave birth to twins which were conceived using her deceased husband's genetic material. Ms. Woodward tried to obtain social security benefits for her children but all her applications were rejected. She decided to address to the court, requesting to recognize her daughters as legal successors of Warren Woodward. The Supreme Court ruled that post- mortem conceived children may enjoy the right to inheritance if: '(1) the surviving parent or the child's other legal representative demonstrates a genetic relationship between the child and the decedent, (2) the survivor or representative must establish that the decedent affirmatively consented to posthumous conception and to the support of any resulting child, (3) the proper time

[32]Nakaz Ministerstva Ohorony Zdoroviya 'Pro Zatverdzhennya Poryadku Zastosuvannya Dopomizhnyh Reproduktyvnyh Tehnologiy v Ukrayini' No 787 (2013) https://zakon.rada.gov.ua/laws/show/z1697-13#Text.

[33]Anikina (2013), p. 8

limitations are met, and (4) notice is given to all parties'.[34] Scholars consider it justified to establish a 2 year term from the moment of the testator's death, because it is possible to ensure due exercising of rights of all the successors: new-born child, conceived after the death of the testator and the other successors.[35]

The Uniform Probate Code of the USA was amended in 2008, allowing children which are conceived post-mortem to inherit. The last revised version of the Uniform Probate Code dated 2019 provides in Section 2-104 the following provision: 'If the decedent dies before the start of a pregnancy by assisted reproduction resulting in the birth of an individual who lives at least 120 hours after birth, that individual is deemed to be living at the decedent's death if the decedent's personal representative received 8 notice or had actual knowledge within 6 months after the decedent's death of intent to use genetic material in assisted reproduction and thereby affect the distribution of the decedent's estate and: (A) the embryo was in utero not later than 36 months after the decedent's death; or (B) the individual was born not later than [45] months after the decedent's death'.[36]

Some scholars argue that children conceived after the death of the parent (s) should be denied the right to inherit. Anikina G. thinks that it is irrational to entitle children conceived and born after the death of the testator to inherit, because it will destroy the concept of the law on succession.[37]

According to Art. 1222 of the CC of Ukraine both natural persons who were alive at the moment of commencement of succession and persons who were conceived during the life of the testator and born alive after commencement of succession can inherit by law and in accordance with the will. The national Ukrainian legislation excludes the children, conceived after the death, from the circle of successors. This approach of the legislator is well balanced, because in order to allow the children conceived posthumously to inherit, it is necessary to amend the legislation to ensure protection of rights and interests of all the interested parties. When drafting such amendments, the legislator should foresee the term during which posthumous conceiving is possible, and consider the question of financial support for such children. It may be possible, for example, to open a bank deposit, which may be used to maintain the future child. The legal vacuum must be filled up and all mentioned difficulties can be resolved in a special law 'On Assisted Human Reproduction' that should be drafted and adopted by the legislator. Relevant drafts were submitted to the Verkhovna Rada for consideration, yet none has been adopted so far.

---

[34] Woodward v. Commissioner of Social Security. https://www.casebriefs.com/blog/law/wills-trusts-estates/wills-trusts-estates-keyed-to-dukeminier/intestacy-an-estate-plan-by-default/woodward-v-commissioner-of-social-security/.

[35] Steeb (2000), p. 161.

[36] Revised Uniform Probate Code dated 2019. https://www.uniformlaws.org/HigherLogic/System/DownloadDocumentFile.ashx?DocumentFileKey=ea6eb709-a22b-87c7-1c42-4336cfeb8148&forceDialog=0.

[37] Anikina (2013), p. 8.

5 Conclusions

Applying post-mortem AHR in Ukraine would require amendments to current legislation, because the common European model for regulation has not been developed yet and there are no legal provisions on the possibility of post-humous gametes' retrieval; the possibility to use gametes of the deceased person to conceive a child and the possibility of such child to inherit the estate of the deceased parent. The mentioned problems can be resolved by adopting a special law 'On Assisted Human Reproduction'. An analysis of foreign legislation and foreign court practices in the cases on posthumous reproduction shows that such a law should contain the following provisions:

- Retrieving biomaterial of the deceased person shall be allowed only in case of express written consent of the person to this medical interference;
- The patient should expressly consent to posthumous reproduction in writing;
- If post-mortem conceived children are to inherit, the lawmaker must foresee the term during which posthumous conceiving is possible, and consider the question of financial support of such children.

References

Anikina GV (2013) K Voprosu o Pravovom Regulirovanii Postmortalnoi Reproduktsii. Nauka, Obschestvo, Gosudarstvi 2:1–11

Exclusive: Diane Blood on family life 20 years later after she won the right to use her dead husband's sperm. http://www.telegraph.co.uk/women/family/exclusive-diane-blood-family-life-20-years-won-right-use-dead/

Israeli Woman's Eggs Can Be harvested And Frozen After Her Death, Court Rules. https://www.huffingtonpost.com/2011/08/08/israeli-woman-eggs-harvested-frozen-death_n_921639.html

Leon G, Papetta A, Spiliopoulou C (2011) Overview of the Greek legislation regarding assisted reproduction and comparison with the EU legal framework. Reprod BioMed Online 23:820–823

Parizer-Krief K (2016) Postmortem procreation in French and British Law. Cult Res 5:91–111

Pennings G (2007) Belgian law on medically assisted reproduction and the disposition of supernumary Embryos and Gametes European. J Health Law 14:250–260

Press Release issued by the Registrar of the ECtHR. Refusal to allow Claude Lanzmann's widow to export her deceased son's sperm with a view to artificial insemination: inadmissible. https://nostal.ge/wp-content/uploads/2019/12/Decision-Petithory-Lanzmann-v.-France-refusal-to-allow-Claude-Lanzmanns-widow-to-export-her-deceased-sons-sperm.pdf

Pushing the dead into the next reproductive frontier: post mortem gamete retrieval under the uniform anatomical gift act. https://pubmed.ncbi.nlm.nih.gov/19493077/

Report on Pre-Legislative Scrutiny of the General Scheme of the Assisted Human Reproduction Bill (2019) https://data.oireachtas.ie/ie/oireachtas/committee/dail/32/joint_committee_on_health/reports/2019/2019-07-10_report-on-pre-legislative-scrutiny-of-the-general-scheme-of-the-assisted-human-reproduction-bill_en.pdf

Sabatello M (2014) Posthumously conceived children: an international and human rights perspective. J Law Health 27:29–67

Steeb LA (2000) Child conceived after his father's death: posthumous reproduction and inheritance rights – an analysis of Ohio Statutes. Cleveland State Law Rev:137–167

Steinbock B (2011) Life before birth: the moral and legal status of embryos and fetuses. Oxford University Press, Oxford, p 328

Vardanyan LG (2016) Sovremennyie Problemy Postmortalnoi Reproduktsii v Respublike Armenia. Visnyk Zaporizkogo natsionalnogo universytety. Yurydychni Nauky. 1:18–25

Woodward v. Commissioner of Social Security. https://www.casebriefs.com/blog/law/wills-trusts-estates/wills-trusts-estates-keyed-to-dukeminier/intestacy-an-estate-plan-by-default/woodward-v-commissioner-of-social-security/

Zupancic K, Meden H, Tomazevic T, Znidarsic V (2000) The future law on infertility treatment and on biomedically assisted procreation in Slovenia. J Assisted Reprod Genet 17(9):496–497

Legal and Regulatory Aspects of Assisted Reproductive Technologies in Ukraine and the EU Member-States

Anna Golovashchuk

Contents

Abstract Legal and regulatory issues in assisted reproductive technologies (ART) are numerous and complex. Our aim is to discuss some aspects of the assisted reproduction in the Ukraine legal system, while differing approaches to regulation by the other EU member states. Assisted reproductive technologies and the law Internationally there are different main approaches to the regulation of ART. Some countries such as France, Italy, Germany have passed laws covering most aspects of ART. Other countries, have fewer laws in this area. This chapter reviews the legal and regulatory aspects of ART, analyzes the laws regulating ART in European countries, and identifies regulatory approaches to assisted reproductive technologies in different countries. Regulatory acts that govern the use of ART are the focus of this article. Through such analysis, this chapter seeks to draw attention to the field of assisted reproductive technologies assessment and regulation in general as applicable to medical technologies, in a context of overall problem using ART of medical.

A. Golovashchuk (✉)
Kyiv, Ukraine

© The Author(s), under exclusive license to Springer Nature Switzerland AG 2022
R. Maydanyk et al. (eds.), *Ukrainian Healthcare Law in the Context of European and International Law*, European Union and its Neighbours in a Globalized World 7,
https://doi.org/10.1007/978-3-031-05690-1_11

1 Introduction

With advances in science, technology, and related social relations, globalization has impacted the health law as well.

Procreation, high fertility, and reproductive health have always been in the limelight for the society. Falling birth rates and rising infertility rates have spurred numerous studies and researches that have raised a number of ethical and legal issues.

According to Eurostat, the birth rates in EU Member States had been steadily declining from the mid-1960s to the early twenty-first century. In the early 2000s, however, the overall birth rate again showed signs of improvement. The rise stopped in 2010, with a further decline to a relatively low level in 2013, followed by a slight increase until 2017. In 2018, the overall fertility rate in the European Union was 1.55 live births per woman, against 1.56 in 2017.[1]

The modern science and technology unleash many opportunities for people and help address a variety of issues. One of the opportunities is the infertility treatment with assisted reproductive technologies. Deteriorating reproductive health has spurred new researches and developments in medicine that require greater attention to the legal aspects of the use of ART and to the related legal relations, reproductive rights, and reproductive health.

The need for an effective regulation of legal relations in the assisted reproductive technologies depends on how clearly these social relations are regulated, namely on whether relevant regulatory acts effectively governing various aspects in the use of ART are in place both at the international level and at the level of individual countries.

This study seeks to analyze approaches of the European Union and Ukraine to regulation of the ART usage and related legal relations.

2 Definition and Regulation of Assisted Reproductive Technologies

International regulatory acts on human rights give considerable attention to, among other things, reproductive health, reproductive rights, and various aspects of the use of assisted reproductive technologies. These acts include, in particular: UDHR of December 10, 1948; Declaration on the Use of Scientific and Technological Progress in the Interests of Peace and for the Benefit of Mankind of November 10, 1975; UN Convention on the Elimination of All Forms of Discrimination against Women of December 18, 1979; Statement on In-Vitro Fertilization and Embryo Transplantation adopted by the 39th World Medical Assembly on October 1, 1987; UN CRC of

[1] Fertility statistics. https://ec.europa.eu/eurostat/statistics-explained/index.php/Fertility_statistics.

November 20, 1989; Oviedo Convention: Convention on Human Rights and Biomedicine of April 4, 1997; Universal Declaration on the Human Genome and Human Rights of November 11, 1997; and UN Millennium Declaration approved by UN General Assembly Resolution 55/2 of September 8, 2000.

The WHO and the International Committee for Monitoring Assisted Reproductive Technologies (ICMART) define ART in the Glossary on Assisted Reproductive Technology as follows: 'Assisted reproductive technology (ART): all treatments or procedures that include the in vitro handling of both human oocytes and sperm or of embryos for the purpose of establishing a pregnancy. This includes, but is not limited to, in vitro fertilization and embryo transfer, gamete intrafallopian transfer, zygote intrafallopian transfer, tubal embryo transfer, gamete and embryo cryopreservation, oocyte and embryo donation, and gestational surrogacy. ART does not include assisted insemination (artificial insemination) using sperm from either a woman's partner or a sperm donor.'[2] Evidently, these international organizations regard assisted reproductive technologies as infertility treatment methods.

Advances in science and technology, which create more opportunities to improve living standards for peoples and nations, can, in some cases, give rise to social issues, as well as threaten human rights and fundamental freedoms. Considering this, Paragraph 3 of the Declaration on the Use of Scientific and Technological Progress in the Interests of Peace and for the Benefit of Mankind adopted by the 30th session of the UN General Assembly on November 10, 1975 establishes that all States shall take measures to ensure that scientific and technological achievements satisfy the material and spiritual needs of all sectors of the population.

Provisions of Paragraph 3 of the Declaration are detailed in Paragraphs 7 and 8 thereof, which require measures, including legislative measures, to ensure that the utilization of scientific and technological achievements promotes the fullest realization of human rights and fundamental freedoms without discrimination whatsoever on grounds of race, sex, language or religious beliefs, and to prevent and preclude the utilization of scientific and technological achievements to the detriment of human rights and fundamental freedoms and the dignity of human person.[3] In the context of ART, the provisions of the Declaration should be regarded as a guarantee of equal access for everyone to the advances in science and technology and as a safeguard against violations of human rights and freedoms. The above provisions mean that States should take the necessary measures, including legislative measures, which include the development and adoption of appropriate regulatory acts aimed at protecting human rights and fundamental freedoms in the area of ART.

On September 24, 1986, the Parliamentary Assembly of the Council of Europe adopted Recommendation 1046 'Use of human embryos and foetuses for diagnostic,

---

[2]The Glossary on Assisted Reproductive Technology (2009).

[3]Declaration on the Use of Scientific and Technological Progress in the Interests of Peace and for the Benefit of Mankind, proclaimed by General Assembly resolution 3384 (XXX) of November 10, 1975. https://www.ohchr.org/EN/ProfessionalInterest/Pages/ScientificAndTechnologicalProgress.aspx.

therapeutic, scientific, industrial and commercial purposes'. This Recommendation states that human embryos and foetuses must be treated in all circumstances with the respect due to human dignity, and that use of materials and tissues therefrom must be strictly limited and regulated to purposes which are clearly therapeutic and for which no other means exist. The use of embryos or foetuses and the removal of their tissues for diagnostic and therapeutic purposes are only justified if the principles and conditions specified in the Appendix to this Recommendation are observed. The document suggests prohibiting any creation of human embryos by the in vitro fertilization for the purposes of research during their life or after death.[4]

Resolution 1399 (2004) and Recommendation 1675 (2004) 'European strategy for the promotion of sexual and reproductive health and rights' establish that the right to sexual and reproductive health implies that people are able to enjoy a mutually satisfying and safe relationship, free from coercion or violence. Individuals and couples should be able to regulate their fertility without adverse or dangerous consequences. In these documents, the Parliamentary Assembly of the Council of Europe calls on Member States to work together to develop a European strategy for the promotion of sexual and reproductive health and rights, as well as to prepare, adopt, and implement comprehensive national strategies for protection of sexual and reproductive health.[5]

The Committee on Women's Rights and Gender Equality states in its report titled 'Sexual and Reproductive Health and Rights' (2013/2040 (INI)):

> ...Reproductive health is safeguarded by reproductive rights. As recognized by Art. 96 of Beijing Platform for Action (1995), those rights are based on human rights of equality and dignity. Reproductive rights, including the right to maternal healthcare and family planning, include both freedoms and entitlements linked to many of the already established civil, political, economic, social, and cultural rights. Although not interchangeable, reproductive rights are one aspect of sexual rights, just as sexual rights are one part of reproductive rights.
>
> The Committee on Women's Rights and Gender Equality calls on EU delegations to work with the relevant governments to elaborate and implement policies that focus on fostering the value of women and girls in society, in order to fight gender inequality, discrimination against women and girls, and the social norms that govern son preference, which constitute the root causes of prenatal sex-selection and abortion, as well as early forced marriage and female genital mutilation; emphasizes that efforts to limit sex selection must not hamper or limit the right of women to have access to legitimate sexual and reproductive health technologies and services.[6]

---

[4]Recommendation 1046 (1986) Use of human embryos and foetuses for diagnostic, therapeutic, scientific, industrial and commercial purposes. http://assembly.coe.int/nw/xml/XRef/Xref-XML2HTML-en.asp?fileid=15080&lang=en.

[5]Resolution 1399 (2004) and Recommendation 1675 (2004) on a European strategy for the promotion of sexual and reproductive health and rights. http://www.assembly.coe.int/nw/xml/XRef/Xref-DocDetails-en.asp?FileID=17257&lang=en.

[6]Report on Sexual and Reproductive Health and Rights (2013/2040(INI)) by Committee on Women's Rights and Gender Equality. https://www.europarl.europa.eu/sides/getDoc.do?pubRef=-//EP//TEXT+REPORT+A7-2013-0426+0+DOC+XML+V0//EN.

Resolution 1394 (2004) 'The involvement of men, especially young men, in reproductive health' states that there are several areas of reproductive health which concern men as much as women: family planning and men's reproductive health (especially the rise in male infertility). In this document, the Parliamentary Assembly of the Council of Europe calls on the governments of Council of Europe member states, in co-operation with relevant partners, to improve men's access to reproductive health services, ensuring that family-planning services offer men-only sessions at their clinics; testing, treatment, advice, and counselling on family planning should be available at such sessions.[7]

Recommendation 675 (1972) 'Birth control and family planning in Council of Europe Member States' suggests that member governments of the Council of Europe should educate about family planning, namely: create family planning advice bureaus in urban and rural areas and encourage the integration of family planning within the general medical and social services; ensure that young people are provided with suitable sex education, subject to respect for parents' rights and, *inter alia*, promote pre-marriage courses; include teaching on family planning in medical, para-medical, and social welfare schools; support the existence and action of national governmental and non-governmental family planning services as coordinating agencies for representatives of relevant professional and other organizations, as a discussion forum and channel for information and education.[8]

It is worth noting that the reproductive health is a pressing issue in European countries, so the WHO has developed a dedicated document for them. Important principles for reproductive health lie at the heart of a strategy developed for all countries in the WHO European Region, 'Health 21: The Health for All Policy Framework for the WHO European Region'. The document has a balanced structure and covers different areas. Chapter 1 outlines the vision, aims, and key values of the policy for health for all (HFA) and sets out the major orientation of the renewed policy.

Chapter 2 focuses on fostering strong solidarity in health development between Member States and greater equity in health among groups within each country.

Chapters 3 and 4 set out the desired health outcome for the peoples of the Region. Chapter 3 focuses on how to enable people to attain a higher level of health sustained over life. Chapter 4 'Preventing and controlling disease and injury' suggests strategies to reduce the incidence, prevalence, and impact of specific diseases and other causes of ill health.

Chapters 5 and 6 identify the range of strategies and actions to reach the overall goal of health. These chapters tell about multisectoral strategies for creating sustainable health; focus on generating action from many sectors to ensure more

[7]Resolution 1394 (2004) The Involvement of Men, Especially Young Men, in Reproductive Health. http://www.assembly.coe.int/nw/xml/XRef/Xref-XML2HTML-EN.asp?fileid=17252&lang=en.

[8]Recommendation 675 (1972) Birth control and family planning in Council of Europe Member States. http://assembly.coe.int/nw/xml/XRef/Xref-XML2HTML-en.asp?fileid=14709&lang=en.

health-promoting physical, economic, social, and cultural environments for people; and orient the health sector to promote better health gain, equity, and cost–effectiveness.

Policies and mechanisms for managing change are described in Chapter 7 that proposes ways of mobilizing political, professional, and public support for health for all at all levels. This policy aims at creating a broad societal movement for health through innovative partnerships, unifying policies, and a health development process tailored to the new realities of the European Region. An objective of this policy is to ensure public access to reproductive health services.[9]

In addition to the regulatory acts above, the following documents address the assisted reproductive technologies, related reproductive rights, and reproductive health:

1. Global Strategy for Women's, Children's and Adolescent's Health 2016–2030 of the World Health Organization. The revised Global Strategy strives to achieve the best possible health for all women, children, and adolescents, transform the future, and ensure that every newborn, mother, and child not only survive, but also prosper. Among the areas of focus in this document are the quality, equity, and dignity in health services; reproductive health and rights.[10]
2. The United Nations Human Rights Council Resolution 21/6 of September 21, 2012 'Preventable maternal mortality and morbidity and human rights'.[11]
3. Arts. 8, 9, and 19 of the Treaty on the Functioning of the European Union that relate to the fight against discrimination on grounds of sex and the protection of human health.[12]
4. Regulation (EC) No. 1567/2003 of the European Parliament and of the Council of July 15, 2003 on aid for policies and actions on reproductive and sexual health and rights in developing countries.[13]

[9]Health 21: The Health for All Policy Framework for the WHO European Region. https://www.euro.who.int/data/assets/pdf_file/0010/98398/wa540ga199heeng.pdf.

[10]World Health Organisation. The Global Strategy for Women's, Children's and Adolescents' Health (2016–2030). https://www.who.int/life-course/partners/global-strategy/global-strategy-2016-2030/en/.

[11]United Nations Human Rights Council Resolution 21/6 of September 21, (2012) Preventable maternal mortality and morbidity and human rights. https://www.right-docs.org/doc/a-hrc-res-21-6/.

[12]The Treaty on the Functioning of the European Union, O.J. C 326, October 26, (2012) p. 0001 – 0390.

[13]Regulation (EC) No. 1567/2003 of the European Parliament and of the Council of July 15, (2003) on aid for policies and actions on reproductive and sexual health and rights in developing countries, O.J. L 224, September 6, (2003), pp. 1–6.

5. The Regulation (EC) No. 1922/2006 of the European Parliament and of the Council of 20 December 2006 on establishing a European Institute for Gender Equality.[14]

The EU documents related to reproductive law and reproductive health focus mostly on reproductive health, namely: protection of reproductive health; accessibility of family planning services and reproductive health services; possibility for an individual to plan a family independently, without pressure.

After analyzing the provisions of international regulations, it becomes clear that they enshrine the right of each person to use the results of scientific progress, in particular, assisted reproductive technologies. Although such use shall be conditioned by respect for human rights and dignity.

We may establish that the core of reproductive rights includes human rights dealing with health, procreation, and access to the necessary information in the field of reproductive health.[15]

The international acts enshrine the freedom of childbirth and procreation and prevent human rights violations in the field of reproduction. They also support the principle of prohibition of discrimination against women in relation to their role in procreation.

The rules of international instruments provide women and men with equal rights to receive information in the field of health and family planning, and therefore to obtain complete and reliable information on issues related to reproductive health, including the effectiveness, benefits and possible risks of assisted reproductive technologies.

From the standpoint of international law, reproductive rights have been enshrined in a number of international regulations. However, at the international level, reproductive rights are not distinguished from other human rights in the system of personal non-pecuniary rights and are considered part of the right to health and the right to health care.

Different aspects of the regulation of relations on the use of ART were considered in the decisions of the ECtHR, namely: cases of Mennesson v. France (application no. 65192/11);[16] cases of Labassee v. France (application no. 65941/11);[17] cases of Paradiso and Campanelli v. Italy (application no. 25358/12).

Consider some aspects of the case of Paradiso and Campanelli v. Italy (application no. 25358/12):

[14] Regulation (EC) No. 1922/2006 of the European Parliament and of the Council of December 20, (2006) on establishing a European Institute for Gender Equality, O.J. L 403, December 30, (2006), pp. 9–17.

[15] Golovashchuk (2017b), pp. 78–81.

[16] Cases of Mennesson v. France (application no. 65192/11). https://hudoc.echr.coe.int/fre#{%22itemid%22:[%22001-145389%22]}.

[17] Cases of Labassee v. France (application no. 65941/11). https://hudoc.echr.coe.int/eng#{%22itemid%22:[%22001-145180%22]}.

. . .The Court notes at the outset that the child T.C. was born from an embryo obtained from an ova donation and a sperm donation provided by unknown donors, and was brought into the world in Russia by a Russian woman who waived her rights to him. There was therefore no biological tie between the applicants and the child. The applicants paid approximately EUR 50,000 to receive the child. The Russian authorities issued a birth certificate stating that they were the parents under Russian law. The applicants then decided to bring the child to Italy and to live there with him. The child's genetic origins remain unknown. The present case thus concerns applicants who, acting outside any standard adoption procedure, brought to Italy from abroad a child who had no biological tie with either parent, and who had been conceived – according to the domestic courts – through assisted reproduction techniques that were unlawful under Italian law.

The Court notes that in the cases of Mennesson v. France (no. 65192/11, ECHR 2014 (extracts)) and Labassee v. France (no. 65941/11, 26 June 2014), two pairs of intended parents had resorted to gestational surrogacy in the United States and had settled with their children in France. In those cases the existence of a biological tie between the father and the children was proven and the French authorities had never envisaged separating the children from the parents. The issue at the heart of those cases was the refusal to register the particulars of a birth certificate drawn up abroad in undisputed compliance with the legislation of the country of origin, and the children's right to obtain recognition of the legal parent-child relationship. The parents and children were all applicants before the Court.

Unlike the above-cited Mennesson and Labassee cases, the present Art. 8 complaint does not concern the registration of a foreign birth certificate and recognition of the legal parent-child relationship in respect of a child born from a gestational surrogacy arrangement. What is at issue in the present case are the measures taken by the Italian authorities which resulted in the separation, on a permanent basis, of the child and the applicants. Indeed, the domestic courts stated that the case did not involve a 'traditional' surrogacy arrangement, given that the applicants' biological material had not been used. They emphasised the failure to comply with the procedure laid down by the legislation on international adoption and the breach of the prohibition on using donated gametes within the meaning of section 4 of the Medically Assisted Reproduction Act.

Therefore the legal questions at the heart of the case are: whether, given the circumstances outlined above, Art. 8 is applicable; in the affirmative, whether the urgent measures ordered by the Minors Court, which resulted in the child's removal, amount to an interference in the applicants' right to respect for their family life and/or their private life within the meaning of Art. 8 § 1 of the Convention and, if so, whether the impugned measures were taken in accordance with Art. 8 § 2 of the Convention.

Lastly, the Court points out that the child T.C. is not an applicant in the proceedings before the Court, the Chamber having dismissed the complaints raised by the applicants on his behalf. The Court is called upon to examine solely the complaints raised by the applicants on their own behalf. . .[18]

Conclusion on the case of Paradiso and Campanelli v. Italy:

. . .The Court does not underestimate the impact which the immediate and irreversible separation from the child must have had on the applicants' private life. While the Convention does not recognise a right to become a parent, the Court cannot ignore the emotional hardship suffered by those whose desire to become parents has not been or cannot be fulfilled. However, the public interests at stake weigh heavily in the balance, while

[18] Cases of Paradiso and Campanelli v. Italy (application no. 25358/12). https://hudoc.echr.coe.int/eng#{%22tabview%22:[%22document%22],%22itemid%22:[%22001-170359%22]}.

> comparatively less weight is to be attached to the applicants' interest in their personal development by continuing their relationship with the child. Agreeing to let the child stay with the applicants, possibly with a view to becoming his adoptive parents, would have been tantamount to legalising the situation created by them in breach of important rules of Italian law. The Court accepts that the Italian courts, having assessed that the child would not suffer grave or irreparable harm from the separation, struck a fair balance between the different interests at stake, while remaining within the wide margin of appreciation available to them in the present case.
>
> It follows that there has been no violation of Art. 8 of the Convention.[19]

3 Legal Regulation of Assisted Reproductive Technologies in Particular Countries

Legal approaches and allowed methods of assisted reproductive technologies vary greatly across countries. Reviewing the ART regulations and guidelines of other countries, we can see that they take different legal approaches to assisted reproductive technologies. Nowadays, we can identify three legal approaches to ART: restriction, permission, and uncertainty.

The restriction approach means that some countries impose restrictions on the use of certain ART methods in their laws. The majority of countries impose various restrictions on the use of such ART methods as artificial insemination, embryo cryopreservation, and preimplantation genetic diagnosis. However, surrogacy is subject to the strictest prohibitions and restrictions in most countries.

Among countries that take the restriction approach are Austria, Holland, Italy, Germany, Norway, France, Switzerland, and Sweden.[20]

Permission is another approach taken to assisted reproductive technologies. With such approach, the majority of ART methods are legally permitted, but there are certain rules to be observed by ART participants. In general, the laws are much more liberal towards the use of ART in these countries. Taking this approach, the nations seek to protect human rights to paternity (maternity) and reproductive rights, as well as prevent discrimination against a human and human rights in health care and ensure access to modern treatment methods.

The approach permits the majority of assisted reproductive technologies and is followed by Australia, Belarus, the UK, Armenia, Greece, Georgia, Israel, Spain, India, Kazakhstan, Canada, Kyrgyzstan, Moldova, Norway, South Africa, Russia, Ukraine, Tajikistan, and some US States.

Uncertainty is the third approach. With this approach, ART are not prohibited on the one hand, but such countries have no statutes or guidelines governing ART on

[19] Cases of Paradiso and Campanelli v. Italy (application no. 25358/12). https://hudoc.echr.coe.int/eng#{%22tabview%22:[%22document%22],%22itemid%22:[%22001-170359%22]}.

[20] Golovashchuk (2017a).

the other hand. Among the countries having uncertainty about ART are Venezuela, Ecuador, Jordan, Colombia, Malaysia, Peru, and Uruguay.[21]

3.1 Italy

In Italy, assisted reproductive technologies are governed by Law No. 40 of February 19, 2004 'Rules on Medically Assisted Procreation' (*Norme in materia di procreazione medicalmente assistita*). This law considerably restricts the use of ART, prohibits surrogacy, and imposes severe sanctions for violations. Pursuant to this act, the use of medically assisted procreation is allowed only on the conditions and in the manner prescribed by this law. The use of medically assisted procreation (artificial insemination) is allowed if there is no other effective treatment methods to remove the causes of infertility. Under Art. 5 of the law, assisted procreation techniques are allowed only for adults of different sex couples, married or cohabiting.[22] Under such restrictive rules, single persons are disallowed to be ART participants. The Italian law also restricts the number of ova that can be fertilized at one time to three and, at the same time, establishes that all embryos must be implanted in a woman. Moreover, this law establishes rules for the embryo protection, prohibits embryo cryopreservation, and imposes general prohibitions and penalties for violations of the law.

We can sum up that Italy has chosen the restriction approach characterized by a very clear and tight regulation of the use of assisted reproductive technologies. It restricts access of certain individuals to ART on the grounds of marital status and prohibits certain ART methods.

3.2 Germany

German laws on assisted reproductive technologies also impose strict rules and a number of prohibitions. In Germany, ART methods are governed by two laws. The first is the Law of July 2, 1976 'On Mediation at Adoption' (*Gesetz über die Vermittlung der Annahme als Kind und über das Verbot der Vermittlung von Ersatzmüttern (Adoptionsvermittlungsgesetz — AdVermiG)*). This act prohibits surrogacy mediation (§ 13 'b' and 'c'), selection of a surrogate mother, search for potential parents, and surrogacy advertising (§ 13 'd'). It imposes criminal liability for surrogacy mediation, in particular imprisonment for up to one year or a fine. If a

[21] IFFS Surveillance 07 (2007).

[22] Rules on Medically Assisted Procreation: Law of Italy of February 19, (2004) No. 40 (*Norme in materia di procreazione medicalmente assistita)* Official Gazette (2004) No. 45. http://www.ieb-eib.org/nl/pdf/loi-pma-italie-english.pdf.

person benefited financially from surrogacy, s/he shall be punished by imprisonment for up to two years or by a fine (§ 14 'b').[23]

The second act is the Law of December 13, 1990 'On the Protection of Embryos' (*Gesetz zum Schutz von Embryonen (Embryonenschutzgesetz — ESchG)*). It prohibits the surrogacy in the country and imposes significant restrictions on the use of ART.[24] International academic literature emphasizes that the Law 'On the Protection of Embryos' is clearly based on the assessment that embryos conceived in vitro must not be used either for research or therapeutic purposes.[25]

3.3 France

French law on ART is no less strict than German regulations. Law No. 2004-800 of August 6, 2004 'On Bioethics' imposed the first prohibitions and restrictions. The act regulated the issues of ethics and biomedicine, genetic expertise, use of human genetic material, childbirth, embryology, and other aspects.[26]

Subsequently, Art. 16-7 of the French Civil Code (*Code civil*) established that any agreement related to procreation or pregnancy at the expense of any third party shall be deemed invalid.[27] Therefore, France prohibits surrogacy at a code level, but allows ART, such as artificial insemination.

Later, France adopted another document on ART, Law No. 2011-814 of July 7, 2011 'On Bioethics'. Much more substantial, this act regulates a wider range of issues, namely: genetic testing for medical purposes; organ and cell donation; prenatal and preimplantation genetic diagnosis, fetal examination; gamete donation; medical assistance in reproduction; and embryo examination.[28]

---

[23] On Mediation at Adoption: Law of Germany of July 2, 1976 *Gesetz über die Vermittlung der Annahme als Kind und über das Verbot der Vermittlung von Ersatzmüttern (Adoptionsvermittlungsgesetz – AdVermiG)*. Bundesgesetzblatt No. 78 dd. July 7, 1976. http://www.bgbl.de/xaver/bgbl/start.xav?startbk=Bundesanzeiger_BGBl&jumpTo=bgbl176s1762.pdf#__bgbl__%2F%2F*%5B%40attr_id%3D%27bgbl176s1762.pdf%27%5D__1446215628622.

[24] On the Protection of Embryo: Law of Germany of December 13, 1990. *Gesetz zum Schutz von Embryonen (Embryonenschutzgesetz – ESchG)*. Bundesgesetzblatt No. 69 dd. December 19, 1990. http://www.bgbl.de/xaver/bgbl/start.xav?startbk=Bundesanzeiger_BGBl&jumpTo=bgbl176s1762.pdf#__bgbl__%2F%2F*%5B%40attr_id%3D%27bgbl190s2746.pdf%27%5D1446215149748.

[25] Christian Starck (2006).

[26] On Bioethics: Law of France of August 6, 2004 No. 2004-800 = *Loi relative à la bioéthique*. https://www.legifrance.gouv.fr/jorf/id/JORFTEXT000000441469.

[27] Civil Code of France enacted on March 21, 1804 = *Le Code civil des Françai* (as amended and supplemented). http://www.legifrance.gouv.fr/affichCode.do?cidTexte=LEGITEXT000006070721&dateTexte=20151022.

[28] On Bioethics: Law of France of July 7, 2011 No. 2011-814 = *Loi relative à la bioéthique*. https://www.legifrance.gouv.fr/jorf/id/JORFTEXT000024323102.

The French Code of Public Health of October 7, 1953 (*Code de la santé publique*) regulates the reproductive health, women's rights in health care, and reproductive donation in the most comprehensive way. This act is directed towards protecting the health of mothers and children. This Code also regulates a number of other important aspects such as the use of ART; working conditions of health care institutions and clinical laboratories dealing with ART; research on embryos; prenatal diagnosis; and artificial insemination.[29]

We can see that the countries that take the restriction approach to ART have developed and adopted special regulations governing ART, prohibited the use of certain ART methods at a legislative level, and imposed strict rules and prohibitions in relation to assisted reproductive technologies. Choosing the restriction approach, the parliament in each of the above countries sought to protect human rights and prevent the use of advances in science and technology to the detriment of human health, dignity, and rights. Nonetheless, current strict laws in these countries have given rise to a new phenomenon and new relations in society. People with reproductive health issues have to travel to other countries with more liberal regulation to undergo the necessary treatment and exercise their reproductive rights. As we can see, the restriction approach and strict prohibitions have given rise to a new phenomenon known as reproductive tourism.

3.4 Ukraine

Today, Ukraine is among countries that allows the majority of ART methods by law. In Ukraine, various aspects of assisted reproductive technologies are regulated by: the CC of Ukraine; the Family Code of Ukraine; Law of Ukraine No. 2801-XII of November 19, 1992 'Fundamentals of the Legislation of Ukraine on Health Care'; Ministry of Health's Order No. 787 of September 9, 2013 'On Approval of the Procedures for the Use of Assisted Reproductive Technologies in Ukraine'; Ministry of Health's Order No. 489 of December 10, 2001 'On Approval of Statistical Documents on Assisted Reproductive Technologies', and a number of other subordinate laws.

Art. 281 of the CC of Ukraine enshrines the right to ART and establishes that an adult woman or man shall have the right, given their medical indications, to undertake medical treatment programs of assisted reproductive technologies according to procedures established by law.[30] Having examined Art. 281 of the Civil Code, we find that ART can be used in Ukraine as medical programs for

[29] On Public Health: Code of France of October 7, 1953 (as amended on October 16, 2020). = *Code de la santé publique.* http://legifrance.gouv.fr/affichCode.do?cidTexte=LEGITEXT000006072665.

[30] The Law of Ukraine Civil Code of Ukraine No 435-IV (2003) (as amended and supplemented). *Vidomosti Verkhovnoyi Rady Ukrainy.* 2003. No. 40-44. Art. 356.

medical reasons, and therefore, the use of reproductive technologies for social reasons is not prescribed by the applicable laws. In addition, the Civil Code also establishes a lower age limit, the full legal age, for the use of ART, omitting to establish the upper age limit. The Code imposes no other conditions or restrictions on the use of ART.

Art. 123 of the FC of UkraineNo. 2947-III of January 10, 2002 (hereinafter referred to as the Family Code) regulates establishment of parentage and parental rights in regard to a child born through assisted reproductive technologies.[31] Analyzing these provisions of Family Code, we should note that the establishment of parentage in regard to a child born through ART is regulated only for spouses, while the use of ART for persons who are in a de facto marital relationship or for an unmarried woman or unmarried man lacks regulation. Therefore, only spouses can be recognized parents of a child born through ART, as the applicable law of Ukraine prescribes. This prevents individuals from exercising their reproductive rights on the grounds of marital status.

Art. 48 of the Law of Ukraine No. 2801-XII 'Fundamentals of the Legislation of Ukraine on Health Care' of November 19, 1992 governs only the use of artificial insemination and embryo implantation, omitting to regulate surrogacy and other ART methods and techniques. Moreover, this law does not define the terms 'assisted reproductive technologies', 'artificial insemination, 'embryo implantation', 'surrogate mother', 'surrogacy', etc.

At the governmental level, various regulations focus on the nation's reproductive health. Among such first regulatory acts was Decree No. 203/2001 'On the Reproductive Health National Program 2001-2005' signed by the President of Ukraine on March 26, 2001. Developed to improve the demographic situation in the country, preserve the nation's reproductive health, protect motherhood and childhood, and strengthen the family relationships, the Program sought to: ensure legal and social protection of the family; monitor the observance by employers of the health and safety laws in regard to women and youth; build a social and economic foundation for measures aimed at improving the demographic situation in the country; and improve the quality and accessibility of reproductive health care.[32]

Subsequently, the Cabinet of Ministers of Ukraine adopted Resolution No. 1849 on December 27, 2006 to approve the Reproductive Health of the Nation State Program 2015. The Program was designed to improve the nation's reproductive health, an important element of the overall health, as the reproductive health has a significant impact on the demographic situation and on the social and economic development of the country. The Program's objectives were to create an enabling environment for safe maternity; strengthen the reproductive health of children and

---

[31] The Family Code of Ukraine No. 2947-III (2002) (as amended and supplemented). *Vidomosti Verkhovnoyi Rady Ukrainy*. 2002. No. 21-22. Art. 135.

[32] The Decree of the President of Ukraine 'On the Reproductive Health National Program 2001-2005' No. 203/2001 (2001) http://zakon0.rada.gov.ua/laws/show/203/2001.

the youth; improve the family planning system; preserve reproductive health of the nation; and ensure effective control over implementation of the Program.[33]

3.5 *Poland*

In Poland, assisted reproductive technologies are regulated by the Law of 25 June 2015 'On the Infertility Treatment'. This act regulates: operation of infertility treatment centers; use of reproductive cells and embryos for medically assisted procreation; collection of reproductive cells and donation of embryos for medically assisted procreation; registration of reproductive cell and embryo donors; reproductive cell and embryo labeling, monitoring, storage, and transportation, as well as safety and quality criteria for reproductive cells and embryos; operation of centers for reproductive medicine and banks of reproductive cells and embryos; export and import of reproductive cells and embryos; tasks and objectives of the Minister responsible for health care, including control and oversight; operation of the Infertility Treatment Council; penalties and administrative fines.

This law outlines: (1) the principles of embryo and reproductive cell protection when embryos and reproductive cells are used in biology and medicine in connection with the infertility treatment; (2) infertility treatment methods, including medically assisted procreation; (3) tasks and objectives of government authorities in relation to the protection and promotion of reproductive health; (4) conditions of donation, procurement, processing, storage, and distribution of reproductive cells and embryos intended for medically assisted procreation; (5) principles governing the operation of centers for reproductive medicine and banks of reproductive cells and embryos.

In Poland, ART is allowed when it is used as an infertility treatment method: '…Infertility treatment using the in vitro fertilization can be undertaken after other treatments were unsuccessful for at least 12 months. The in vitro fertilization can be carried out without other exhausting procedures in less than 12 months after the start of infertility treatment if, as the modern medicine proves it, it is impossible to establish pregnancy with these methods…'.[34]

[33]The Resolution of the Cabinet of Ministers of Ukraine 'On Approval of the Reproductive Health of the Nation State Program' (2015) No. 1849 http://zakon3.rada.gov.ua/laws/show/1849-2006-%D0%BF.

[34]Ustawa z dnia 25 czerwca 2015 r. o leczeniu niepłodności (Dz.U. 2015 poz. 1087). http://isap.sejm.gov.pl/isap.nsf/DocDetails.xsp?id=WDU20150001087.

3.6 Moldova

In Moldova, Law No. 185 of May 24, 2001 'On Reproductive Health Protection and Family Planning' regulates the use of assisted reproductive technologies. This act defines assisted reproductive technologies as a set of medical measures aimed at restoring human reproductive function and regulates the use of such ART methods as reproductive cell donation and artificial insemination. The Law enshrines a number of reproductive health rights: the right to decide freely on procreation; the right to receive information about one's reproductive health and family planning; right to donate gametes; right to artificial insemination and in vitro fertilization. Under Moldovan law, men and women under 35, physically and mentally healthy, have the right to donate gametes after appropriate medical and genetic tests, with anonymity guaranteed to such individuals. The responsibility for the preservation and use of gametes lies with the Government. Gamete preservation and use cannot be a source of income.[35]

When analyzing the legal regulation of ART application in the above countries, we can identify both strong and insufficiently regulated aspects.

The legislation of Italy, France and Germany clearly spells out which types of ART are prohibited, and which are not. The legislation of these countries supports restrictions of certain activities, for instance, Italy prohibits mediation in assisted reproductive technologies, as well as advertising of ART. Italian law limited the number of eggs that can be fertilized at a time down to three and at the same time established the rule by which all resulting embryos must be implanted to a woman. French law clearly spells out the working conditions of healthcare organizations, clinical laboratories operating in the field of ART, performance of research on embryos and prenatal diagnosis.

Although a significant number of restrictions and prohibitions prescribed in the legislation of these countries force their citizens to seek health care services in the field of ART in other countries with more liberal legislation, thereby creating a new public phenomenon called "reproductive tourism".

Ukraine does not restrict the use of surrogacy, which is why a significant number of international couples come here for treatment with this type of ART. However, when using surrogacy for international couples, there is always a risk with regard to the child receiving a birth certificate of the home country of her parents, as well as whether parents will be able to travel to their home country with the child.

The legislation of Ukraine also does not prohibit ART advertising, cryopreservation of embryos, as well as work of mediation agencies that provide consulting and organizational services.

However, unlike the legislation of Germany, the legislation of Ukraine does not regulate the issue of creation of hybrid embryos and chimera embryos. The

---

[35] The Law of Moldova 'On Protection of Reproductive Health and Family Planning' No. 185 (2001) http://lex.justice.md/viewdoc.php?action=view&view=doc&id=312794&lang=2.

unregulated nature of this issue creates opportunities for abuse and requires a speedy resolution.

4 Conclusions

Modern globalization processes have an impact on legal regulation as well. Amid globalization, countries face common problems that bring them together to find solutions. International regulations on reproductive human rights and ART give general recommendations on how to regulate the use of ART. Moreover, these documents emphasize the need to protect human rights in the application of modern advances in science and medicine. The laws in the European Union and individual countries focus on the protection of human reproductive rights and reproductive health.

The analysis of the regulatory acts in the EU Member States shows that many countries have adopted special laws to regulate the use of ART.

Ukrainian regulatory acts on health care in general and on ART in particular regulate a great number of issues, but need improvements and a special law to be adopted to regulate the matters in question.

Legal communications between countries and a common legal understanding in the area of ART regulation encourage learning of the best practices and approaches of other countries in this area.

We believe it is reasonable to pay attention to reproductive rights of both women and men equally. To this end, the practices of the EU Member States can be useful, in particular: France (regulation of health care by a single code); Poland (regulation of operation of banks of reproductive cells and embryos); and Germany (criminal liability for offenses against human reproductive rights and the use of ART).

When comparing the legislation of Ukraine and other countries, we noted that now the legislation of Ukraine in the field of ART use features a number of gaps that require clear regulation, namely:

(1) definition of terms and concepts in the field of ART use, and development of a clear conceptual framework;
(2) development and adoption of the concept of government policy in the field of family planning and the use of ART, taking into account the recommendations provided in international regulations;
(3) development of modern unified clinical protocols for ART treatment;
(4) setting requirements for healthcare organizations where ART can be implemented and for medical personnel capable of performing such treatment;
(5) the rights, obligations and responsibilities of all ART participants (patients, doctors, healthcare organizations and others) should be clearly spelled out at the legislative level;

(6) the procedure and conditions for donation of reproductive cells and embryos, as well as special attention should be paid to the issue of maintaining medical confidentiality during donation of reproductive cells and embryos;
(7) conditions and procedure of cryopreservation of reproductive cells and embryos;
(8) conditions and procedure for shipping (transportation) reproductive cells and embryos within Ukraine and outside;
(9) procedure and conditions for using ART in case of foreign nationals and stateless persons in Ukraine.

All of the above issues and many others require careful consideration and review. There is also a need to amend the legislation of Ukraine, namely the Civil Code of Ukraine and the Family Code of Ukraine. Ukraine also needs to develop a separate law to regulate the use of ART followed by a number of by-laws.

References

Golovashchuk A (2017a) Civil Legal Regulation of Relations Associated with the Use of Assisted Reproductive Technologies. Thesis. Volodymyr Koretsky Institute of State and Law of the National Academy of Sciences of Ukraine, Kyiv, p 61

Golovashchuk AP (2017b) Topical issues of protection of reproductive human rights in modern conditions. *Human Rights: Theory and Practic:* collection of scientific papers of First International educational and scientific forum, Poland, January 23–28, 2017. IASHE, London, pp 78–81.

IFFS Surveillance 07 (2007) Fertility and Sterility 87(2):8–14

Starck C (2006) Embryonic stem cell research according to German and European Law. German Law J 7(7):655–656

Part V
Intellectual Property in Medicine and Pharmacy

Intellectual Property in Medicine and Pharmacy: Harmonization of Ukraine and EU Legislation

Oksana Kashyntseva

Contents

Abstract This chapter is devoted to harmonization of public and private interests in health care by the Intellectual Property mechanisms. This problem has got significance after the proclamation of the UN Millennium Declaration and became even more relevant in the context of the COVID-19 pandemic. The chapter reviews the changes that took place at the beginning of the twenty-first century with the adoption of the Doha Declaration on the TRIPS Agreement and Public Health. The author presents the analysis of the political reasons for additional commitments taken by Ukraine in the sphere of Intellectual Property and outlines ways to overcome them now, as the world tends to liberalize Intellectual Property in health care in general and in the COVID-19 treatment and COVID-19 vaccines in particular. For Ukraine and Eastern European countries, it is important to maintain the sue generis trend laid down at signing the Association Agreement with the EU. Now, Ukraine has changed its approach to shaping an internal position in the market of medicines, trying to use both the experience of the EU and the experience of developing countries in certain areas. Exclusion of methods of treatment, diagnostics and surgical interventions

This paper is prepared on the basis of the reports for the Conference 'Private Healthcare Law: Challenges and Prospects'.

O. Kashyntseva (✉)
Centre for Harmonisation of Human Rights and Intellectual Property Rights of the Scientific and Research Institute of Intellectual Property of National Academy of Law Sciences of Ukraine, Kyiv, Ukraine

© The Author(s), under exclusive license to Springer Nature Switzerland AG 2022
R. Maydanyk et al. (eds.), *Ukrainian Healthcare Law in the Context of European and International Law*, European Union and its Neighbours in a Globalized World 7,
https://doi.org/10.1007/978-3-031-05690-1_12

from patentable objects is the implementation of the EU and Eastern European experience. Ukraine has turned to rethinking its commitments in the field of protection of Intellectual Property rights in medicine in the TRIPS-plus regime. And we are not alone on this way.

1 Introduction: Background and Objectives of the Study

The legal doctrine of the twenty-first century shows global trends for liberalization of Intellectual Property rights in health care. And if in the legal doctrine of the twentieth century the absolute priority is given to Intellectual Property rights of the owner of such rights and their inviolability, since Intellectual Property rights were placed above the public interest, then in the twenty-first century we see a reverse trend—the desire to harmonize human rights and Intellectual Property rights in health care, the sphere which is very sensitive to any monopoly. These issues were covered in detail at the Kyiv legal readings 'Private law in the sphere of healthcare: challenges and prospects'.

The United Nations Millennium Development Goals (MDGs)[1] identify the need to encourage the development of the generic pharmaceutical industry in order to provide access to affordable essential medicines in developing countries. Under the WHO Global Strategy and Action Plan on Public Health, Innovation and Trade, the organization has a key role in balancing Public Health, innovation and Intellectual Property.[2]

The legal aspects of harmonization of public and private interests in health care by the Intellectual Property mechanisms have got significance after the proclamation of the UN Millennium Declaration and became even more relevant in the context of the COVID-19 pandemic.

An estimated 33–50% of the global population had coverage for essential health services, including medicines.[3] Barriers to access medicines disproportionately affect people in low- and middle-income countries due to unaffordable prices, medicines shortages and insufficient health care coverage. These challenges are compounded by insufficient research and medicines development for neglected,

---

[1] United Nations Millennium Development Goals (2000). https://www.un.org/ru/documents/decl_conv/declarations/summitdecl.shtml.

[2] See: The Global Strategy and Plan of Action on Public Health, Innovation and Intellectual Property (2000), Available via DIALOG. https://www.who.int/phi/implementation/phi_globstat_action.

[3] Primary Health Care on the Road to Universal Health Coverage: 2019 Monitoring Report: Executive Summary.

World Health Organization, Geneva 2019 https://apps.who.int/iris/handle/10665/328913.

poverty-related and vaccine-preventable diseases, with COVID-19 being at the top of this list today.[4]

The European Union can potentially have a major influence on the access to medicines in low- and middle-income countries. The EU is a key pharmaceutical exporter to these countries, a trade hub for medicines in transit and a major global health donor for drug development and procurement by international agencies. However, in parallel with the implementation of progressive provisions of European legislation, it is extremely important for Ukraine to maintain a balance and use instruments provided by international acts to weaken or exclude IP rights whose impact is growing in a pandemic. The experience of EU countries, in particular Germany and France, which during the pandemic improved IP legislation in order to overcome patent barriers is indicative for Ukraine.

2 Trends in the Liberalization of Intellectual Property Rights

The beginning of the twenty-first century is marked by amendments to the TRIPS Agreement[5] and the adoption of the Doha Declaration on the TRIPS Agreement and Public Health. Today, this issue is even more sensitive in connection with the COVID-19 pandemic, which has become a catalyst for global trends in the liberalization of Intellectual Property rights in health care. As stated by the WHO, COVID-19 puts immense pressure on the health care system. In these circumstances rapid and large-scale research is required, while traditional randomized clinical trials take years. Humanity has no time for that now. Solidarity clinical trials, which were proclaimed by WHO in the COVID-19 treatment, should reduce the duration of studies to 80%, and involving patients in a single global randomized trial will help facilitate a rapid comparison of unproven treatments worldwide.

The WHO states that solidarity clinical trials for COVID-19 treatment call for simplified procedures that allow even overcrowded hospitals to participate without completing all the documents required for traditional trials. As of March 27, 2020, more than 70 countries have already confirmed their readiness to contribute to the research, and many other countries are on their way to joining this effort. The WHO emphasizes that the more countries participate in solidarity clinical trials, the faster the results will be obtained. WHO facilitates access to thousands of trial treatment courses donated from a number of manufacturers. WHO also invites researchers and companies to work together to ensure disclosure of treatment variability if effective.[6]

---

[4]Wirtz et al. (2017).

[5]TRIPS Agreement. http://zakon3.rada.gov.ua/laws/show/981_018.

[6]See: Solidarity' clinical trial for COVID-19 treatments. https://www.who.int/emergencies/diseases/novel-coronavirus-2019/global-research-on-novel-coronavirus-2019-ncov/solidarity-clinical-trial-for-covid-19-treatments.

It should be noted that EMA insists that compassionate use[7] is not a part of an experiment or a clinical trial required for the authorization of a medicinal product.[8]

IFLA (International Federation of Library Associations and Institutions) also wrote an open letter to the WIPO urging it to use all available flexible Intellectual Property mechanisms to maximize worldwide access to information (research data) on COVID-19 treatment.[9]

For Eastern European countries it is important that the *sue generis* trends were laid down at the time of signing the Association Agreement with the EU. Thus, in particular, in the EU-Ukraine Association Agreement[10] the sphere of Intellectual Property and Public Health is regulated by Art. 219—Patents and Public Health. Similar provisions can be found in the Association Agreement between Moldova and the EU—Art. 313[11] and in the Association Agreement between Georgia and the EU—Art. 185.[12]

For Ukraine, as for most Eastern European countries, the problem of access to treatment is an urgent concern. When fulfilling the strategic task of acquiring membership in the WTO, we have introduced instruments for the protection of Intellectual Property in the field of medicine without taking into account the experience of the EU countries in terms of the priority of the human right to access to treatment and not taking into account the experience of low- and middle-income countries in terms of implementing the flexible provisions of the TRIPS Agreement. However, the TRIPS Agreement sets minimum requirements for the legal protection of Intellectual Property in a WTO member-state. Ukraine has made additional commitments (TRIPS-plus provisions) in the part that was not mandatory and the EU experience should have been the main argument in the search for balance, instead Ukraine introduced legal protection in the field of medicine, allowing patenting of therapeutic and surgical methods of treatment and diagnostics, patenting

[7] Compassionate use is a treatment option that allows the use of an unauthorised medicine. Under strict conditions, products in development can be made available to groups of patients who have a disease with no satisfactory authorised therapies and who cannot enter clinical trials. See: https://www.ema.europa.eu/en/human-regulatory/research-development/compassionate-use.

[8] European Medicines Agency. https://www.ema.europa.eu/en/human-regulatory/research-development/compassionate-use.

[9] International Federation of Library Associations and Institutions. Available via DIALOG. https://www.ifla.org/node/92993.

[10] Association Agreement between the European Union and the European Atomic Energy Community and their Member States, of the one part, and the Ukraine, of the other part. https://zakon.rada.gov.ua/laws/show/984_011.

[11] Association Agreement between the European Union and the European Atomic Energy Community and their Member States, of the one part, and the Republic of Moldova, of the other part. https://eur-lex.europa.eu/legal-content/EN/TXT/?uri=uriserv%3AOJ.L_.2014.260.01.0004.01.ENG.

[12] Association Agreement between the European Union and the European Atomic Energy Community and their Member States, of the one part, and Georgia, of the other part. Available via DIALOG. https://eur-lex.europa.eu/legal-content/en/TXT/PDF/?uri=CELEX:22014A0830(02).

of a previously known product or method for a new purpose[13] and introducing a patent linkage for authorization of medicines,[14] etc. The countries of Eastern Europe did not undertake such obligations and paved their way to the EU much faster than Ukraine, that is under pressure from the side of Russian Federation due to integration into the economic and political area of the EU.

Currently, Ukraine has changed its approach to shaping an internal position in the market of medicines, trying to use both the experience of the EU and the experience of developing countries in certain areas.

3 Content of Eastern European Patent Legislation in Health Care and Patent Reform in Ukraine

Exclusion of methods of treatment, diagnostics and surgical interventions from patentable objects is implemented into of the EU and Eastern European legislation. For example, in such Eastern European countries as Serbia (Art. 9 of the Serbian Patent Law),[15] Albania (Art. 6 of the Industrial Property Law),[16] Northern Macedonia (Art. 26 of the Industrial Property Law)[17] and other PCT[18] countries, treatments, diagnostics and surgical interventions are also excluded from the objects of patenting.

Today, Ukraine has turned to rethinking its commitments in the field of protection of Intellectual Property rights in medicine in the TRIPS-plus regime. And we are not alone on this way. Ukraine has received expert support from international organizations—WHO and the United Nations Development Program, whose mandate includes expanding access to treatment. High-level political dialogues on reforming Intellectual Property legislation in the field of medicine have shaped the basis of modern patent reform in Ukraine.

Low-income and developing countries[19] have advocated for a special Intellectual Property regime in the field of medicine, which is called in legal doctrine the 'TRIPS-flexibility provisions'. In addition, the EU has given us an excellent example having not included therapeutic and surgical treatment methods as well as methods

[13] See the Law of Ukraine 'On Protection of Inventions and Utility Models'.

[14] See: Art. 9 The Law Of Ukraine 'On Medicines'.

[15] Patent Law of Serbia. http://www.zis.gov.rs/upload/documents/pdf_en/pdf_patenti/zakon%20pat.%20eng%2020.1.20.pdf.

[16] See: Law On Industrial Property of Albania.URL: https://www.wipo.int/edocs/lexdocs/laws/en/al/al069en.pdf.

[17] Law On Industrial Property of North Macedonia. http://ippo.gov.mk/EN/LegislationPreview.aspx?lang=EN&id=47&cat=NAT.

[18] European Patent Convention. https://www.epo.org/law-practice/legal-texts/epc.html.

[19] See: Low-income countries. https://iwa-network.org/wp-content/uploads/2019/01/2019-Country-Classification-Update-2018-08.

of diagnostics as the objects of patenting. And this has been done from the standpoint of inconsistency of such monopolization with fundamental human rights - the right to life and the right to health.

Active scientific research, in-depth analysis of the implementation of the TRIPS-flexibility provisions in national legislation has begun in Ukraine more than 10 years ago and evolved from finding legal grounds for liberalization of Intellectual Property in medicine to shaping political will to implement them.

Ukraine exercised its sovereign right to formulate its own policy in the domestic market of Intellectual Property in the field of health care guided by Art. 8 'Principles' of the TRIPS Agreement:

1. Members may, in formulating or amending their laws and regulations, adopt measures necessary to protect Public Health and nutrition, and to promote the public interest in sectors of vital importance to their socio-economic and technological development, provided that such measures are consistent with the provisions of this Agreement.
2. Appropriate measures, provided that they are consistent with the provisions of this Agreement, may be needed to prevent the abuse of Intellectual Property rights by right holders or the resort to practices which unreasonably restrain trade or adversely affect the international transfer of technology.

Thus, with the adoption on July 21, 2020 of the Law of Ukraine 'On Amendments to Certain Legislative Acts of Ukraine on the Reform of Patent Legislation', Ukraine laid foundation for a new Intellectual Property policy in the field of medicine. Despite that, *Damocles gladius* still hangs over some of the provisions, and this is not so much due to legal uncertainty, but more because of lobbying certain business interests. It should be noted however, that the Ukrainian patent reform has received support from WHO and UNDP experts in the issue of ensuring access to treatment namely by Intellectual Property mechanisms. Relevant letters with recommendations and support for the implementation of the TRIPS-flexibility provisions can be found in the archives of the interagency working groups.

For the sake of objective coverage of all aspects of the patent reform in Ukraine and the current situation with Intellectual Property in medicine, we shall present both controversial and non-controversial provisions of the reform.

Let's start with the non-controversial norms of the Law of Ukraine 'On Protection of Rights to Inventions and Utility Models', which is fundamental in balancing Intellectual Property rights and Health Care. Such novels contain provisions that exclude therapeutic and surgical methods of treatment and diagnostics from legal protection. At one time, the therapeutic and surgical methods of treatment, taken out of the patent legislation, significantly reduced the number of patents in this class in European countries, which, as we can see, did not affect in any way the innovative level of European medicine.

Though Ukraine, Moldova, Russia and Belarus have the highest percentage of patents issued in the class 'Medicine' and 'Medicines', they, unfortunately, have nothing to do with the innovative sphere of health care.

The *pre-grant opposition,* provided for as a possibility in WIPO,[20] also belongs to non-controversial provisions. It is defined in the same way in European Patent Convention.[21]

However, Bosnia and Herzegovina, taken as an example, despite the fact that it belongs to EPO area, has no formal pre- or post-grant opposition procedure which is available in the case of patents. In the case of consensual patents (patents which are granted without substantive examination—Art. 41, 42 Patent Law) any person may, within 6 months, file notice of opposition to the grant of a consensual patent (Art. 42 Patent Law). The applicant for a consensual patent may, within 6 months from receipt of notification of the opposition, file a request for the grant of a patent on the basis of the substantive examination procedure. If the applicant for a consensual patent does not file a request, the Institute rejects the patent application.

In accordance with Art. 246 of the Industrial Property Law of Poland, the opposition may be filed on the same grounds on which a patent, may be revoked, i.e.: (i) the requirements for the grant of a patent have not been satisfied, or (ii) the invention has not been disclosed in a manner sufficiently clear and complete for it to be carried out by a person skilled in the art, or (iii) the patent has been granted for an invention not covered by the contents of the application or of the original application.[22]

In Ukraine, Art. 16 of the Law of Ukraine 'On Protection of Inventions and Utility Models' is supplemented by paragraph 17: 'Within six months from the date of publication of the information on the application for the invention, any person may file with the examination body a reasoned notice of opposition to the application.'

Therefore, we have the opportunity to appeal submitted applications for the inventions for compliance with their inventive step without the need to wait for granting a patent for *post-grant opposition.* The possibility of appealing applications exists in the EU legislation in the *pre-grant opposition* regime at the level of directives regulating legal protection of industrial property objects. This legal instrument is effective both for preventing abuse of patent rights and for helping in the examination process at Ukrpatent.[23] It should be noted that any interested person who believes that the grant of a patent may violate his rights or legally protected interests, from the moment of publication of information about the filed application for invention, may read the arguments of the applicant or the person objecting to the grant of the patent (if any) or file his own objections.

[20] See: Opposition Systems. https://www.wipo.int/scp/en/revocation_mechanisms/opposition/index.html.

[21] See: European Patent Convention. https://www.epo.org/law-practice/legal-texts/html/epc/2016/e/ar52.html.

[22] See: Industrial Property Law of Poland. https://www.wipo.int/export/sites/www/scp/en/revocation_mechanisms/opposition/pdf/opposition_poland.pdf.

[23] State Enterprises 'Institute of Intellectual Property (Ukrpatent)'.

It's worth to mention, that the very fact of including the provision on the possibility to appeal an application into the national legislation prompted the withdrawal of some applications from Ukrpatent immediately after the adoption of the Law in its first reading, apparently anticipating their rejection. As the rest of the provisions of the Law were discussed between the first and second readings, the issue of *pre-grant opposition* was raised only by supporters of maintaining *status quo* in Patent Law, but it was overridden by the pro argument about the effective use of *pre-grant opposition* in EU practice. While the effect of the implemented novels is mostly delayed in time, the absence of monopoly on the ways and methods of treatment and *pre-grant opposition* will explicit immediately.

Let's turn to controversial issues. Among them the most sensitive one is the novel of determining the inventive step in the applications for authorization of inventions with a medicinal product as an object. In line with the opportunities provided to countries by Art. 8 of the TRIPS Agreement, Art. 7 of the Law of Ukraine 'On protection of rights to inventions and utility models' was amended by introducing paragraph 7, which states:

> ...An invention involves an inventive step, if it is not obvious for a specialist, i.e., does not result from the level of technology. The contents of applications mentioned in part five of this article shall not be taken into account in the course of the assessment of the inventive step. As those that obviously result from the level of technology can be recognized new forms of known technology of medication, including salts, esters, ethers, compositions, combinations and other derivatives, polymorphs, metabolites, pure forms, particle sizes, isomers, if they do not differ significantly in efficacy.

Such formulation at the level of the law implies the need for further amendments to the Guidelines for the Examination of Patent Applications for inventions and utility models[24] on the basis of the Recommendations of the UN Development Program (Guidelines for the Examination of Patent Applications Relating to Pharmaceuticals of the UNDP[25]). Relevant recommendations were also developed by the South Center[26] (Guidelines on Examination of the Patent Application in the field of Medicine and Pharmaceuticals based on the recommendations of the WHO[27]).

[24] On approval of the Rules for consideration of applications for inventions and applications for utility models of the Ministry of Education and Science of Ukraine; Order, Rules of 15.03.2002 No 197. http://zakon5.rada.gov.ua/laws/show/z0364-02/page3.

[25] See: Guidelines for the Examination of Patent Applications Relating to Pharmaceuticals of the UNDP. https://www.undp.org/content/undp/en/home/librarypage/hiv-aids/guidelines-for-the-examination-of-patent-applications-relating-t.html.

[26] South Center was established for the Achieving the Sustainable Development Goals (SDGs), particularly poverty eradication, requires national policies and an international regime that supports and does not undermine development efforts. The South Centre is an intergovernmental policy research think-tank composed of and accountable to developing country Member States. It conducts policy-oriented research on key policy development issues, and supports developing countries to effectively participate in international negotiating processes that are relevant to the achievement of SDGs. The Centre promotes the unity of the South in such processes while recognizing the diversity of national interests and priorities.

[27] See: Guidelines on Examination of the Patent Application in the field of Medicine and Pharmaceuticals based on the recommendations of the WHO. file:///C:/Users/Lenovo/AppData/Local/Temp/rp61-guidelines-on-patentability-and-a2m-en.pdf.

It should be noted that in Ukraine the issue of differences in 'efficacy' will be resolved jointly with the expert of the State Expert Center of the Ministry of Health of Ukraine. Such a novelty is necessary since for a chemist, the formula of the invention may appear formally new, while for the clinician questions of obviousness and a new distinctive effect may be decided differently. Similar experience can be found in Brazil in the process of examination in the ANVISA office—Agência Nacional de Vigilância Sanitária.[28]

4 'Bolar Exemption' as a Mechanism to Expand Access to Medicines

The issue of expediting access to any domestic market in general, and to the Ukrainian market of generic medicines in particular, is solved by the implementation into the Ukrainian legislation so called the 'Bolar exemption'.[29] Bolar exemption is presented in US, Canadian and EU law. In EU legislation the Bolar exemption is determined by European Directive 2001/83/EC on the Community Code relating to medicinal products for human use. Art. 10(6) excludes from infringement of patent rights or supplementary protection certificates (SPCs): 'Conducting the necessary studies and trials with a view to the application of paragraphs 1, 2, 3 and 4.' Paragraphs 1–4, i.e. Arts. 10(1)-(4) of the Directive, concern the provision of data during the marketing approval process.[30]

According to Ukrainian lawyers who were part of the working group on the development of the draft law in the field of patenting, the Bolar exemption in Ukrainian law fully complies with the provisions of Art. 28 of the TRIPS Agreement and was confirmed by the WTO Dispute Settlement Body in its decision in the EU-Canada case.[31]

June 2, 2020, the Verkhovna Rada of Ukraine adopted the Law of Ukraine 'On Amendments to Certain Laws of Ukraine on Elimination of Artificial Bureaucratic Barriers and Corruption Factors in Health Care', which is extremely important for domestic patients and national pharmaceutical manufacturers. The novelties introduced by this Law into national legislation (in Art. 31 of the Law of Ukraine 'On Protection of Rights to Inventions and Utility Models' and in Art. 9 of the Law of Ukraine 'On Medicinal Products') in terms of limiting patent rights and exclusivity of pharmaceutical data dossiers are present in the legislation of many countries and are a well-established practice in the EU, USA, Canada and 48 other countries.

[28] Agência Nacional de Vigilância Sanitária. https://www.gov.br/anvisa/pt-br.

[29] See: the Bolar exemption is in the p. 5 Art. 31 of the Law of Ukraine 'On Protection of Inventions and Utility Models'.

[30] Sterne Kessler Goldstein & Fox PLLC. Bolar Exemption in Europe and Asia.

[31] See: WTO. Canada Patent Protection of Pharmaceutical Products, Report of the Panel. WTO WT/DS114/R, 2000.

However, such independence in shaping one's own policy on the domestic market of medicines is quite unexpected for those who do not want to see the Ukrainian pharmaceutical industry as an independent player.

The following are no longer recognized as an infringement of the rights arising from the patent: lawful import of goods manufactured using the invention (utility model) for the purpose of research and/or use of the invention (utility model) in research conducted with the purpose to prepare and submit information for marketing authorization of the medicinal product (par. 5 Art. 31 of the Law of Ukraine 'On Protection of Rights to Inventions and Utility Models'). Similar provisions are to be found, in particular, in Directive 2001/83 /EC of the European Parliament and of the Council of 6 November 2001 on the Community code relating to medicinal products for human use (hereinafter—Directive 2001/83/EC).

Opponents of the proposed formulation of the Bolar exemption accuse the legislator of the infringement of pharmaceutical data exclusivity regime, referring to the Art. 222 norm of the EU-Ukraine Association Agreement. In return, national and international Intellectual Property experts involved in the development of this provision do not see any violations here and set out the following reasons.

On the market, a medicinal product is protected by patent right and the right for protection information on the data of the pharmaceutical (authorization) dossier. It is important that both legal doctrines (institutions) complement each other. For example, after the expiration of patent rights (valid for 20 years plus 5 years of additional legal protection), the countdown of 5 years of data exclusivity begins from the moment of filing an application for the first authorization of an original medicine with the State Expert Center of the Ministry of Health of Ukraine (hereinafter SEC of the Ministry of Health of Ukraine). Therefore, in practice there is a situation that even after the exhaustion of patent rights, data exclusivity does not allow the generic drug to enter the market, as it will not be authorized until the expiration of the 5-year term of protection.

Thus, the amendments introduced by the Law to Art. 31 of the Law of Ukraine 'On Protection of Rights to Inventions' and Art. 9 of the Law of Ukraine 'On Medicinal Products' apply only when both the patent and data exclusivity have exhausted themselves in Ukraine.

These novels do not violate the provisions of Art. 222 of the EU-Ukraine Association Agreement, as it is guarded by the provisions of the Art. 9 Law of Ukraine 'On Medicinal Products', stating that the information contained in the application for marketing authorization of medicinal products with annexes to it, in accordance with the provisions of this Law and other regulations of Ukraine, is subject to government protection against disclosure and unfair commercial use.

And what are namely the illegal actions mentioned in Art. 222 of the EU-Ukraine Association Agreement? First, disclosure, and second, unfair commercial use.

As for the disclosure, it should be noted that when applying for marketing authorization of a generic medicinal product, the applicant refers to the publicly available information from the dossier of the original product which is no longer protected in data exclusivity regime. The application shall be also accompanied by bioequivalence research conducted by the manufacturer of the generic himself.

Therefore, the applicant's reference to the information contained in the published part of the dossier of the original medicinal product and its use by the experts for analysis as part of their professional activities cannot be considered as the disclosure, and even more so, unfair commercial use.

Consequently, in accordance with the amendments introduced by the Law to the Ukrainian legislation, the entry of a generic medicinal product on the market is possible only the day after the expiration of patent protection or data exclusivity, or both protection regimes at the same time. As of now, it is possible to start only a research on bioequivalence next day after the expiration of these legal protection regimes and then, after receiving positive results, submit an application to the SEC of the Ministry of Health of Ukraine.

When the result is negative, we should continue the research, improve production, etc. Therefore, the release of a generic drug is delayed for years because of inability to be ready to enter the market the day after the end of the market monopoly ensured by the patent and the originator's data exclusivity.

5 Compulsory Licenses, Government Use and IP Waivers in a Pandemic

The application of the flexible provisions of the TRIPS Agreement in line with the spirit of the Doha Declaration on the TRIPS Agreement and Public Health is primarily aimed at ensuring access to medicines in low- and middle-income countries. The importance of these provisions and at the same time the differences in their understanding were highlighted by the pandemic. At the same time, due to the latter the international community has stepped on the road of improving existing and developing new mechanisms to expand access to medicines and vaccines through Intellectual Property rights. And if in the previous pre-pandemic period the changes in the Ukrainian legislation received controversial assessments, nowadays, the practice proves the correctness of our approaches in introducing the expanded access to treatment through the flexible provisions of the TRIPS Agreement. Today, the Trade Representative of Ukraine in the TRIPS Council supports IP waivers during the pandemic.

In the process of implementing the flexible provisions of the TRIPS Agreement, Ukraine faces the task of moving towards the provisions of the EU-Ukraine Association Agreement, and it was quite difficult to keep in line with it in terms of compulsory licensing and government use, as the grounds foreseen for a low- and middle-income country have not yet been used in the EU. Compulsory licenses in the EU were rather based on the principles of the anti-monopoly law and consumer protection, which is a complete gap in Ukrainian legislation as of today. Instead, along with Ukraine's European integration aspirations, the stakeholders in reforming IP legislation in pharmacy and medicine faced the challenges of a low-income country suffering from aggression in part of its territory. Time will tell whether

Ukraine managed to maintain this balance, but negotiations between Ukraine and the EU on establishment of a so-called 'visa-free entrance for medicines' are already underway.[32]

Declaration of the pandemic forced also the EU countries to reconsider conceptual approaches to compulsory licensing and government use towards the application of the grounds specifically on intellectual property rights as described below. In addition, the world in general and Ukraine in particular participated in the discussion on the possibility of restricting intellectual property at the facilities related to the diagnosis, prevention and treatment of COVID-19. Obviously, the most acute issue was the access to vaccines due to the overcoming of the patent monopoly and the disclosure of trade secrets. IP waivers have become a new challenge for the doctrine of Intellectual Property law, which now requires a solution.

With a monopoly, patent and know-how holders are unable to meet the demand for vaccines today. Thus, according to pharmaceutical industry data, the industry expects to produce a total of about ten billion vaccine doses by the end of 2021. According to researchers at the International Monetary Fund in Washington DC who review the current trends, this is unlikely to happen. In the paper published on May 19, they report that the industry is likely to produce about six billion doses by the end of 2021.[33]

Today, the revision of compulsory licensing opportunities is being so rapid that it requires an equally dynamic tracking of new trends in balancing IP property rights and the right to life and health.

The doctrine (institution) of temporary alienation of patent rights for an invention on medicinal product as an object of intellectual property is one of the main legal instrument in ensuring access to treatment. Unfortunately, the doctrine has not undergone the necessary changes for its effective function. It has become extremely necessary in the context of a pandemic, although it was prudently written out at the level of international law back in the last century.

Art. 5 of the Paris Convention for the Protection of Industrial Property of 1883 provides that each country of the Union shall have the right to take legislative measures providing for the grant of compulsory licenses to prevent the abuses which might result from the exercise of the exclusive rights conferred by the patent.

Art. 31 of the TRIPS Agreement provides for the right to use a patent without the authorization of the patent owner by the government of the member state or a third party with the permission of the government in case of national emergencies or in other circumstances of extreme urgency.

Art. 219 of the EU-Ukraine Association Agreement states that the parties recognize the importance of the Doha Declaration. In interpreting and exercising the rights

[32] Костюк Володимир. Безвіз для ліків: чого очікує українська фарміндустрія від самміту ЄС. https://www.eurointegration.com.ua/experts/2021/10/11/7128780/.

[33] https://www.imf.org/en/Publications/Staff-Discussion-Notes/Issues/2021/05/19/A-Proposal-to-End-the-COVID-19-Pandemic-460263.

and obligations under Chapter 9 'Intellectual Property', the Parties shall ensure consistency with the Doha Declaration.

It is important that the legal grounds for using the compulsory licensing mechanism under subparagraph (b) of paragraph 5 of the Doha Declaration are determined by each member-country at its own discretion. Some examples of possible grounds are set out in Art. 31 of the TRIPS Agreement, such as:

- public non-commercial use;
- use in case of emergency in the country or other circumstances of extreme urgency;
- use to prevent anti-competitive practices;
- interdependence of patents.

In addition, the Paris Convention permits compulsory licensing in case of non-use or insufficient use of the invention. If we take as an example possible future non-use of patented drugs for COVID-19 in Ukraine due to unwillingness to spend on obtaining an authorization certificate for a drug, it may serve as a ground for compulsory licensing and production or supply of a generic version of such a drug, or biosimilar, if it is a biological preparation. It should be noted that in health care all these grounds can have place.

Reviewing the world practice of applying compulsory licensing mechanisms in health care we can conclude that the first two grounds are widely used in developing and least-developed countries.

In contrast to Ukraine, in the EU the most common ground for compulsory licensing in the healthcare sector is to prevent anti-competitive practices on the basis of Anticompetitive legislation. Unfortunately, such legislation and as a result a practice does not exist in Ukraine at all. The development of relevant provisions in Competition Law is currently among the legislator's priorities, especially given that the prevention and/or correction of anti-competitive practices that impede access to medicines is one of the important TRIPS-flexibility provisions. Thus, the interpretation of this provision is included in Art. 8, paragraph 2, Art. 31, paragraph 1 (k) and Art. 40 of the TRIPS Agreement. It is noteworthy that the TRIPS Agreement does not contain a definition of anti-competitive behavior and thus leaves the WTO members free to determine anti-competitive actions and develop their own policy on them and it is the main task for Ukraine in a pandemic.

The granting of compulsory licenses under Art. 31 (1) (k) of the TRIPS Agreement as a remedy for anti-competitive practices, as opposed to compulsory licenses under Art. 31 (1) (b) of the TRIPS Agreement, does not require prior negotiation with the patent owner. There is no requirement to notify the patent owner, as in the case of using a patent in the interests of the country.

As per subparagraph (k) part 1 Art. 31 of the TRIPS Agreement, the need to correct anti-competitive practices may be taken into account in determining the amount of remuneration to the patent owner. This means that in particularly serious cases of anti-competitive practices, remuneration may not be paid at all. In practice, competition authorities also resort to imposing fines on violators, which serves as another deterrent to anti-competitive behaviour.

Thus, the TRIPS Agreement does not limit the possibility to determine the grounds for compulsory licensing at the level of national legislation, however, it requires their proper consolidation at the level of national law.

According to Art. 31 of the TRIPS Agreement, there are several possible scenarios for the use of patented inventions without the authorization of the right holder, depending on the initiator of the compulsory license:

- use *initiated by the third party* and authorized by the government;
- use by the *government* or a government-authorized contractor at the initiative of the government in cases of public non-commercial use.

With regard to the entity that issues a permit for a compulsory license, each country has different legislative approaches based on the national form of government and public administration:

- in countries where such powers are delegated to the executive, the entity is appointed by the executive as represented by the government or the relevant ministry/ ministries, minister/ministers (USA, France);
- in some countries, other competent authorities have been identified (in the People's Republic of China—the Department of Patent Rights under the State Council of the People's Republic of China, in the Arab Republic of Egypt—the Patent Office of Egypt);
- in monarchies, the authority to grant permission to use the invention in the interests of the country is mainly transferred to the monarch (Australia);
- in some countries it has historically been the case that such powers are vested in the judiciary (Germany, the United Arab Emirates, Croatia, Madagascar, Kyrgyzstan).

Thus, the entity making decisions on the use of a patented invention without the consent of the patent owner is the relevant body (bodies) or official (officials) of the public authority (executive, judicial, etc.), defined by national law in different jurisdictions.

In the context of Art. 31 of the TRIPS Agreement, compulsory licenses may be issued:

- under the general procedure with obligatory prior measures taken to obtain authorization from the patent owner;
- under the simplified procedure without prior measures, but with post factum notification of the patent owner on the issuance of a compulsory license (only in cases of compulsory licensing on the grounds of public non-commercial use, in case of emergency, other circumstances of extreme urgency);
- under the simplified procedure without prior measures and without notifying the patent owner on the issuance of a compulsory license (only in cases of compulsory licensing to prevent anti-competitive practices).

International experience in the implementation of some TRIPS-flexibility provisions shows that the effective mechanism for compulsory licensing consolidated in the legislation of a WTO member country and clear legislation on free competition make it possible to achieve the main goal—the provision of medicines—sometimes without compulsory measures, through voluntary licensing on reasonable terms.

In Ukraine, the procedure for implementing Art.30 of the Law of Ukraine On Inventions and utility models (Patent Law) is determined by the Resolution of the Cabinet of Ministers of Ukraine No. 877 of December 4, 2013 ‘ On Approval of the Procedure for Granting Permission by the Cabinet of Ministers of Ukraine to Use the Patented Invention (Utility Model) concerning Medicines ‘ (hereinafter - ‘Procedure No. 877’).

The effective Procedure No. 877 does not apply to legal relations governed by the provisions of Art. 31 of the Law on Inventions, there is legal uncertainty with respect to it. The health care emergency is not obligatory required for compulsory authorization of the use of a patented invention in accordance with the current Procedure No.877, it is sufficient to refer to one of the components of the purpose: Public Health, national defence, environmental safety and other public interests in accordance with Art. 30 of the Law on Inventions.

In accordance with national law, the details of the circumstances giving grounds for compulsory licensing are set forth in Arts. 30 and 31 of the Law on Inventions: in the first case it is the need to ensure public health and national defence, environmental safety and other public interests, and in the second case it is government actions to ensure public health in emergencies.

As noted above, freedom of interpretation of the mentioned norms at the national level is provided by the Doha Declaration. Each Member has the right to determine what constitutes a national emergency or other circumstances of extreme urgency, it being understood that Public Health crises, including those relating to HIV/AIDS, tuberculosis, the COVID-19 pandemic, and other circumstances of extreme urgency. However, in Art. 31 of the Law on Inventions such grounds are not clearly defined, and the relevant clarifications have not yet been made by the Law as amended on July 21, 2020.

As we can see, the conditions for compulsory licensing include such grounds as: ensuring the Public Health, the inability of the patent owner to satisfy the need for medicines and the unjustified refusal to grant a license voluntarily. In the current context of the COVID-19 pandemic, this basis has been used by potential manufacturers of a generic version of remdesivir, patented by Gilead. Being aware of the risks of compulsory licensing, the patent owner voluntarily granted a license to eight manufacturers. And this is a clear example of the fact that the very existence in national legislation of a mechanism for compulsory licensing or the government use in the public interest with a clearly defined implementation algorithm serves as an incentive for voluntarily licensing by patent owners.

Negotiations with the patent owner which end up with an unmotivated refusal from the latter are an important condition for granting a compulsory license. Negotiations on the prospects of granting a compulsory license significantly differ from the negotiations on Managed Access Agreements. First, for compulsory licensing, all stages of negotiations and the content of such a license are transparent: the price and the number of doses of the drug. Secondly, for legal granting of a compulsory license, the refusal has to be unmotivated and it has to exist as a fact.

The passive silence of the patent owner will not be interpreted by the court as an unmotivated refusal. And the latter is actually a stumbling block for the implementation of Art. 30 of the Law on Inventions, as it is not defined legally which actions or absence of those can be considered an unmotivated refusal, as well as what period without any reaction from the patent owner shall be considered a refusal.

In case of granting a permit to use a patented invention on the basis of Art. 31 Law on Inventions, it is possible to temporarily waive the above requirement about making efforts to negotiate with the patent owner. However, the right holder shall be notified of the use of his invention as soon as possible.

Unfortunately, the Law of Ukraine 'On Amendments to Certain Legislative Acts of Ukraine (regarding Patent Law Reform)' adopted on July 21, 2020 by the Verkhovna Rada of Ukraine does not make appropriate changes to the legislation on compulsory licensing and use of inventions in the public interest in emergencies. Therefore, the issue of 'motivated refusal' and the specifics of the use 'in the national interests' remained open, and these gaps shall be addressed as soon as possible. Much wealthier countries (as compared to Ukraine) have used these legal mechanisms to ensure access to generic drugs in a pandemic.[34]

Several countries have already publicly considered compulsory licensing as part of their COVID-19 response. On March 24, 2020, Israel granted a compulsory license to import generic versions of lopinavir/ritonavir. The Israeli Ministry of Health has determined that an antiretroviral drug may be a possible treatment for patients with COVID-19. Unlike Thailand and Brazil, Israel issued a compulsory license not because of the price of the drug, but because the patentee (AbbVie) failed to provide enough lopinavir/ritonavir.

In Canada, the COVID-19 Emergency Response Act amended the Patent Act of Canada to expedite the compulsory licensing process based on the need to ensure Public Health. The amendment allows the Government of Canada to license the necessary innovations and later agree on remuneration.[35]

In the wake of the COVID-19 pandemic, the German government recently adopted the so-called 'Coronavirus Crisis Package'. The law on the protection of the population in the event of an epidemic provides for measures to restrict German patents, for example, covering medicines or medical products.[36]

Moreover, today countries have gone much further and started a debate on expanding the mechanisms of intellectual property rights in order to get access to the only available now way to overcome the pandemic—IP rights exemptions for vaccines.

Analysis of TRIPS Council papers, which provide arguments of the countries advocating for a temporary exemption from intellectual property rights concerning the facilities used for diagnostics, therapy and prevention of COVID-19, gives us

[34] FAIR Health. The Projected Economic Impact of the COVID-19 Pandemic on the US Healthcare System (2020).

[35] See: COVID-19 Emergency Response Act, S.C. 2020, C-13 (Can.).

[36] Gesetz zum Schutz der Bevölkerung bei einer epidemischen Lage von nationaler Tragweite.

grounds to conclude that such measures shall be introduced in order to provide mankind with vaccines as soon as possible, as well as to develope domestic production of vaccines and medicines, which is a component of the biological safety of the country.[37]

Observing global trends, we understand that countries are preparing to produce medicines in emergencies. Voluntary licensing issues are raised by the Technology Access Partnership TAP, administered by UN Technology Bank or through the Open COVID Pledge Initiative. However, so far we do not see significant progress in this direction. We are witnessing a tense situation regarding access to COVID-19 prevention technologies.

The analytical report 'Accelerating COVID-19 Vaccine Production via Involuntary Technology Transfer' presented by South Center is extremely valuable to us. It states that 'currently discussed proposals at the WTO related to increasing the production of COVID-19 vaccines, including the EU proposal to clarify the use of compulsory licensing and the submission by South Africa and India on the intellectual property (IP) waiver, require complementary mechanisms to rapidly improve the production of COVID-19 vaccines that are urgently needed today.'[38]

However, the governments opposing the waiver argue that current WTO rules already allow countries to apply for 'compulsory licensing' to override IP during emergencies.

And it is important to note here that compulsory licensing provides access to a patent, but under conditions that are not always possible to achieve. As noted, TRIPS Art. 31 requires negotiations with the patent owner, but as of October 2021, in most cases such negotiations are not successful. In addition, the disclosure of a patent for vaccines is absolutely insufficient without the transfer of access to know-how and technology in general. Therefore, in order to overcome the limited access to vaccines two proposals were submitted to the WTO: the first one concerns the interpretation of the flexible provisions of the TRIPS Agreement, the second one—the possibility of disclosing not only the patent but also the technology.

As for the first proposal, it concerns the clarification for a uniform interpretation of the TRIPS Agreement flexible provisions, agreed in Marrakesh back in 1994 and foresightedly detailed in 2017. Today, in a pandemic they can be used to introduce IP rights exemptions in the form of compulsory licensing.[39] South Africa and India were the first to step up with the initiative to temporarily waive IP rights in the TRIPS

[37] Waiver from certain provisions of the TRIPS agreement for the prevention, containment and treatment of covid-19. Retrieved from: https://docs.wto.org/dol2fe/Pages/SS/directdoc.aspx?filename=q:/IP/C/W669.pdf&Open=True.

[38] Olga Gurgula. Accelerating COVID-19 Vaccine Production via Involuntary Technology Transfer. https://www.southcentre.int/wp-content/uploads/2021/09/PB102_Accelerating-COVID-19-Vaccine-Production-via-Involuntary-Technology-Transfer_EN.pdf.

[39] WTO Agreement on Trade-Related Intellectual Property Rights, Marrakesh Agreement Establishing the World Trade Organization, Annex 1C, 15 April 1994, as amended on 23 January 2017.

Agreement,[40] the EU joined the discussion later on and now it is partially supported by the US.[41]

As for the second key proposal, it concerns the disclosure and transfer of know-how. The urgency of expanding access to such knowledge through C-TAP is the key to accelerating the release of vaccines in the required amounts, which will allow to vaccinate a critical number of people to stop the mutation of the virus. However, at the time of writing, negotiations on such a transfer have failed. For example, negotiations between Biolyse (Canada's powerful cancer drug maker), which can produce two million doses a month and Johnson & Johnson (J&J), were unsuccessful. J&J refused to license its technology to Biolyse.[42]

Representatives of some law schools currently acknowledge that there are no specific provisions in international and national IP laws, similar to the compulsory licensing mechanism developed for patents, that would allow access to trade secrets held by pharmaceutical companies if they are not willing to share this information voluntarily.[43] Lawyers are categorical in their assessments: 'Unlike patents, regulatory entities do not grant or confirm trade secrets; rather, one has a trade secret by keeping valuable information secret. Trade secrets are not meant to be shared unless the owner authorizes it and then, usually, under a requirement of secrecy by the authorized party. Thus, the core trade secret legal action is one for misappropriation of it by a former employee/competitor through commercial espionage or sloppy trade secret management.'[44]

Instead, it seems to us legitimate to consider the provisions of Article 73 'Security Exceptions' of the TRIPS Agreement as possible grounds for disclosure and use of know-how in a pandemic. However, the application of this norm at the level of national legislation also requires appropriate changes in national legislation. We also believe that the principles of the TRIPS Agreement contained in Article 8 allow us to use trade secrets for public health purposes.

[40] Communication from India and South Africa, "Waiver from Certain Provisions of the TRIPS Agreement for the Prevention, Containment and Treatment of Covid-19" (2 October 2020) IP/C/W/669 https://docs.wto.org/dol2fe/Pages/SS/directdoc.aspx?filename=q:/IP/C/W669.pdf&Open=True. The revised proposal was submitted on 21 May 2021. See "Waiver from Certain Provisions of the TRIPS Agreement for the Prevention, Containment and Treatment of COVID-19. Revised Decisionю Text". Available from https://docs.wto.org/dol2fe/Pages/SS/directdoc.aspx?filename=q:/IP/C/W669R1.pdf&Open=True.

[41] Biden backs COVID-19 vaccine patent waivers. Available from: https://thehill.com/policy/healthcare/551992-biden-backs-covid-19-vaccine-patent-waivers.

[42] Arianna Schouten, "Canada based Biolyse Pharma Seeks to Manufacture COVID-19 Vaccines for Low Income Countries, may test Canada's compulsory licensing for export law", KEI, 12 March 2021. Available from https://www.keionline.org/35587.

[43] Olga Gurgula. Accelerating COVID-19 Vaccine Production via Involuntary Technology Transfer. https://www.southcentre.int/wp-content/uploads/2021/09/PB102_Accelerating-COVID-19-Vaccine-Production-via-Involuntary-Technology-Transfer_EN.pdf.

[44] David S. Levine, "Covid-19 Trade Secrets and Information Access: An Overview", InfoJustice, 10 July 2020. Available from http://infojustice.org/archives/42493.

In conclusion, it should be mentioned, that although it is extremely important for Ukraine to be able to use the flexible provisions of the TRIPS Agreement both for the production of vaccines and over time for the production of specific COVID treatment medicines, the Government should have in mind the need to clarify production capacities of the national manufacturer, to allow the production of such vaccines and medicines exclusively for the national market, at least in the first stage, as the priority is to meet the needs of the national patient. And, of course, compulsory know-how licenses (trade secrets) should contain provisions limiting the time and number of doses produced similar to compulsory licenses for inventions.

References

Agência Nacional de Vigilância Sanitária. https://www.gov.br/anvisa/pt-br.

Arianna Schouten, "Canada based Biolyse Pharma Seeks to Manufacture COVID-19 Vaccines for Low Income

Art. 9 The Law Of Ukraine 'On Medicines'

Association Agreement between the European Union and the European Atomic Energy Community and their Member States, of the one part, and Georgia, of the other part. Available via DIALOG. https://eur-lex.europa.eu/legal-content/en/TXT/PDF/?uri=CELEX:22014A0830(02)

Association Agreement between the European Union and the European Atomic Energy Community and their Member States, of the one part, and the Republic of Moldova, of the other part. https://eur-lex.europa.eu/legal-content/EN/TXT/?uri=uriserv%3AOJ.L_.2014.260.01.0004.01.ENG

Association Agreement between the European Union and the European Atomic Energy Community and their Member States, of the one part, and the Ukraine, of the other part. https://zakon.rada.gov.ua/laws/show/984_011

Biden backs COVID-19 vaccine patent waivers. Available from: https://thehill.com/policy/healthcare/551992-biden-backs-covid-19-vaccine-patent-waivers

Bolar exemption is in the p. 5 Art. 31 of the Law of Ukraine 'On Protection of Inventions and Utility Models'

Communication from India and South Africa, "Waiver from Certain Provisions of the TRIPS Agreement for the Prevention, Containment and Treatment of Covid-19" (2 October 2020) IP/C/W/669 https://docs.wto.org/dol2fe/Pages/SS/directdoc.aspx?filename=q:/IP/C/W669.pdf&Open=True. The revised proposal was submitted on 21 May 2021. See "Waiver from Certain Provisions of the TRIPS Agreement for the Prevention, Containment and Treatment of COVID-19. Revised Decisionю Text". Available from https://docs.wto.org/dol2fe/Pages/SS/directdoc.aspx?filename=q:/IP/C/W669R1.pdf&Open=True

Compassionate use is a treatment option that allows the use of an unauthorised medicine. Under strict conditions, products in development can be made available to groups of patients who have a disease with no satisfactory authorised therapies and who cannot enter clinical trials. See: https://www.ema.europa.eu/en/human-regulatory/research-development/compassionate-use

Countries, may test Canada's compulsory licensing for export law", KEI, 12 March 2021. Available from https://www.keionline.org/35587

COVID-19 Emergency Response Act, S.C. 2020, C-13 (Can.)

European Medicines Agency. https://www.ema.europa.eu/en/human-regulatory/research-development/compassionate-use

European Patent Convention. https://www.epo.org/law-practice/legal-texts/epc.html

European Patent Convention. https://www.epo.org/law-practice/legal-texts/html/epc/2016/e/ar52.html

FAIR Health. The Projected Economic Impact of the COVID-19 Pandemic on the US Healthcare System (2020)

Gesetz zum Schutz der Bevölkerung bei einer epidemischen Lage von nationaler Tragweite

Guidelines for the Examination of Patent Applications Relating to Pharmaceuticals of the UNDP. https://www.undp.org/content/undp/en/home/librarypage/hiv-aids/guidelines-for-the-examination-of-patent-applications-relating-t.html

Guidelines on Examination of the Patent Application in the field of Medicine and Pharmaceuticals based on the recommendations of the WHO. file:///C:/Users/Lenovo/AppData/Local/Temp/rp61-guidelines-on-patentability-and-a2m-en.pdf

https://www.imf.org/en/Publications/Staff-Discussion-Notes/Issues/2021/05/19/A-Proposal-to-End-the-COVID-19-Pandemic-460263

Industrial Property Law of Poland. https://www.wipo.int/export/sites/www/scp/en/revocation_mechanisms/opposition/pdf/opposition_poland.pdf

International Federation of Library Associations and Institutions. Available via DIALOG. https://www.ifla.org/node/92993

Law of Ukraine 'On Protection of Inventions and Utility Models'

Law On Industrial Property of Albania.URL: https://www.wipo.int/edocs/lexdocs/laws/en/al/al069en.pdf

Law On Industrial Property of North Macedonia. http://ippo.gov.mk/EN/LegislationPreview.aspx?lang=EN&id=47&cat=NAT.

Low-income countries. https://iwa-network.org/wp-content/uploads/2019/01/2019-Country-Classification-Update-2018-08

Olga Gurgula. Accelerating COVID-19 Vaccine Production via Involuntary Technology Transfer. https://www.southcentre.int/wp-content/uploads/2021/09/PB102_Accelerating-COVID-19-Vaccine-Production-via-Involuntary-Technology-Transfer_EN.pdf

On approval of the Rules for consideration of applications for inventions and applications for utility models of the Ministry of Education and Science of Ukraine; Order, Rules of 15.03.2002 No 197. http://zakon5.rada.gov.ua/laws/show/z0364-02/page3

Opposition Systems. https://www.wipo.int/scp/en/revocation_mechanisms/opposition/index.html

Patent Law of Serbia. http://www.zis.gov.rs/upload/documents/pdf_en/pdf_patenti/zakon%20pat.%20eng%2020.1.20.pdf

Primary Health Care on the Road to Universal Health Coverage: 2019 Monitoring Report: Executive Summary

Solidarity' clinical trial for COVID-19 treatments. https://www.who.int/emergencies/diseases/novel-coronavirus-2019/global-research-on-novel-coronavirus-2019-ncov/solidarity-clinical-trial-for-covid-19-treatments

South Center was established for the Achieving the Sustainable Development Goals (SDGs), particularly poverty eradication, requires national policies and an international regime that supports and does not undermine development efforts. The South Centre is an intergovernmental policy research think-tank composed of and accountable to developing country Member States. It conducts policy-oriented research on key policy development issues, and supports developing countries to effectively participate in international negotiating processes that are relevant to the achievement of SDGs. The Centre promotes the unity of the South in such processes while recognizing the diversity of national interests and priorities.

State Enterprises 'Institute of Intellectual Property (Ukrpatent)'

Sterne Kessler Goldstein & Fox PLLC. Bolar Exemption in Europe and Asia

The Global Strategy and Plan of Action on Public Health, Innovation and Intellectual Property (2000) Available via DIALOG. https://www.who.int/phi/implementation/phi_globstat_action

TRIPS Agreement. http://zakon3.rada.gov.ua/laws/show/981_018

United Nations Millennium Development Goals (2000). https://www.un.org/ru/documents/decl_conv/declarations/summitdecl.shtml

Waiver from certain provisions of the TRIPS agreement for the prevention, containment and treatment of covid-19. Retrieved from: https://docs.wto.org/dol2fe/Pages/SS/directdoc.aspx?filename=q:/IP/C/W669.pdf&Open=True

Wirtz VJ, Hogerzeil HV, Gray AL (2017) Essential medicines for universal health coverage. Lancet. https://www.thelancet.com/journals/lanepe/article/PIIS2666-7762(21)00196-4/fulltext?fbclid=IwAR17j8v6y8dMvdmWTT0YykXlgTjFRyQ0W6wgpK_eyOaxGLHTswRpCp0tR2c

World Health Organization, Geneva 2019. https://apps.who.int/iris/handle/10665/328913

WTO. Canada Patent Protection of Pharmaceutical Products, Report of the Panel. WTO WT/DS114/R, 2000

WTO Agreement on Trade-Related Intellectual Property Rights, Marrakesh Agreement Establishing the World Trade Organization, Annex 1C, 15 April 1994, as amended on 23 January 2017.

Костюк Володимир. Безвіз для ліків: чого очікує українська фарміндустрія від саммiту С. https://www.eurointegration.com.ua/experts/2021/10/11/7128780/

Intellectual Property Protection of the DNA Sequence of a Living Organism in the Era of Artificial Intelligence and Other Social Challenges

Liubov Maidanyk

Contents

Abstract This chapter shows the problems of protecting the intellectual property of a living organism's DNA sequence in relation to contemporary social and legal shifts. U.S. Supreme Court decisions in Mayo Collaborative Services v. Prometheus Laboratories and Association for Molecular Pathology v. Myriad Genetics Inc. have challenged U.S. and European law on what constitutes patentable subject matter. Thus, we argue that accepted patent legal protection for DNA is no longer the best option for the legal framework. In doing so, we draw three main conclusions. First, we discuss the relevance of patent legal protection under the current practice of court decisions in various countries. As a second conclusion, we show that copyright law, as an alternative approach for protecting DNA intellectual property, offers more advantages than patent law. We discuss the advantages of copyright protection in light of the application of open source, possible involvement of artificial intelligence. To do this, we analyze Ukrainian legislative proposals on artificial intelligence within the copyright framework. The third conclusion proposes leaving DNA out of intellectual property protection, which is most controversial because of the obvious harm to scientific progress in this regard.

This chapter is prepared on the basis of the report for the Conference 'Private Healthcare Law: Challenges and Prospects'.

L. Maidanyk (✉)
Intellectual Property and Informational Law Depatment, Law School of Taras Shevchenko National University of Kyiv, Kyiv, Ukraine
e-mail: liubov_maidanyk@knu.ua

© The Author(s), under exclusive license to Springer Nature Switzerland AG 2022

R. Maydanyk et al. (eds.), *Ukrainian Healthcare Law in the Context of European and International Law*, European Union and its Neighbours in a Globalized World 7,
https://doi.org/10.1007/978-3-031-05690-1_13

1 Introduction

Historically, intellectual property law was designed to promote innovation and human progress. Through the legal monopoly granted under intellectual property rights, it is believed that the right holder can recover and increase his or her contribution. For many years there has been a steady practice of protecting DNA sequences through patenting, but recent scientific and social changes, especially in light of the COVID-19 pandemic, pose crucial new challenges. The news of the possible successful modification of human embryo genes for resistance to HIV[1] evokes ambiguous perception: on one hand, there is hope for substantial progress in treatment of incurable diseases, and on the other—raises moral and ethical questions about the possibility of legalization of such bioengineering results, contrary to the legal prohibition in many countries and the need to protect the intellectual property rights of human DNA and other living organisms.

This raises again the question of the relevance of established approaches to the protection of intellectual property rights for the results of 'synthetic biology' and the feasibility of intellectual property protection of such subject matter in general. The problem of protecting DNA primarily under patent law covers two opposing interests: scientists welcome open access to information for research purposes, but at the same time would like to enjoy all the financial benefits of patenting such research results. The ability to patent genes has the effect of deterring innovation.[2] The risk of patent infringement holds the company back from launching research, such as developing cancer testing methods. One of the possible ways to resolve some of the discussed problems, is to presume that DNA (including human engineered DNA or cDNA) can't be patented. But another question arises—does such an approach imply an alternative regime of intellectual property right protection? Because, as mentioned above, the scientist would still like to use the monopoly granted by intellectual property rights to satisfy his economic interests. Or, only the public interest should be taken into account and intellectual property law protection in principle should be excluded.

In this regard, it is seen that the legal regime of protection of DNA of a living organism can be framed in the following ways:

(a) protection by patent law (although it is obvious that this approach is no longer fully consistent with current trends in society;
(b) copyright protection as a possible alternative - with no requirements for mandatory state registration, small fees, and the possibility of distribution through open source;
(c) exclusion from the intellectual property protection.

[1]For more details see Raposo (2019), pp. 197–199.
[2]For more details see. Sax (2012), p. 326.

Each approach will be discussed in more detail below. However, the chapter concludes that none of the discussed approaches provides a perfect solution.

2 Patent Protection

The protection of such intellectual property is conducted through patent law, but due to the very rapid development of science in this area, there are more indicators of the inconsistency of this approach due to the long procedure of registration and high cost of fees. Besides, some researchers have suggested that protection under patent law only hinders the development of technologies in this area, and therefore requires significant restrictions. In this regard, there are similarities with the legal debate on the possibility of computer programs protection under copyright in the 1970s. Such discussion led to changes in the legislation of most countries introducing the protection of computer program code as a literary work without covering its functional purpose. The question of the origin of copyright in the DNA sequence was discussed in the scientific community at the same time as the question of the legal regime of intellectual property rights to a computer program.[3] The DNA sequence and the computer program are very similar in nature, as they are a set of instructions in the form of symbols to achieve a certain result. It was economically viable to provide a simpler mechanism for obtaining protection compared to patent law for computer programs, which was due to the beginning of the era of personal computers and software. There are benchmark judgments of the US Supreme Court in *Gottschalk v. Benson* 1972[4] and *Parker v. Flook* of 1978[5] on the impossibility of protecting a computer program with patent law. Over time, the jurisprudence has taken the position that the rights to DNA sequences, including modifications, can be protected under patent law. For agribusiness, the so-called 'genetic patents' for genetically modified plant varieties occupy a prominent place. An example is the GAT (Roundup Ready) gene, derived from the resistance of individual plants (such as soybeans) to glyphosate, a herbicide that effectively fights pests known as ROUNDUP (Monsanto owns the rights to this gene in certain plant varieties).

The legislation of Ukraine allows patent protection of bioengineering results—DNA sequence. In particular, such an object is defined as a material object—a result of human activity: a product, in particular, is... cell culture of plants and animals and other biological material, including transgenic plants and animals. The Supreme Court of the United States has ruled that patent protection does not protect human DNA sequences. This decision radically changed the decades-old practice of patenting genes. The Court ruled that 'a naturally occurring DNA segment is a product of nature and not patent eligible merely because it has been isolated, but that

[3] See Smith (1988), pp. 1096–1108. Burk (1989), pp. 531–563.

[4] See Gottschalk v. Benson, 409 U.S. 63 (1972).

[5] See Parker v. Flook, 437 U.S. 584 (1978).

the cDNA is patent eligible because it is not naturally occurring'. High Court of Australia undertook similar position in *D'Arcy v Myriad Genetics*[6] case. High Court decided that Myriad's claims relating to isolated BRCA1 nucleic acid were not patentable subject matter. In particular, High Court noted that any naturally occurring subject matter which merely claims genetic information, be it isolated DNA, RNA, whether human or non-human, coding or non-coding, is excluded as patentable. Besides, they point out that although the isolation of nucleic acid comprising the BRCA1gene is a man-made process, it does not involve any element of inventiveness. Besides, the court held that the grant of a monopoly for such a claim has the potential to inhibit other researchers and medical practitioners from diagnostically testing the BRCA1 gene for an entirely different purpose.

Currently, EU Directive 94/44/EC (the 'Biotech Directive') states that '[a]n element isolated from the human body or otherwise produced by means of a technical process, including the sequence or partial sequence of a gene, may constitute a patentable invention, even if the structure of that element is identical to that of a natural element.' This is opposite to the mentioned above decision of the US Supreme Court in Myriad which held that although the inventors had discovered a useful DNA sequence, merely isolating DNA from a naturally-occurring genome did not make it patent eligible—anything significantly different from nature had been created. Historically patent protection could be given to isolated living forms (e. g. as did Pasteur to bacterias). In this sense, the naturally-occurring genome can be recognized as a discovery but not an invention. Under the Ukrainian Civil Code discovery is determined as an establishment of previously unknown, but objectively existing laws, features, and phenomena of the material world, which make radical changes in the level of scientific knowledge.

This question has been raised in the practice of the EPO in the case of Howard Florey Institute[7] regarding the grant of a patent for human hormone relaxin. The Howard Florey Institute of Experimental Physiology and Medicine filed a patent application for an invention of the molecular cloning and charachterization of a further gene sequence coding for human relaxin. A patent was issued in Europe in 1991, then opposed in 1992.[8] EPO noted, that a discovery of a DNA occurring in nature was not patentable; but if the substance was newly isolated and characterized, then it was not a mere discovery; it was an industrially applicable technical solution to a technical problem. The DNA was considered as new, due to fact it was complementary DNA. The form of relaxin that it coded for was also unknown until the inventor isolated it for the first time.[9]

Law of Ukraine 'On protection of inventions and utility models' draws similar provisions to art. 5 of the 'Biotech Directive'. In particular, Art. 6 states that: 'Patent

[6]See D'Arcy v. Myriad Genetics Inc & Anor, S28 (2015).

[7]For more detail see T 0272/95 (Relaxin/HOWARD FLOREY INSTITUTE) of 23.10.2002.

[8]See opposition T 0272/95 (Relaxin/HOWARD FLOREY INSTITUTE) of 23.10.2002.

[9]More detais on bioethical issues of patenting the human genes in mentioned case see in 'Bioethics and patent law: the Relaxin case' (2006), WIPO Magazine.

protection does not extend to the simple detection of one of the elements of the human body, in particular a sequence or part of a gene sequence. However, the effect of this provision does not affect the granting of legal protection to the invention, the object of which are elements of the human body outside the body or otherwise obtained, using a technical process, including the sequence or partial sequence of a gene, even if the structure of this element is identical to naturally-occurred element'.

In the light of recent US practice of excluding DNA from patent protection, the question arises about the social role of such a legal monopoly and its benefits to society. Primarily intellectual property rights are intended to be an incentive for inventors for the benefit of society as a whole. Johnathon Liddicoat, Kathleen Liddell, and Mateo Aboy conducted in 2019 research concerning the negative effects of Myriad and Mayo cases for the industry. The study set out to explore at the organizational level by interviewing patent practitioners, executives at molecular-test companies, and managers in technology-transfer offices at research institutes (Liddicoat et al. 2019, p. 835). Three main negative effects were found: several organizations deliberately chose to forgo developing tests; small patent-precarious organizations (those that rely heavily on patents for competitive advantage) have been more affected by the decisions than other; US-headquartered organizations have been more affected by the cases than European organizations (Liddicoat et al. 2019, p. 837). However, researchers focused only on negative effects at the same time they state that the most obvious potential positive effect is the one argued by the Supreme Court: that the decision would unshackle 'basic tools of scientific and technological work.'

3 Copyright Protection

If we assume that the DNA sequence can be protected by copyright as a literary work, then only if it meets the generally accepted criteria: originality and expression in an objective form. If a cell biologist came up with his own original sequence, this sequence could be protected by copyright (assuming a sufficient length of such a sequence, its originality, etc.). However, in the case of a biologist sequencing a natural DNA fragment, copyright protection does not arise because such an object is not original: there is simple copying of what already existed in nature. There is no doubt that to reproduce such a DNA sequence also requires considerable effort, the use of skills and technologies, but this is not enough for originality. An example of a technology using DNA reproduction of a sequence of natural origin is the cloning of a living organism. Cloning of pets: cats, dogs, and horses are becoming more common. The DNA sequence of the dead animal is reproduced to conduct cloning. Chinese company Sinogene in 2019, at the request of a client, it created the country's first cloned cat, based on the genetic material of his deceased pet, nicknamed Garlic. Famous Hollywood actress Barbara Streisand has repeatedly approached the animal cloning company to recreate her favorite dog breed Cotton de Tulear. Although human cloning is outlawed in more than 30 countries, and all research is questionable in terms of ethics and morality, we can assume in the future legal use of DNA correction of the human embryo for legitimate purposes. For example, with development of artificial intelligence technologies the possible positive effect is viewed in the treatment of serious diseases, such as Alzheimer's disease.

Opponents of copyright protection of biotechnology often argue about lack of originality, since DNA sequences are chemical compounds that exist in nature, attempting to copyright a sequence would be like trying to copyright a fact.[10] In this regard, sui generis rights regime is seen as an appropriate legal policy tool, especially in the era of artificial intelligence. Assuming the creation of a new DNA sequence using an autonomous computer system, immediately raises the question of the possibility of protection by intellectual property rights of such subject matter. Formally objects created by artificial intelligence can be covered by intellectual property rights if they meet the criteria of originality and form of expression under Ukrainian law. Although, such recognition forces us to reconsider concepts of 'creator' and 'inventor'. To date, the approach of patent protection of the results of artificial intelligence is doubtful, in particular in the European Union. Negative position is expressed in the EPO decision of 27 January 2020 on EP 18 275 163 and the EPO decision of 27 January 2020 on EP 18 275 174. The decisions concern the refusal of the European patent applications EP 18 275 163[11] and EP 18 275 174[12] in which an AI system called 'DABUS' was designated as the inventor. The EPO considered provisions of the European Patent Convention and the term 'inventor'. The EPO held that the term refers to a natural person and noted that this appears to be an internationally applicable standard and that various national courts have issued decisions to this effect. Decision T 0161/18 (Äquivalenter Aortendruck/ARC SEIBERSDORF) of 12.05.2020. In this decision, the EPO did not grant a patent on determining cardiac output by the aid of an artificial neural network. The decision points to a lack of descriptive sufficiency because a subject matter expert could not reproduce the training of an artificial neural network. In case *Shenzhen Tencent v. Shanghai Yingmou* Beijing Intellectual Property Court decided that computer-generated content is copyrightable as there was human intervention in created work. The Tencent Technology personnel used companies' own independently developed artificial intelligence computer program "Dreamwriter" to write articles on sports, weather and other issues. The Shanghai Yingmou published one of the articles on its website, which was considered as copyright infringement in ongoing court decision. Nanshan District People's Court, Shenzhen, Guangdong Province on December 24, 2019 held that an article completed by an artificial intelligence program is covered by copyright of China.

[10] Resnik (2004), p. 51.

[11] Grounds for the EPO decision of 27 January 2020 on EP 18 275 163 https://register.epo.org/application?documentId=E4B63SD62191498&number=EP18275163&lng=en&npl=false.

[12] Grounds for the EPO decision of 27 January 2020 on EP 18 275 174 https://register.epo.org/application?documentId=E4B63OBI2076498&number=EP18275174&lng=en&npl=false.

On October 27, 2020, the United States Patent and Trademark Office (USPTO) released a report titled 'Inventing AI: Tracing the diffusion of artificial intelligence with U.S. patents.' The study shows that artificial intelligence patent applications increased by more than 100% between 2002 and 2018, from 30,000 to over 60,000, and the overall share of patent applications containing artificial intelligence subject matter rose from 9% to nearly 16%.[13] Thereby changes in legal policy on artificial intelligence are only a matter of time and legislative flexibility.

Obviously, IP policy on artificial intelligence is on the issue, so some countries have already introduced the legislative strategy. The draft Law of Ukraine 'On Copyright and Related Rights'[14] among other proposals, contains Art. 35 entitled 'Sui generis right to non-original objects generated by a computer program'. The authors of this provision have chosen this approach of legal protection for computer-generated works—through the 'sui generis'—law of a special kind, which still attracts copyright.

Authors of draft law propose the following meaning of computer-generated work: '... is a non-original object created as a result of the activity of a computer program without the direct involvement of an individual in the creation of this object'. The draft law proposes to grant the rights to persons who have the exclusive intellectual property rights to this computer program: to the authors of the computer program, their heirs, or persons to whom the authors or their heirs transferred (alienated) their property rights to the computer program. Such special rights holders will receive the same amount of rights as copyright holders, except for personal non-property rights (moral rights). The term of protection of property (economic) rights is proposed for 25 years. The rules on the free use of copyrighted works also apply to computer-generated works. The authors of Ukrainian draft Law chose the least revolutionary approach to determining the results of the work of artificial intelligence—in fact, they recognized it as a tool. In order to avoid the recognition of artificial intelligence as an independent rightholder—the subect of legal relations, they designated the legal regime only for the results of its activities. Some scholars proposed to grant AI a legal status of capable subject of law, however with some restrictions: by analogy with slaves in Roman law or with legal entities.[15] In particular was argued the joint ownership of intellectual property rights between the computer program (artificial intelligence) and the human.[16]

When analyzing the form of expression of DNA as a potentially copyrighted subject matter, attention should be paid to the following. The DNA sequence can be expressed in writing as a literary work in the form of letters. However, does

---

[13] Inventing AI: Tracing the diffusion of artificial intelligence with U.S. patents. Report of USPTO. https://www.uspto.gov/sites/default/files/documents/OCE-DH-AI.pdf.

[14] Draft Law of Ukraine 'On Copyright and Related Rights' https://www.me.gov.ua/Documents/Detail?lang=uk-UA&id=cf7b9e32-1995-4b66-995a-4ab3dcac1a8f&title=ProktZakonuUkrainiproAvtorskePravoISumizhniPrava.

[15] Nekit et al. (2020), p. 247.

[16] Morkhat (2017), p. 123.

copyright arise when the sequence is created as a molecule? The legislation of Ukraine on copyright allows any objective form of expression of the work. So this is an argument in favor of the position that the expression of DNA sequences in a molecule could potentially be covered by copyright. On the question of the form of expression of a DNA sequence, K. Holman also points out the similarity between a computer program and a DNA sequence. The most coherent and convincing theory for copyright protection engineered DNA sequences seems to be the one that equates gene function to a sort of biological software.[17] Thus, the genetic sequence provides a number of instructions that guide the living cell to perform the functions dictated by these instructions. Genetic engineering allows a person to set these instructions. Like a computer program, a genetic sequence can be expressed in a form that can be reproduced by a human, although instead of a series of zeros and ones, it is a sequence of A, T, C, and G that corresponds to the four primary nucleotides that make up DNA.[18] The functional purpose of such a DNA sequence (similar to the computer program protection) will not be covered by copyright protection. For example, resistance to certain harmful plants—the primary functional purpose, is excluded from copyright scope. This is certainly a disadvantage for companies producing such varieties of plants. At the same time, genetic engineering in general, in contrast to computer programs, is more closely related to fundamental human rights and ethical and moral aspects of the treatment of living beings.

We do not presume copyright protection of synthetic biology results as an intentional overlap in intellectual property rights since it is considered as a proper legal mechanism corresponding to modern conditions. Copyright protection of DNA sequences leaves space for society to apply limitations and exceptions to certain rights (free use cases under Ukrainian legislation), which is generally considered positive for the development of science and balance of rights as a whole. Copyright protection is capable of producing a socially desirable balance of restricted and permissible uses of DNA sequences.[19] Similar to computer program copyright exceptions and limitations system provided in Ukrainian law 'On copyright and related rights' special exceptions can be introduced for copyrighted DNA sequence.

One more advantage of copyright protection of DNA is full application of open source approach. Open source biology becomes especially relevant in the context of the global COVID-19 pandemic. Despite the initiative of some researchers, similar success with computer programs has not been achieved. It is seen that one of the reasons is the protection of the results of research in synthetic biology by patent law, which has different approaches compared to copyright. Unlike copyright protection that emerges without any formalities, intellectual property rights in the invention are registered under the costly and long procedure.

[17] Bonadio and Lucchi (2018), p. 377.

[18] Holman (2011), p. 713.

[19] Torrance (2012), p. 27.

4 Conclusions

It is seen that the protection of DNA sequences by intellectual property rights is in the process of fundamental change, and this process is irreversible. Thus there is a need to rethink old approaches and find alternatives following the social demand of the new times.

Three approaches to development of DNA protection are concluded:

1. Withhold the protection of DNA sequences of living organisms within existing patent law framework. But, this approach has been increasingly questioned in recent years by both scholars and practice (following the example of the US Supreme Court decisions) for the next reasons. One of the arguments against this approach is to slow down the development of technological progress, and as a result, patients have limited access to technology using patented products.
2. Exclusion of the DNA sequence of a living organism from intellectual property protection. This approach, on the one hand, will allow the use of any experience without regard to the limitations of intellectual property rights and may reduce the cost of the final product for the user, such as tests. However, such an approach will reduce the number of new studies due to the lack of funding and general encouragement.
3. The extension of copyright protection to DNA sequence is seen as a compromise in the case of exclusion of such an object from patent protection due to the lack of formalities for the validity of intellectual property rights, long term legal protection. At the same time, it is possible to use open source and anticipate certain cases of free use of such an object. However, such an approach requires additional arguments in terms of economic feasibility, since such developments will significantly affect the activities of companies producing products using DNA technology.

References

Bonadio E, Lucchi N (2018) Non-conventional copyright: do new and atypical works deserve protection? Edward Elgar Publishing

Burk DL (1989) Copyrightability of recombinant DNA sequences. 29 JURIMETRICS J 469:531–563

Holman CM (2011) Copyright for engineered DNA: an idea whose time has come. West VA Law Rev 113:699–738

Liddicoat J, Liddell K, Aboy M (2019) The effects of myriad and mayo on molecular test development in the US and Europe: interviews from the frontline. Vanderbilt J Entertain Technol Law 22:785–837. https://doi.org/10.2139/ssrn.3381553

Morkhat P (2017) Iskusstvenníy intellekt. Pravovoy vzglyad. Buki Vedi, Moskva

Nekit K, Tokareva V, Zubar V (2020) Artificial intelligence as a potential subject of property and intellectual property relations. Ius Humani. Law J 9(1):231–250. https://doi.org/10.31207/ih.v9i1.227

Raposo VL (2019) The first chinese edited babies: a leap of faith in science. JBRA Assist Reprod 23(3):197–199. https://doi.org/10.5935/1518-0557.20190042

Resnik DB (2004) Owning the genome: a moral analysis of DNA patenting. State University of New York Press, Albany
Sax JK (2012) Financial conflicts of interest in science. Annals Health Law 21:291
Smith D (1988) Comment, copyright protection for the intellectual property rights to recombinant deoxyribonucleic acid: a proposal. St Mary's Law J 1083, 1096–1108
Torrance AW (2012) DNA copyright Valparaiso university law review. St Mary's Law J 46:1–41

Part VI
Healthcare Contracts

Europe Towards a Pan-European Treatment Contract

Roman Maydanyk and Nataliia Popova

Contents

Abstract The pan-European treatment contract shall be a legal instrument of approximation and unification of national law of European countries and EU-law. This instrument shall provide a unified concept of medical services, their scope and

---

This paper is prepared on the basis of the reports for the Conference 'Private Healthcare Law: Challenges and Prospects'.

R. Maydanyk
Department of Civil Law at the Law School, Taras Shevchenko National University of Kyiv, Kyiv, Ukraine
e-mail: roman.maydanyk@knu.ua

N. Popova (✉)
Department of General Legal Disciplines, Civil Law and Tourism Legislative Regulation at the Economics and Law School, Kyiv University of Tourism, Economics and Law, Kyiv, Ukraine

© The Author(s), under exclusive license to Springer Nature Switzerland AG 2022

R. Maydanyk et al. (eds.), *Ukrainian Healthcare Law in the Context of European and International Law*, European Union and its Neighbours in a Globalized World 7,
https://doi.org/10.1007/978-3-031-05690-1_14

main obligations of a medical services provider taking into account common features as well as peculiarities of European countries. The integral prerequisite of the forthcoming pan-European treatment contract shall be the general provision for rendering of medical services provided in the European law, acts of 'soft law' and jurisprudence at national and international levels, which corresponds to the recognized values and operative principles of the EU. At international level, the pan-European treatment contract should be regarded as a basic legal standard of medical care, provided by the instruments of harmonization of the EU-law and the law of European countries. It should set a minimum level of medical services for all European countries, regardless of whether these services are paid by individuals or are state-funded. It should also aim at combining of recognized values and operative principles of the EU with quality, institutional ability, affordability and traditions of the healthcare systems of the European countries. At national level, it is advisable to unify a treatment contract by introducing general conditions for providing medical services into the legislation of European countries (in the Civil Codes or special laws).

1 Introduction: Background and Objectives of the Study

The need for improvement of European medical care in terms of globalization necessitates the approximation of national law of European countries and unification of EU-law concerning a treatment contract at different levels—national and international—to efficiently combine European values and principles with national variety and traditions. EU Member State and Member Association Agreements and Neighbourhood should have effective and predictable provisions on a treatment contract as an important component of the national healthcare system.

The ideological basis of any national treatment contract is a system of basic provisions for rendering medical services. The decisive role in this system plays a general understanding of medical services and typical conditions for their rendering. The legal uncertainty of this understanding hinders the effectiveness and predictability of legal provision on a treatment contract.

At present, EU's acquis and national law of the European countries on general provisions of a treatment contract and their decisive components are not unified.

The additional relevance of these issues is due to the differences between the national Law of EU-member states and other European countries in terms of understanding medical services as an important component of any national healthcare system. This makes it difficult to establish uniform laws, case law and doctrine on the treatment contract.

Codified acts, other laws governing relationships of property turnover (Civil Codes, etc.) do not always contain the general provisions for providing medical services and the legal grounds for their providing as one of the main characteristics of the healthcare system.

The special laws of many European countries, especially Central and Eastern Europe, often contain fragmented general provisions about treatment contracts. For instance, in the legislation of Ukraine on health care, the characteristics of these agreements are limited by the provisions on the concept, essential conditions, and procedure for concluding an agreement on medical care covered by the program of medical guaranties.[1] General conditions on the provision of medical services—the concept and scope of their action, the main duties of the parties, the means of protection against breaches of obligations under this agreement, law, or regulations—are not provided.

The lack of general conditions for providing medical services prescribed by law complicates the understanding and scope of legal norms on medical services, the list of basic duties of the service provider, the legal consequences of the breach of obligations to provide medical services and remedies for their violation. The national legal doctrines of the European countries do not always adequately address these issues.

To approximate and harmonize the national law of European countries and EU-law on the treatment contract, it is essential to form a pan-European model of a treatment contract. It should include, in particular, general provisions for rendering of medical services as a decisive determinant (characteristic) of this model.

Thus, in our article, we will try to outline the concept and main characteristics of a pan-European model of a treatment contract which will combine the recognized values and principles in the EU with high quality and affordability of medical services, taking into account national variety, institutional ability and traditions of the European healthcare systems. The comparative component of this study should help identify the peculiarities of a treatment contract in the European countries and formulate main components of a general provision for providing medical services which should be taken into account in the unified model of a treatment contract.

2 Legal Analysis of a Pan-European Treatment Contract

2.1 Pan-European Treatment Contract as a Unified Standard of Law

The selection of the most effective and consistent pan-European provisions of the contract for medical services has updated the task of unification and uniform application of legal norms concerning the basic responsibilities of the health care

[1] Art. 18 of the Law of Ukraine 'Osnovy Zakonodavstva Ukrainy Pro ohoronu zdorovja' (1992) (Fundamentals of the legislation of Ukraine on health care) https://zakon.rada.gov.ua/laws/show/2801-12#Text.; Part 3 of Art. 26 of the Federal Law of the Russian Federation of 21 Nov 2011 № 323-FZ 'Ob osnovah ohrany zdorovja grashdan Rossijskoj Federazii' FZ (About basics of health care of citizens in Russian Federation) https://zakonbase.ru/content/base/2494.

provider, other general (typical) provisions of this contract. To this end, the general conditions for the provision of medical services have been adopted at the legislative level in some countries, and model legal norms on the contract for the provision of medical services have been developed at the European level with the help of soft law instruments. These model norms can be seen as the national prototypes of a pan-European treatment contract.

Systematization of legislation on general conditions of medical services, along with standardization of medical care, licensing of economic activities in medical practice, control of compliance with licensing conditions and accreditation of health care facilities, is one of the integral legal tools to ensure the quality and legal certainty of medical services regardless of national features of the health care system of European countries.

In its own sense, the standardization of medical care involves the regulation of mainly clinical aspects of medical care by determining the procedure for providing medical care in medical industry standards.

The law of some East European countries (Ukraine, Russia, etc.) industry standards in the sphere of health care include the standard of medical care (medical standard), clinical protocols, table of material and technical equipment, medical formulary, as well as other norms, rules and regulations, provided by the laws governing activities in the sphere of health care (Art. 14-1 of the Fundamentals of Legislation of Ukraine on Health Care).

Unlike industry standards in the sphere of health care, legal norms on general conditions for the provision of medical services should be referred to general standards in the sphere of health care, as they, although regulating health care activities, do not directly determine the procedure for providing medical care, requirements for methods (measures) of medical care and their sequence.

The legal norms on the general conditions for the provision of medical services contain a list of the main legal obligations of the provider of medical services defined by law, which applies to all health care facilities and types of medical care. These general conditions do not directly determine the procedure for providing medical care,[2] medical standards (clinical protocols, medical forms, etc.),[3] which, in particular, contain average indicators of frequency of use of medical services, medicine, medical devices, blood components, medical nutrition, indicators of the quality of medical care of the appropriate type, requirements for diagnostic, therapeutic, preventive methods of medical care, rehabilitation measures and their sequence, requirements for rehabilitation measures and their sequence, a list of equipment, facilities and tools needed to equip a particular type of health care institution, a list of drugs that are cost-effective.

---

[2] Art. 37 of the Federal Law of the Russian Federation. № 323-FZ 'Pro osnovy okhorony zdorovya gromadyan u Rosiyskiy Federatsiї.;. https://minzdrav.gov.ru/documents/7025-federalnyy-zakon-ot-21-noyabrya-2011-g-323-fz-ob-osnovah-ohrany-zdorovya-grazhdan-v-rossiyskoy-federatsii.

[3] Art. 14-1 'Osnovy Zakonodavstva Ukrainy Pro ohoronu zdorovja' (1992) ((Fundamentals of the legislation of Ukraine on health care) № 2801-XII. https://zakon.rada.gov.ua/laws/show/2801-12#Text.

The general conditions for the provision of medical services in the pan-European treatment contract are designed to serve as a basic standard of law for the provision of medical services, proposing the unified understanding and application of legal norms for rendering of medical services in accordance with recognized values and operative principles in the EU.

2.2 *National Legislation of European Countries and Model Rules of the DCFR on a Treatment Contract as Prerequisites for the Upcoming Pan-European Unification of a Treatment Contract*

The decisive legal prerequisites for the future pan-European Unification of a treatment contract include: the treatment contract provided in the national law of the most European countries (national level of the European Unification); provisions of the international legal acts of the EU-law and of the 'soft law' acts, in particular, the Draft Common Frame of Reference (DCFR)[4] which allows the parties to conclude a medical services agreement under Art. i.V.-8:101 and 8:111 (international level of the European Unification).

The DCFR, which is a particular instrument developed in the 1980s in the legislation of the European Community—now the European Union—has the purpose to protect the parties, inter alia, the consumers in private contractual situations, and above all, when one party is in a weaker position (the patient) in comparison to the medical provider (the Services Directive does not apply to the medical services).[5]

As it says in the DCFR, the 'DCFR is developed on the basis of comparative studies of community law and the laws of the Member States, it has to reflect the underlying values to be found in the existing laws, that are not the same in each system.' As far as there are differences between the underlying values in individual jurisdictions, or between the laws of the Member States and the EU law, the DCFR mediates between them and takes a balanced position. Any attempt to work in principles of private law will at least have to deal with the following core aims and the expressed in them provisions on: Justice; Freedom; Protection of Human Rights; Economic welfare; Solidarity and Social Responsibility; Promotion of the Internal Market; Preservations of Cultural and Linguistic Plurality and so on.[6]

The DCFR is to be interpreted and applied in consistency with the aims and principles of not only the laws of the Member States, but also the principles on which the European Union is based on, such as the Internal Market with free and fair

---

[4]Von Bar et al. (2009), Book IV ('Specific Contracts and the rights and obligations arising from them'), Part C ('Services'), Chapter 8 (Treatment), p. 1930.

[5]Council Directive 2006/123/CE, 12 December 2006, OJ 2006, L 376.36.

[6]Von Bar et al. (2009), p. 8.

competition and free movements of goods, people, services and capital, and the protection of consumers and others in need of protection.[7]

The jurisprudence of the European countries and the EU interpreted that the legal provision on a treatment contract shall be an important prerequisite that determines the future unified legal model of the said contract.

Thus, the treatment contract provided in European laws, acts of the 'soft law' and jurisprudence at the national and international levels should be considered as the integral prerequisites for the forthcoming pan-European Unification of a treatment contract.

2.3 The Framework of the Rules of Chapter 8 DCFR and of the European National Codified Acts on a Treatment Contract. Legal Nature of Medical Services

The DCFR was elaborated on the basis of national comparative law and the study of the EU acquis in private law. The aim is to harmonize European legislation in the EU and to be a 'toolbox' for both legislation and judicial actors.[8]

The mentioned provisions of the DCFR are characterised as soft law, but are very important in the doctrine and jurisprudence, inter alia, in services contracts or when some countries don't have regulated services contracts.[9]

DCFR, in Art. IV.C. – 8:101, covers the scope of application of the rules in Chapter 8. This Chapter applies to contracts under which one party, the treatment provider, undertakes to provide medical treatment for the patient, which is a contracting party or a third person, where the patient is not the contracting party, another party, the patient, or undertakes any other service in order to change the physical or mental condition of a person. The most common application will be that of a patient entering into a contract with a treatment provider in order to receive treatment. However, an important policy issue is whether the Chapter should apply to situations where a clear contractual link is lacking. On the one hand, it may be argued that for conceptual reasons only treatment provided after a treatment provider and a patient concluded a contract should fall within the scope of this article. On the other hand, not broadening the scope of these rules to the aforementioned situations would amount to discrimination without any practical reason. In fact, it often

[7]Helga Fonseca (2016) An overview of the treatment contract in the DCFR. https://officialblogofunio.com/2016/04/14/an-overview-of-the-treatment-contract-in-the-dcfr/.

[8]General Provisions (Book I); Contracts (Book II); Obligations (Book III); Specific Contracts (Book IV); Benevolent Intervention in another affairs (Book V) et al.

[9]Jansen and Zimmermann (2009), pp. 98–112; Von Bar (2007).

happens that the patient and the person concluding the treatment contract are not the same.[10]

The scope of application is extended to treatment provided on behalf of a person who is not a contractual party.[11] The reason is the protection of patients in equal situations. In exceptional circumstances, where treatment must be performed immediately to serve the best interests of the patient and the patient cannot express agreement to the contract, the rules on benevolent intervention in another's affairs may apply.

In principle, the Chapter applies only in so far as there is a contractual relationship between a treatment provider and the patient. However, if under national law the relationship cannot be qualified as a private law contract, the present Chapter does not apply; administrative courts may, irrespective of its private law nature and of their own accord, apply and act by analogy.

In most European countries, the contract for treatment falls into existing categories of contracts for services (Spain and Portugal), or contracts for work (France). In some legal systems it is not clear if treatment is qualified as a contract for work or services or if it is a specific innominate *sui generis* contract (Greece). Countries regulating the contract for treatment as a nominate contract in the CC are the Netherlands, Germany (in BGB since 2013) and some Eastern countries (Moldova). In Portugal, when the treatment takes place in a public hospital, administrative law applies. It means, that 'there's no medical contractual liability of the doctor, for his duty, in the public hospital, unless he works there in a private practice', there is only contractual liability of the hospital.[12] It would be desirable to considerate as a contract this contractual relationship whether it is private or public,[13] since this contractual relationship should be subject to the general rules of the Civil Code on the performance of obligations.

In the Netherlands there are two contracts: one with the doctor and one with the clinic. This implies that the patient sometimes has two contracts: one with the hospital authorities for nursing and care and one with the physician for examination and treatment.[14]

In the European countries, medical services are considered an intangible asset that is subject to civil law (France, the Netherlands), the general provisions of which, including its concept, turnover, rules for providing these services, should be determined by a national civil codification act (Civil Code, etc.).

In some European countries (Germany, Portugal), medical services can be provided in both public and private law. Medical services provided within the regulations of public law belong to the sphere of public administration for the provision of

[10] DCFR, Full Edition, p. 1934.

[11] See par (3).

[12] Monteiro (1984), p. 33, Bentes et al. (2004).

[13] Fonseca (2016).

[14] Hondius and Hooft (1996), p. 2.

public services,[15] which ensures the availability of medical care as a manifestation of a sufficient social standard of living in society. In this case, medical services are provided on behalf of the state or a territorial public body (federal state in Germany) and at their expense. In private law, medical services are provided on behalf of a private provider of medical services, and not on behalf of the state, regardless of whether these services are funded by the state or by private individuals.[16] In this case, medical services are recognized as a type of civil law services to which the general provisions on services apply, taking into account the peculiarities of their provision provided by the BGB (§§ 630a – 630h of the BGB).[17]

The doctrine of law of European countries in transition substantiates the thesis of the provision of private and public medical services (Russia), or the recognition of medical services in the sphere of civil law and enshrining general provisions on medical services in national Civil Codes (Moldova, Ukraine).

Thus, the legislation and doctrine of law of the Russian Federation consider medical services as a sphere of public law or civil law. The following types of public services in the sphere of medical care are recognized: medical services that have a social purpose—they are positively evaluated by society and are guaranteed by the state (availability of medical care); medical services, the need for which is caused by a combination of private and public interests, which are fixed due to the obligations of the citizen to take certain actions for their own benefit (vaccination); services related to a purely public interest or public functions aimed at satisfying the private interest (licensing of medical practice, information services).[18]

The law of Ukraine recognizes medical services as an object of civil rights, to which the general provisions of the Civil Code on services apply. The legislation of Ukraine does not explicitly provide for the extension of provisions on public services to certain medical services. The CC of Ukraine does not contain special norms on medical services.

In European countries in transition, there are no two separate agreements on medical services: with a doctor and a health care institution. In these countries, a single agreement is concluded on medical services (with private health care facilities), or on medical care for the population (with public or municipal health care facilities). The parties to this agreement are the provider of medical services and the customer (patient or other customer in the interests of the patient). If the customer is a person other than the patient, such a contract is considered a contract in favour of a third party—the patient. In this case, the patient is a third party and not a party to the contract. The subject of these agreements is the provision of medical care, examination and treatment services. Therefore, the contract between the patient and the doctor for examination and treatment is not concluded.

---

[15] Maurer (1995), p. 3.

[16] Winkhart-Martis (2014), p. 122.

[17] Der Behandlungsvertrag im BGB – Neue Regelungen im Jahr 2013. http://www.medizinrecht-ratgeber.de/medizinrecht/vertrag/behandlungevertrag.html.

[18] Gritsenko and Shevelevoy (2007), p. 12.

2.4 *Legislative Regulation and Structure of the Chapter of the Civil Codification Act on Provision of Medical Services Agreement*

In European countries, the relationship of the contract for the provision of medical services is governed by special laws (France, Portugal), or special laws and the Civil Code (Holland, Germany, Moldova). Thus, in Germany and Moldova, the provisions on medical services are provided for by separate chapters of the Civil Codes of these countries (§§ 630a – 630h of the BGB)[19] and the Civil Code of Moldova (Arts. 1400–1410).[20]

In these provisions of civil codes is, to some extent, reflected the idea inherent, first of all, to German contract law about the right of approximate (general) conditions of performance of contracts (transactions). This right is to be understood as the system of norms defining the legal nature, value, content and other manifestations of potential and current conditions that are considered exemplary (general).[21]

The provisions of the BGB (§§ 630a – 630h) and the Civil Code of Moldova (Arts. 1400–1410) on the general conditions for the provision of medical services define the legal nature, scope and content of the main (basic) responsibilities of the medical service provider, which apply to all types of medical services and their performers.

The tendency to enshrine in the Civil Code provisions on the contract for the provision of medical services is gradually spreading to other European countries. Thus, the doctrine of the law of Ukraine proposes to introduce general conditions for the provision of medical services in a separate chapter of the CC of Ukraine 'Medical Services.' This chapter will contain provisions on the concept and scope of the contract on medical services, as well as a list of responsibilities, norms and principles regarding the behavior of the health care provider[22] following the example of the legislation of some European countries, in particular Germany (§§630a – 630h BGB),[23] Moldova (Arts. 1400–1410 of the Civil Code of Moldova).[24] It will also take into account 'soft law' of the EU (DCFR, Chapter 8: Medical Services).[25]

It is substantiated that the chapter of the CC of Ukraine 'Medical Services' should determine the provisions on the scope of medical services; preliminary examination;

---

[19] Der Behandlungsvertrag im BGB – Neue Regelungen im Jahr 2013. http://www.medizinrecht-ratgeber.de/medizinrecht/vertrag/behandlungevertrag.html.

[20] Civil Code of Moldova. The Law of the Republic of Moldova in the wording № 133 of 15.11.2018. http://www.legis.md/cautare/rezultate/112573.

[21] Zhalinskiy and Roericht (2001), p. 383.

[22] Maydanyk (2020b).

[23] Der Behandlungsvertrag im BGB – Neue Regelungen im Jahr 2013. http://www.medizinrecht-ratgeber.de/medizinrecht/vertrag/behandlungevertrag.html.

[24] Civil Code of Moldova. The Law of the Republic of Moldova in the wording № 133 of 15.11.2018. http://www.legis.md/cautare/rezultate/112573.

[25] Von Bar et al. (2009).

responsibilities related to tools, medicines, materials, devices and premises; the duty to exercise competence and prudence; duty to inform; obligation to inform in case of optional or experimental medical services; exceptions to the obligation to inform; the obligation not to provide medical services without consent; medical documents; remedies in case of non-compliance; obligations of executors under the contract for the provision of medical services.[26]

2.5 *Scope of Medical Services. Legislative Definition of the Basic Model of the Contract for the Provision of Medical Services*

At the present stage, the law of European countries in the sphere of medical care is characterized by a tendency to expand the scope of the contract for the provision of medical services, which leads to the extension of general provisions of this agreement to all contracts for the provision of medical services, regardless of whether they are paid for by individuals or budget funds of the state or local community.

The tendency to universalize contracts for the provision of medical services presupposes the possibility of forming a pan-European agreement for the provision of medical services, the content of which envisages universal general provisions on rendering medical services, paid by individuals or the state/territorial community. In both cases there is a contractual obligation, which is a matter of civil law. Obligations to provide medical services at the expense of individuals are regulated by acts of civil law, in particular, the general provisions of the Civil Code on the contract for services (§ 611 BGB, Art. 901 of the CC of Ukraine, Art. 1375 of the Civil Code of Moldova, Art. 779 of the Civil Code). State-guaranteed free medical services, which are also contractual, are provided as part of compulsory social insurance. Thus, under the law of Ukraine, these medical services are provided on the basis of a contract of medical care concluded by an authorized state body for the benefit of an individual patient with a health care institution to provide medical services under medical guarantees (in Ukraine - National Health Service of Ukraine).[27]

In some European countries in transition (Ukraine), state-guaranteed medical services are recognized as civil law services, with some features of public social services. The agreement on the provision of these services for the population under the program is an agreement on the provision of medical services for the benefit of third parties. This agreement is civil in nature.[28]

The state-guaranteed medical service is characterized by an increased level of public-law influence on these legal relations and the use of the construction of the

---

[26] Maydanyk (2020b).

[27] Art. 8 of the Law of Ukraine 'Pro dershavni finansivi harantiji medychnoho obsluhohuvannja naselennja" of 19 October 2017 № 2168-VIII. https://zakon.rada.gov.ua/laws/show/2168-19#n109.

[28] Senjuta (2018).

medical service contract, which are subject to the general rules on the contract and provision of medical services provided by the Civil Code.[29]

A contract for the provision of medical services at the expense of individuals is a contract for the provision of services. It is distinguished from the contract for work by the criterion of the target direction of the obligation. Under the contract for work, the contractor must provide the result of the work (§ 631 BGB; Art. 946 of the Civil Code of Moldova; Art. 702 of the Civil Code of Russia; Part 1 of Art. 837 of the CC of Ukraine), and under the service contract (§ 611 BGB; Art. 1375 of the Civil Code of Moldova); Art. 779 of the Civil Code of Russia; Part 1 of Art. 901 of the CC of Ukraine) he/she must provide a service that is consumed simultaneously with its provision, i.e. to perform certain work. Thus, the surgeon during the amputation of a leg should give the patient not the result (absence of the leg), but to perform the necessary operation in accordance with the medical standard. A doctor cannot be obliged to achieve a certain result, because despite the commercialization of the modern social system and the medical sphere, in some cases the disease is a fate that cannot be changed by the best doctor. Therefore, a contract between a health care facility/doctor and a patient is not in any case a contract for work, except for certain medical activities, such as laboratory work, where the obligation may be to obtain a specific result - the analysis data.

The doctrine of law of some countries of Western and Eastern Europe (in particular, Germany, Ukraine) substantiates the position that the contract for the provision of services can not fully cover the complex nature of contracts in the medical sphere. In particular, when it comes to medical services that have a tangible result (implantation of a dental crown, artificial valve in the heart, etc.). Proponents of this approach suggest the use of a mixed contract (with elements of a contract for work and a service contract),[30] sui generis or administrative contract, referring to the non-legal or public-law nature of medical activities and the nature of the doctor-patient relationship.[31]

Judicial practice in Ukraine separates the contract for work from the contract for the provision of services on their subject matter. Thus, the Decision of the Commercial Court of Kyiv dated 13.04.2017 in case № 910/1092/17 states: ‘Services are a certain intangible good that is consumed in the process of committing a certain activity or carrying out a certain activity without acquiring a material form. The result of the contractor’s work is a materialized object, which is embodied in individually-made things. Analysis of the terms of the contract shows that the service of the person who signed it meant the plaintiff's performance of dental materials from their own materials, the result of which is the manufacture of prostheses, crowns, etc., to be transferred to the Defendant. Thus, the subject matter of the contract is the achievement of the result, which is the manufacture of dental products. In view of the foregoing, despite the fact that the contract is called a

[29] Maydanyk (2013); Gudushyna (2006), pp. 34–35; Andreev (2007), p. 79.

[30] Smotrov (2003), p. 44.

[31] Deutsch, Spickhoff (2003), p. 42.

contract for the provision of services, the legal relationship governed by it is a contractual obligation, and, accordingly, this transaction by its very nature is a contract for work.'[32]

It is worth supporting the statement that in practice it does not matter how to classify the type of these contracts (as the provision of services, sui generis or administrative contract). The judge should still consider the doctor, the patient, and others involved. The legal consequences, including the consequences of the application of the general part of the law of obligations and the institution of damages, are the same. Accordingly, it is necessary to take into account the peculiarities of the above existing relations, but this does not affect the civil law relations, which are 'enveloped' by the public law system[33] in the case of a contract for medical care.

The doctrine of law draws attention to the civil nature of the obligations under the agreement on medical care within the programs guaranteed by the state and the lack of rules on medical services in the CC of Ukraine.

In this regard, plausible is the idea of extending the provisions of the Civil Code on obligations to all contracts for the provision of medical services, including the contract for medical care, taking into account the features provided by law and the essence of this agreement.[34]

It is believed that this approach will provide an opportunity to legalize and universalize the contract on medical services as a single institution of law in the sphere of health, help to equalize differences between the two existing systems of medical services, increase the efficiency of medical services in compulsory social insurance, strengthen the infrastructural support of medical activity and supervision over its quality.[35]

In view of this, the Ukrainian legal doctrine substantiates the expediency of applying the chapter of the CC of Ukraine 'Medical Services' to contracts under which one party, the contractor, undertakes to provide medical services to the other party, the patient. The provisions of this chapter shall also apply to contracts under which the contractor undertakes to provide any other services aimed at changing the physical or mental condition of the person. If the patient is not a party to the contract, he is considered a third party who has the right to demand from the executor performing of contractual obligations under the law. Peculiarities of execution of agreements on medical care for the population under medical guarantee programs should be determined by law.

[32] Decision of commercial court of Kyiv of 13.04.2017, case № 910/1092/17. https://zakononline.com.ua/court-decisions/show/67096996.

[33] Deutsch and Spickhoff (2003), p. 43; Roericht (2011), p. 160.

[34] Maydanyk (2020b); Maydanyk (2020a), pp. 146–154.

[35] Roericht (2011), p. 154.

2.6 *Preliminary Examination*

The civil codes of some European countries and the model norms of the DCFR provide for the provisions of the preliminary examination (Art. 1401 of the Civil Code of Moldova, Art. IV.C.-8: 102 DCFR).

Thus, the provisions of Art. IV.C.-8: 102: Preliminary DCFR examination provides:

> The Contractor shall, to the extent reasonably deemed necessary for the provision of the Services, shall:
>
> (1) obtain information from the patient about his health, symptoms, previous illnesses, allergies, previous or current treatment, as well as about the patient's preferences and priorities for medical services;
> (2) perform the examinations necessary to diagnose the patient; and
> (3) consult with other persons providing medical services to the patient.[36]

In Ukraine, the legal norms on preliminary examination are provided in various laws and regulations, which contain mainly procedural and technical norms on medical examinations, determine the grounds and procedure, types of medical examinations, documents on the results of medical examinations, responsibilities of the employer.[37]

In particular, the mandatory preventive medical examination includes a general examination by specialists (physician—therapist, dermatovenereologist, otolaryngologist and other specialists if necessary), laboratory and functional examination according to the List approved by the order of the Ministry of Health of Ukraine from 23.07. 2002 № 280. In some cases, individual additional examinations are prescribed to clarify the person's diagnosis.

It is the responsibility of the healthcare institution/private practitioner to examine the patient and prescribe the necessary examinations provided for in the relevant treatment protocol. Based on the information received, the doctor decides on the treatment of the patient. If necessary, the doctor gives referrals to specialized specialists.

The Instruction on Mandatory Preliminary and Periodic Psychiatric Examinations stipulates that mandatory preliminary and periodic psychiatric examinations provide for mandatory examination: possible complaints and history of mental disorders, clinical examination, which is part of the specified program, and, in this case needs

[36] Von Bar et al. (2009).

[37] Stattya 169 Kodeksu zakoniv pro prazju Ukrajiny ta st. 17 Zakonu Ukrajiny 'Pro okhoronu prazi' vid 14 zhovtnya 1992 r. № 2694-KHII; stattya 21 Zakonu Ukraïni "Pro zakhyst naselennya vid infektsiynikh khvorob" vid 6 kvitnya 2000 r. № 1645-III; stattya 11 Zakonu Ukrajiny "Pro zasady zapobigannya i protydiji korupziji" № 3206-VI vid 7 kvitnya 2011 r.; Poryadok provedennya medichnikh ohlyadiv pratsivnikiv pevnikh kategoriy, zatverdzhenomu nakazom Ministerstva okhoroni zdorov'ya Ukrajiny vid 21 travnya 2007 r. № 246; nakaz Ministerstva okhorony zdorov'ya Ukraji vid 23.07.2002 r. № 280. https://zakon.rada.gov.ua/laws/show/322-08#Text.

additional examinations in accordance with the Mandatory Protocol of preliminary and periodic psychiatric examinations.[38]

The unified clinical protocol of primary, emergency and secondary (specialized) medical care 'Arterial hypertension' provides for the responsibilities of the health care institution for a preliminary examination at the stages of the organization of medical care and diagnosis.

At the stage of organization of medical care, primary care institutions are obliged to: (a) perform the examinations necessary to verify the diagnosis and conduct dispensary supervision of patients with hypertension; (b) if necessary, ensure that the patient is referred to a secondary care facility for a definitive diagnosis and optimal treatment; (c) provide the patient with information on the state of his health in an accessible form with recommendations on non-drug and drug treatment, tactics of behavior in case of sudden deterioration of the disease orally and in writing; (d) to provide dispensary supervision for patients with high and very high risk of hypertension, to fill in a standard card form for this category of patients; (d) ensure that patients have the necessary laboratory tests. If it is impossible to perform research in a primary care facility, the doctor must refer the patient to a facility that provides secondary care.

At the stage of diagnosis, the primary care institution is obliged to conduct clinical, laboratory and instrumental examination of patients with hypertension, which provides the following necessary actions of the doctor to diagnose hypertension: (a) blood pressure measurement; conducting a medical examination for all; (b) laboratory tests provided for in the clinical protocol. If it is impossible to perform research in primary care facilities, the patient should be referred to a facility that provides secondary care.[39]

The conducted analysis shows that the legislation of Ukraine does not contain unified legal norms on preliminary examination, which stipulate the content of the general obligation of the medical service provider during any preliminary examination.

According to its content, the preliminary examination involves the duty of the service provider (health care institution/private practitioner) to obtain history of illness, i.e. to obtain information from the patient about his health, to conduct examinations necessary to diagnose the patient and consult with other persons providing medical services to the patient.

In view of this, we consider it expedient to introduce in the CC of Ukraine unified provisions on preliminary examination, which provide for the duty of the service provider (health care institution/private practitioner) (a) obtain from the patient

[38]Mandatory Protocol of preliminary and periodic psychiatric examinations 'Instrukziya pro provedennya obov'yazkovikh poperednikh ta periodichnikh psikhiatrichnikh ohlyadiv' approved by the Order of the Ministry of Health of Ukraine of 17.01.2002 № 12. https://zakon.rada.gov.ua/laws/show/z0094-02#Text.

[39]Order of the Ministry of Health of Ukraine of 24 May 2012 № 384 'Pro zatverdzhennya ta vprovadzhennya mediko-tekhnologichnikh dokumentiv zi standartizatsiji medichnoji dopomohy pry arterialniy hipertenzijy'. https://ips.ligazakon.net/document/MOZ15826.

information about the patient's state of health, treatment, benefits and priorities for medical services, (b) conduct the examination necessary to diagnose the patient; and (c) consult with other persons providing the patient with medical services.

2.7 Contractor's Obligations with Respect to Instruments, Medicines, Materials, Devices and Premises

Legal norms on the obligations of the executor concerning instruments, medicines, materials, devices and premises as the general condition of rendering medical services are provided in the Civil Code of Moldova (item 1402), DCFR (item IV. C.-8: 103).

Art. IV.C.-8: 103: 'Obligations' relating to DCFR instruments, medicines, materials, devices and premises provides:

(1) The Contractor shall use such tools, medicines, materials, devices and premises, the quality of which at least corresponds to what is required in accordance with generally accepted and reliable professional practice, which are line with applicable regulations, and which are suitable for achieving the specific purposes for which they are commonly used.
(2) The parties may not, to the detriment of the patient, exclude the application of this Art. in whole or in part or change its effect.[40]

In European countries in transition, the legal provisions on the obligations of the performer relating to instruments, medicines, materials, devices and premises are not usually provided for by a special rule of law.

Thus, according to the legislation of Ukraine, these legal relations are subject to the provisions of the CC of Ukraine on justice, good faith and reasonableness (paragraph 6 of Part 3 of the Civil Code), good faith performance of obligations (Part 3 of Art. 509 of the Civil Code) and liability for damages, in particular, caused by a source of increased danger (Arts. 1166, 1187 of the Civil Code), as well as laws and bylaws (Cabinet of Ministers of Ukraine, Ministry of Health, etc.) on the quality of medical services.[41]

Under Ukrainian law, the principle of fairness, good faith and reasonableness applies to negotiations at the conclusion of the contract, performance of the contract and general tortious liability. Manifestations of fairness, good faith and reasonableness of performance of the obligation include the obligation of the parties to act in respect to each other honestly and fairly (subjective criterion) and the requirement of

[40] Von Bar et al. (2009).

[41] Order of the Ministry of Health of Ukraine 'Pro poryadok kontrolyu yakosti medichnoï dopomogi' (On procedure for healthcare quality control) of 28.09.2012 № 752. https://zakon.rada.gov.ua/laws/show/z1996-12#Text.

observance by the parties of reasonable standards of honesty in contractual relations (objective criterion).[42]

Judicial practice in Ukraine adheres to the position that in applying the applicable law, the provider must be guided by internal criteria, good faith, in relation to the counterparty-patient (to act in such a way as not to cause harm, to prevent the conclusion of an obligation on the basis of fraud, violence, abuse of trust, to comply with the legal conduct of the parties, to do everything dependent on the party actions for proper performance of obligations and non-violation of the rights of others) and adhere to external criteria, fairness and reasonableness, which is expressed in the equal legal scale of conduct and in the proportionality of legal responsibility for the offense. That is, each party in the performance of civil obligations must adhere to such procedural behavior that would exclude biased (unfair) actions of the parties to the obligation in relation to each other.[43]

According to the law of Ukraine, a good quality medical service is considered to be one that meets the achievements of modern science and best practice, has a positive effect on the patient's health and meets his needs with maximum efficiency, safety and without unnecessary costs.[44]

The WHO European Office, in its report on the principles of quality assurance in health care, pointed out the need to take into account four elements in addressing this issue:[45] (1) Qualification of the specialist; (2) Optimal use of resources; (3) Risk to the patient; (4) Patient satisfaction with the interaction with the medical subsystem.

The quality of medical care is a property of the process of doctor and patient interaction associated with the qualifications of staff, i.e. the doctor's ability to reduce the risk of disease progression and new pathological process, to optimally use medical resources and ensure patient satisfaction with his interaction with the medical system.[46]

Health care quality is a broad term that encompasses many aspects of patient care. On the basis of several definitions in the literature, the WHO definition of quality of care is 'the extent to which health care services provided to individuals and patient populations improve desired health outcomes. In order to achieve this, health care must be safe, effective, timely, efficient, equitable and people-centred.'[47]

---

[42] Valigura (2020), p. 13.

[43] Act of The Supreme Court of Ukraine (2019) in a case № 761/41709/17. http://reyestr.court.gov.ua/Review/82001379.

[44] Martinenko (2006), p. 36.

[45] Boyko (2001).

[46] Sistema kontrolya kachestva i effektivnosti meditsinskoy pomoschi (uchebno-metodicheskoe posobie), Tomsk 1999 g. Sibirskiy Gosudarstvennyy Meditsinskiy Universitet. Fakultet usovershenstvovaniya vrachey. Kafedra sotsialnoy meditsiny, ekonomiki i upravleniya zdravookhraneniya. http://www.ssmu.ru/ofice/f7/soc/met2.htm.

[47] World Health Organization (2006) Quality of care: a process for making strategic choices in health systems, p. 9. https://www.who.int/management/quality/assurance/QualityCare_B.Def.pdf.; World Health Organization (How do we define quality of care? https://www.who.int/teams/maternal-newborn-child-adolescent-health-and-ageing/quality-of-care#:~:text=On%20the%20

In Ukraine and some other European countries in transition, there is currently no modern unified approach to the quality of medical care, which would include the quality of tools, medicines, materials, devices and premises that the contractor is obliged to use. Only certain instructions of action of medical workers, as well as clinical guidelines, standards and unified clinical protocols of medical care are valid.

It is also allowed to use international protocols. These are important tools, but they are only some elements of the quality management system that needs to be created in each health facility. To do this, the heads of institutions need to learn quality management and promote the training of hospital staff.

Therefore, the provider is obliged to use such tools, medicines, materials, devices and premises, the quality of which corresponds to applicable regulations and generally accepted norms of business turnover, to act in relations with the contractor (patient, etc.) honestly and fairly, to adhere to reasonable standards of honesty in a binding relationship. The instruments, medicines, materials, devices and premises used by the contractor in the provision of medical services must be safe, effective, timely, cost-effective, equitable and human-oriented.

The absence at the legislative level of a legal norm on the obligations of the executor concerning instruments, medicines, materials, devices and premises, makes it expedient to introduce this general condition of medical services to the CC of Ukraine,[48] national acts of civil codification of other European countries in transition.

2.8 *Model of a Pan-European Treatment Contract: Concept, Levels, Components*

The pan-European treatment contract shall be a legal instrument of approximation and unification of EU-law and national law of European countries at a different levels—national and international—providing a unified concept of medical services, their scope and main obligations of medical services provider, which correspond to the recognized values and operative principles in the EU, taking into account common features and peculiarities of European countries.

At the international level, the pan-European treatment contract should be regarded as a pan-European basic legal standard of a medical care, which sets a minimum allowable level of medical services for all European countries, regardless of whether these services are paid by the individuals or funded by the state, in order to succeed better in combining of recognized values and operative principles in EU

basis%20of%20several,populations%20improve%20desired%20health%20outcomes. Committee on Quality of Health Care in America, Institute of Medicine (2001). Crossing the Quality Chasm: A New Health System for the 21st Century. Washington, D.C., National Academy Press, Chapter 1. from http://www.nap.edu/catalog/10027/crossing-the-quality-chasm-a-new-health-system-for-the.

[48] Maydanyk (2020a), pp. 146–154.

with quality, institutional ability, affordability and traditions of healthcare systems of European countries.

At the national level, it is advisable to unify a treatment contract by introducing into the legislation of European countries (in the Civil Codes or special laws) of general conditions for providing medical services, which should contain provisions on: the scope of medical services; preliminary examination; duty relating to instruments, medicines, materials, devices and premises; the relationships between the manifestation of competence and prudence; duty to inform, duty to inform in case of optional or experimental medical services, exceptions to the duty to inform; duty not to provide medical services without consent; medical records remedies in case of default; duties of providers under contract on rendering of medical services.

3 Concluding Remarks

The integral prerequisite of the forthcoming pan-European treatment contract shall include general provisions for rendering of medical services provided in the European laws, acts of the 'soft law' and jurisprudence at the national and international levels, which correspond to the recognized values and operative principles in the EU.

The Pan-European treatment contract shall be a legal instrument of approximation and unification of EU-law and national law of European countries at a national and international levels, which sets a basic legal standard of a medical care, a minimum allowable level of medical services for all European countries, regardless of whether medical services are paid by the individuals or state-funded, provide a unified concept of medical services, their scope and main obligations of medical services provider taking into account common features and peculiarities of European countries.

References

Bentes M, Dias CM, Sakellarides C, Bankauskaite V (2004) Health care systems in transition: Portugal. Copenhagen, WHO Regional Office for Europe on behalf of the European Observatory on Health Systems and Policies. 120 p. https://www.euro.who.int/__data/assets/pdf_file/0005/107843/e82937.pdf

Boyko AT (2001) Kachestvo meditsinskoy pomoschi. Problemy obespecheniya. Mir Meditsiny. N 1. C. 24–30

Deutsch E, Spickhoff A (2003) Medizinrecht. Arztrecht, Arzneimitteltecht, Medizinproduktrecht und Transfusionsrecht. Springer, 854 s

Fonseca H (2016) An overview of the treatment contract in the DCFR. The Official blog of UNIO. https://officialblogofunio.com/2016/04/14/an-overview-of-the-treatment-contract-in-the-dcfr/

Gritsenko EV, Shevelevoy NA (2007) Publichnye uslugi: pravovoe regulirovanie (rossiyskiy i zarubezhnyy opyt). Volters Kluver, Moscow

Gudushyna OY (2006) Pravovoj reshym publichnogo dogovora i dejateljnostj medizinskih organizazij po okazaniju platnyh medizinskih uslug: sootnoshenije. Medizinskoje pravo 2:34–35

Hondius E, Hooft A (1996) The new dutch law on medical services. Netherlands Int Law Rev XLIII:2

Jansen N, Zimmermann R (2009) A European civil code in all but name. Cambridge Law J 98–112

Martinenko LV (2006) Yakist medichnoï dopomogi patsientu – yakist zhittya medika. Zhinochiy likar 1:36. https://z-l.com.ua/ua/article/75

Maurer H (1995) Allgemeines Verwaltungsrecht. 10 Aufl. Muenchen, p 3

Maydanyk RA (2020a) Rekodifikatsiya tsivilnogo zakonodavstva Ukraïni: medichni poslugi. In: Maidanyk RA, Moskalenko KV et al (eds) Privatne pravo v sferi okhoroni zdorov'ya: vikliki ta perspektivi. Kiïvski pravovi chitannya. Conference abstracts, 17 September 2020. LOBF 'Meditsina i parvo', Lviv, pp 146–154

Maydanyk RA (2020b) Reforma vitchusnjanoi modeli ohorony zdorovja: jakoju vona malab buty? Legal Newspaper. Online 13(719). https://yur-gazeta.com/publications/practice/medichne-pravo-farmacevtika/reforma-vitchiznyanoyi-modeli-ohoroni-zdorovya-yakoyu-vona-mala-b-buti.html

Maydanyk RA (2013) Dohovir pro bezoplatne nadannja hromadjanam medychnoji dopomohy. Ponjattja, pryroda, elementy. Yurydychna hazeta online 45(387). https://yur-gazeta.com/publications/practice/medichne-pravo-farmacevtika/dogovir-pro-bezoplatne-nadannya-gromadyanam-medichnoyi-dopomogi.html

Monteiro S (1984) Responsibilidade Medica em Portugal. Boletim do Ministerio da Justica 332:33

Roericht AA (2011) Teoreticheskie osnovy meditsinskogo prava: problemy formirovaniya i razvitiya. RAN INION, Moscow, 456 p. https://books.google.com.ua/books

Senjuta IY (2018) Dohovir pro medychne obsluhohuvannja naselennja za prohramoju medychnyh harantij: okremi shtryhy do 'normatyvnoho portretu.' Ukrainskyj medychnyj chasopys, 28 May 2018. https://www.umj.com.ua/article/125801/dogovir-pro-medichne-obslugovuvannya-naselennya-za-programoyu-medichnih-garantij-okremi-shtrihi-do-normativnogo-portretu

Smotrov OI (2003) Dohovir shchodo oplatnoho nadannja medychnyh posluh. Dissertation, Nazionaljnyj un-t vnutr. sprav, Kharkiv. 213 p

Valigura K (2020) Printsip dobrosovisnosti yak kategoriya tsivilnogo prava. Pidpryjemnyztvo, gospodarstvo i pravo 4(11–15):13. http://pgp-journal.kiev.ua/archive/2020/4/3.pdf

Von Bar C (2007) Coverage and structure of the common frame of reference. ERCL

Von Bar C, Clive E, Schulte-Nölke H et al (2009) Principles, Definitions and Model Rules of European Private Law Draft Common Frame of Reference (DCFR). Outline Edition Prepared by the Study Group on a European Civil Code and the Research Group on EC Private Law (Acquis Group). Based in part on a revised version of the Principles of European Contract Law. https://www.law.kuleuven.be/personal/mstorme/2009_02_DCFR_OutlineEdition.pdf.

Winkhart-Martis M (2014) Arzthaftungs-recht. Fallgruppenkommentar von Ruediger 4. Auflage Verlag Dr. Otto Schmidt, Koeln, p. 122

Zhalinskiy A, Roericht A (2001) Vvedenie v nemetskoe pravo. Spark, Moscow, 383 p. https://rusneb.ru/catalog/000199_000009_000735783/

Andreev YN (2007) Platnyje medizinskije uslugi. Pravovoje regulirovanije u sudebnaja praktika. Izdatelstvo Osj-89, 400 s. https://www.twirpx.com/file/225256/

The Legal Nature of Managed Entry Agreements (MEAs) in the Coronavirus Response System

Vitalii Pashkov

Contents

Abstract This article elaborates on the admission procedure for vaccines against COVID-19 in various European countries and the United States. Neither the EU countries nor the United States has applied for a full license to manufacture or issue a coronavirus vaccine registration certificate. At best, it is an emergency use authorization or conditional marketing authorization. A particular focus will be on the Legal Nature of Managed Entry Agreements (MEAs) in the Coronavirus Response System. The use of MEAs allows not only to legalize emergency use authorization or conditional marketing authorization as a way to combat coronavirus infection, but also others, including for treating, preventing, or diagnosing seriously debilitating or life-threatening diseases. That includes orphan medicines. However, Ukraine and Russia have followed the path of simplifying the registration and full admission of vaccines for further use. Russia registered vaccines against COVID-19 of its own development, however, in Ukraine, there is a situation when it fully legalizes

This paper is prepared on the basis of the reports for the Conference 'Private Healthcare Law: Challenges and Prospects'.

V. Pashkov (✉)
Department of Civil, Commercial and Environmental Law, Poltava Law Institute and Laboratory for the Study of National Security Problems in the Field of Public Health, Poltava, Ukraine

© The Author(s), under exclusive license to Springer Nature Switzerland AG 2022

R. Maydanyk et al. (eds.), *Ukrainian Healthcare Law in the Context of European and International Law*, European Union and its Neighbours in a Globalized World 7,
https://doi.org/10.1007/978-3-031-05690-1_15

vaccines against COVID-19 earlier than the countries of this vaccine's origin. This is due to ignoring the regulations and the experience of using MEAs both by Ukraine and Russia.

1 Introduction

According to experts from the World Health Organization, the situation with COVID-19 remains unstable following the declaration of a pandemic. Although vaccination against coronavirus infection has already begun in most European countries. According to the Global Alliance for Vaccines and Immunization (GAVI), created with the participation of WHO, in 2020, there were more than 170 vaccine-candidates under development.[1] *The most known are vaccine of* Pfizer/BioNTech, Oxford/AstraZeneca, Johnson & Johnson, Sanofi/GSK, CureVac, Moderna.[2] Including two vaccines from Russia,[3] one of them is known under the trade name Sputnik V[4] and Chinese coronavirus vaccines CanSinoBio and Sinovac.[5]

However, all vaccine-candidates have the status of incompletely tested drugs and are approved for use under simplified procedures. The main criterion for vaccine admission is the excess of the risk of morbidity over the risk of using the vaccine in the absence of other alternative therapies. At the same time, regulators in developed countries understand that using these products may cause severe unexpected side effects in the future. In turn, in the process of using drugs, developers are obliged to continue researching drugs and monitoring patients' condition.

In such circumstances, it is Managed entry agreements (MEAs) that are a set of instruments to facilitate access to new vaccines. Experience in implementing MEAs varied substantially across the region.

Analysis of the "Managed entry agreements (MEAs") concept use in the EU, USA, and Ukraine shows different understandings and applications.

In the European Union and the United States, the legal nature of Managed entry agreements is to speed up the marketing authorization procedure to minimize threats

[1] COVAX explained. 3 September—by Dr Seth Berkley, CEO of Gavi, the Vaccine Alliance. URL: https://www.gavi.org/vaccineswork/covax-explained.

[2] Belgian secretary of state accidentally reveals EU vaccine prices. URL: https://www.politico.eu/article/belgian-secretary-of-state-accidentally-reveals-eu-vaccine-prices/?fbclid=IwAR3OXidyWlhE56iLmdQkszF_JEOt3G5BLRKIOCIkRlv8QfxNDfgL-_ADbaI.

[3] Информация Федеральной службы по надзору в сфере защиты прав потребителей и благополучия человека от 14 октября 2020 г. "О регистрации вакцины ФБУН ГНЦ ВБ "Вектор" Роспотребнадзора "ЭпиВакКорона". URL: http://base.garant.ru/74754034/.

[4] Вакцина от короновируса: что происходит в России и мире. VADEMECUM. URL: https://vademec.ru/news/2020/09/13/vaktsina-ot-koronavirusa-chto-proiskhodit-v-rossii-i-v-mire/.

[5] China slips in COVID-19 vaccine race on doubts over effectiveness. URL: https://asia.nikkei.com/Spotlight/Coronavirus/China-slips-in-COVID-19-vaccine-race-on-doubts-over-effectiveness.

to public health (analysis of most publications shows that by 2020 these were separate forms of cancer and/or of an orphan).

We are talking primarily about patients' access to experimental drugs with unproven efficacy.

EU pharmaceutical legislation ensures that vaccines are only approved after a scientific assessment that their overall benefits outweigh the risks. The benefits of the vaccine in protecting humans from COVID-19 should far outweigh any side effects or potential risks.[6]

The European Medicines Agency's (EMA) website makes it clear that during the COVID-19 pandemic, the EMA's conditional marketing authorization is used to expedite the approval of safe and effective COVID-19 drugs and vaccines in the EU. In their view, conditional marketing authorization is the most appropriate tool for granting access to COVID-19 vaccines to all EU citizens simultaneously and to support mass vaccination campaigns. Once a temporary marketing authorization has been granted, its holder must meet certain obligations in a timely manner, which may include the completion of current or new research or the collection of additional data to confirm that the benefit-risk balance remains positive.[7]

From the EMA's point of view, a conditional marketing authorization is a tool that allows regulators to approve drugs quickly and pragmatically in a medical emergency.[8]

In the United States, the emergency use authorization mechanism allows the Food and Drug Administration (FDA) to protects health care practices by facilitating the availability and use of essential drugs during emergencies. Under section 564 of the U.S. Federal Food, Drug, and Cosmetic Act, an FDA commissioner may allow the use of unapproved (i.e., unregistered) drugs or off-label (for unapproved indications) in emergencies to diagnose, treat, or prevent serious or life-threatening diseases or conditions where there are no adequate, approved and available treatment alternatives.

In the U.S. (in the E.U., it is not available), there is another mechanism for the use of unapproved (unregistered) drugs and the use of off-label (for unapproved indications)—permission for emergency use authorization. The FDA Commissioner may authorize their use during emergencies to diagnose, treat, or prevent serious

[6]European Medicines Agency. Human regulatory. Robust regulatory framework and scientific expertise in the EU. URL: https://www.ema.europa.eu/en/human-regulatory/overview/public-health-threats/coronavirus-disease-covid-19/treatments-vaccines/covid-19-vaccines-development-evaluation-approval-monitoring#scientific-evaluation-and-approval-section.

[7]Human regulatory. Conditional marketing authorisation. URL: https://www.ema.europa.eu/en/human-regulatory/marketing-authorisation/conditional-marketing-authorisation#use-during-covid-19-pandemic-(new)-section.

[8]European Medicines Agency. Human regulatory. URL: https://www.ema.europa.eu/en/human-regulatory/overview/public-health-threats/coronavirus-disease-covid-19/treatments-vaccines/covid-19-vaccines-development-evaluation-approval-monitoring#scientific-evaluation-and-approval-section.

life-threatening diseases or conditions when there are no approved and available treatment alternatives.

That is, in the E.U. and the U.S., Managed entry agreements (MEAs) are agreements between pharmaceutical companies and healthcare payers that provide for the possibility of using new drugs, taking into account uncertainties about their effectiveness and financial costs.

To ensure rapid access to new, potentially useful healthcare technologies, it is necessary to obtain the best value for money and ensure affordability. As a result, health care providers use several innovative approaches to cost recovery.

It is essential that no country in the world has announced the full implementation of all stages of clinical trials of coronavirus vaccine-candidates. At best, it is a conditional permit for use in the E.U., emergency use in the U.S. and the U.K., or simplified registration in Russia.

In EU countries, in the interest of public health, applicants may be granted a conditional marketing authorisation for such medicines on less comprehensive clinical data than typically required, where the benefit of immediate availability of the medicine outweighs the risk inherent in the fact that additional data are still required.[9]

Conditional marketing authorisations are valid for 1 year and can be renewed annually. Once a conditional marketing authorisation has been granted, the marketing authorisation holder must fulfill specific obligations within defined timelines.

In the United States and the United Kingdom, there is emergency use authorization for the use of vaccine-candidates. For example, this is the case with the COVID-19 Pfizer/BioNTech vaccine for emergency use in the United States. The same can be said about the emergency use authorization granted by the Medicines and Healthcare products Regulatory Agency (MHRA).[10]

Conditional marketing authorization is different from an emergency use permit, which some countries use to allow temporary use in an emergency. An emergency use permit is not a marketing permit.[11]

[9]European Medicines Agency. Human regulatory. Conditional marketing authorisation. URL: https://www.ema.europa.eu/en/human-regulatory/marketing-authorisation/conditional-marketing-authorisation#use-during-covid-19-pandemic-(new)-section.

[10]AstraZeneca's Covid-19 vaccine approved in the U.K. URL: https://www.nbcnews.com/news/world/astrazeneca-s-covid-19-vaccine-approved-u-k-n1252418.

[11]European Medicines Agency. Human regulatory. URL: https://www.ema.europa.eu/en/human-regulatory/overview/public-health-threats/coronavirus-disease-covid-19/treatments-vaccines/covid-19-vaccines-development-evaluation-approval-monitoring#scientific-evaluation-and-approval-section.

2 Legal Characteristics of the Admission of COVID-19 Vaccines-Candidates in Europe and the United States

2.1 Legal Bases for Access to COVID-19 Vaccines in the EU, the US and the UK

We are talking about permissive procedures for access to vaccines for patients as a way to combat coronavirus disease.

Thus, in the EU, there is also a particular procedure for the admission to the market of certain groups of drugs without the issuance of a manufacturing license and / or registration certificate. That is the so-called conditional marketing authorization. Such authorization is granted when immediate drug availability benefits outweigh the risks associated with the need for additional research. The legal basis is Article 14 (7) of Regulation (EC) No 726/2004 of the European Parliament and of the Council of 31 March 2004 laying down Community procedures for the authorisation and supervision of medicinal products for human and veterinary use and establishing a European Medicines Agency (Text with EEA relevance). The Regulation stipulates that following consultation with the applicant, an authorisation may be granted subject to certain specific obligations, to be reviewed annually by the Agency. The list of these obligations shall be made publicly accessible. The provisions for granting a conditional marketing authorisation are further elaborated in Regulation (EC) No 507/2006.

According to Regulation (EC) No 507/2006,[12] in order to meet the unmet medical needs of patients and in the interests of public health, it may be necessary to grant marketing authorisations based on less complete data than is normally the case and subject to specific obligations, hereinafter 'conditional marketing authorisations.'

Although the data upon which an opinion on a conditional marketing authorisation is based may be incomplete, the risk-benefit balance, as defined in Article 1(28a) of Directive 2001/83/EC, should be positive. Furthermore, the benefits to public health of making the medicinal product concerned immediately available on the market should outweigh the risk inherent in the fact that additional data are still required.

Where conditional marketing authorisations are granted, they should be restricted to situations where only the clinical part of the application dossier is less complete than usual. Incomplete pre-clinical or pharmaceutical data should be accepted only in the case of a product to be used in emergencies, in response to public health threats.

Conditional marketing authorisations are distinct from marketing authorisations granted in exceptional circumstances in accordance with Article 14(8) of Regulation

[12]EUR-Lex. Commission Regulation (EC) No 507/2006 of 29 March 2006 on the conditional marketing authorisation for medicinal products for human use falling within the scope of Regulation (EC) No 726/2004 of the European Parliament and of the Council (Text with EEA relevance). URL: https://eur-lex.europa.eu/legal-content/EN/TXT/?uri=CELEX%3A32006R0507.

(EC) No 726/2004. In the case of conditional marketing authorisation, authorisation is granted before all data are available. The authorisation is not intended, however, to remain conditional indefinitely. Instead, once the missing data are provided, it should be possible to replace it with a marketing authorisation, which is not conditional, that is to say, which is not subject to specific obligations. In contrast, it will typically never be possible to assemble a full dossier in respect of a marketing authorisation granted in exceptional circumstances.

According to the European Medicines Agency, conditional marketing authorizations are valid for one year and can be renewed annually.[13]

At the same time, the EMA website has information on granting conditional marketing authorization for the Pfizer/BioNTech vaccine on December 21, 2020. That was granted in the interest of public health because the medicine addresses an unmet medical need and the benefit of immediate availability outweighs the risk from less comprehensive data than usually required. Later, on January 6, 2021, the vaccine by Moderna Biotech Spain, S.L. received a conditional marketing authorisation.

As for any medicine, if new data show that the medicine's benefits no longer outweigh its risks, EMA can take regulatory action, such as suspending or revoking the marketing authorisation.[14]

However, the EMA statement states that vaccines' safety and effectiveness will continue to be monitored in EU member states through a system of pharmacovigilance and additional research conducted by the company and European authorities. That is, as of January 2020, no pharmaceutical company in the EU has received a license for the production or registration certificate of the COVID-19 vaccine.

Once a temporary marketing authorization has been granted, its owner must meet certain obligations in a timely manner, which may include the completion of current or new research or the collection of additional data to confirm that the benefit-risk balance remains positive.[15]

EU pharmaceutical legislation ensures that vaccines are only approved after a scientific assessment will demonstrate that their overall benefits outweigh the risks. The benefits of the vaccine in protecting humans from COVID-19 should far outweigh any side effects or potential risks.[16]

---

[13] European Medicines Agency. Human regulatory. Conditional marketing authorisation. URL: https://www.ema.europa.eu/en/human-regulatory/marketing-authorisation/conditional-marketing-authorisation#use-during-covid-19-pandemic-(new)-section.

[14] European Medicines Agency. Human regulatory. Conditional marketing authorisation. URL: https://www.ema.europa.eu/en/human-regulatory/marketing-authorisation/conditional-marketing-authorisation#use-during-covid-19-pandemic-(new)-section.

[15] Human regulatory. Conditional marketing authorisation. URL: https://www.ema.europa.eu/en/human-regulatory/marketing-authorisation/conditional-marketing-authorisation#use-during-covid-19-pandemic-(new)-section.

[16] European Medicines Agency. Human regulatory. Robust regulatory framework and scientific expertise in the EU. URL: https://www.ema.europa.eu/en/human-regulatory/overview/public-

US legislation on the use of drugs in a restricted legalization regime is different.

Under section 564 of the Federal Food, Drug, and Cosmetic Act (FD&C Act), the FDA Commissioner may allow unapproved medical products or unapproved uses of approved medical products to be used in an emergency to diagnose, treat, or prevent serious or life-threatening diseases or conditions caused by CBRN threat agents when there are no adequate, approved, and available alternatives.[17]

The Emergency Use Authorization (EUA) authority allows the FDA to help strengthen the nation's public health protections against CBRN threats by facilitating the availability and use of MCMs needed during public health emergencies.

The FDA clarified that emergency use authorization means what its name suggests: a medical product gets special authorization by the FDA to be used during an emergency—but it is short of a full approval. Pfizer would have to file a separate application for its vaccine to be fully licensed by the FDA.[18] According to FDA regulations, we are talking about the so-called "compassionate use," expanded access is a potential pathway for a patient with an immediately life-threatening condition or severe disease or condition to gain access to an investigational medical product (drug, biologic, or medical device) for treatment outside of clinical trials when no comparable or satisfactory alternative therapy options are available.[19] The legal basis for extended access is the PREP Act of 31.01.2020. The PREP Act amended the Public Health Service Act (PHS Act) to add section 319F-3 (42 U.S.C. 247d-6d).[20]

PREP Act - COVID-19 Related Information: (1) Notice of Declaration under the Public Readiness and Emergency Preparedness Act for medical countermeasures against COVID-19 (February 4, 2020). (2) Amended April 10, 2020, to add countermeasures under the CARES Act. (3) COVID-19 - Medical Countermeasures (effective February 4, 2020) Amended April 10, 2020, to add countermeasures pursuant to the CARES Act OGC Advisory Opinion on PREP Act Declaration. (4) Advisory Opinion 02-02 on the PREP Act and the Secretary's Declaration under

health-threats/coronavirus-disease-covid-19/treatments-vaccines/covid-19-vaccines-development-evaluation-approval-monitoring#scientific-evaluation-and-approval-section.

[17] *Emergency Use Authorization. About Emergency Use Authorizations (EUAs). URL:* https://www.fda.gov/emergency-preparedness-and-response/mcm-legal-regulatory-and-policy-framework/emergency-use-authorization?fbclid=IwAR3EBrAELMmTeUl_IPtmHZNl_veTMN6tL2-CUJcrz0nS6AOxjAvBktKICy8.

[18] FDA issues emergency use authorization for Pfizer/BioNTech Covid-19 vaccine. By Jacqueline Howard, CNN Updated 0840 GMT (1640 HKT) December 12, 2020. URL: https://edition.cnn.com/2020/12/11/health/covid-vaccine-fda-eua/index.html?utm_medium=social&utm_content=2020-12-12T02%3A44%3A51&utm_term=link&utm_source=twcnnbrk.

[19] Expanded Access FDA. URL: https://www.fda.gov/news-events/public-health-focus/expanded-access?fbclid=IwAR25HGmQDMhkp6PQgNp2DPfzLQR9AWELoAE4bcnnfhqXRq5nVsepWIYJTl4.

[20] Emergency Use Authorization. About Emergency Use Authorizations (EUAs).FDA. URL: https://www.fda.gov/emergency-preparedness-and-response/mcm-legal-regulatory-and-policy-framework/emergency-use-authorization?fbclid=IwAR3EBrAELMmTeUl_IPtmHZNl_veTMN6tL2-CUJcrz0nS6AOxjAvBktKICy8.

the Act. (5) Second Amendment to Declaration under the PREP Act for Medical Countermeasures against COVID-19. (6) Third Amendment to Declaration under the PREP Act for Medical Countermeasures Against COVID–19.

Based on the above-mentioned regulations, on December 11, 2020, the FDA granted a temporary permit for the emergency use of the Pfizer/BioNTech vaccine for the prevention of coronavirus disease.[21] 95 percent efficiency is emphasized for patients from 16 years of age.[22] Information on the research is publicly available. Also, on December 18, 2020, it granted a temporary permit for the emergency use of the Moderna vaccine to patients over 18 years of age with 95 percent of effectiveness.[23]

Although relevant specialists prepared the draft regulations, a significant burden was placed on lawyers, of course, those who have experience in medical law.[24]

That is, the United States, as of December 2020, established a limited legal status of vaccines (Pfizer/BioNTech and Moderna) from COVID-19, intended for emergency use on the basis of a special temporary permit for production and release. That involves continuing the production licensing procedure and/or obtaining a registration certificate, which requires high costs and time limits.

The legislation of Great Britain conceptually corresponds to the legislation of the USA. Medicines and Healthcare products Regulatory Agency, when allowing the use of not thoroughly investigated drugs, applies to regulatory flexibilities.[25]

Flexibilities do not displace or diminish any other obligations applicable to the relevant products. Any medicinal product which benefits from these regulatory flexibilities remains subject to marketing authorisation.

Requirements set out for each of the regulatory flexibilities may vary (for example, pre-conditions and notifications). Manufacturers should take great care to meet the relevant requirements and must satisfy themselves that the product remains safe to use before putting flexibility in place.

None of these flexibilities amount to authorisation or a recommendation by the MHRA for the purposes of the Human Medicines Regulations.

---

[21] Emergency Use Authorization. Drug and Biological Products. URL: https://www.fda.gov/emergency-preparedness-and-response/mcm-legal-regulatory-and-policy-framework/emergency-use-authorization?fbclid=IwAR3EBrAELMmTeUl_IPtmHZNl_veTMN6tL2-CUJcrz0nS6AOxjAvBktKICy8.

[22] Safety and Efficacy of the BNT162b2 mRNA Covid-19 Vaccine. URL: https://www.nejm.org/doi/full/10.1056/NEJMoa2034577.

[23] Emergency Use Authorization. Drug and Biological Products. URL: https://www.fda.gov/emergency-preparedness-and-response/mcm-legal-regulatory-and-policy-framework/emergency-use-authorization?fbclid=IwAR3EBrAELMmTeUl_IPtmHZNl_veTMN6tL2-CUJcrz0nS6AOxjAvBktKICy8.

[24] Legal Authority. Public Health Service Act | Social Security Act |Federal Food, Drug and Cosmetic Act | Robert T. Stafford Disaster Relief and Emergency Assistance Act. URL: https://www.phe.gov/Preparedness/planning/authority/Pages/default.aspx.

[25] GOV.UK. MHRA guidance on coronavirus (COVID-19). URL: https://www.gov.uk/government/collections/mhra-guidance-on-coronavirus-covid-19#regulatory-flexibilities.

These regulatory flexibilities are: (1) temporary and will be kept under review; (2) offered to protect people's health in exceptional circumstances; (3) effective immediately.

Some UK flexibilities, while aligned with those of the EU, are not limited to treatments for COVID-19 products but cover the supply of other essential products that have been affected by the outbreak by factors such as travel and transportation restrictions or shortages of starting materials.

The first COVID-19 vaccine for the UK, developed by Pfizer/BioNTech, has 2 December 2020 been given approval for use following a thorough review carried out by the Medicines and Healthcare products Regulatory Agency (MHRA).

30 December 2020, the vaccine Oxford/AstraZeneca has been approved after meeting the required safety, quality, and effectiveness standards.[26]

2.2 *Legal Bases for Access to Vaccines in Other Countries*

The legal procedure for access to vaccines-candidates in Russia is quite different. Thus, in the Resolution of the Government of the Russian Federation of 03.04.2020 N 441 "On features of circulation of medicines for medical use which are intended for use in the conditions of the threat of emergence, emergence, and emergency response situation and for the organization of medical care to the victims of emergencies situations, prevention of emergencies, prevention and treatment of diseases that pose a danger to others, diseases and lesions resulting from adverse chemical, biological, radiation factors "(as amended). The resolution was prepared in pursuance of Art. 13 of the Russian Federation's Federal law from 12.04.2010 "On circulation of medicines". Part 8 of Art. 13 of this legal act of the Russian Federation was stated in the new edition of 01.04.2020: "State registration of drugs intended for use in hostilities, emergencies, prevention of emergencies, prevention and treatment of diseases that pose a danger to others, diseases and injuries, obtained as a result of adverse chemical, biological, radiation factors, and which are developed, including on behalf of the federal executive authorities, authorized in the field of national defence and security, is carried out in the manner prescribed by the Government."

The main point is that these regulations in Russia have introduced the so-called "accelerated registration" of drugs, simplifying the procedure for submitting a registration dossier, and conducting clinical and preclinical studies. That is, it is not a temporary emergency use or a temporary marketing authorization.

While registering of medicines, including vaccines before completion of clinical trials of the Ministry of Health of Russia, some specific conditions (one or several) are established, for instance, carrying out post-registration clinical researches that result in the evaluation of expected benefit and possible risk of drug use, conducting

[26] Medicines & Healthcare products Regulatory Agency. URL: https://www.gov.uk/government/organisations/medicines-and-healthcare-products-regulatory-agency.

of post-market serial selective quality control of this drug, requirements for its labelling, notification of Federal Service for Surveillance in Healthcare about each fact of drug use, submission of information on side effects, adverse reactions in connection with the use of the drug, the peculiarities of its interaction with other drugs, individual intolerance and other circumstances that affect the change in the ratio of the expected benefits to the possible risk of use, identified at any stage of the drug circulation.[27]

Besides, it is necessary to subsequently carry out the procedure of registration confirmation of the drug registered under these conditions—the applicant must send to the Ministry of Health of Russia a statement by December 1 of the current year (paragraphs 17.2–17.4 Peculiarities of drugs). The reason for the refusal to confirm registration is the decision of the Ministry of Health of Russia, adopted based on the examination of the expected benefits and the possible risk of using the drug, that the risk of harm due to using these drugs exceeds the effectiveness of its use.

The above accelerated and simplified procedure was used in the registration in the Russian Federation of the first and second vaccines against COVID-19: (1) the first, developed by the National Research Center for Epidemiology and Microbiology named after N.F. Gamalia, (combined vector vaccine for the prevention of coronavirus infection caused by SARS-CoV-2 virus), which was registered on 11.08.2020 (registration number: LP-006395); (2) the second, developed by the State Scientific Center of Virology and Biotechnology "Vector" of Federal Service for Surveillance on Consumer Rights Protection and Human Wellbeing (vaccine based on peptide antigens for the prevention of COVID-19), registered on 13.10.2020 (registration number: LP-006504).

The Federal Service for Surveillance on Consumer Rights Protection and Human Wellbeing on 14.10.2020 published information on the registration of the vaccine and indicated the plans of the developers to conduct post-registration clinical trials.[28] That is, it is clear that this is not a full-fledged registration of vaccines against coronavirus infection.

It is also necessary to pay attention to the open appeal of the Association of Russian Clinical Trials Associations, which strongly opposes the simplified procedure for registration of the vaccine against coronavirus infection.[29] From their perspective, there are high risks of drug registration before the end of phase III. This phase provides the primary evidence of efficacy and information on the side

---

[27] Новые возможности регистрации и патентования лекарственных средств. Гарант.ру. URL: https://www.garant.ru/article/1418220/.

[28] Информация Федеральной службы по надзору в сфере защиты прав потребителей и благополучия человека от 14 октября 2020 г. "О регистрации вакцины ФБУН ГНЦ ВБ "Вектор" Роспотребнадзора "ЭпиВакКорона". URL: http://base.garant.ru/74754034/.

[29] Ассоциация Организаций по Клиническим Исследованиям. Открытое обращение Ассоциации организаций по клиническим исследованиям в связи с анонсированной государственной регистрацией вакцины «Гам-Ковид-Вак» НИЦЭМ им. Н.Ф. Гамалеи Минздрава России. URL: http://acto-russia.org/index.php?option=com_content&task=view&id=411.

effects that the drug can cause in certain groups of patients: people with weakened immune systems and people with comorbidities.

Recent legal initiatives in Ukraine show that the country, unfortunately, in these matters is on the path of implementing the legislative model of the Russian Federation rather than the EU.

Thus, in accordance with Art. 9 of the Law of Ukraine "On Medicinal Products", medicinal products are allowed for use in Ukraine after their state registration, except as provided by this Law. According to the same article, there is a simplified procedure for medicines, registered, for example, in the USA and the EU, but we have already stated above that no COVID-19 vaccine has received full legal status and is not registered in these countries. The only exception is the Russian Federation with its own vaccines.

Also, the Law of Ukraine of 04.11.2020 № 4314 "On Amendments to Certain Legislative Acts of Ukraine on the Prevention of Coronavirus Disease (COVID-19)" like the relevant legislation of the Russian Federation establishes, in fact, simplified registration of new medicines by simplifying the clinical trial program for drugs intended for the specific prevention of coronavirus disease (COVID-19). In Ukraine, there may be a situation that vaccines that are not registered in any country of the world but are only temporarily restricted will already be registered in Ukraine.

In this regard, we can mention a criminal case: according to the decision of the Court of Appeal of Kyiv (case №10-71 of 20.10.2010 on sending materials for a new trial), the First Deputy Minister of Health of Ukraine, going beyond his rights and powers, made and signed a one-time permit to import into the customs territory of Ukraine vaccine against measles and rubella produced by Serum Institute of India Ltd. That was imported into the customs territory of Ukraine on April 11, 2008, and subsequently distributed in sanitary-epidemiological and medical institutions for use without a state registration in a total of 9 million doses. As a result, 69 people were hospitalized due to vaccination complications and deteriorating health. In fact, such actions were some kind of "anti-vaccine advertising," and the credibility of vaccination in Ukraine has deteriorated.

Thus, today Ukraine plans to introduce COVID-19 vaccines with no legal status, thus not assuming any responsibility. Individual officials will be responsible in such a situation, but not the state. In our opinion, it is still necessary to seriously study the EU and US legislation with the possibility of experience using. However, today Ukraine introduces only the Russian Federation's experience without any comparison with the legislation of the above countries. In other countries, there is also no registration of vaccines against coronavirus infection.

The inactivated COVID-19 vaccine developed by Beijing Institute of Biological Products of Sinopharm CNBG has been granted conditional registration by the NMPA of China, the Chinese equivalent of FDA, on December 31, 2020.[30] This vaccine, in addition to China, has undergone clinical trials in the UAE and Bahrain.

[30]China grants conditional market approval for Sinopharm CNBG's COVID-19 Vaccine. URL: http://www.sinopharm.com/en/s/1395-4173-38862.html.

An analysis of the legislation of most countries of the world gives grounds to claim that without conducting all phases of clinical trials, no country registers vaccines but only provides conditional permits for use.

3 The Impact of International Governmental and Non-Governmental Organizations on COVID-19 Vaccination Policy

The World Health Organization (WHO) listed the Comirnaty COVID-19 mRNA vaccine for emergency use, making the Pfizer/BioNTech vaccine the first to receive emergency validation from WHO since the outbreak began a year ago.[31] That is despite the fact that the EU, the UK, and the US have granted conditional permits for the use of other vaccines.

Besides, COVAX announced the signing of an advance purchase agreement with AstraZeneca for 170 million doses of the AstraZeneca/Oxford candidate and a memorandum of understanding (MoU) with Johnson & Johnson for 500 million doses of the Janssen candidate, which is currently being investigated as a single-dose vaccine. These deals are in addition to existing agreements COVAX has with the Serum Institute of India (SII) for 200 million doses—with options for up to 900 million doses more—of either the AstraZeneca/Oxford or Novavax candidates, as well as a statement of intent for 200 million doses of the Sanofi/GSK vaccine-candidate.[32]

COVAX is a special program created by the Global Alliance for Vaccines and Immunization (GAVI) together with the Coalition for Epidemic Preparedness Innovations (CEPI) and with the participation of the World Health Organization (WHO). This program is designed to protect both low-income countries that would not otherwise be able to afford these vaccines, as well as individual higher-income countries that do not have bilateral agreements with vaccine manufacturers. Today, COVAX monitors the largest and most diverse portfolio of COVID-19 vaccines in the world, with nine vaccines-candidate already under development and nine more under evaluation. At the same time, COVAX guarantees to provide up to 20 percent of vaccines to the country's population. It should be noted that the COVAX program not only guarantees low-income countries that they will be able to receive a certain amount of vaccine over time but also guarantees pharmaceutical manufacturers that a certain number of their vaccines will be sold. That is, COVAX

---

[31] WHO issues its first emergency use validation for a COVID-19 vaccine and emphasizes need for equitable global access. URL: https://www.who.int/news/item/31-12-2020-who-issues-its-first-emergency-use-validation-for-a-covid-19-vaccine-and-emphasizes-need-for-equitable-global-access.

[32] COVAX Announces additional deals to access promising COVID-19 vaccine candidates; plans global rollout starting Q1 2021. URL: https://www.who.int/news/item/18-12-2020-covax-announces-additional-deals-to-access-promising-covid-19-vaccine-candidates-plans-global-rollout-starting-q1-2021.

also protects the interests of the large pharmaceutical business from possible risks. This is understandable, given that vaccine production is a very risky type of pharmaceutical production.

Ukraine plans to receive the vaccine from Oxford University (UK) and AstraZeneca under the COVAX program. The affordability and temperature regime of these vaccines are the most favourable.[33] Although it is worth recalling that AstraZeneca stated before the end of the tests that their vaccine was 70% effective.[34] But the vaccine-candidate from AstraZeneca/Oxford is part of the COVAX research and development portfolio, which is overseen by the Coalition for Epidemic Preparedness Innovations (CEPI).[35] The Ministry of Health of Ukraine has declared the COVAX initiative to supply Ukraine with 8 million doses of COVID-19 vaccine for 4 million people.[36] The Ministry of Health of Ukraine, through the Department of Economic Cooperation of the Ministry of Foreign Affairs of Ukraine, addressed the subjects of the Federal Republic of Brazil, which may be potential producers of vaccines from COVID-19, and received a negative response.[37] Earlier it was reported that the most promising vaccines at the testing stage are AstraZeneca/Oxford (Brazilian partner is the State Institute of Immunobiological Technologies "Bio-manguinhos"), Sinovac (Brazilian partner is the State Butantan Institute), Pfech/BioNT, Johnson & Johnson. In addition, one of the states has signed an agreement with the Russian Investment Fund to test the Sputnik V vaccine.

The above entities responded that after obtaining a permit for the production of these vaccines in partnership with foreign companies, Brazil's Government would primarily meet the needs of the domestic market of more than 250 million people.

It seems that international organizations do not have established contacts between themselves and governments. However, this issue is essential not only in the context of ensuring the right to health of low-income citizens but also in discussing the introduction of vaccination passports or vaccination certificates.

Situations, when access to individual countries and flights is available only with certain documents on vaccination are spreading. Therefore, the recognition of

---

[33] Oxford–AstraZeneca COVID-19 vaccine efficacy. URL: https://www.thelancet.com/journals/lancet/article/PIIS0140-6736(20)32623-4/fulltext.

[34] *Gavi statement on AstraZeneca/Oxford interim efficacy data. URL:* https://www.gavi.org/news/media-room/gavi-statement-astrazenecaoxford-interim-efficacy-data.

[35] *Gavi statement on AstraZeneca/Oxford interim efficacy data. URL:* https://www.gavi.org/news/media-room/gavi-statement-astrazenecaoxford-interim-efficacy-data.

[36] Центр громадського здоров'я. COVAX верифікував першу частину заявки України на вакцини від COVID-19. URL: https://phc.org.ua/news/covax-verifikuvav-pershu-chastinu-zayavki-ukraini-na-vakcini-vid-covid-19.

[37] StateWatch. Посольство України у Федеративній Республіці Бразилія надіслало запити щодо перспектив експорту вакцини проти COVID-19 на бразильські державні інститути, які є партнерами їх виробників, а також надіслало в Україну докладну інформацію про іноземних виробників, які тестують вакцину на території Бразилії. URL: https://statewatch.org.ua/publications/ukraina-shukaie-mozhlyvosti-zakupyty-vaktsynu-proty-covid-19-cherez-brazyliiu-tam-testuiut-i-rosiys-ku/.

vaccines not only by individual countries but also by international organizations is critical.

For instance, large tech firms are also getting in on the act. IBM (IBM) developed its own app, called Digital Health Pass, which allows companies and venues to customize indicators they would require for entry, including coronavirus tests, temperature checks, and vaccination records. Credentials corresponding to those indicators are then stored in a mobile wallet. Early on in the pandemic, Apple (AAPL) and Google (GOOG) set aside their smartphone rivalry to jointly develop a Bluetooth-based system to notify users if they'd been exposed to someone with Covid-19. Many countries and state governments around the world also developed and used their own apps".[38]

4 Conclusion

This study provides an overview that leads us to the conclusion of the specificity of each country's approach to protect its population from COVID-19. At the same time, international organizations are slowly interfering in providing vaccines to low-income countries. One can also admit the first steps in restricting citizens' rights to travel in the case of the vaccination passport's introduction. We should admit a positive step that on 19.08.2021 the European Commission finalized the process of mutual recognition of digital COVID-certificates of Ukraine and the European Union, adopting a Decision on their technical compatibility. Ukraine, along with other European countries, became one of the first countries outside the EU to receive EU approval to connect to the digital trust network. This is an additional step towards the globalization of health legislation. It should also be noted that the fact of mutual recognition of COVID-19 vaccine candidates serves in favor of the gradual globalization of legislation in this direction. At the same time, studying the experience of some countries, including Ukraine, we can observe artificial restrictions on the legalization of vaccines-candidates, which indicates not only the low level of specialists involved in law-making but also the problem of staffing among the representatives of the state.

References

Asociaciya Organzacij po Klinicheskim Issledovaniyam. Otkrytoe obrashenie Associacii organizacij po klinicheskim issledovaniyam v svyazi s anonsirovannoj gosudarstvennoj registraciej vakciny "Gam-Kovid-Vak"

[38] If you want to travel next year, you may need a vaccine passport. URL: https://edition.cnn.com/2020/12/27/tech/coronavirus-vaccine-passport-apps/index.html.

AstraZeneca's Covid-19 vaccine approved in the U.K. URL: https://www.nbcnews.com/news/world/astrazeneca-s-covid-19-vaccine-approved-u-k-n1252418

Belgian secretary of state accidentally reveals EU vaccine prices. URL: https://www.politico.eu/article/belgian-secretary-of-state-accidentally-reveals-eu-vaccine-prices/?fbclid=IwAR3OXidyWlhE56iLmdQkszF_JEOt3G5BLRKIOCIkRlv8QfxNDfgL-_ADbaI

China grants conditional market approval for Sinopharm CNBG's COVID-19 Vaccine. URL: http://www.sinopharm.com/en/s/1395-4173-38862.html

China slips in COVID-19 vaccine race on doubts over effectiveness. URL: https://asia.nikkei.com/Spotlight/Coronavirus/China-slips-in-COVID-19-vaccine-race-on-doubts-over-effectiveness

COVAX Announces additional deals to access promising COVID-19 vaccine candidates; plans global rollout starting Q1 2021. URL: https://www.who.int/news/item/18-12-2020-covax-announces-additional-deals-to-access-promising-covid-19-vaccine-candidates-plans-global-rollout-starting-q1-2021

COVAX explained. 3 September – by Dr Seth Berkley, CEO of Gavi, the Vaccine Alliance. URL: https://www.gavi.org/vaccineswork/covax-explained

Emergency Use Authorization. About Emergency Use Authorizations (EUAs). URL: https://www.fda.gov/emergency-preparedness-and-response/mcm-legal-regulatory-and-policy-framework/emergency-use-authorization?fbclid=IwAR3EBrAELMmTeUl_IPtmHZNl_veTMN6tL2-CUJcrz0nS6AOxjAvBktKICy8

Emergency Use Authorization. About Emergency Use Authorizations (EUAs).FDA. URL: https://www.fda.gov/emergency-preparedness-and-response/mcm-legal-regulatory-and-policy-framework/emergency-use-authorization?fbclid=IwAR3EBrAELMmTeUl_IPtmHZNl_veTMN6tL2-CUJcrz0nS6AOxjAvBktKICy8

Emergency Use Authorization. Drug and Biological Products. URL: https://www.fda.gov/emergency-preparedness-and-response/mcm-legal-regulatory-and-policy-framework/emergency-use-authorization?fbclid=IwAR3EBrAELMmTeUl_IPtmHZNl_veTMN6tL2-CUJcrz0nS6AOxjAvBktKICy8

EUR-Lex. Commission Regulation (EC) No 507/2006 of 29 March 2006 on the conditional marketing authorisation for medicinal products for human use falling within the scope of Regulation (EC) No 726/2004 of the European Parliament and of the Council (Text with EEA relevance). URL: https://eur-lex.europa.eu/legal-content/EN/TXT/?uri=CELEX%3A32006R0507

European Medicines Agency. Human regulatory. Robust regulatory framework and scientific expertise in the EU. URL: https://www.ema.europa.eu/en/human-regulatory/overview/public-health-threats/coronavirus-disease-covid-19/treatments-vaccines/covid-19-vaccines-development-evaluation-approval-monitoring#scientific-evaluation-and-approval-section

European Medicines Agency. Human regulatory. URL: https://www.ema.europa.eu/en/human-regulatory/overview/public-health-threats/coronavirus-disease-covid-19/treatments-vaccines/covid-19-vaccines-development-evaluation-approval-monitoring#scientific-evaluation-and-approval-section

European Medicines Agency. Human regulatory. Conditional marketing authorisation. URL: https://www.ema.europa.eu/en/human-regulatory/marketing-authorisation/conditional-marketing-authorisation#use-during-covid-19-pandemic-(new)-section

Expanded Access FDA. URL: https://www.fda.gov/news-events/public-health-focus/expanded-access?fbclid=IwAR25HGmQDMhkp6PQgNp2DPfzLQR9AWELoAE4bcnnfhqXRq5nVsepWIYJTl4

FDA issues emergency use authorization for Pfizer/BioNTech Covid-19 vaccine. By Jacqueline Howard, CNN Updated 0840 GMT (1640 HKT) December 12, 2020. URL: https://edition.cnn.com/2020/12/11/health/covid-vaccine-fda-eua/index.html?utm_medium=social&utm_content=2020-12-12T02%3A44%3A51&utm_term=link&utm_source=twcnnbrk

Gavi statement on AstraZeneca/Oxford interim efficacy data. URL: https://www.gavi.org/news/media-room/gavi-statement-astrazenecaoxford-interim-efficacy-data

GOV.UK. MHRA guidance on coronavirus (COVID-19). URL: https://www.gov.uk/government/collections/mhra-guidance-on-coronavirus-covid-19#regulatory-flexibilities
Human regulatory. Conditional marketing authorisation. URL: https://www.ema.europa.eu/en/human-regulatory/marketing-authorisation/conditional-marketing-authorisation#use-during-covid-19-pandemic-(new)-section
Human regulatory. Conditional marketing authorisation. An official website of the European Union. European Medicines Agency. URL: https://www.ema.europa.eu/en/human-regulatory/marketing-authorisation/conditional-marketing-authorisation#use-during-covid-19-pandemic-(new)-section
If you want to travel next year, you may need a vaccine passport. URL: https://edition.cnn.com/2020/12/27/tech/coronavirus-vaccine-passport-apps/index.html
Informaciya Federalnoj sluzhby po nadzoru v sfere zashity prav potrebitelej i blagopoluchiya cheloveka ot 14 oktyabrya 2020 g. "O registracii vakciny FBUN GNC VB "Vektor" Rospotrebnadzora "EpiVakKorona". URL: http://base.garant.ru/74754034/
Legal Authority. Public Health Service Act | Social Security Act |Federal Food, Drug and Cosmetic Act | Robert T. Stafford Disaster Relief and Emergency Assistance Act. URL: https://www.phe.gov/Preparedness/planning/authority/Pages/default.aspx
Medicines & Healthcare products Regulatory Agency. URL: https://www.gov.uk/government/organisations/medicines-and-healthcare-products-regulatory-agency
NICEM im. N.F. Gamalei Minzdrava Rossii. URL: http://acto-russia.org/index.php?option=com_content&task=view&id=411
Novye vozmozhnosti registracii i patentovaniya lekarstvennyh sredstv. Garant.ru. URL: https://www.garant.ru/article/1418220/
Oxford–AstraZeneca COVID-19 vaccine efficacy. URL: https://www.thelancet.com/journals/lancet/article/PIIS0140-6736(20)32623-4/fulltext
Safety and Efficacy of the BNT162b2 mRNA Covid-19 Vaccine. URL: https://www.nejm.org/doi/full/10.1056/NEJMoa2034577
StateWatch. Posolstvo Ukrayini u Federativnij Respublici Braziliya nadislalo zapiti shodo perspektiv eksportu vakcini proti COVID-19 na brazilski derzhavni instituti, yaki ye partnerami yih virobnikiv, a takozh nadislalo v Ukrayinu dokladnu informaciyu pro inozemnih virobnikiv, yaki testuyut vakcinu na teritoriyi Braziliyi. URL: https://statewatch.org.ua/publications/ukraina-shukaie-mozhlyvosti-zakupyty-vaktsynu-proty-covid-19-cherez-brazyliiu-tam-testuiut-i-rosiys-ku/
Vakcina ot koronovirusa: chto proishodit v Rossii i mire. VADEMECUM. URL: https://vademec.ru/news/2020/09/13/vaktsina-ot-koronavirusa-chto-proiskhodit-v-rossii-i-v-mire/
WHO issues its first emergency use validation for a COVID-19 vaccine and emphasizes need for equitable global access. URL: https://www.who.int/news/item/31-12-2020-who-issues-its-first-emergency-use-validation-for-a-covid-19-vaccine-and-emphasizes-need-for-equitable-global-access
Центр громадського здоров'я. COVAX верифікував першу частину заявки України на вакцини від COVID-19. URL: https://phc.org.ua/news/covax-verifikuvav-pershu-chastinu-zayavki-ukraini-na-vakcini-vid-covid-19